OUR
RELIGION
AND OUR
NEIGHBORS

OUR RELIGION AND OUR NEIGHBORS

A Study of
Comparative Religion
Emphasizing
the Religions
of the
Western World

Illustrated by
WILLIAM STEINEL

By
RABBI MILTON G. MILLER,
M.A., M.H.L.,
Temple Beth El, Elizabeth, N. J.
and
RABBI SYLVAN D. SCHWARTZMAN,
Ph.D., Professor, Jewish Religious Education,
Hebrew Union College—Jewish Institute of Religion

Union of American
Hebrew Congregations
New York, N. Y.

EDITOR'S INTRODUCTION

THE BIBLE DENIES THE VALUE OF IDOLATRY passionately and without qualification. Some have mistakenly taken this to mean Judaism rejects all other religions. Such people know neither the Bible nor the Jewish tradition. It is one thing to reject idolatry though many peoples practice it. It is another to say heathens cannot know God. This Judaism does not say. To the contrary, it has continually affirmed that the non-Jew can know God.

Genesis tells the story of God's covenant with Noah. Under it men were required to be ethical and pious, and God in return promised them His protection from total annihilation. This mutual responsibility is the Bible's understanding of religion, and since all men are descendants of Noah, it is clear all men can have a true religion.

The rabbis affirmed this principle of biblical Judaism and made it a cardinal concept in Jewish Law. The Sons of Noah, as distinguished from the idolaters, are given special recognition and status by the rabbis. Down to this day this ancient category provides the means by which Judaism measures and evaluates its neighbors' religions.

We teach comparative religion to our children within this Jewish context. We are not dispassionate observers of the various activities on the religious scene. We are devoted Jews, who, precisely because of the intensity of our faith, likewise believe that others may know and worship God. Because we believe in Judaism, we practice tolerance—or even more, live brotherhood. For us, comparative religion is a legitimate authentic Jewish discipline, the search for the Sons of Noah.

We carry it on not for academic reasons alone. If we seek to bring all men to fulfil the covenant of Noah and live by God's law, we must know how close to Him they have come. If we wish to live in brother-love with all our neighbors—and who in this shrinking world is not our neighbor?—knowledge will open the way to understanding, and understanding will prepare us for love.

There is no simple way to fulfil the *mitzvah* of loving our neighbors, least of all that counsel which calls for the obliteration of differences to facilitate brotherhood. God does not call us to love our neighbors only when he is just like us, or vice versa. This would hardly be love, and is too selfish a thought to be ascribed to God. Rather the commandment is given because my neighbor is different from me, and just because he is different I must come to see that he is yet like me and thus love him.

To compare means primarily to note the similarities of different things; and in seeing what they have in common, we also see their unique qualities emerge. We would not teach a course in contrasting religions, for we are not primarily concerned with what separates us from others. We would rather compare, and see our differences in the light of our similarities.

Some would not undertake this quest for fear they may lose their faith. If they can believe only by the prejudice of excluding all others from the truth or by tightly closing their eyes to their own real doubt and confusion, they have lost more in integrity than they can ever hope to gain from the bliss of narrow-mindedness. Such attitudes stem only from insecurity in Judaism. The believing Jew can meet the religions of the world and their adherents with ease and confidence. Nothing true in them is alien to his tradition; and his religious faith, he knows, is as valid for him today as it has been for his ancestors in their day for nearly 4,000 years. All that he learns will make him the better, the more devoted, the more faithful Jew, for he is confident that his Judaism is true—and indeed has often been the source of truth for others.

It is no accident that this pioneering effort to explain the religions of the world to the young Jew appears within Reform Judaism. At home in the contemporary world, as it is in the Jewish tradition, this movement is secure enough in faith to reach out to its brothers in all faiths. May the undertaking bring us closer to the day "when all who dwell on earth shall know that to Thee alone. . . ."

Rabbi Eugene B. Borowitz

PREFACE

THIS VOLUME IS BASED UPON A RABBINICAL thesis prepared by Milton G. Miller for the Department of Jewish Religious Education of the Cincinnati School of the Hebrew Union College–Jewish Institute of Religion. With some revision the original material was used experimentally for several years as a religious school text at Temple Israel, Memphis, Tennessee. It has since been thoroughly revised three times and greatly expanded.

In connection with the preparation of his thesis in 1953, Rabbi Miller conducted an extensive survey of Reform Jewish religious schools. The results indicated that the teaching of Comparative Religion was wide-spread at the upper grade levels, and that a variety of texts was being used. The findings also revealed the lack of a generally suitable student text. These facts, coupled with the authors' conviction about the importance of the subject for modern American Jewish youth, prompted the preparation of this volume.

To a large extent, this book has been shaped by the opinions and interests of the religious school students themselves. In a poll of some six hundred of them, the topics that evoked the greatest response concerned the beginnings of religion, the development of Christianity, the beliefs and practices of the Protestant and Roman Catholic, and the similarities and differences between Judaism and Christianity. This

volume, therefore, has concentrated upon these subjects. The evolutions of Eastern Orthodoxy, Islam, and the great religions of the East have been given a much more limited treatment.

For ease and simplicity of presentation, the text follows a combined historical-topical approach. Careful selectivity and the use of the most reliable scholarly research have been employed to insure objectivity and accuracy. The attempt also has been made throughout to sustain a respectful attitude toward the beliefs and practices of all faiths. At the same time, recognizing that this volume is designed for use in the Jewish religious school, the authors have taken special care to focus attention upon the development and teachings of Judaism in relation to the different faiths.

It is sincerely hoped that the approach and contents of this volume will enable the student to develop a deeper appreciation of religion in general and a better understanding of the beliefs of his fellow man. More than this, however, we voice the hope that, through the study of Comparative Religion, each Jewish youth will derive fresh insights into his own faith and appreciate more deeply the relevance and significance of Judaism as his way of life.

The authors wish to express their deep indebtedness to the Editor, Rabbi Eugene B. Borowitz, and to the following members of the Reading Committee of the Commission on

Jewish Education—Rabbis Bernard J. Bamberger, Leon Fram, and Sidney M. Lefkowitz. Their comments, judgments, and criticisms have proven invaluable in the preparation of this volume.

We are grateful, too, to the various scholars who were invited by the Commission to share with us their reactions to our efforts. Our thanks therefore go to Professor Horace L. Friess, Professor of Religion, Columbia University, for reading the chapters on the origins of religion; to Dr. Harry M. Orlinsky for reading the chapters on the development of Judaism in biblical times; to Father Gerard Sloyan, Chairman of the Department of Religious Education, the Catholic University of America, for reading the chapters on Roman Catholicism; to Dr. John C. Bennett, Dean of Faculty, Union Theological Seminary, who read the chapters dealing with Protestantism; and to Professor Archie J. Bahm, Professor of Philosophy, the University of New Mexico, who read the chapters dealing with the Eastern religions. Naturally, the authors bear full responsibility for all questions of fact and opinion. While the scholars' suggestions have been carefully considered, we have presented the material in our own way and wish clearly to relieve our advisers of any errors the authors may have made.

We also wish to thank numerous rabbinical colleagues, religious school directors, teachers, and others for utilizing the volume in its experimental stages and giving us the benefit of their suggestions for its improvement.

A special word of appreciation goes to Mrs. Esther P. Kaplan for overseeing the preparation of the typescript, to Mr. William Steinel for the attractive art work, to Mr. Ralph Davis for supervising the production and design of this edition, to Dr. Jerome J. Kanner for his careful copy editing and to Miss Myrna Pollak for her research in obtaining the photographs. We also thank the many organizations, named on pages 295-296, who furnished us with so many fine photos.

Finally, although the information for this volume has been drawn from innumerable sources, we wish especially to thank the authors and publishers for permission to use brief selections from the following: (The page numbers listed refer to the pages of *Our Religion and Our Neighbors* where the material has been cited.)

ALBRIGHT, WILLIAM F., *From the Stone Age to Christianity*, Doubleday Anchor, p. 30.

American Jewish Yearbook, 1961, American Jewish Committee and Jewish Publication Society of America, pp. 8, 9-10.

ARCHER, JOHN CLARK, and CARL E. PURINTON, *Faiths Men Live By*, Ronald Press, pp. 14-15, 18, 244.

BAHM, ARCHIE J., *Philosophy of the Buddha*, Harper, pp. 231-233.

———, *Tao Teh King*, Frederick Ungar Publishing Co., pp. 242, 244, 246.

———, *Yoga, Union with the Ultimate*, Frederick Ungar Publishing Co., pp. 219-220, 247.

BALLOU, ROBERT O., *The Bible of the World*, Viking Press, pp. 203, 204, 205, 207, 216, 217, 219-220, 228-229, 231, 232, 242, 244, 247.

BENEDICT, RUTH, "Religion," in Franz Boas, *General Anthropology*, Heath and Co., pp. 17, 18.

BOWRA, C. M., *The Greek Experience*, World Publishing Co., p. 30.

BUBER, MARTIN, *Tales of the Hasidim—The Early Masters*, Schocken Books, pp. 174, 176.

CHWOROWSKY, KARL M., "What Is a Unitarian?" in Leo Rosten, *A Guide to the Religions of America*, Simon and Schuster, pp. 130-131.

CLARK, ELMER T., *The Small Sects in America*, Abingdon-Cokesbury, pp. 149-151.

COGLEY, JOHN, "What Is a Catholic?" in Leo Rosten, *A Guide to the Religions of America*, Simon and Schuster, pp. 100-101.

COHON, SAMUEL S., *Theology Lectures: I. Theology and Religion*, Hebrew Union College Cooperative Store, p. 268.

EDWARDS, D. MIALL, *The Philosophy of Religion*, Harper, p. 17.

FRIEDLANDER, M., *The Guide of the Perplexed of Maimonides*, Hebrew Publishing Co., pp. 166-167.

JAMES, E. O., *Prehistoric Religion*, Thames and Hudson, p. 17.

KITAGAWA, JOSEPH M., *Religions of the East*, Westminster Press, p. 252.

LIETZMANN, HANS, "Creeds," *Encyclopedia Britannica*, Encyclopedia Britannica, Inc., p. 77.

MANWELL, REGINALD D., and SOPHIA L. FAHS, *The Church Across the Street*, Beacon Press, p. 130.

MARCUS, JACOB R., *The Jew in the Medieval World*, Sinai Press, p. 171.

MORGAN, KENNETH W., editor, *The Path of the Buddha*, Ronald Press, pp. 234, 236.

———, *The Religion of the Hindus*, Ronald Press, p. 221.

NOSS, JOHN B., *Man's Religions*, Macmillan, pp. 18, 23-24, 26, 210, 212, 246, 247, 249.

PIKE, E. ROYSTON, *Encyclopaedia of Religion and Religions*, World Publishing Co., p. 239.

REMMERS, H. H., "Purdue Opinion Poll," Purdue University Press, p. 2.

SCHAFF, PHILIP, *History of the Christian Church*, Wm. B. Erdmans Publishing Co., pp. 110-111.

SCHROEDER, H. J., *Canons and Decrees of the Council of Trent*, B. Herder Book Co., p. 138.

SCHWARTZMAN, SYLVAN D., *Reform Judaism in the Making*, Union of American Hebrew Congregations, pp. 185-188.

SMITH, HUSTON, *The Religions of Man*, New American Library, pp. 217-218, 221, 231, 236-237, 246.

SPENCE, HARTZELL, *The Story of America's Religions*, Holt, Rinehart, Winston, pp. 83-84, 105, 116-117, 119, 121, 127, 128-129, 133, 134, 136, 142, 144, 146.

The Apocrypha, An American Translation, Trans. Edgar J. Goodspeed, University of Chicago Press, p. 50.

The Book of Common Prayer, The Church Pension Fund, p. 126.

The Book of Mormon, Mission of the Church of Jesus Christ of Latter-Day Saints, p. 144.

The Holy Scriptures, Jewish Publication Society of America, pp. 32, 40, 43-44, 45, 54, 58, 254.

The Official Catholic Directory, 1961, P. J. Kenedy and Sons, p. 105.

The Old Testament, Revised Standard Version, Thomas Nelson and Sons, pp. 32, 40, 43-44, 45, 54, 58, 254.

The New Testament, Revised Standard Version, Thomas Nelson and Sons, pp. 55, 57, 68, 147, 150.

The World's Great Religions, Time, Inc., pp. 8, 236, 249.

Union Prayerbook, I, Central Conference of American Rabbis, p. 269.

World Almanac, 1961, New York World-Telegram, and *Encyclopedia Britannica's Book of the Year, 1961*, Encyclopedia Britannica, Inc., pp. 3, 4-7, 201.

Yearbook of American Churches, 1961, National Council of the Churches of Christ in the USA, pp. 6, 7, 120.

YELLIN, DAVID, and ISRAEL ABRAHAMS, *Maimonides*, Jewish Publication Society, pp. 165, 166.

MILTON G. MILLER
SYLVAN D. SCHWARTZMAN

CONTENTS

xi

CHARTS AND MAPS

OUR
RELIGION
AND OUR
NEIGHBORS

1 RELIGION IN THE WORLD TODAY

The Interest in Other Religions   There's a growing interest in other religions today.

An opinion poll of young people conducted by Purdue University confirms it. Ninety per cent of all those participating declared that they wanted to know more about the various religions.

And, if we may judge from the quantity of new books, magazine and newspaper articles, and radio and television programs, this also holds true of adults. For instance, some years ago *Look* magazine published a series of articles on seventeen different religions in the United States. The response was so enthusiastic that a second series was begun shortly after. During the same period *Life* also ran accounts of six of the world's great religions: Hinduism, Buddhism, Confucianism, Islam, Judaism, and Christianity. The articles featured by both magazines, and now published in book form, are a good indication of the interests of many millions of their readers.

But why this concern with other religions?

One reason, certainly, is curiosity. In the course of school, business, community activity, recreation, ordinary conversation, all of us are exposed to people of different religions. On the golf course a Protestant friend may mention that he is going to attend Communion later. Or perhaps someone has watched a Catholic mass or Passover seder on television. All of this makes people wonder about their neighbors' beliefs and practices.

A second reason, undoubtedly, is our increasing preoccupation with religion in general. Within recent years more and more people have come to feel the need for something worthwhile to believe in, a faith to sustain them in these difficult times. As a result there has been a substantial growth in the membership of American churches and synagogues. A great many individuals are actively searching for faith, some out of dissatisfaction with the religion of their birth, others out of a desire to experience religious belief for the first time. Consequently they want to know more about the different faiths—about Judaism, for instance, and the teachings of Martin Buber, one of its great modern thinkers, or the beliefs of Zen Buddhism, the doctrines of Roman Catholicism, or the rites of particular Protestant sects.

But today's interest in the various religions arises largely out of the changed nature of the modern world. The development of high-speed communication and transportation has reduced the earth to the size of a large neighborhood. With everyone a neighbor, most of us find it necessary to know much more about one another. And since religion is an essential part of most people's way of life, to know something about his particular faith is to understand the other fellow better.

THE MAJOR RELIGIONS OF THE WORLD *

● ▯ represents 25 million followers

JUDAISM 12,750,000 — ½%

EASTERN ORTHODOXY 137,000,000 — 5½%

BUDDHISM 152,000,000 — 6%

PROTESTANTISM 214,000,000 — 8½%

CONFUCIANISM 301,000,000 — 12%

HINDUISM 332,000,000 — 13¼%

ISLAM 431,000,000 — 17¼%

ROMAN CATHOLICISM 537,000,000 — 21½%

ALL OTHER KNOWN RELIGIONS about 387,000,000 — 15½%

*Figures are for 1960

Hence the growing concern to learn about "Comparative Religion."

Our Study of Comparative Religion What exactly do we mean by the term "Comparative Religion"?

Technically, it is that branch of knowledge which deals with the study of all the different religions of mankind. It covers a vast area and involves the research of a great many specialists, including historians, archeologists, anthropologists, linguists, and others. So extensive is the knowledge required that, even with a full lifetime of study, few are able to master the entire field.

Naturally, therefore, our study of Comparative Religion must be a limited one. We will deal with just eight of the important modern religions, concentrating mainly upon the three major faiths of the Western world, Roman Catholicism, Protestantism, and Judaism. The remaining five religions—Eastern Orthodoxy, Islam, Hinduism, Buddhism, and Confucianism—will be considered only briefly.

To start with, we will look into some of the *basic facts about the size and age of the different religions* in the world today.

Then, realizing that all modern faiths are the outgrowth of more primitive forms of belief

PRIMITIVE RELIGION. Here in Tahiti, a South Pacific island, primitive peoples dance as part of their ancient ritual.

and practice, we will investigate the *origins of religion* in general.

In connection with the different faiths we shall also want to explore something of *their historical development*. For we know that we cannot really understand them without some knowledge of their past.

This, in turn, will lead us to a consideration of *their essential beliefs and practices*.

Finally, we will want to *compare the basic teachings* of the various religions with Judaism as well as with one another, and note in what respects they differ.

So to commence our study of Comparative Religion let us inquire into some of the key facts about present-day religion. In the process we shall try to answer the following five questions:

—Which are the major religions from the standpoint of numbers?

—Where chiefly do their followers live?

—Which are the largest religious bodies in the United States?

—What in particular are the facts about our own religion, Judaism?

—Which of the major faiths is the oldest?

The World's Major Religions Of the nearly three billion people in the world at the end of 1960, about two and a half billion were associated with some religion. Naturally the figures cannot be exact, but we are presenting our best estimate.

All told, there are about a thousand known religions. Many are only tribal religions, like those of the aborigines of Australia or the natives of the South Sea Islands. Others may be branches of larger religious groupings, such as Presbyterianism, which is part of Protestantism.

However, the vast majority of people today are found within only eight different religions. These eight religions have a total membership of more than two billion and constitute about 85 per cent of all religious individuals. Turning back to the chart that appeared on the previous page, you will find the facts as best we can determine them. . . .

4

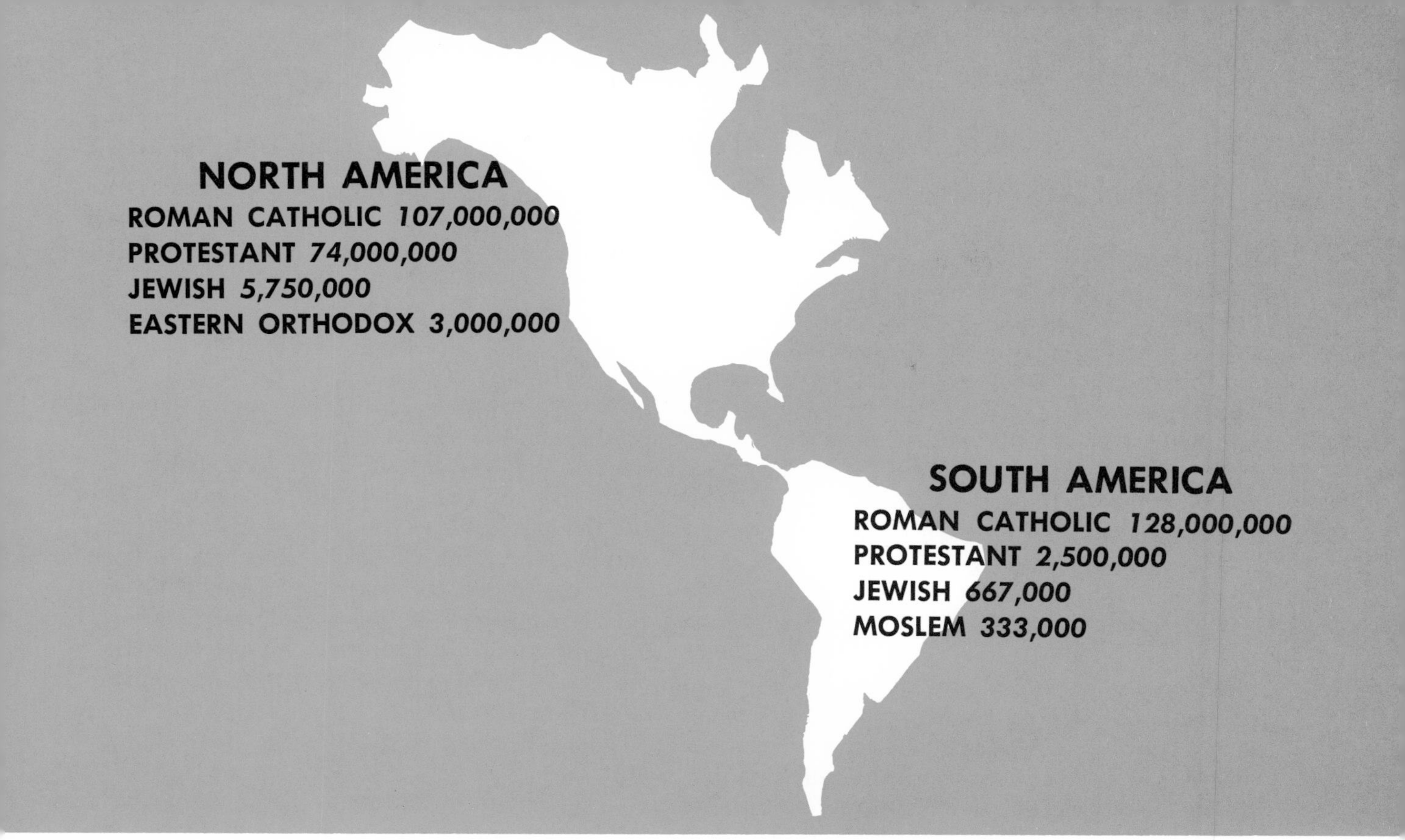

THE WORLD'S MAJOR RELIGIONS, BY CONTINENTS *

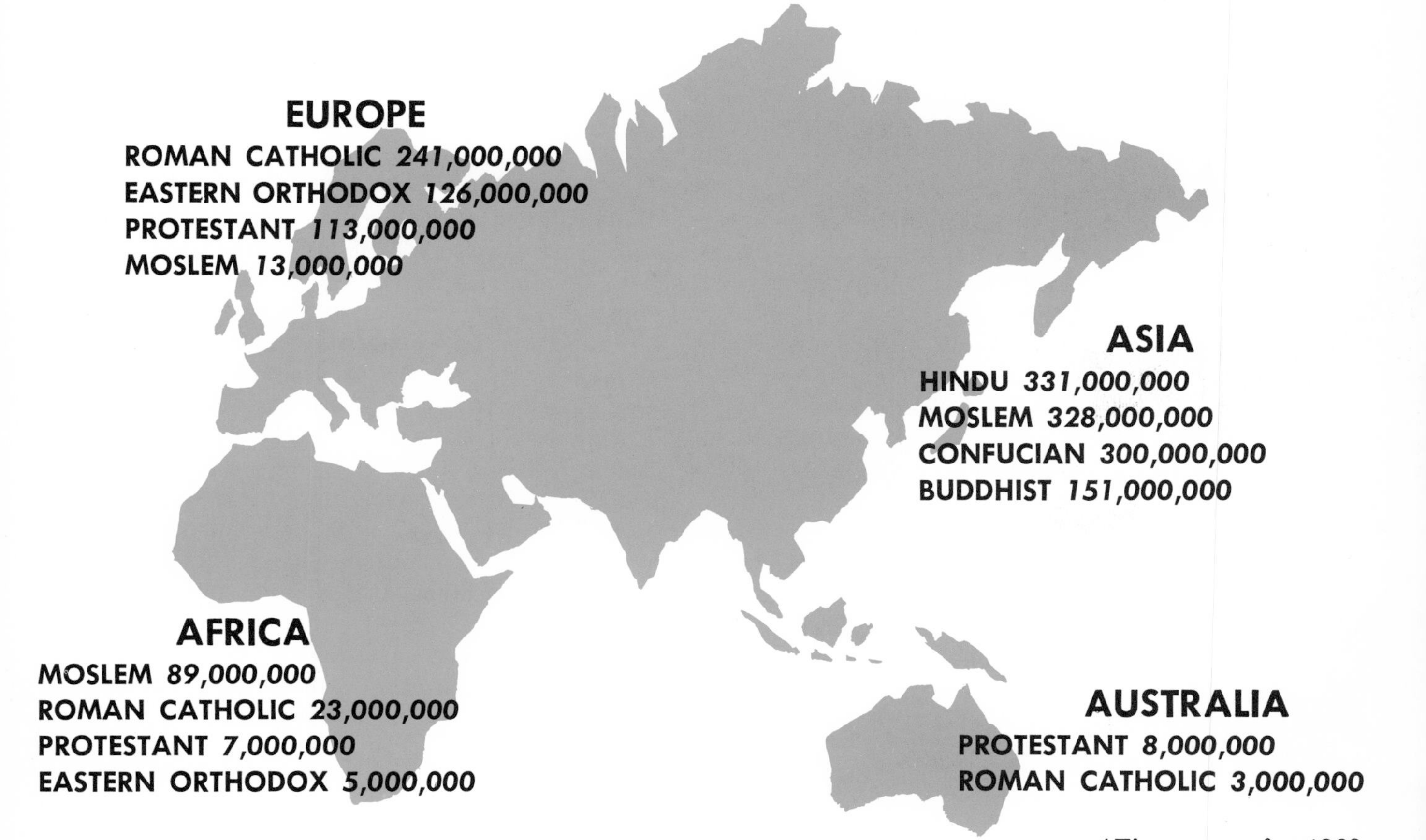

NORTH AMERICA
ROMAN CATHOLIC *107,000,000*
PROTESTANT *74,000,000*
JEWISH *5,750,000*
EASTERN ORTHODOX *3,000,000*

SOUTH AMERICA
ROMAN CATHOLIC *128,000,000*
PROTESTANT *2,500,000*
JEWISH *667,000*
MOSLEM *333,000*

EUROPE
ROMAN CATHOLIC *241,000,000*
EASTERN ORTHODOX *126,000,000*
PROTESTANT *113,000,000*
MOSLEM *13,000,000*

ASIA
HINDU *331,000,000*
MOSLEM *328,000,000*
CONFUCIAN *300,000,000*
BUDDHIST *151,000,000*

AFRICA
MOSLEM *89,000,000*
ROMAN CATHOLIC *23,000,000*
PROTESTANT *7,000,000*
EASTERN ORTHODOX *5,000,000*

AUSTRALIA
PROTESTANT *8,000,000*
ROMAN CATHOLIC *3,000,000*

*Figures are for 1960

In addition to the specific information about each of the major faiths, we discover four other significant facts:

First, Roman Catholicism, with some 537 million followers, is the largest religious group in the world. Actually, more than one-fifth of all the religious people on earth are Roman Catholics.

Second, Christianity as a whole accounts for over one-third of all religious people. For adding together the figures for Roman Catholicism, Protestantism, and Eastern Orthodoxy, we get a total of some 888 million individuals.

Third, almost half of all people associated with religion belong to the major faiths of the Middle and Far East. Together they number almost a billion and a quarter.

Finally, the figures confirm what a very small group the Jews really are. Jews comprise about one-half of one per cent of all the religious people in the world. This is often quite surprising to many because of the great influence Judaism has had upon the development of other religions.

Where the Religions Are Located   Where do the followers of these eight major religions live?

Actually some live in practically every country of the world, but in many instances they seem to be concentrated in certain particular areas. This we observe from the picture-map on the preceding page which listed the four religions with the greatest number of followers on each continent. (In the case of Australia, because of its relatively small population, only two religions were mentioned.)

Thus we see that some faiths, chiefly Roman Catholicism, Protestantism, and Islam, have sizable numbers of followers in most parts of the world. Others, like Hinduism and Buddhism, are concentrated in one principal area.

There are some other interesting facts worth noting. For instance, the Roman Catholic faith is the dominant religion on half of the six continents of the world: North and South America and Europe. The Hindus, Confucianists, and Buddhists live mainly on the continent of Asia, and the Moslems in Africa and Asia. The Eastern Orthodox faith is centered chiefly in Europe.

Once again the small size of the Jewish group is confirmed. On only two continents, North and South America, are the Jews found within the top four religions, but nowhere are they the dominant faith.

The Religions of America   So far all of our information has dealt with religion in the world as a whole, and at this point we may be wondering about the situation in our own country.

Of the approximately 190 million people in the United States at the close of 1960, it is estimated that about 63 per cent, or roughly 120 million, are affiliated with well over 300 different religious groups. These include followers of all the major world religions as well as numerous Protestant denominations, the Christian Science Church, the so-called universal faiths like Baha'i, all the many little-known sects, and others.

However, only four main religious bodies in the United States have a million or more members. In 1960, Protestantism as a whole, with some 62½ million members, represented over half of all religious Americans. And as we note from the diagram on the next page, the Roman Catholics were the second largest group, and the Jews the third. . . .

Observe, too, how the numerical proportion of the various major religious bodies in the United States is considerably different from that of the world at large. For one thing, here the Protestants, and not the Roman Catholics, are the dominant faith. For another, we do not find any sizable number of followers of the religions that predominate elsewhere in the world, notably Islam and the Far Eastern faiths. Only Christianity in its various forms, and Judaism are of significance on the American religious scene.

Finally, here, in contrast to its standing in the world as a whole, Judaism occupies a much more prominent position. This is the result, of course, of the comparatively large concentration of Jews in this country.

To see this even more clearly, suppose at this point we review the facts about our own faith. . . .

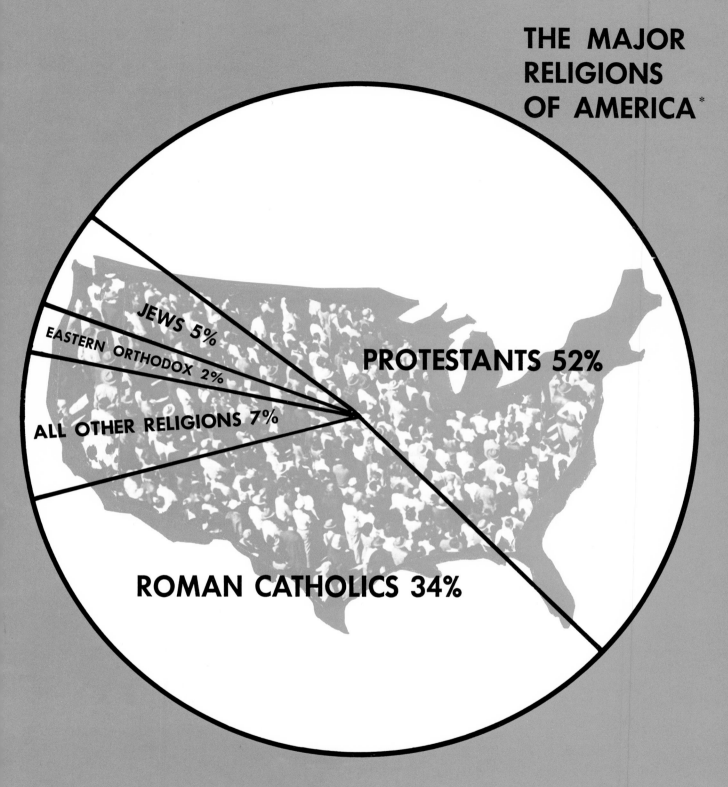

THE MAJOR RELIGIONS OF AMERICA*

JEWS 5%

EASTERN ORTHODOX 2%

ALL OTHER RELIGIONS 7%

PROTESTANTS 52%

ROMAN CATHOLICS 34%

PROTESTANTS
62,500,000

ROMAN CATHOLICS
40,750,000

ALL OTHER RELIGIONS
(Universalist faiths, religions of the East, non-Protestant and non-Catholic Christianity, etc.)
About 8,500,000

JEWS
5,500,000

EASTERN ORTHODOX
2,750,000

*Figures are for 1960

SOVIET RUSSIA. Outside one of the few remaining synagogues stands a Jew who still tries to practice his faith despite official opposition to religion.

Some Facts about the Jews   In 1960, in a world of approximately three billion people, there were only slightly more than 12¾ million Jews. The 1961 edition of the *American Jewish Yearbook* lists 12,800,000 to be more exact, or about one-third of one per cent of the world's entire population.

The picture-map on the next page reveals how the Jews are distributed over the world. . . .

As we observe, Jews are found on every continent; some live in practically every country. However, 90 per cent are concentrated on just three continents, North America, Europe, and Asia.

And, as far as countries are concerned, just three account for about three-quarters of world Jewry. These are the United States, the Soviet Union, and the State of Israel, which three, as we note from the chart appearing on page 10, contain the largest settlements of Jews. . . .

Which Religion Is the Oldest?   Which of the world's major religions is the oldest?

The answer is not easy for numerous reasons. Many religions boast of their antiquity. Judaism, as we know, dates its religious calendar from the traditional "beginning of the world" over 5700 years ago, or 3761 B.C.E. (Before the Common Era). The Hindus for their part claim that "their sages stood on the river banks of India to sing their religious hymns long before the time of Moses."

The issue is also complicated by the fact that the roots of certain religions seem to go back to

very primitive times. For example, archeologists in India have found figurines of male and female deities dating before 2500 B.C.E., and some believe them to be forms of the later Hindu gods. Certain characteristics of present-day Confucianism, too, such as ancestor worship, go back many thousands of years. Moreover, back of all religions lie certain prehistoric beliefs and practices upon which they originally drew and then reinterpreted in the light of their own teachings. Among these undoubtedly were the observance of the winter and spring seasons, and birth and death, all of which are still commemorated by practically every faith in existence.

Still it is helpful to distinguish between the first traces of a particular religion and that point in history when we can say that it exists as a distinct and fully-organized faith. Otherwise every religion's roots could be traced back to the most remote period of mankind.

With this principle in mind, we find the evidence pointing to Judaism as the oldest of the great modern faiths. Though the tales in the Bible about Abraham, Isaac, and Jacob are traditions that were written down long after they lived, they do contain sufficient fact to justify this conclusion. Archeological discoveries in Mesopotamia and Egypt, as well as the known facts about the history of the ancient Near East, date the period of the Patriarchs at between 2000 and 1700 B.C.E. The Exodus of the Hebrews from Egypt under Moses is considered to have taken place around 1300 B.C.E. By then Judaism was certainly a well-established faith.

That religion flourished in very ancient India is unquestionably true. But Hinduism as such could not have come into being until after the invasion of the Aryans, a people living northwest of India. They are believed to have entered India sometime between 1500 and 1200 B.C.E., and there produced certain Hindu writings known as the *Vedas*, books of religious "knowledge." The oldest, going back to the period between 1500 and 1000 B.C.E., is a collection of more than a thousand hymns to the gods. Hence we may consider Hinduism the second oldest faith.

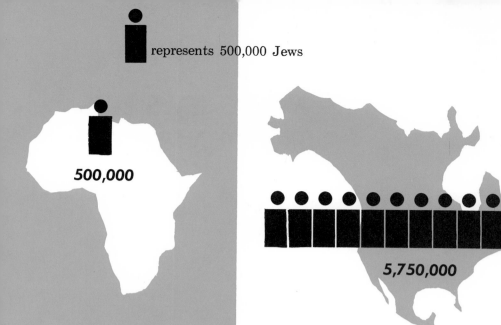

represents 500,000 Jews

AFRICA

500,000

NORTH AMERICA

5,750,000

SOUTH AMERICA

667,000

WHERE JEWS LIVE, BY CONTINENTS*

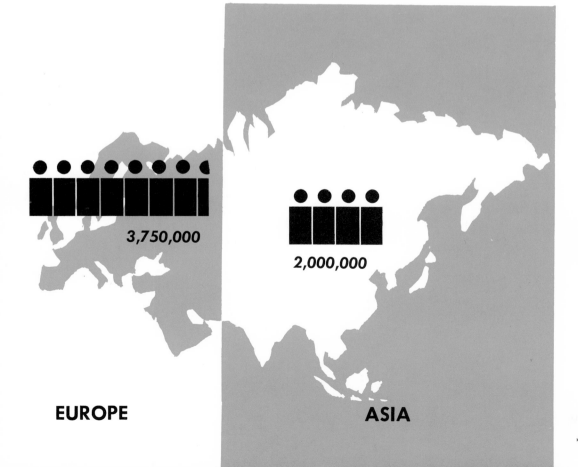

EUROPE

3,750,000

ASIA

2,000,000

AUSTRALIA

68,000

*Figures are for 1960

WHERE JEWS LIVE, BY COUNTRIES *

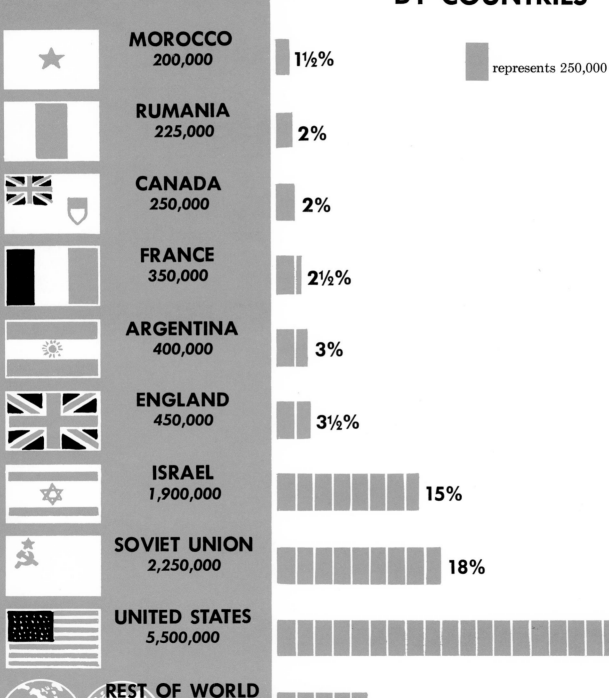

MOROCCO 200,000 — 1½%

RUMANIA 225,000 — 2%

CANADA 250,000 — 2%

FRANCE 350,000 — 2½%

ARGENTINA 400,000 — 3%

ENGLAND 450,000 — 3½%

ISRAEL 1,900,000 — 15%

SOVIET UNION 2,250,000 — 18%

UNITED STATES 5,500,000 — 43

REST OF WORLD 1,225,000 — 9½%

represents 250,000

*Figures are for 1960

AN ANCIENT LAND. Even today the fields near Bethlehem, in Jordan, look very much as they did in ancient times. It was near this very spot that Ruth first met Boaz, her relative by marriage. See Chapter 2 of the Book of Ruth.

Originating at considerably later periods, the other major religions can be dated with greater ease. We know that the founder of Buddhism, Siddhartha Gautama, known as Buddha, was born around 563 B.C.E. Confucianism originated about a decade later when, Chinese tradition claims, its founder, Kung-Fu-Tse, or Confucius as we have come to know him, was born.

The beginnings of Christianity, of course, go back to the birth of Jesus, about the year 4 B.C.E. Hence the Christian religion as a whole can be said to begin its particular career then. A distinct Roman Catholic Church as such did not come into existence until at least the fourth century of the Common Era.

Eastern Orthodoxy and Protestantism are both offshoots of the Roman Catholic faith. The Eastern Orthodox Church and Roman Catholicism finally parted company in 1054 C.E. (Common Era). Protestantism as such began in the sixteenth century with Martin Luther's act of defiance against the Church, although other dissident Christian movements had appeared as early as the first century of the Common Era. However, Protestants regard 1517 as the start of the Reformation because it was in that year that Luther nailed his statement challenging certain Catholic practices to the door of a church in Wittenberg, Germany.

Moslems reckon the beginning of their religion as the year 622 C.E. This is when Mohammed, who had already begun to preach his religion in the city of Mecca, was forced to flee to Medina, several hundred miles away. There his message was warmly received and he attracted a considerable following.

Summarized in chart-form on the next page are all these basic facts about the origins of the various religions. . . .

Long Before the Patriarchs Summarizing, then, here are some important observations we may make about religion in the world today:

—All told, there are eight major faiths: Roman Catholicism, Islam, Hinduism, Confucianism, Protestantism, Buddhism, Eastern Orthodoxy, and Judaism.

—The religion with the largest number of followers is Roman Catholicism. The faith with the fewest is Judaism.

—Although the major faiths have followers throughout most of the world, all but Roman Catholicism are centered in one or two main areas.

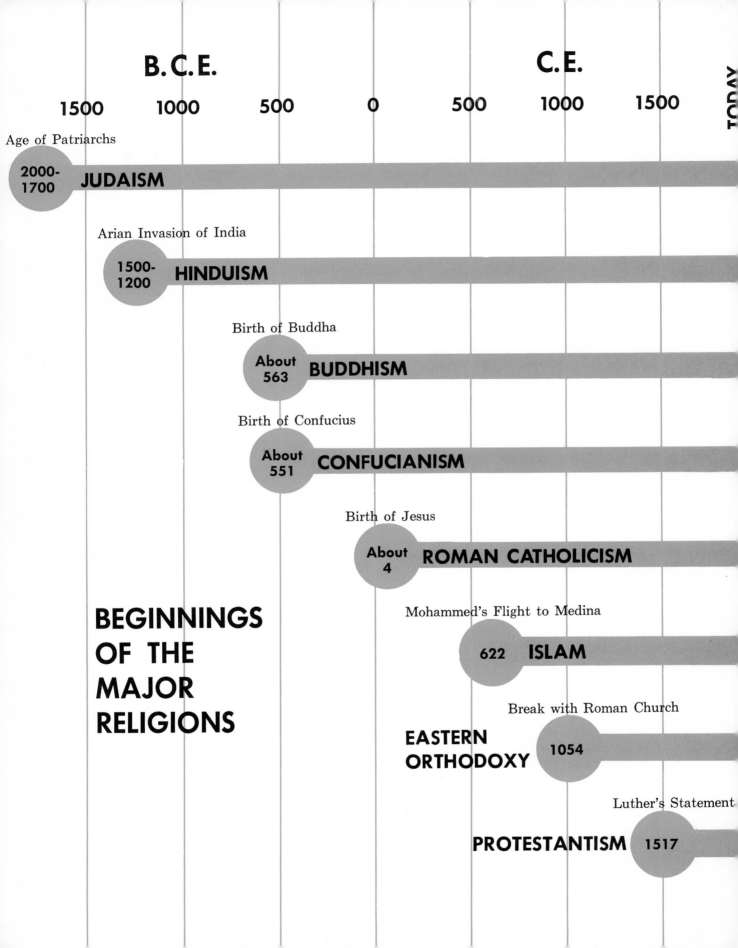

B.C.E.   **C.E.**

1500   1000   500   0   500   1000   1500   TODAY

Age of Patriarchs

2000-1700   **JUDAISM**

Arian Invasion of India

1500-1200   **HINDUISM**

Birth of Buddha

About 563   **BUDDHISM**

Birth of Confucius

About 551   **CONFUCIANISM**

Birth of Jesus

About 4   **ROMAN CATHOLICISM**

Mohammed's Flight to Medina

622   **ISLAM**

Break with Roman Church

EASTERN ORTHODOXY   **1054**

Luther's Statement

PROTESTANTISM   **1517**

BEGINNINGS OF THE MAJOR RELIGIONS

RELIGION IN THE WORLD TODAY

—In the United States, Protestantism, Roman Catholicism, and Judaism are the dominant faiths. The majority group is the Protestants.

—As compared with the other great religious bodies, the Jews are a tiny minority. The major population center of Judaism is in the United States.

—Judaism appears to be the oldest of the great religions, and Hinduism is next. Protestantism is the youngest.

Though Judaism is the most ancient of the major world religions, we know from the brief mention of certain early practices in India and China that the origins of all religion go back to very early prehistoric times. Consequently, to follow the development of the great religions we need first to know something about the beliefs and practices of primitive man from which they grew.

For this we must go far back into time . . . long before the Hebrew patriarchs appeared on the scene. . . .

TOPICS TO DISCUSS

1. Why should Jews today be interested in learning about Comparative Religion?
2. In what important ways can society as a whole benefit from a wider knowledge of all the various faiths?
3. What effect has the particular religious composition of your community had upon you?
4. How does the fact that the Jews constitute such a small group in comparison with the followers of other religions affect us?

THINGS TO DO

1. The figures on the followers of the major religions given in the text are for the year 1960. Using the *World Almanac* or *Encyclopedia Britannica Book of the Year* for the current year, bring the charts dealing with religion in the world and in the United States up to date. From the changes that appear, what seem to be the trends in the growth of the major religions?
2. With information secured from the local Chamber of Commerce or Council of Churches, prepare a picture-chart comparing the size of the major religious groups in your own community. How does this information compare with that of the world at large and of the United States as a whole?
3. Using the latest issue of the *American Jewish Yearbook*, bring the facts about Jewish population in 1960 up to date. What significant changes, if any, do you observe? Where the Jewish population shows a sizable increase or decrease, see if you can explain the reason?

OTHER THINGS TO READ

American Jewish Yearbook, American Jewish Committee and Jewish Publication Society—latest edition, "World Jewish Population."

ARCHER, JOHN CLARK, and CARL E. PURINTON, *Faiths Men Live By,* Ronald Press, "Introduction," pp. 3-20.

LANDIS, BENSON Y., *World Religions,* Dutton—latest edition, "Statistical Tables."

SMITH, HUSTON, *The Religions of Man,* Mentor, Chapter 1, "Point of Departure," pp. 11-22.

The World's Great Religions, Time, "Introduction," pp. 1-9, by Paul Hutchinson.

2

HOW RELIGION BEGAN

Man Becomes Aware of the Supernatural

Near the top of a mountain a big boulder suddenly started to slide. It tumbled forward and shot upward each time it hit other rocks. Gathering speed, the boulder sent smaller stones scattering ahead; other rocks and boulders were loosened and started crashing down the mountainside.

A small human figure wearing an animal skin stood midway up the mountain. He was stalking a big brown bear just ahead of him. Suddenly the hunter heard the roar up above. He looked up, terror-stricken, to see an avalanche hurtling down upon him.

In an instant he bounded forward to the protection of a sheltering precipice. The mass of boulders, stones, and earth came smashing past him with a deafening roar. Amid the dust and the rocks, the hunter saw the bear hurtling by.

Cautiously and fearfully the hunter inched out of his shelter, his eyes fixed to the mountaintop to make certain the danger was over. Then, looking down, he watched the landslide crashing and falling to the valley far below. Part way down the mountain, broken and lifeless, was the bear.

Trembling, the hunter once more looked up to the very top of the mountain which had so recently threatened his destruction. Suddenly he felt a strange sense of awe as though he were in the presence of something too wonderful for words. He sensed some mysterious Power, a great Force that seemed everywhere. It was in the mountain, in the avalanche; yes, even in himself. Of this he was sure!

Could this be how man first experienced religion?

We cannot tell, of course. But we can be sure that it all began with a sense of the Supernatural, a Power or Being controlling everything in his world.

Some Facts and Theories   How long ago religion began and why, are questions that cannot be definitely answered. We simply do not know. However, thanks to important archeological discoveries and studies of primitive peoples who still inhabit the earth, we do have certain facts and theories about the subject.

We know, for example, that religion existed a great many thousands of years ago. In fact, some experts feel that humans had some religious belief as early as 100,000 years ago. As evidence they point to the graves of Neanderthal men. The bodies are always arranged a certain way and are accompanied by various objects, such as flints and weapons, as well as the charred bones of animals. This seems to indicate that some sort of burial rites with food offerings took place. From this they conclude that a type of primitive religious ceremony was connected at least with death.

HOW RELIGION BEGAN

Evidence points with far more certainty to the fact that religion was practiced during the Stone Age of 50,000 to 15,000 years ago. Prehistoric man of this period not only engaged in more elaborate burial customs, including painting the corpse red, but performed certain magical rites as well. Some very old cave drawings and clay figures found in Spain and Southern France testify to this. For instance, the clay figure of a bear covered with spear-thrusts reveals that Stone Age man attempted to insure good hunting by means of primitive ritual. The caves themselves may even have served as shrines, comparable in certain respects to the Gothic cathedrals of much later times.

That man turned to religion at a very early period, then, is fact. But *why* he did is a matter of theory.

Perhaps the nature of the world in which he lived was responsible, for it was a time of violent physical change and upheaval. The earth was marked by many smoking volcanoes which frequently erupted, and earthquakes were common. Early man was subject also to extreme weather changes due to the effects of a series of Ice Ages. Fierce animals, terrifying storms, and other hazards threatened man at every turn. The world represented constant lurking danger which caused primitive man to feel himself at the mercy of some mighty supernatural Force. To cope with his fears, he instinctively turned to a Power beyond himself that he felt was capable of protecting and helping him.

Or perhaps the answer is to be found more within man himself. Unlike other creatures, man possesses the capacity for awe. As man's body and mind developed, he grew to the point where he came to look upon his world with wonder and awe. Certain natural events like the growth of crops, and birth and death were beyond his knowledge and understanding. He conjectured about the things he experienced— where did the sun, the heavens, the seas come from? What was responsible for the changing seasons, sleep, the growth of the individual into manhood, and many other things? As he thought about these, something within him recognized that there were mighty unseen forces in the universe, and he was overcome with a mystical feeling.

But these are only two of the theories which seek to explain how religion began. Other the-

EARLY CAVE-ARTISTS. On the walls of their caves, Cro-Magnon men, who lived more than 25,000 years ago, painted pictures of some of the beasts they hunted.

springing up simultaneously even in different localities.

Many hold that prehistoric man's initial feeling for the Supernatural led him to think of it as a general, indefinable form of mysterious power found in nearly everything. This is attested to by careful studies of very primitive groups in Australia, Africa, India, the islands of the South Pacific, and elsewhere. Here, among some of these peoples even to this day, the Supernatural is precisely this kind of impersonal power or force. Authorities have given it the name "mana," which is the term used by the natives of Melanesia, the small islands north of New Guinea and Australia.

Mana is not a particular god or spirit. Rather it is a vague spiritual power which attaches itself to persons or things and accounts for the success of an individual. Mana is more like electricity or energy than a specific thing like an engine or a motor. A canoe will not be swift unless mana sends it forward. A fine deer may be caught because the hunter possesses mana or because the stone used for the arrowhead has mana. Mana is believed capable of being transmitted through elaborate and strange ceremonies, especially at important periods of life, such as when a boy enters upon manhood.

Other primitive peoples, however, view the Supernatural in terms of what is commonly called "animism." The word is derived from the Greek, *animos*, "soul" or "spirit," and is used to describe a belief in religious forces that have become personalized.

Moved by awe and fear of what they experienced, certain prehistoric peoples evidently came to conceive of the Supernatural as something alive and inhabiting everything. Consequently, whatever happened became the work of "spirits," and all things, alive or not, possessed such a living force, or "soul."

There was a spirit or soul in the tiger that hunted people, and in the deer that they hunted. There were spirits in the trees and hills about them. There were spirits in each person, even in the dead. All of these were "alive" and could harm or protect people. The mountain that could kill them with a landslide could also feed

ANCIENT MAGIC. From Spain come these prehistoric drawings of deer-hunters at work. Perhaps these were also designed to insure the success of some future hunt.

ories see religion growing out of ancestor worship, or man's dreams and visions, or spontaneous excitement over some remarkable happening. Some theories hold that religion originated as man's reaction to his own difficulties and dissatisfactions, or in response to the more pressing needs of the group for food and other necessities.

Though some or all of these factors may well have played a part, the real facts about the birth of religion must remain shrouded in the mists of the past.

Early Conceptions of the Supernatural
What form religion originally took is likewise a matter for speculation. As the experts see it, there could be several possibilities, with each

16

them with the fruits, berries, and animals on its slopes.

Naturally, certain spirits, like those of the bushes, grasses, or tiny stones, could be regarded as less powerful. But others, like the spirits of the sky, mighty rivers, or some huge mountain, were far more important and worthy of special veneration.

Yet, as still other experts maintain, it is just as likely that man first came to conceive of the Supernatural as a supreme Being, most probably a sky-deity. Undoubtedly early man was impressed with the ever-present heavens under whose favor or hostility he lived, and it represented a mighty Being to him.

Studies of certain primitive peoples seem to support this view. For common among numerous tribes are beliefs about some all-powerful sky-god who, over the years, has been pushed into the background by other objects of worship. Archeological finds coming out of prehistoric Egypt and Mesopotamia confirm the fact that almost the entire Near East once shared this belief in a sky-deity as a supreme Power.

Since most religions of ancient times were purely local in nature, it is likely that each had its own special character. With whatever form religion actually began, rarely for long did any maintain pure worship of mana, spirits, or a sky-god. Eventually each became a mixture of various kinds. Still, why religion developed as it did in one place and not in another, we cannot say. All we can assume is that very early in man's history his awareness of the Supernatural led him to conceive of it in one of these ways.

Traces of all three varieties are still found in present-day religion. For example, the wearing of the cross by a Christian or a m'zuzo-charm by a Jew implies certain special power in these objects which the individual considers helpful. Though the meaning of each has been thoroughly reinterpreted, they do remind us of very ancient practices associated with the idea of mana.

Many remnants of animism, too, have persisted. Buddhists, for instance, still revere the holy tree under which their teacher, Buddha,

is said to have preached. However, there is good reason to believe that the tree had been worshipped by people who lived long before Buddha. We also know that the Moslems, who venerate a large black stone in the middle of their great mosque at Mecca, are following a practice that existed hundreds of years before Mohammed. Evidently, primitive peoples once believed that both the tree and the black stone possessed powerful spirits.

And, as for reminders of man's early belief in an all-powerful Being of the heavens, many are still found in Western religion, though their meaning has, of course, been reinterpreted. For instance, stars are important symbols in both Judaism, with its "Star of David," and Christianity, with its "Star of Bethlehem." Church spires that reach skyward, as well as the common notion of God "dwelling in heaven," could well have grown out of such very old beliefs.

Varieties of Early Religious Practice To early man the existence of the Supernatural in one of its several forms accounted for his successes or failures. The good catch of fish proved that he had an abundance of mana; the illness of his children was the work of the spirits or punishment by the sky-god. So the chief concern of primitive religion was to develop the means by which people could gain benefits from their relationship with the Supernatural.

From place to place a bewildering variety of religious practices sprang up. Many involved magic by which primitive man sought to influence or compel the Supernatural to do his will. By making a figurine of his enemy and melting it in the fire he could insure his destruction. Or, as in the case of the cave paintings and images, he besought success in his hunts by piercing a representation of a bear or buffalo with numerous spears.

The use of fetishes and amulets was another feature of his religion. A fetish is an object believed to possess special power and hence capable of insuring personal success; an amulet is any fetish that can be worn by the individual. Both were believed to possess something of the Supernatural. A peculiarly shaped stone, a tree, even a river could become fetishes. Often they were spoken to as though they were persons. So, among certain West African tribes today, a native about to set out on a hunt may spend days talking to his spear and urging it to produce good results.

Frequently religious acts were accompanied by the use of special words. Even today in Melanesia it is believed that one's garden cannot grow without the use of certain word formulas. But whether connected with magic or not, prayer as an expression of dependence upon the Supernatural was one of the very early religious practices. Often it was accompanied by offerings and sacrifices. Here, for example, is a portion of a prayer voiced by certain Indians who live in the neighborhood of the Great Lakes: ". . . Here I stand with tobacco in my hand. Grant us what you granted our grandfathers! Accept our humble offering of tobacco. . . ."

Rituals of all kinds were introduced, especially in connection with major events in the individual's life—birth, manhood, marriage, and death—and with the cultivation of food. Thus certain primitive African tribes commemorate the eating of the first fruits of their crops with week-long festivals, and one Australian tribe celebrates the approaching manhood of its boys by knocking out two of his front teeth.

Prominent in the rites of early religion were also singing and dancing. In this respect the well-known snake-dance of the Hopi Indians, a rain-making ceremony, is characteristic.

Early religion involved "taboos," persons or objects believed to be so charged with supernatural power or so contaminated that all contact with them had to be avoided. Almost anything at some time or other could become taboo. It might be a woman in childbirth, the food of a tribal chief, or someone who had recently come into contact with the dead. To ignore the taboo was, of course, to invite dreadful consequences.

Ancestor worship and ceremonies connected with death were likewise part of early religion. To prehistoric man it was difficult to believe that the dead were really not alive. Certainly if living people possessed a portion of the Supernatural, some part of it must remain after death. So unless proper concern for the dead was shown, the souls of the dead, it was feared, might become displeased and cause harm. Or appealing to their spirits could insure success in important ventures. So in primitive religion we find all sorts of practices involving the dead. Some rites are designed to keep the dead from doing mischief—acts like placing a heap of stones on the body or throwing thorns on the grave so that their spirits may not walk about. Other practices, such as providing their burial places with food, clothing, and even weapons, are intended to please the dead.

Again, it is interesting to see how some of our present-day practices can be traced back to early religion. Of course, these practices are all differently interpreted today, but the customs of placing flowers at the grave, wearing a cross or holy medallion, observing dietary restrictions, and even praying and singing hymns may have very old roots indeed!

The Appearance of Tribal Communities The development of primitive religion was unquestionably influenced by man's social development. When tribes appeared, religion no longer remained the concern of merely the individual and his family. It now became a matter for the community as well.

But how men came to band together in tribal communities is another mystery. The following may be as good an explanation as any. . . .

The wild wheat and barley were ripening in the fields. Primitive man saw them and he was curious. He plucked a few grains and tasted them. They were good; also they were nourishing. He carried some back to his family, and they welcomed the new food, too.

An idea dawned in his brain. He moved his family nearer to the fields where the grain was ripening. Perhaps he found a cave nearby where they might live, or else he set up temporary tents of skin upon the field itself. At any event, for several months he was able to feed himself and his family upon the produce of the land. Now every fall he came to look forward to gathering a supply of food that would sustain him over the critical winter months.

EARLY VILLAGE LIFE. A scene of what communal life was like in Denmark about 5,000 years ago. In order to survive, everyone had many different tasks to perform.

Eventually he learned that the grain could be sowed. Though he could grow it on the slopes of hills and mountains, he found it much easier to plant in the valleys where there was flat level land, a good supply of water, and rich soil that seemed to grow things better. He chose a piece of level ground for himself and his family, and there he planted and reaped. Of course, it was still necessary for him to hunt and fish, but slowly his life became more and more concerned with farming. Soon he built a hut near the field where he and his family could live permanently.

Other families observed what he was doing. Some came and settled nearby, choosing a piece of land for themselves. Slowly a community of settlers began to spring up, and as time passed the whole valley was occupied.

Naturally the people had contact with one another. The women would meet at the river or wells where they would talk about many things—their children, their husbands, food, homes. Sometimes the men, who busied themselves with hunting, fishing, planting, and harvesting, would share information with each other. Occasionally they would also join with their neighbors against common enemies—wild beasts, plunderers, or natural catastrophes, like locusts. Eventually the settlers banded themselves into a loosely organized tribe, with the men meeting occasionally and agreeing upon certain rules for their protection.

It was probably then that the practice de-

veloped of having the group offer tribal sacrifices and prayers for the success of its activities. It seemed natural to believe that the more who participated, the greater would be the effect upon the Supernatural.

Slowly the various phases of religion involved the whole tribal community. Commonly accepted customs and rituals began to develop. Now that the group was concerned with all things having to do with its own preservation, common prayers and rituals connected with rain and good harvests, marriage, birth and death, suc-

PREHISTORIC FARMERS. In Germany, some 5,000 years ago, Neolithic families had only the most primitive stone-tipped plows and hoes with which to plant and cultivate the land.

19

cessful hunts, destruction of enemies, and the like, were adopted.

The Development of Totemism   The growth of the tribal community undoubtedly stimulated the belief that certain animals possessing an abundance of the Supernatural were special guardians of the group. Thus, for a tribe that depended largely upon buffalo for food, upon its fur for clothing, and upon its skin for tents, the animal might become an important object of worship. Its spirit would be appealed to for the welfare of the group, and the people would even come to feel that they were originally descended from the buffalo. Often the tribe would then be prohibited from eating the animal except on certain special religious occasions.

Sometimes the tribe erected poles with the symbols of various sacred animals, faces, or signs upon them. The Algonquin Indians called them "totem" poles, derived from a word meaning "group affinity" or "brother-sister relationship." In this way they indicated a sense of close kinship between these animals and the members of a certain tribe, clan, or family.

The word "totem" forms the basis for "totemism." This refers to the kind of religion in which people feel themselves mystically bound up with the spirit of a specific animal, plant, force of nature, or other object which has been adopted as the totem.

Totemism is still practiced in the modern world. Among certain primitive tribes, such as the Aruntas of Australia, each native feels himself united with some animal or plant, which he regards as his particular totem. The whole tribe bears the name of the totem as its ancestor, and its living representatives are held sacred. They are also taboo except as part of the tribe's religious observances.

Remnants of totemism persist even among more civilized peoples. We observe that in certain religions, animals—such as the cow in Hinduism—are considered sacred. In our own Western society totemism is reflected in the use of coats of arms. As they employ designs of animals, flowers, symbols, and colors to represent

TOTEMS. Figures of humans, animals, reptiles, and birds go to make up this totem pole that stands today in the State of Washington.

20

a particular clan or family, they may be considered to be outgrowths of primitive totemism.

The Rise of Religious Specialists Once the tribal community was formed, it was inevitable that members should recognize that some men were better hunters, farmers, fishermen, or craftsmen than others. Of course, the whole community benefited if a man who was a fine hunter but a poor farmer did not have to waste his talents on farming. So it was to everyone's advantage that he be encouraged to exchange some of the deer or buffalo he killed for wheat or fruit raised by a more skilful farmer. Gradually, then, as community life developed, men devoted themselves more to their "specialities."

Religion tended to produce specialists, too. Some people were clearly better at religion than others; special circumstances revealed them to have more intimate relationships with the Supernatural. They were the ones who possessed a greater abundance of mana, or knew the various ways of influencing the spirits or the sky-deity. They appeared to be more successful in getting rain when it was needed, or keeping lightning from striking the village, or healing the sick.

It was natural that all of the members of the community should call upon these individuals to intercede with the Supernatural. Thus a kind of "priesthood" emerged, particular specialists who knew all the effective rites.

All the while, religious practice had grown more complicated. Now a great many special chants and prayers were needed. The faces of participants in ritual dances had to be painted in a certain way. All of the numerous sacrifices and prayers had to be performed in a specified manner, and the exact times and seasons for particular rites had to be observed.

The priest's time became more and more taken up with performing religious functions so that he soon had little time to fish and hunt for himself. Now in the interests of the community, the people brought him food and drink, clothed him, and even provided him with shelter in order that he might be free to carry on his religious duties.

As time passed, the ordinary person knew less and less about specific rituals. He became increasingly more dependent upon the priest to instruct him in offering sacrifices and presenting prayers, and in guiding him about what customs and rites were necessary to carry on farming, hunting, fishing, and living more effectively. Henceforth, supervision of religion was transferred into the hands of professionals; that is, specialists supported by the community. They jealously guarded the knowledge of the proper rites and tribal customs. Often the priesthood became hereditary, with priestly knowledge being passed on exclusively from father to son.

In the medicine man of African tribes we find this primitive type of professional priest. Wearing special garb and often working himself into trances, he is recognized by everyone as the religious authority. He possesses special religious knowledge; he is in charge of the various ritual dances and sacrifices. He is believed capable of improving the lot of his people in many ways, among them, using rituals and medicines to heal sick tribesmen.

The more highly-developed religions of the world today also maintain a professional religious leadership, although its character is naturally quite different from medicine men of primitive tribes. Catholicism has its priests; Protestantism, its ministers; Judaism, its rabbis. Although the nature of their offices and functions differ considerably, they are all specialists in religion and are supported by their religious communities.

The Achievements of Primitive Religion . . . and Its Need By now religion had struck deep roots within primitive society. Growing out of prehistoric man's sense of awe and wonder, his critical struggle for survival, his fears, and his many physical and social needs, religion had begun with a feeling of some supernatural Power responsible for much of what happened to him.

From a belief in impersonal mana, or in a world peopled by spirits, or controlled by an invisible sky-god, man derived a sense of closeness to the Supernatural. To it, in whatever form he conceived of it, he felt he owed his well-being or misfortune. Consequently it became the object of his worship, meriting his respect and personal attention through rituals, sacrifices, and prayers.

As human society passed from the family stage into that of the tribal community, religion became the common concern of a larger group. Now the means of worship and the various ceremonial rites grew more elaborate and were prescribed in precise manner. And with the appearance of specialization generally, religion produced its professional priesthood. All of this was no small accomplishment.

However, further religious progress depended upon man's development of a higher conception of the Supernatural. For in the long run, the powers that he worshipped would determine the nature of his religion. Those who prayed to mana, spirits of animals, rocks or streams, or to some mysterious sky-deity, were bound to carry on with only the most superstitious kinds of beliefs and primitive rites.

Many peoples never advanced much beyond this stage. But in certain others, the concept of the Supernatural slowly underwent change. And with it the course of religion took new turns. . . .

TOPICS TO DISCUSS

1. What significance is to be found in the fact that religion was universal in very early times?
2. Had early man not discovered religion, in what ways might your life be different today?

3. How does modern man meet those essential needs that were satisfied by primitive religion? Does this mean that we have outgrown the need for religion? Why?
4. In what fundamental ways is modern Judaism different from the faith of primitive peoples?

THINGS TO DO

1. Draw up a list of some of the present-day Jewish practices that you believe may be traced back to early forms of religion. In two columns alongside each, state first, what you consider its origin to have been, and, second, in what ways Judaism has modified or reinterpreted the practice.
2. Using stick-figure drawings or illustrations from old magazines, prepare the first portion of a chart presenting the development of Judaism from prehistoric times down to the present.
3. Imagine that you lived during prehistoric times. Write a page of a diary showing how religion would play its part in the daily life of your family and yourself.

OTHER THINGS TO READ

ALBRIGHT, WILLIAM F., *From the Stone Age to Christianity*, Doubleday Anchor, pp. 128-137.

ARCHER, JOHN CLARK, and CARL E. PURINTON, *Faiths Men Live By*, Ronald Press, Chapter 2, "Primitive Religion," pp. 22-51.

GAER, JOSEPH, *How the Great Religions Began*, Signet, "In the Beginning," pp. 9-14.

NOSS, JOHN B., *Man's Religions*, Macmillan, Chapter 1, "Religion in Prehistoric and Primitive Cultures," pp. 5-43.

PIKE, E. ROYSTON, *Encyclopaedia of Religion and Religions*, Meridian, "Amulets," p. 16; "Animism," p. 19; "Fetishism," pp. 152-153; "Shamanism," p. 349; "Taboo or Tabu," p. 367.

3

RELIGION DEVELOPS MANY GODS

The Spirit-God Answers The hot sun burned down upon the parched land. The people gazed sadly about their wheat fields; already the tender shoots were starting to wilt. Then they looked up into the sky. Not a cloud marred its brilliant blueness.

There was only one thought in their minds as they gathered outside the hut of the priest. "Pray to the spirits!" they called. "They must send us rain!"

In a short while the priest came out. He carried a small pitcher and over his shoulder he bore the skin of a lion. Now he began to sway back and forth, crying out, "Hear me, spirit of the lion, friend of our tribe! I offer you drink, for you are very thirsty. . . ." With this he spread the skin upon the ground and began pouring from the pitcher. "Drink, friend of our tribe, drink. . . ." The water trickled over the lion skin, and some of it spilled upon the ground. The people watched in silent awe.

"See, we are giving you water for your thirst!" cried the priest. "For you, O spirit of our tribe, are our friend." Now, one by one, the people came forward with pitchers which they took turns in emptying upon the skin. "See our offering!" the priest called out.

For more than an hour the ceremony continued. Then the priest cried, "And we, your people, are thirsty, too. As we have given you drink, now you will give us rain, water for our thirsty lands. Send the clouds. Send the rain. Give us water and you shall have offerings of the first of our grain. . . ." All day the prayers continued and far into the night. Then the priest called for the special rain dances.

The first light of dawn streaked across the sky. The dancing ceased; the voices died away. All eyes looked upward toward the heavens. For hours no one moved or made a sound. Now a small cloud passed over the sun, and behind it other clouds appeared, dark and heavy. A drop of rain fell, then another. Suddenly a torrent poured down, and from every throat went up a triumphant cry.

"The lion-spirit is a powerful god!" they said to one another afterward. "He conquers the sun and brings the rain. . . ."

How Spirits Became Gods This tale, of course, is fictional, but it suggests how spirits or totems may have become gods. For it was not too big a step for certain primitive peoples to have transformed a particularly powerful spirit into a deity with a distinct personality of its own, or to have distributed certain functions of a sky-god to other beings.

Some of these early deities were pictured in animal form, and in various parts of the world, the lion, tiger, eagle, bear, bull, buffalo, serpent, and others, came to be venerated. Deities were also conceived of in combinations of human and animal features. For example, in early Egypt, Anubis, the guardian of the dead, had a jackal's head and a human body. Horus, the sun-god, bore the head of a hawk.

More generally, the deities took on the appearance of humans and there are various theories to explain why. Some seem to think it was the result of the tribe's appealing to the spirits of former heroes who were felt to possess special powers. Undoubtedly, among the Greeks, Hercules had enjoyed such a heroic existence before the people made him a divinity. Others believe that it arose out of the worship of the souls of dead ancestors in general. For, like the living, the dead also possessed spirits to whom people could turn for help in time of trouble.

Or perhaps, as a great many more think, the gods came into being when people began to project some of their own characteristics upon the spirits so that the deities eventually appeared as "super-humans." Thus, in early Egypt, the god Re was pictured as a tremendously powerful hunter paddling himself in a boat across the reedy marshes. And in Greece,

EGYPTIAN DEITIES. Anubis, pictured on the left, bears a jackal's head, while Osiris, on the right, appears entirely in human form.

Hera, originally perhaps a cow-goddess, was seen as a constantly jealous wife, seeking to protect her marriage to the powerful sky-god.

Various natural forces especially were deified, like the sun and rain. In Egypt, Re was a sun-god, and Osiris is thought originally to have been the "life-giving water." The Greek god Zeus, who began as the great sky-father, became the ruler of the upper heavens and giver of rains, and at one time Pallas was the thunder-goddess.

At what point in the development of prehistoric man all this started we cannot be sure. But that it had already taken place by 3000 B.C.E. is clear because we have ample evidence of actual gods and goddesses who were then worshipped in Mesopotamia. Through archeological discovery, we know, for instance, that the ancient Sumerians, who inhabited that region more than 5000 years ago, carried on a religion that centered about the worship of a large group of deities with human characteristics.

The Gods and Their Worship   The number of gods multiplied rapidly. In ancient Sumeria, we hear of nearly 4000 different god names representing practically every phase of nature. It was also usual for male gods to be linked with goddesses. In fact, some of the oldest figurines we have are those of goddesses.

Like the humans who worshipped them, the gods were eventually gathered together into a full-fledged family. The sky was the powerful Father-god; the earth was thought of as the great Mother-goddess. Among the ancient Sumerians, Anu, god of the encircling sky, was called "father of the gods," and another of the more important deities was named Ki, "earth," or Nintu, "the lady who gives birth." Among certain peoples the natural forces of sun, rain, sea, storm were no longer isolated deities, but became the divine offspring of the parent gods.

Numerous myths about the deities also came into being. Thus, the world, said the Sumerians, was born out of the struggle between the dragons of darkness and the gods of light, headed by the warrior-deity Ninurta. A particularly common myth, told of Osiris by the Egyptians, and

24

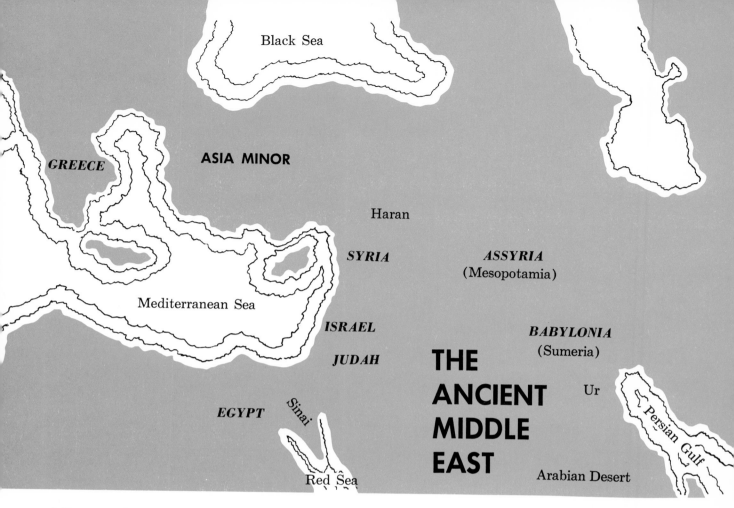

Black Sea

GREECE

ASIA MINOR

Haran

SYRIA

ASSYRIA
(Mesopotamia)

Mediterranean Sea

ISRAEL

JUDAH

BABYLONIA
(Sumeria)

THE
ANCIENT
MIDDLE
EAST

Ur

EGYPT

Sinai

Persian Gulf

Red Sea

Arabian Desert

of Tammuz by various peoples of the Middle East, accounted for the revival of nature in the spring through the god's resurrection from a tragic death.

The development of humanized gods stimulated artists to produce visual representations of them, sacred images of the deities in human and semi-animal form. It was not long before these became objects of worship in temples and other special places set apart for the purpose. Carried over, too, were most of the practices of earlier religion, such as the professional priesthood, prayer, sacrifice, taboos, and a variety of rites. Charms, amulets, and talismans or "good-luck pieces" were also cherished. Like the rabbit's foot or four-leaf clover today, they were supposed to bring success and good fortune to the possessor.

With the appearance of so many deities, the process of specialization which had produced the professional priesthood also set in among the gods. More and more, individual gods were

assigned specific duties. Among the early peoples of India, for instance, Surya, originally the sun-spirit, became the god of birth, and it was to him that petitions were addressed by those seeking children. Among the Sumerians, Enki was the lord of the life-giving waters, and Enlil, the god of storms. Among the Greeks, Poseidon was lord of the sea, and Demeter, goddess of the earth. Those seeking help were expected to turn to the appropriate god or goddess with prayer and sacrifice. Though often several gods might be expected to do one job, they tended more and more to be put in control of specific areas of nature and human activity.

Not every civilization reached this stage. Where it did, we call its kind of religion "polytheism," a word coming from the Greek and meaning "belief in many gods."

The Birth of National Gods All the while the number of tribal communities continued to multiply. With good harvests providing a regu-

THE PANTHEON was originally dedicated to the worship of "all gods" when it was first built in Rome in 27 BCE in honor of the nation's heroes. In 609 it was converted into a church.

lar supply of food, with plenty of water, adequate shelter from the heat, rain, and cold, and greater protection from wild beasts and other enemies, many of the tribal communities prospered. Eventually some sizable cities came into existence.

Expanding population meant that some communities outgrew their supply of land. It now became necessary to conquer the territory of neighboring tribes in order to survive. At the same time, the more a community thrived, the more envious grew the less fortunate people of nearby areas. The result was an increase in tribal warfare.

For mutual protection or conquest, we now think, it became common for several tribal communities to band together. As time passed, they often found it to their advantage to remain together, first in loose federations, and later in more tightly-knit nations. In the beginning, nations may have consisted of only a few tribes or several cities. But gradually they came to contain larger numbers of people, including many who were defeated in battle and were absorbed into the conquering tribal community or nation.

Where nations came into being, new religious problems arose, for within the nation each of the tribes or cities continued to worship its own gods. Rival claims were made for them which sometimes created confusion and friction. However, as members of the various groups continued to intermingle and the peoples gradually merged together, religious beliefs and practices tended to fuse into a more-or-less common faith. It generally provided for a single family of gods who represented a collection of the deities of the various tribes or communities.

Usually special prominence was given to the main gods of the more powerful tribes or cities, and they often became the chief gods of the nation. So, among the Sumerians, the gods of the six largest cities were the most important, and three of them, Anu, Enlil, and Ea, became a trio of national deities in control of the whole universe. Sometimes chief gods came into being through a merger of several powerful tribal deities. Among the early peoples of India, the gods of fire, rain, and sun, each with his own particular name, were amalgamated into one supreme god. However, the people of various localities continued to call him by his different names.

Often, too, important cities continued to worship their own gods as well as those of the nation. So in ancient Egypt, the city of Memphis carried on with its worship of Ptah, the creator who made the world out of mud, even though the sun-god was the national deity.

Each nation, of course, had its own particular collection of deities. The gods of the Aztecs in Mexico, for instance, were Huitzilopochtli, god of agriculture and war, Tezcatlipoca, god of law and justice, Quetzalcoatl, god of culture and good living. They were not the same deities as those worshipped by the Incas of Peru, the sun-god and the gods Viracocha and Pachacamac. Similarly, in the Near East, the Canaanite people worshipped their own particular gods; so did the Syrians, the Assyrians, and the Egyptians.

And with the development of national deities, somewhat different religious ideas appeared.

26

TRIAD OF GODS. Pictured here are three of the most important Egyptian deities: Osiris, Isis, and Horus.

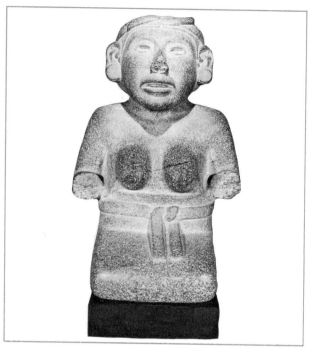

AZTEC IDOL. Worship of such deities was common in ancient Mexico. There each god was in charge of some particular function.

The Beliefs of National Religion   In the main, the people's beliefs about religion were now intimately bound up with the experience of the nation.

For instance, people believed that when their nation was successful in warfare, it was the gods who fought on their side and defeated the gods of the enemy. This we clearly observe in a very old passage of the Bible. The Book of Judges tells us that when the ancient Hebrews under the prophetess Deborah were able to defeat the army of the Canaanite general, Sisera, she thanked her people's God for participating in the battle and giving them such a glorious victory (Judges 5).

For a people to be conquered meant that its gods had also been defeated. Consequently, vanquished nations would generally adopt the worship of the more powerful deities of their victors. So, when conquering invaders from the north entered Greece around the twelfth century B.C.E., their chief deity, Zeus, promptly became the god of many sections of the country. The Assyrian kings symbolized their power over subject peoples by bringing the defeated gods in a captive train to their capital city.

It was now accepted that the gods of each nation were supreme within its territory. But the deities' power extended only to these boundaries. Ancient peoples who moved to another country gave up their former worship, seeing that they were now in the province and under the protection of the gods of a new land. Hence, when the Kingdom of Israel, already weakened by the worship of other gods, was conquered in 721 B.C.E. and the people were taken captive to Assyria, there seemed no alternative but to abandon the worship of their own deity for the religion of Assyria.

"National religion," as this type of belief is called, quickly spread among the peoples of the ancient world. To some extent, it has also lived on into modern times. The Nazi movement, in Germany, claimed some ties to the ancient Germanic forms of worship. Under the leadership of Hitler and the Nazis, the attempt was made to reintroduce the cult-worship of Wotan and Thor, gods of the ancient Teutonic peoples.

But remnants of national religion persist in other forms. Certain lands have special patron saints, such as Saint Patrick in the case of Ireland. Others, like the Scandinavian countries, still maintain their own national churches, in this instance the state-supported Lutheran faith. The ruler of Great Britain, too, bears as one of the royal titles, "Protector of the Faith," the "faith" being Christianity as carried on by the Church of England, a state religion supported by the government.

The Circulation of Religious Ideas Over the centuries new nations continued to be formed, and they varied considerably in size and might. Some were small, like tiny Israel and Judah in the years before their destruction; some were larger and more powerful, like Syria, Israel's neighbor to the north. Others, like Assyria and Egypt, became vast empires through the conquest of weaker peoples.

The steady growth of nations and the rise of empires led to more contact between the peoples of the ancient world. This, in part, was the result of the flourishing trade that sprang up, for most of the nations had special talents or goods that were greatly in demand. We learn from the Bible, for instance, that the people of Tyre produced the finest kinds of woods and were noted as such excellent builders that King Solomon employed them to construct his palace and Temple (I Kings 5:15-25). Solomon, in turn, is known to have exported great quantities of copper in return for certain products of the East.

Constant warfare as well brought different peoples into contact. Nations were forced to develop diplomatic relations with one another for their own protection, and frequently alliances were formed. Soldiers of different armies moved from land to land. Sometimes they joined with the forces of other nations to fend off attacks of some mighty empire. Sometimes they were sent to police the peoples of conquered countries with whom they mingled and often intermarried. It was also the policy of certain empires, such as Assyria, to transplant defeated peoples to other regions of their vast territory.

As a result, knowledge of other people's beliefs and practices were circulated over wide areas. Traders carried their religions as well as their goods wherever they went. Soldiers spread religious ideas and observances from land to land. Even the formation of alliances contributed to the transmission of religion. In the ancient world an alliance generally involved the marriage of the king to a foreign princess, who brought her own religion to the new land. So when King Ahab of Israel entered into an alliance with the King of Tyre, he married the latter's daughter, Jezebel. Then, much to the anger of the prophet Elijah, the queen promptly introduced the worship of her own gods, Melkart and Astarte, into the country (I Kings 16:29-33; 18).

By this same process, various myths came to be shared in common throughout the ancient Middle East. Those particularly having to do with agriculture and the deities responsible for the fertility of the earth became wide-spread. In general, they told of the death of some god in the fall and of his rebirth in the spring, thanks to the efforts of a great Mother-goddess. In Egypt, Babylonia, Palestine, Greece, and many other lands, we find similar types of gods and goddesses being worshipped in much the same way.

Shortcomings of National Religion The circulation of many common beliefs and practices, however, had no effect upon the basic character

KING SOLOMON'S MINES. Located in the Negev, the southern part of Israel, these cliffs contain the copper that was mined in Solomon's day.

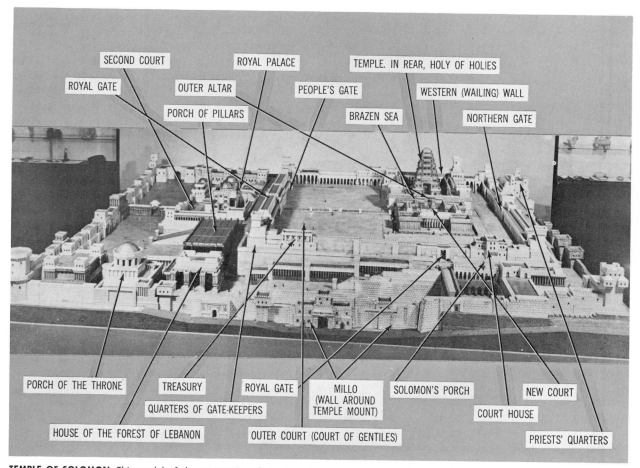

SECOND COURT — ROYAL PALACE — TEMPLE. IN REAR, HOLY OF HOLIES

ROYAL GATE — OUTER ALTAR — PEOPLE'S GATE — WESTERN (WAILING) WALL

PORCH OF PILLARS — BRAZEN SEA — NORTHERN GATE

PORCH OF THE THRONE — TREASURY — ROYAL GATE — MILLO (WALL AROUND TEMPLE MOUNT) — SOLOMON'S PORCH — NEW COURT

QUARTERS OF GATE-KEEPERS — COURT HOUSE

HOUSE OF THE FOREST OF LEBANON — OUTER COURT (COURT OF GENTILES) — PRIESTS' QUARTERS

TEMPLE OF SOLOMON. This model of the ancient Temple in Jerusalem was reconstructed on the basis of the details found in the Bible, especially Chapters 6 and 7 of I Kings.

of national religion. Each country continued to worship its own numerous deities represented in human form and specializing in particular functions. Each called for a wide variety of rites designed to appease, bribe, or coerce the gods. And each limited the authority of their gods to the boundaries of its own nation or empire.

Certain more sensitive individuals began to object to these limitations and shortcomings. In the area of practice, for example, some of the demands of the gods as determined by the priesthood were repulsive and barbaric. Some forms of religious worship called for human sacrifice, especially of children. Others demanded self-whipping or cutting one's flesh. Temple worship, too, often involved acts of the worst

kind of immorality. To the more spiritually minded, these practices appeared revolting.

They also found serious difficulties with the accepted notions about the nature and authority of deity. Was it really true that the deity possessed human form, or that there were so many different gods, each with separate functions? And was the authority of the deity restricted only to the territory of the nation?

Somehow the facts seemed to run counter to these notions. For example, all peoples seemed to have similar religious wants. Essentially the same kind of help and protection that one nation sought from its gods was desired by every other. And despite the fact that peoples dwelt in different lands, they all shared many things in common, like the dawn and sunset, storms

EGYPT AND MESOPOTAMIA. On the left, Ikhnaton and his queen worship the sun-god. In the relief on the right, the Mesopotamian goddess Ishtar stands atop a lion, symbolic of her great power.

and rainclouds, the changing seasons, the growth of crops, joy at the birth of children, and sorrow in the presence of death. How then could the deity's authority end at the borders of the nation or even an empire?

How, too, could the functions of an orderly universe be parcelled out among so many gods, all of whom listened to the requests of their worshippers? And how could gods whose behavior was no better than that of ordinary human beings be respected?

Though most people were perfectly content with national religion, there were a few who were troubled by these questions.

Enter: The Hebrew People   Some of these individuals appeared in various parts of the world at different times. For instance, as early as about 1370 B.C.E., a certain Egyptian king named Ikhnaton came to the conclusion that the sun-god, Aton, was the only deity. To him it was the sun in the heavens that alone merited the people's reverence, and the Pharaoh himself was its incarnation on earth, "born anew every morning like the sun-god his father." Though Ikhnaton introduced no fundamental changes

in the practices of Egyptian religion, he did try to put a stop to the worship of all other gods, removing their names from public monuments and persecuting their priests. However, the effects of his efforts did not outlive him. As soon as he died, the worship of the old gods was promptly restored.

Much later, among the Greeks, there were men like the great philosopher Xenophanes of the sixth century B.C.E., who questioned whether all of the different gods really existed. He concluded that deity was neither human-like nor more than one. "One God," he declared, "the greatest among gods and men, like unto mortals neither in form nor in thought."

But the break-through from national religion to belief in a single moral God of the world was accomplished by a unique group of people who eventually settled in two tiny nations at the eastern end of the Mediterranean. These were the Hebrews.

Among them sprang up the patriarchs and Moses, who introduced certain new conceptions of religion. Then came men like Amos, Hosea, Micah, and the First Isaiah, who appeared in the kingdoms of Israel and Judah around 750 B.C.E. It was they who proclaimed radically different answers to the fundamental questions involving proper religious conduct, the nature of deity, and the extent of divine authority.

Amos, for one, indicted the people of the Northern Kingdom for failing to see the direct relationship between moral conduct and the worship of the deity. Their religion, he insisted, required justice and righteousness in addition to sacrifice and ritual.

At the same time, he also indicated that the Deity of the Hebrew people possessed powers beyond the territorial limits of the land. For their God was able to use other nations to chastise His own people!

Thus, particularly under the influence of the prophets, the Hebrew people formulated answers to some of the most difficult religious problems of all times.

We may wonder why among all peoples the Hebrews should have been so concerned with such things. . . .

RELIGION DEVELOPS MANY GODS

TOPICS TO DISCUSS

1. Why are polytheism and idolatry undesirable forms of religion?
2. In what particular ways have the beliefs and practices of modern religion been affected by the developments that took place in the ancient Middle East?
3. What evidences of national religion do we still find in present-day America? In Judaism?
4. How does your own concept of God differ from those that were current in ancient religion?

THINGS TO DO

1. Imagine that you are living in the ancient world. Prepare a prayer that would be appropriate to the beliefs of people of those days. Then, coming back to the present, rewrite that prayer according to modern Jewish belief.
2. Conduct a debate on the subject: *Resolved,* That Ikhnaton was the founder of all monotheistic religion.

3. Continuing your picture-chart of the development of Judaism from prehistoric times to the present, add the pertinent details concerning the background, beliefs, and practices of national religion.

OTHER THINGS TO READ

ALBRIGHT, WILLIAM F., *From the Stone Age to Christianity,* Doubleday Anchor, pp. 200-236.

FRANKFORT, HENRI, *Ancient Egyptian Religion,* Harper Torchbooks, Chapter 1, "The Egyptian Gods," pp. 3-29.

NOSS, JOHN B., *Man's Religions,* Macmillan, Chapter 2, "Representative National Religions of the Past," pp. 45-106.

PIKE, E. ROYSTON, *Encyclopaedia of Religion and Religions,* Meridian, "Atonism," p. 37; "Babylonian Religion," p. 42; "Egyptians, Ancient," pp. 137-138; "Greek Paganism," pp. 167-168; "Sun Worship," p. 364.

SILVER, ABBA HILLEL, *Moses and the Original Torah,* Macmillan, pp. 16-22 (a view of Ikhnaton).

4

THE HEBREW GOD DEMANDS RIGHTEOUSNESS

The Man at Beth-El   A crowd gathered around the shepherd who began to speak outside the king's sanctuary at Beth-El, in Israel, just north of the Judean border.

The Israelites listened. It was plain by his speech that he came from Judah, and he was saying the strangest things. Not only was he condemning the people for oppressing the poor and for committing other misdeeds, but he was even accusing them of carrying on the wrong kind of religion. For this, he told them, is what their God had ordered him to say:

> I hate, I despise your festivals, and take
>   no delight in your solemn gatherings.
> Even though you offer Me your burnt-
>   offerings and your flour-offerings,
> I will not accept them, nor the
>   peace-offerings of your fatted beasts.
> Take away from Me the sound of your
>   songs; I will not listen to the music of
>   your harps.
> But let justice rise up like waters,
>   and righteousness like a mighty
>   stream.

Furthermore, the man warned, if the people failed to listen, their God would surely destroy them.

The people shook their fists at him. What did he mean by such talk? Would their God destroy His own nation? This was treason!

The priest of Beth-El came forward and confronted the shepherd. "Go back to your own land of Judah," he ordered, "and henceforth stay away from the royal shrine of Beth-El. You are speaking outrageous things against our nation!"

The herdsman merely shook his head sadly and replied, "Your sons and daughters will perish by the sword, and your nation, Israel, will be carried off captive to a foreign land."

The year was about 750 B.C.E. The shepherd was the prophet Amos.

A Great Mystery   It was this man and the other Hebrew prophets who insisted that righteous conduct was an indispensable part of religion. Now it was established that the worship of the Deity demanded not merely the performance of rites and rituals, but a high standard of moral behavior as well. For the first time religion required ethical conduct.

This was only one of the important religious contributions that the Jews were to make. This development is one of the great mysteries of human history. Why, among all the peoples of the world, were the Jews responsible for so many important contributions to religion? And why was it the Jews who first came to know God, the God that all the Western world accepts as the true God?

32

THE HEBREW GOD DEMANDS RIGHTEOUSNESS

Varying explanations for the religious genius of the Jews have been propounded. One links this genius with their early way of life. Subject to the stern hardships of shepherds who lived in desert-like regions, the early Hebrews were compelled to cooperate with one another in order to survive. Out of desert necessity, then, came a stricter code of right-doing toward their fellow man. And even after the Hebrews settled in Palestine, the memories of that desert life with its approved standards of conduct lived on in the people's consciousness. It made them more sensitive to the need for righteous behavior and a higher conception of deity. But many other peoples lived in the desert and they never developed these religious standards.

Another explanation is rooted in the Jews' experiences in the land of Canaan. Living in Palestine, the crossroads of trade, travel, and warfare between the nations and empires of the Middle East, the Jews were exposed to all kinds of pressures. As a tiny group, their polit-ical existence seemed always in doubt, their religion in constant danger of being swallowed up by the faiths of their neighbors.

Self-preservation, then, forced them to cling more determinedly to their own ways, and the seriousness of their situation compelled them to think in terms different from those of other peoples. For instance, once the Hebrews realized that they were unable to compete militarily with the great empires of their day, the concept of their Deity as "victorious in battle" had to undergo change. But there were many other peoples similarly endangered who did not come to know God.

Finally, a third explanation claims that the Jews were directly inspired by God Himself. It was He, many feel, who endowed certain gifted, sensitive individuals with special religious insights. Among them were Abraham and the other patriarchs, Moses, and the prophets. But that a few people should be geniuses, while most are not, is always a mystery. And we are still left with no explanation of why such gifted individuals appeared only in Israel. At best, all of this simply recognizes their remarkable uniqueness.

Perhaps the answer is to be found in a combination of all three. Certainly, as we shall see, without their early desert background, the experiences in Palestine, and the appearance of certain inspired individuals, the Jews could hardly have developed their genius for religion.

The First Hebrews Judaism traces its origins back to the patriarch Abraham, whom it regards as the first Jew.

The only direct information we have about him comes from the Bible and various traditions created by later generations. However, most scholars today believe that the biblical account is generally reliable.

The ancestors of Abraham were Mesopotamians, who dwelt in the fertile region watered by the Tigris and Euphrates Rivers. Originally living in Ur of the Chaldees, an important city located not far from the Persian Gulf, they migrated to Haran, midway between Babylonia and Palestine. From here Abraham took up a

BEDOUINS IN THE NEGEV. Desert peoples continue their old ways of living, in contrast to the modern tractor in the background.

ARCHEOLOGISTS AT WORK. At an ancient site near Beersheba, shafts dug by Israeli archeologists reveal still earlier settlements below the surface.

OUR RELIGION AND OUR NEIGHBORS

The development of such traditions is easily understandable. Later generations were deeply impressed with Abraham's role as the "father of his people," and wished not only to glorify him but to credit him with as many of Judaism's teachings as possible. Among early peoples this was not uncommon. The Mesopotamians, for instance, attributed many of their religious practices to their ancient hero, Gilgamesh, and within the Bible itself we have instances where later teachings were ascribed to other early heroes. Thus the Book of Deuteronomy, which probably was prepared shortly before it was discovered in the Temple in 621 B.C.E., was said to have been written entirely by Moses, who lived some 700 years before.

So, though it is hard for us to believe that Abraham could have made all the contributions that later tradition claimed for him, it is undoubtedly true that he was a pioneer in developing certain religious ideas that mark the beginnings of Judaism. Under his leadership the Hebrew people came into being and with

new kind of life in and around Palestine. This is believed to have taken place sometime around 2000 B.C.E. Most likely not only Abraham and his family, but a larger group of people, perhaps a whole tribe or more, migrated with him.

The Bible tells us that Abraham was the father of Isaac, the grandfather of Jacob, and the great-grandfather of all of Jacob's sons, who formed the twelve Hebrew tribes. There are some problems with this simple theory since an interval of about 600 years exists between the time Abraham left Haran and the tribes appeared. But we can certainly accept the fact that the Hebrew people came into being with Abraham.

Jewish tradition produced many stories about the greatness of its ancient forefather. The stories insisted particularly that it was Abraham who first arrived at a belief in the one and only God, who demanded righteous conduct of His people.

AKKADIAN EPIC. One of a dozen large clay tablets recounting in verse the story of Gilgamesh, an ancient Mesopotamian hero.

34

them a kind of religion that was markedly different from all others.

Trying these thousands of years later to discover what really happened to him or to Moses is a most difficult task. Many theories have been produced by scholars, but what follows seems to us to be the most reasonable explanation we have.

Abraham Requires a New Religion   In the city of Ur, from which Abraham's ancestors came, the Sumerians, and after them the Babylonians, worshipped numerous gods, represented with human faces and forms. Some, as we have seen, were portrayed as men, others as women; and each had certain specified functions. Enlil, for instance, was the god of the storm; Enki, the god of the water that made life and agriculture possible. There were already certain deities who were more widely worshipped than others, chiefly a great Father-god and a great Mother-goddess.

In his youth in Haran, Abraham undoubtedly practiced the religion his family had brought with them from Ur. However, when he and his group left for Palestine, circumstances forced them to adopt a non-agricultural kind of religion. They were unable to settle as farmers in Palestine because of the tight control of the region by the powerful Pharaohs of Egypt of the Twelfth Dynasty. Instead, they had to live on the fringes of Canaan, where the limited water supply and sparse vegetation compelled them to become shepherds.

In this desert-like region, Abraham and his people became nomads, moving about from place to place to feed their flocks. Abraham, himself, became what we see today in a Bedouin sheik, the respected authority of his people. Evidently he also served as the patriarch, or fatherly-leader, of a number of tribes.

The religion that he had known in his native land had been closely identified with agriculture. However, now that he and his people were involved in nomadic life, constantly moving on from place to place, a different form of religion was necessary. For shepherds, the deity must help locate water, increase the flock, provide

male offspring, settle quarrels with other nomadic tribes, and the like.

Inevitably Abraham found himself practicing a religion that was quite distinct from that which his forebears had carried on in Mesopotamia.

The Religion of Abraham   In developing his new faith, Abraham was unquestionably influenced by the beliefs of the other nomadic peoples among whom he now lived. In the main, their religion stood midway between animism, the belief in spirits, and polytheism, the worship of numerous gods.

For centuries the peoples of the region had believed various localities and landmarks to be inhabited by spirits. These landmarks included certain large stones and pillars, most wells and springs. Trees, in general, were venerated and groves were especially sacred. Many creatures, too, such as wolves, hyenas, panthers, lions, foxes, serpents, and others, were thought to possess dangerous spirits.

As with other primitive folk, some of the spirits had already been assigned human characteristics. These were known as *elim* (plural of *el*), "supernatural beings" or gods. Particu-

ANCIENT ALTAR. A reconstruction of a sacrificial altar in ancient Palestine, based upon archeological discoveries.

lar *elim* were associated with certain wells, trees, and even places. So in the Bible we find localities named Beth-El (the home of an *el*), where Jacob built an altar, and Penu-El (the presence of an *el*), where he was said to have wrestled with an angel.

As desert peoples travelled about, they tended to find some particular *el* with whom they established a close relationship. He became a personal, father-like deity to the tribe or group of tribes, and protector of his people. Often he was given a special name, such as Baal, "owner of the land," or Moloch, "ruler." Though his followers continued to believe in the existence of other deities and spirits, it was to this one particular god that they felt especially bound and to him they offered their sacrifices.

Attracted to such beliefs, Abraham and his people may very possibly have adopted as their own deity a god whose name was probably "El Shaddai," "the mountain spirit." He appeared to them as a desert people might picture Him, powerful, stern, wrathful, and just, who required strict adherence to the code of desert life. He insisted, for example, upon generous hospitality to strangers and upon honesty in business dealings. He also demanded His share of the increase of the flocks, and perhaps originally even of the children.

Likewise, in patriarchal religion, we find references to "teraphim," which may have been amulets or images of household gods. Thus, when Jacob fled his father-in-law's home, his wife Rachel carried off with her the family's teraphim. We even find hints of possible totemism as well, as, for instance, in Jacob's blessing in the forty-ninth chapter of the Book of Genesis, where some of the Hebrew tribes are identified with particular animals.

Nonetheless, in many respects the religion of Abraham seems to have differed significantly from that of the peoples who lived in the more settled areas of the Middle East. The god of the patriarchs was always a male deity, and he seemed to have control over the other existing spirits. As part of his worship he demanded obedience to a rather strict code of justice. Particularly noteworthy was the very close rela-

tionship which he established between his people and himself. For, from the very beginning, it was this tie, this covenant, as later generations called it, that closely bound the Hebrews to one another and to their faith.

In this respect, then, the religion of Abraham foreshadowed later developments in Judaism and justifies his traditional prominence as the founder of the Hebrew faith.

The Covenant with Yahveh The thunder roared and the top of the mountain seemed on fire with repeated lightning flashes. There, near the summit, stood a tiny figure whom the people watched fearfully.

Thick clouds came down and covered the mountain-top. The man could no longer be seen.

Down below, the people waited anxiously for his return. The more the thunder roared and the lightning blazed, the more frightened they grew. So powerful was the storm that the very ground under their feet seemed to be quaking.

Then out of the midst of the cloud the man reappeared. In his arms he carried two large stone tablets engraved with letters. Slowly he made his way down the mountain.

The people were reassured. Their leader was returning. The covenant with the great mountain god had been completed.

This, in essence, is the scene the biblical writers described as the Hebrew people stood at the foot of Mt. Sinai. Here they had entered into a covenant, an agreement, with their god. The letters of his name were Y-H-V-H, and we think it was pronounced "Yahveh." (Jewish tradition has never read this name as written, but said instead, "Adonoi," "My Lord." However, the early Christians mistakenly read it as "Jehovah.")

Moses, some believe, discovered Yahveh through his marriage into a tribe of Kenites, a nomadic people similar to the Hebrews. Apparently Yahveh was a powerful mountain god who was thought to dwell in the region of Mt. Sinai, in the southern part of the Sinai Peninsula, between Egypt and Palestine. Because El Shaddai, whom Abraham probably worshipped, had also been a mountain deity, scholars conclude that the Hebrew people identified Yahveh, or "the Lord" as He came to be known, with him.

Successful in leading the Hebrew tribes out of Egypt where they had been slaves, Moses saw behind this deliverance the power and love of God. It was He who had compelled the Egyptians to free Israel. But now the Hebrews must once more agree to accept Him as their God, as had the patriarchs. To this end Moses had led the tribes to the deity's mountain to establish the covenant.

As His part of the agreement, the Lord accepted the Hebrews as His people and promised to protect them and help them in battle. In return, the Hebrews pledged themselves to worship only Him and to obey His commandments. Not only did He demand certain types of sacrifices, but a particular code of conduct which may have also included the Ten Commandments, as later tradition has made them known to us. Worship of Him was to center around a special symbol of the presence of the deity, a portable "Ark of the Covenant," which the Hebrews promptly constructed. The people of other nations might continue to worship other gods, but not the Hebrews. They were pledged only to the Lord, and their belief in Him was strengthened by later victories under Joshua which made it possible for the tribes to settle in Palestine.

Loyalty to this covenant with their God was, therefore, basic to the Hebrew religion. Moreover, the Deity was a "jealous" God, who threatened the destruction of His people if they should adopt the worship of other gods.

The Establishment of a National Religion

As yet the worship of the Lord was simply the religion of a few tribes, for many scholars believe that not all of the Hebrews went to Egypt. Now, on their return to Palestine, the religion of these tribes faced its most serious test. Could the worship of the Hebrew God survive in the midst of Canaanite religion?

Like the people of Mesopotamia, the Canaanites, who were the Hebrews' chief neighbors, practiced an agricultural religion that involved numerous gods and goddesses. The father of the gods was an *el* who was often pictured in the form of a bull. With his wife Asherah, he sired some seventy gods and goddesses, among whom was Baal, the chief god responsible for rain and the growth of the crops. According to certain legends, each year after the life-giving rainy season, Baal was supposed to be murdered by Mot, the god of death, only to come alive again the following year when he once more brought the rains.

Associated with this religion were the sacrifice of children, the worship of snakes, and many immoral practices. This was in sharp contrast to the conduct demanded by the God of the Hebrews. At first the Hebrews resisted its influences. But as the tribes settled down to agricultural life, certain elements of Baal-worship crept into their religion.

Among some of the Hebrew tribes, especially those, it is felt, who had not gone to Egypt, the tendency to adopt Canaanite practices seems to have been more pronounced. The tribes of the South, who had certainly come out of Egypt, appear to have had a greater loyalty to the religion of their own God, although they, too, were influenced by certain features of Baal-worship.

For nearly two hundred years, the Hebrews continued to live in separate tribes. Occasionally they banded together in the name of the Lord under certain military leaders, called "Judges," to fight against common enemies. Eventually, through the united efforts of most of the tribes under Saul and David, the power of their greatest enemy, the Philistines, was broken and a kingdom of all the Hebrew people was established.

To a large extent the worship of the Lord followed the pattern of a national religion. Solomon established a magnificent sanctuary in Jerusalem with an organized priesthood and impressive rituals. Many saw the Lord as the God essentially of the Hebrew nation, with His power extending over the very land itself. We observe this in the biblical story of Naaman, a Syrian leader who was cleansed of leprosy by one of the early prophets. Out of gratitude he wished to continue the worship of the Hebrew God in his native land. Therefore, he carried

DAVID FACES GOLIATH. Here, etched in Steuben Glass, is a modern conception of the famous contest described in Chapter 17 of I Samuel.

back with him two mule-loads of Palestinian soil (II Kings 5).

Meanwhile, elements of other religions continued to creep into the worship of the Hebrews. For example, the Hebrew kings' respect for the deities of their foreign wives served to spread the worship of foreign idols. But more persistent was the influence of Baalism. The fact that the Bible continually protests against a variety of Baalistic practices, and that Saul, the first King of Israel, gave his son the name of Ish-Baal, "the man of Baal," indicate the wide influence of Baal-worship.

The Appearance of Prophets After the death of Solomon, the national religion suffered by the division of the kingdom. Now the Lord became the God of two separate nations that often clashed.

By and large, the Northern Kingdom of Is-

rael, more populous and prosperous than its neighbor to the south, was more susceptible to the influences of Canaanite religion. In addition, many of its foreign princesses encouraged the practice of their own religions. Thus, as we have already noted, Jezebel, Queen of Israel, publicly sponsored the worship of her Tyrian god, Melkart.

Judah, the kingdom to the south, with its more nomadic population and its control of the sanctuary at Jerusalem, tended more faithfully to preserve the Hebrew religion. Yet even here foreign elements managed to creep in.

In both nations certain individuals now began to appear who spoke in the name of the Hebrew God and demanded changes in the people's conduct, worship, and beliefs. These were the prophets, and their emphasis, in general, was upon righteousness as required by God. Some of the earlier prophets, like Samuel, Nathan, and Elijah, dared to challenge even the acts of the kings themselves. Nathan condemned King David for having taken away Bathsheba, another man's wife; Elijah berated King Ahab for stealing Naboth's vineyard.

But it was the prophets of the period around 750 B.C.E., men like Amos, Hosea, Micah, and the first Isaiah (known as "literary" prophets because they left written records of their messages), who carried this theme to the highest point of religious thought and feeling. They told the people of Israel and Judah that their conduct made them faithless to their covenant with the Lord. They warned that, if the people continued in their ways, their God would punish them and allow other nations to conquer them. For He had influence over the actions of other peoples as well.

What exactly was it that the Deity demanded of His followers? Briefly, it was to cease worship of idols and other gods, and to halt all foreign practices, especially those connected with the religion of Baal. But beyond this, the Lord called upon the people to be righteous in their relations with one another. He wanted Israel to live by its covenant, to be loyal to Him, and to show this in their actions with other men.

Here is the way the prophet Micah stated it:

THE DEVELOPMENT OF JUDAISM TO THE DEUTERONOMIC REFORM

EVENTS IN JEWISH HISTORY	DEVELOPMENTS IN JUDAISM	OTHER RELIGIOUS EVENTS
about 2000 B.C.E. Abraham and beginning of the Age of the Patriarchs. 	Beginnings of the Hebrew religion. 	National religion already in existence. Gradual development of empires. **After 1500 B.C.E.** Beginnings of Hinduism.
about 1300 B.C.E. Exodus from Egypt under Moses.	Establishment of the Covenant with Yahveh and the people.	Continued development of national religions among the peoples of the Middle East.
about 1000 B.C.E. Start of the Hebrew Kingdom with Saul and David.	Development of a national Hebrew religion with Temple and priesthood. Beginnings of prophecy (Samuel).	
926 B.C.E. Division of the kingdom.	Increasing Canaanite and foreign religious influence. Prophecy continues (Elijah, Elisha).	
around 750 B.C.E. Activity of Amos, Hosea, Isaiah and Micah.	Literary prophecy begins. Growing emphasis upon righteous conduct. Growing authority of the Deity.	
?1 B.C.E. Assyrian destruction of the Northern Kingdom of Israel.	Assyrian exiles eventually disappear.	
?1 B.C.E. Book of Deuteronomy discovered. Activity of Jeremiah.		

DEAD SEA SCROLLS. A fragment of two selections from the Book of Deuteronomy. The column on the right is Deut. 29:12-20; the one on the left is Deut. 30:19-31:6.

It has been told you, O man, what is
    good,
And what the Lord does require of you.
Only to do justly, to love mercy and to
    walk humbly with your God.
    —Micah 6:8

Toward a Higher Stage of Religion Though the people of the Northern Kingdom paid little attention to the prophets, those in the South did heed them. The result was a great religious reformation. In the year 621, King Josiah of Judah introduced sweeping religious reforms based upon a book that suddenly turned up in the Temple.

This discovery seems in major part to have been what today we call the Book of Deuteronomy. It contains many laws that reflect the teachings of the prophets. The book also con-

tains the Sh'ma, which, among other things, and in keeping with the prophetic message of the times, declared that the Lord alone was the God of the Hebrews and His worship permitted no other gods.

The Bible informs us that King Josiah's reformation did not put an end to Baal-worship or the misconduct of the people. Indeed, the Southern Kingdom was itself conquered only 35 years later. But by now the idea of a Deity who insisted upon righteousness and who could influence the actions of other nations was firmly implanted in Judaism.

This marked an important advance, a major milestone in the development of religion. Now, according to this scholarly theory, there was but one more step to the concept of a completely universal God, a God of the whole world, who demanded righteousness from all mankind.

THE HEBREW GOD DEMANDS RIGHTEOUSNESS

However, it was to take one of the worst disasters in Jewish history, and the efforts of two of Israel's greatest prophets to arrive at this higher form of religion. . . .

TOPICS TO DISCUSS

1. How do you account for the particular religious genius of the Jewish people?
2. To what extent is our present-day Judaism still based upon the teachings of Abraham, Moses, and the prophets?
3. What elements of the earliest and national phases of religion do we still observe in Judaism?
4. Within present-day Jewish life, what conflicts do we still find between the teachings of the prophets and (a) the absorption of other religious ideas; (b) the conduct of the Jewish people; and (c) the practices of institutionalized religion?

THINGS TO DO

1. Imagine that the prophet Amos returned to your community. Write a speech that he might deliver at the city hall.
2. As a student of religion, investigate the following passages of the Bible and prepare a brief report on the character of patriarchal religion: Genesis 11:31-32; 12:5-6; 13:18; 15:1-18; 16:9; 17:1-14; 19:24-25; 22:1-18; 24:1-4; 28; 31:13-20.
3. Continuing with your picture-chart of the development of religion, add the pertinent items now contributed by the Hebrews.

OTHER THINGS TO READ

BALLOU, ROBERT O., *The Portable World Bible*, Viking, "The Old Testament," pp. 246-298; 333-339.

BAMBERGER, BERNARD J., *The Story of Judaism*, UAHC, Chapter 1, "Seeds and Roots," pp. 5-10; Chapter 2, "Growth of a National Religion," pp. 11-15; Chapter 3, "The Great Revolution," pp. 16-19; Chapter 4, "The Great Revolution (continued)," pp. 20-25; Chapter 5, "The Beginnings of Torah," pp. 26-31.

NOSS, JOHN B., *Man's Religions*, Macmillan, pp. 463-498.

SCHWARTZMAN, SYLVAN D., and JACK D. SPIRO, *The Living Bible*, UAHC, Chapter 2, "Who Is God?" pp. 17-41.

SILVER, ABBA HILLEL, *Moses and the Original Torah*, Macmillan, Chapter 2, "The Torah That Men Had Rejected," pp. 7-15; Chapter 3, "Moses Who Gave This Torah," pp. 16-38; Chapter 4, "The Prophets Who Championed It," pp. 39-44; Chapter 5, "The Bene Israel Whom Moses Led," pp. 45-63.

WOLFE, ROLLAND E., *Men of Prophetic Fire*, Beacon Press, Chapter 1, "The Prophets—Who Were They?" pp. 3-13; Amos, pp. 17-68; Hosea, pp. 71-98; Isaiah, pp. 101-131; Micah, pp. 133-150.

5

JUDAISM BECOMES A MISSIONARY FAITH

Disaster Strikes the Hebrews   Wedged in between the mighty powers of Mesopotamia to the east and Egypt to the south, the small Hebrew nations of Palestine had little chance of survival. For the Kingdoms of Israel and Judah stood directly in the path of the two great rival empires of the ancient Middle East.

The Northern Kingdom of Israel was destroyed first. In 721 B.C.E. its people were taken captive and were dispersed among the lands of the victorious Assyrians. It was there that the so-called "Lost Ten Tribes" disappeared from history. Evidently believing that their national Deity had failed them, the captives probably turned to the worship of the more powerful gods of their conquerors, and were finally completely assimilated into the Assyrian population.

The people of Judah were not taken by the Assyrians. Prophets like Jeremiah pointed to the example of Israel and promised the Judeans the same fate as their northern brothers if they failed to remain true to the covenant with their God and worship Him according to His demands.

Some listened to the prophets. In fact, it was during this period that the sweeping religious reforms inspired by the discovery of the Book of Deuteronomy in the Temple took place. As a result, local shrines which had been centers of Baal-worship were closed, and special laws to protect the laboring man and the poor were introduced. However, the effect of these reforms was only temporary. Once more Jeremiah began to prophesy the eventual destruction of the Kingdom of Judah.

Unfortunately his words proved true. In 586 B.C.E. mighty Babylonia, the successor to the Assyrian Empire, captured Jerusalem and carried off most of the Judeans as captives.

Thus twice within a period of 135 years disaster struck the Hebrews. Now the people of Judah seemed about to suffer the same fate as their kinsmen of the Northern Kingdom.

Two Prophets Save the Jews   Belief in their God grew fainter as the weary captives trudged toward Babylonia. To most of them it was plain that He had failed them in a time of national crisis. Either He had abandoned them because of their faithlessness to the covenant, or perhaps it was true that Marduk, the chief god of the Babylonians, was more powerful than the Lord.

As they caught their first glimpse of the great cities of Mesopotamia, the reality of their situation sank in. Now they were helpless exiles, far from their homeland of Palestine, far from the soil over which their God had control. What choice had they but to relinquish their own religion for the faith of the Babylonians?

Undoubtedly these were some of the thoughts

that passed through the minds of the captives. We catch their mood in this passage from the Book of Psalms:

> By the waters of Babylon,
>   There we sat; yes, we wept
> When we remembered Zion.
>   There they that took us captive . . .
> Asked of us mirth . . .
>   But how can we sing the Lord's song
>   in a foreign land?—Psalm 137:1-4

This indeed was the question. For even if they wanted to, how could they continue to worship their own God when they now lived so far from His only sanctuary?

Except for two prophets the question might have remained unanswered, and the Jews and Judaism might have disappeared.

The first prophet was Jeremiah, whom the Babylonians permitted to remain behind in Palestine. He wrote to the captives, advising them to settle down to a normal life in Babylonia and continue to worship their own God there. The Lord, he explained, had not really forsaken them; He was only punishing them for their failure to keep the covenant with Him. But the covenant itself would never be destroyed. Because of it, eventually He would bring the exiles back to their native land.

Thus Jeremiah made the people understand that they could carry on their religion even though they lived on foreign soil. He based his message in part upon the teachings of the earlier prophets who had taught that God's power extended over other nations. But Jeremiah also voiced a new message: punishment did not put an end to Israel's relationship with its God, and the Lord would some day restore the Jews to their country.

Some thirty-five years later another prophet appeared, this time, many believe, among the exiles in Babylonia. We know him only as the Second Isaiah since his message was simply added on to the writings of the original Isaiah who had lived two centuries before.

The Lord, this prophet told the people, was by no means a national god, the deity of a particular land or people. He was the God of the

JERUSALEM. Enclosed in glass for protection, these Dead Sea Scrolls were written a century or more before the Common Era.

entire universe, the God who created the world and everything in it. This is how the Second Isaiah stated it:

> Thus God the Lord says,
> Who created the heavens and stretched
>   them out,
> Who spread out the earth and all that
>   comes from it,
> Who gave breath to all the people
>   upon it,
> And spirit to all who walk upon it. . . .
> Thus says the Lord, the King of Israel,
> And his Redeemer, the Lord of hosts:
> I am the first, and I am the last,
> And beside Me, there is no God.
>   —Isaiah 42:5; 44:6

What did this prophet have to say about the captives from Judah? Their suffering in exile, he taught, was intended to purify them for their great task as God's "servant." He explained:

> I am the Lord, I have called you in
>   righteousness,

I have taken you by the hand and kept
    you;
I have given you as a covenant to the
    people, a light to the nations. . . .
You are My witnesses, says the Lord, and
    My servant whom I have chosen. . . .
      —Isaiah 42:6; 43:10

Now the captives have been charged with a "mission" to all mankind. They must spread the truth that the Lord, the God of Israel, is the one and only God of the universe, and His will is supreme!

Champions of Ethical Monotheism   Thanks to the teachings of Jeremiah and Second Isaiah, the Jewish people were able not merely to survive, but also to become the bearers of "ethical monotheism" to all mankind.

What is the meaning of "ethical monotheism"? The word "ethical," of course, means "doing the right thing," or "being righteous." "Monotheism" comes from two words, Greek in origin, *mono*, "one," and *theos*, "god." "Monotheism," then, means "one God." Thus the term "ethical monotheism" describes that form of religion which believes in the existence of only one God, a God whose power extends over the entire universe and who, completely righteous Himself, demands righteous conduct from His followers as an essential part of their worship.

Though this concept is quite familiar to us today, it was a new and revolutionary idea in the ancient world. It required the surrender of the old notions about a variety of national deities and the substitution of a single God who could be worshipped everywhere. It also insisted that religion extended beyond the boundaries of the nation, that the same code of conduct applied to everyone, and that the well-being of all mankind was the concern of the worshipper.

For if the Deity was indeed the God of the entire universe, then He was equally interested in what happened to all peoples. Consequently the proper worship of Him meant seeking the good of humanity, everywhere striving to overcome evil, which always produces misery and suffering, and helping all men to live together in brotherliness and peace.

ISAIAH'S PROPHECY. A modern sculptor portrays the Prophet beating his sword into a ploughshare. See Isaiah 2:2-4.

JUDAISM BECOMES A MISSIONARY FAITH

True, earlier prophets had already spoken of the time when nations would "beat their swords into ploughshares and their spears into pruning-hooks," when nation would not "lift up sword against nation, nor learn war anymore" (Isaiah 2:4). They had promised, too, that the day would come when everyone would "sit under his vine and under his fig-tree, and none shall make them afraid" (Micah 4:4).

But now, as a consequence of the belief in a universal God, new emphasis was placed upon the welfare of all peoples. Such works as the Books of Jonah and Ruth began to appear. In the former, God sends His prophet Jonah to preach to the people of Nineveh, a city of Babylonia, and by so doing He reveals His concern for the well-being of the non-Jew as well as the Jew. "Shall I not take pity on Nineveh," God asks Jonah, "that great city which has more than 120,000 inhabitants? . . ." And the Book of Ruth points to the fine qualities of a Moabite woman (that is, not a Jewess) who eventually became the great-grandmother of King David himself!

Later Jewish literature shows how deeply these new teachings took root. For instance, at about the time of the Common Era, the rabbis, in commenting upon the Exodus from Egypt, pictured God as rebuking His angels for rejoicing over the destruction of the Egyptians at the Red Sea. "How can you be happy," He sadly asks the angels, "when My children, the Egyptians, are drowning?" Thus, by the time of the Common Era, the teachings of ethical monotheism were so thoroughly a part of Judaism that even the long-standing Egyptian enemy had become precious to the God whom the Jews worshipped.

By about this time, too, as champions of ethical monotheism, the Jews interpreted their ancient covenant with God to mean something more. The covenant represented Israel's promise to show loyalty to God by living according to His laws in the sight of all men. Through the example of the Jews, all the world might come to know Him. As a result, Israel was forever charged with serving as a "living witness" to its faith in the Lord.

The Spread of Ethical Ideals   The Jew's concept of ethical monotheism and his dedication to it were unique among the peoples of the ancient world. And they were destined to remain so down to the very present.

Many religions, like Hinduism, Buddhism, and Confucianism, never arrived at this stage. Even the daughter religions of Judaism, Christianity and Islam, adopted only more limited forms of ethical monotheism. Consequently, over the centuries the Jew alone has maintained it in its purest state.

Nonetheless, certain common ethical ideals gradually made their way into the faiths of other peoples as part of a more desirable way of life. One was the so-called "Golden Rule," and it is interesting to see how it arose among the various religions.

In Judaism the principle, "You shall love your neighbor as yourself," first appears in the Book of Leviticus, coming chiefly from about the sixth century B.C.E. The teaching of this "Golden Rule" was further emphasized by Hillel, one of the great scholars of rabbinic Judaism who lived around the beginning of the Common Era. When asked by a non-Jew to define the essence of Judaism, Hillel replied, "What is displeasing to yourself, do not do to your fellow man."

We find practically the same principle expressed by Confucius, who lived in the sixth century B.C.E. When he was asked by one of his disciples for a single word to serve as a guide to life, he answered, "Perhaps the word *Shu*,

HILLEL'S ANSWER. The learned Sage summarizes the essence of Judaism while his non-Jewish questioner stands on one foot.

45

'reciprocity,' or 'replying in the same manner,' will do. Do not unto others what you do not want others to do unto you."

Both Buddhist and Moslem literature offer similar teachings, and so does Christianity. The Gospel of Matthew, which is part of Christian Scriptures, has Jesus instruct those who have come to listen to him, "Whatever you wish that men would do to you, do so to them."

Gradually, then, various important ethical teachings began to appear within the different religions. But a significant difference remained. Only in the case of Judaism was ethics uniquely interwoven with belief in a single universal God so that ethics constituted an essential of His worship. And only Israel was pledged to exemplify God's righteous demands in everyday living.

Some Significant Developments in Judaism

These new beliefs as well as the vastly different kind of Jewish way of life in Babylonia led to four significant developments in Judaism.

The first development was the creation of the synagogue. Many scholars believe this originated during the Babylonian Exile. With the destruction of the Temple in Jerusalem, worship with sacrifices and burnt-offerings was no longer possible. Instead, the Jews substituted a service of prayer and study. Now, following the former daily routine of Temple sacrifices, the people would gather together to recite a number of prayers, of which the "Sh'ma" was one, and to read selections from their growing religious literature. Sometimes, too, particular laws would be discussed so that the exiles would be informed more precisely about the demands of God.

The place where the people gathered for worship was known as the *bes ha-k'neses*, "place of assembly," and, physically, it was either a special room or a building set aside for the purpose. At a later period it came to be called a "synagogue," from the Greek word meaning "assembly-place." Unlike the Temple which was in Jerusalem and was unique, Jews placed no limit on the number of synagogues that might exist.

The second development was the growth of a sacred literature. Because the exiles were eager to preserve their identity, they undertook the collecting and editing of many of their early traditions and the writings of the prophets, and this marked the start of the Bible. Though the process was not completed until sometime after the first century of the Common Era, the Five Books of Moses and a number of prophetic books now began to take shape. Even certain new writings were produced. For instance, in view of the promise that the Jews would shortly return to Palestine, the prophet Ezekiel and the priests took great pains to record all of the details of Temple worship for that day when the Jerusalem sanctuary would be restored. This information is found in our present Books of Leviticus and Ezekiel.

Gradually, then, and in contrast to the other religions that centered mainly about a temple-cult, Judaism came more and more to be based upon the teachings of its Bible. For it contained a sacred literature that the people believed to be the very word of God Himself.

The third development was the emergence of a special kind of religious leader. As the Jews became a "people of the Book," individuals known as "scribes" began to appear. These were learned men who were capable of explaining the

ARCHEOLOGICAL SEARCH. At the site of this archeological expedition, scores of men sift the soil for the remains of ancient civilization.

contents of the Bible and interpreting its laws in the light of life in Babylonia. The scribes' wide knowledge of Jewish traditions enabled them to determine precisely what God's law demanded. And, as interpreters of His word, they became the forerunners of the much later "rabbis," who served in essentially the same capacity.

Unlike the Temple priests whose office was handed down from father to son, the family background of the scribe or rabbi was unimportant. As the translation of the title "rabbi," "my teacher," shows, his essential qualification was a wide knowledge of Judaism. These new religious leaders arose out of practically every class of society. Learning, not family tree, was the most important consideration.

The fourth and final development was the principle of study. The focus of attention upon the Bible prompted the exiles to emphasize study as an important aspect of the worship of God. As a result, places of study for the young as well as for adults were established as part of the synagogue proper or in buildings attached to it. Here, in the *beis ha-midrosh*, "house of study," the scribes taught the moral, ethical, and ceremonial laws of Judaism. Study was also introduced into the worship, and parts of the sacred Bible were read aloud and interpreted. Now, in addition to righteous conduct and prayer, study became an indispensable feature of the Jewish religion.

Thus, with the development of the synagogue, the Bible, the scribe and rabbi, and the study of sacred literature, the Babylonian exiles had produced a new and lasting form of Judaism.

The Return to Palestine   Loud cheers for Cyrus, the great Persian general, king, and conqueror of the Babylonians, rang out in the streets of Babylon. As the chariots and horses of Cyrus' mighty army thundered past, a roar went up from the many thousands of captives whom the Babylonians had deported from their homelands.

"Home, we're going home," sighed an old man, a Jew who had been taken off to Babylonia as a youth from the ruins of Jerusalem.

But many years were to pass before any sizable number of Jews returned to Palestine. Most of the people never went back because Judaism had found a home in Babylonia, and for many centuries Babylonia continued to be a great spiritual center of the Jewish religion. Many of Judaism's most famous scholars were trained in its schools. Their study and work formed the basis, centuries later, for the famous Babylonian Talmud, the great work that served to reinterpret the teachings of the Bible in subsequent generations.

However, with the consent of Cyrus and the prodding of certain prophets as well as of Ezra and Nehemiah, two prominent Jewish leaders, small bands of pioneers slowly began to return to Palestine. When the first group finally reached Jerusalem, all they found were the ruins of the city. What is more, the inhabitants looked upon them as invaders, rather than as exiles returning home after a long absence.

Nevertheless, with support of their fellow-Jews back in Babylonia, the pioneers commenced their work of rebuilding Jerusalem. Slowly, arduously, the walls were put up, and eventually, about 515 B.C.E., the Second Temple was erected. The priestly ritual was reintroduced and the practice of sacrifices restored. Now the priestly class sought to reestablish its

TORAH SCRIBES. Religious Jews, trained for the task, devote their lives to the preparation of accurate Torah scrolls.

THE DEVELOPMENT OF JUDAISM FROM EXILE TO COMMON ERA

EVENTS IN JEWISH HISTORY

586 B.C.E. Destruction of First Temple. Fall of the Southern Kingdom of Judah and Babylonian exile commences. Activity of Ezekiel.

Around 550 B.C.E. Activity of Second Isaiah.

About 538 B.C.E. Cyrus permits the return of the exiles.

About 515 B.C.E. Jerusalem Temple completed.

About 450 B.C.E. Ezra and Nehemiah return to Palestine.

331 B.C.E. Alexander the Great of Greece takes over control of Palestine.

167 B.C.E. Beginning of Maccabean revolt.

63 B.C.E. Romans take over control of Palestine.

DEVELOPMENTS IN JUDAISM

National religion gives way to a universal faith based upon ethical monotheism. A return to Palestine promised. Beginnings of the scribes, Bible, synagogue, study of Scripture, etc.

Functions of the priesthood reestablished. Beginning of religious struggles between scribes and priests.

Beginnings of the rabbinate.

OTHER RELIGIOUS EVENTS

About 563 B.C.E. Birth of Buddha

About 551 B.C.E. Birth of Confucius.

From 450 B.C.E. on Period of Greek philosophy begins with Socrates, Plato, and Aristotle.

Beginning from about 200 B.C.E. on Growth of the great mystery religions of Cybele, Isis, and Mithra.

About 4 B.C.E. Birth of Jesus.

authority over the Jewish religion. But this brought them into conflict with the scribes and, some centuries later, with the rabbis under whom Judaism continued to develop in Palestine as well as Babylonia.

In the religious disputes that subsequently took place, there were numerous points at issue. For instance, in their emphasis upon righteousness, kindness, and charity, the scribes and rabbis reflected the universal teachings of Judaism to a much greater extent than the priests, who were more inclined to look upon Judaism as a national religion. The priests also felt that God's worship should center about the elaborate Temple ritual of sacrifices, but the scribes and rabbis placed great stress upon prayer and study in the synagogue. Moreover, the priests objected to reinterpretations of Jewish belief that were not mentioned by the Torah. So they opposed the teachings of the scribes and rabbis about resurrection, the concept that some day the dead would be restored to life in bodily form.

Eventually, by the first century B.C.E., the two groups formed separate religious parties. The priests, supported generally by the wealthier landowners and ruling classes, comprised a group known as the Sadducees, probably named after Sadok, the founder of the priestly line in King Solomon's time. Those who sided with the scribes and rabbis were known as the Pharisees, a name derived from a Hebrew word meaning to "separate" or "interpret." By and large, the Pharisees had much greater popular support, and, despite the opposition of the Sadducees, Judaism continued to grow through the process of scribal and rabbinical interpretation.

How Judaism Differed from Other Religions

By the time of the Common Era, Judaism differed from the other religions of the ancient world in five principal ways:

First, many of the Jewish practices were unique. Judaism's insistence upon study, non-sacrificial worship, Sabbath rest, circumcision, dietary laws, the various holiday observances, and the like, set the Jews apart from the other peoples.

Second, Judaism was distinctive because of its development of original religious institutions like the synagogue, the Bible, the rabbinate, and the whole process of Jewish law.

Third, Judaism contained a number of beliefs that were in direct contrast to those of other faiths. One was the Jew's insistence upon a strict ethical code of conduct as central to religious practice. Others were the concept of a universal God whose power extended over all mankind; belief in a Deity who could not be seen or represented in any visible form; and the conviction that the people of Israel had been especially chosen by God to live a holy, righteous life.

Fourth, there was the Jews' unwillingness to compromise in matters of religion. In the Maccabean revolt beginning in 167 B.C.E., the Jews had shown themselves prepared to die rather than obey the commands of the Syrian overlord of Palestine, Antiochus Epiphanes, to worship idols or eat forbidden food. While the Jews were willing to carry out his political demands, they refused to accede to any that violated their religious convictions. From the point of view of national religion, this insistence upon freedom to worship God in their own way, and unwillingness to accede to the religious edicts of a ruling power was something unheard of. Their belief that their God was really the only God prohibited them from bowing to a mere flesh-and-blood ruler.

Fifth, the Jews' sense of obligation to convert the other peoples to their faith ran counter to the religious sentiments of the ancient world. For it was customary to accept the existence of the gods of other nations. Hence the contention of any group, and especially of a tiny, helpless people like the Jews, that it alone possessed the true God and that all others must come to believe in Him was looked upon as the height of arrogance.

Furthermore, because the Jews were firmly convinced that this was the "Mission" for which their God had chosen them, they became a missionary people.

The Jews Become Active Missionaries

Through commerce, travel, and war, word about

THE EDICT OF CYRUS. Pictured here is the ancient King of Persia granting the Jews permission to rebuild their Temple in Jerusalem.

the Jews spread among the peoples of the ancient world. But some Jews also took it upon themselves to circulate as much information about their religion as possible.

Living in different parts of the then-known world, they attempted to do this through day-to-day contacts with their neighbors and the circulation of various writings. There were the works of Philo, which presented the teachings of Judaism to the Greek-speaking world, and those of Josephus, which explained the history of the Jews to the Romans. Another was "The Wisdom of Solomon," now contained in the Apocrypha, a collection of writings that were not considered sufficiently sacred to be included in the Bible. Among other things this work attacked the worship of many gods and attempted to persuade their followers to adopt the beliefs of the Jews. For thus declared the writer of "The Wisdom of Solomon":

. . . All men are foolish by nature, and

had no perception of God,
And from the good things that were visible they had not the power to know Him who is,
Nor through paying attention to His works did they recognize the Workman,
But either fire, or wind, or swift air,
Or the circle of the stars, or rushing water,
Or the heavenly lights, the rulers of the world, they considered gods.
And if through delight in their beauty they supposed that these were gods,
Let them know how far superior is the Lord of these. . . .
—Wisdom of Solomon 13:1-3

At first the Jews appeared to others as a very strange group indeed. Their ethical ideas were in startling contrast to the often immoral and superstitious rites of the others; and to those who prayed to idols, the Jews' worship of an invisible God seemed sheer nonsense. Apparently Titus, a cruel Roman emperor, did not believe it, for when he conquered Jerusalem he thrust a sword in the Holy of Holies in the Temple to try to kill the Jewish God who lived there. The peoples were also mystified by the Jews' refusal to worship idols or to bow down before powerful emperors who regarded themselves as gods.

But to the more thoughtful these very aspects of Judaism and the Jews had special appeal, and some adopted the Jewish religion. Many became full converts. Many more, however, accepted only certain portions of Judaism, such as its ethical ideals, or the Sabbath as a day of rest, or its teachings about the one, universal God, without binding themselves to observe the dietary laws, or practice circumcision.

Now an increasing number of Jewish missionaries began to travel about the Roman world. The New Testament states that they would "compass sea and land to make one convert," and undoubtedly they did convince many to accept the religion of Israel. Certain Roman authors, including Cicero, Horace, Seneca, and Tacitus, testify to their wide-spread and successful missionary activities. Sometimes they pursued their mission so intensively that they

50

JUDAISM BECOMES A MISSIONARY FAITH

antagonized the authorities. On two occasions at least, Jews were expelled from Rome for vigorously carrying on their propaganda.

The Growing Religious Unrest   With the arrival of the Common Era, the tempo of Jewish missionary activity mounted. The times, it seemed, were ripe for Judaism's distinctive teachings, for it was a period of considerable religious unrest.

Actually, doubt about the merit of the existing religions had arisen several centuries earlier when certain of the Greek philosophers began questioning various beliefs. Ultimately they even challenged the very existence of the gods themselves. Some poked fun at many of the ancient myths about them, and Plato, who lived during the fourth century B.C.E., spoke of the "Idea of the Good" as the supreme force in the universe. For him, however, God was simply a lesser deity who had created the world.

A century after Plato, one school of Greek philosophy, the Stoics, began teaching about a universal force, really representing nature, whom they called God. They sought to apply to all men rules based on "Natural Laws" and thereby to unite them in one great brotherhood of humanity.

Thus, though Greek philosophy did not arrive at a conception of ethical monotheism, it did succeed in undermining belief in existing religions.

Meanwhile the triumphant armies of the Greeks under Alexander the Great were spreading these teachings and others to the various lands they conquered. The victorious Romans who followed carried Greek thought to practically every part of the ancient world. With it also went the general discontent of the conquered peoples with the stern and often brutal rule of Roman emperors who demanded that they be worshipped as deities. All the while, the influence of Judaism, with its condemnation of idol-worship and of gods that behaved like sinful humans, began to be felt.

Slowly, more and more people were affected by the sweep of these new and different ideas. Though they continued to worship their old

ROMAN REMAINS. Still standing in Rome is this Arch of Titus showing some of the spoils from the Temple, including the Menorah (candelabrum), being carried off.

gods, many began to doubt old beliefs and practices, and over the years the power of the gods was sapped. Nor was the imperial religion of Rome able to replace the old national faiths, for it offered nothing more than the same set of gods with new names.

A Vacuum to Be Filled   Thus, the period around the beginning of the Common Era was a time when many people were prepared to abandon their old beliefs and observances for something else. Many were searching for a more satisfactory answer to their spiritual needs than that offered by their national cults.

There was the possibility, of course, that Judaism might become that religion. Jewish missionaries were carrying the teachings of their faith to all parts of the Roman Empire with increasing effect.

However, as things turned out, Jewish mis-

51

sionaries were simply setting the stage for the birth of a new religion. For certain events were taking place among the Jews of Palestine that were destined to fill the religious void of the ancient world. . . .

TOPICS TO DISCUSS

1. Some people have claimed that one cannot truly be a religious Jew without living in the State of Israel. From the standpoint of Second Isaiah, how would you answer this?
2. To what extent does modern Judaism draw upon the contributions of the Babylonian Jews?
3. How have the beliefs and practices of the modern Jew been affected by the appearance of scribes and rabbis?
4. How do you account for the fact that Judaism failed to capture the ancient world? In what ways has this affected Jewish life today?

THINGS TO DO

1. Imagine that you were a Jewish missionary during the period around the beginning of the Common Era. Draw up a list of arguments that you would use to convince people of Judaism's superiority over the national religions.
2. Conduct a debate on the subject: *Resolved,* That the Jews should again become missionaries.

3. As a student of religion, investigate the following biblical passages and from them describe the role of the Jews as seen by Second Isaiah: Isaiah 42:1-13; 43:1-15; 44:1-5; 49:1-12, 22-23; 52:13-15.

OTHER THINGS TO READ

BALLOU, ROBERT O., *The Portable World Bible,* Viking, "Old Testament," pp. 337-345.

BAMBERGER, BERNARD J., *The Story of Judaism,* UAHC, Chapter 5, "The Beginnings of Torah," pp. 26-31; Chapter 6, "Exile," pp. 32-37; Chapter 7, "Hopes and Disappointments," pp. 38-41; Chapter 8, "Judaism Is Complete," pp. 42-47; Chapter 9, "Particularism and Universalism," pp. 48-51; Chapter 12, "Judah and Hellas: Palestine," pp. 65-69; Chapter 14, "The Struggle for Religious Democracy," pp. 76-82; Chapter 15, "Judah and Hellas: Alexandria," pp. 83-93.

BROWNE, LEWIS, *The Wisdom of Israel,* Modern Library, "The Story of Bel," pp. 116-118; "The First Rabbis," pp. 125-132; "The Hellenized Jews," pp. 133-144.

MOORE, GEORGE FOOT, *Judaism,* Harvard University, Volume I, Chapter 1, "The Foundations of Judaism," pp. 3-28; Chapter 2, "Ezra and the Great Synagogue," pp. 29-36; Chapter 3, "The Scribes," pp. 37-47; Chapter 4, "The Religious Crisis," pp. 48-55; Chapter 5, "Rise of the Pharisees," pp. 56-71.

NOSS, JOHN B., *Man's Religions,* Macmillan, pp. 495-528.

SCHWARTZMAN, SYLVAN D., and JACK D. SPIRO, *The Living Bible,* UAHC, pp. 30-40; Chapter 3, "Does God Have a Favorite People?" pp. 42-63.

6

THE BIRTH OF CHRISTIANITY

Jesus—The Messiah? The discussion between the two farmers who had traveled to Jerusalem to celebrate Passover grew more heated.

"I tell you, Isaac," a red-faced peasant from Galilee in northern Palestine was saying, "I saw this man Jesus myself. He says the Kingdom of God is coming soon. . . ."

"Nonsense!" shouted his companion, a small man whose face was also weather-beaten from work in the fields.

"No, Isaac. His followers claim he is the Messiah. The real Messiah, do you hear?"

"Claims!" the second man said contemptuously. "Ignorant peasants! He's not the first they've called the Messiah. . . ."

"Well, he could be," answered his companion. "How do we know they're not right this time?"

"Jonathan, don't be a fool! This man's a poor carpenter, not a mighty descendant of King David. Sure, the poor Galileans who listen to him would like to believe he's the Messiah. But wait until the Romans get wind of it. They'll kill him for being a troublemaker, just like they've done with all the others who thought they were the Messiah."

"Maybe you're right," the red-faced man admitted. "But who knows? You could be wrong, too. . . ."

"Not me!" Isaac shot back. "You're wrong, you and all the others who are ready to believe anyone who comes along and says he's the Messiah. And what more proof have you about this Jesus? Why, he doesn't even promise to get rid of the Romans!"

Jonathan was silent. Perhaps his friend Isaac was right. After all, what did he really know about Jesus? And how different was he from all the other "Messiahs"?

Jewish Hopes for Deliverance It is very likely that among some of the Jews of Palestine such arguments took place during the period around the turn of the Common Era. Undoubtedly they centered not only about the man called Jesus, but about others who were looked upon as the long-awaited Messiah. For who knew? Perhaps one of them *was* the descendant of King David of old who had come to deliver the nation out of the hands of the Romans and usher in the glorious Kingdom ruled by God!

These were troubled times for the Jews. Roman rule was harsh, taxes were extremely high, and the Romans were quick to strike down anyone who dared to object. Moreover, the conqueror did not always respect the Jews' religious feelings. Sometimes their military leaders mocked the most cherished Jewish beliefs, and on occasions they deliberately provoked the people by bringing the image of their emperor-god into the holy city of Jerusalem.

How the Jews longed to be free from Roman

rule! Surely, they felt, deliverance must come eventually. Didn't the prophets promise that some day all of the Jews would live undisturbed in their own land? Then God would establish His Kingdom on earth, and all peoples would be happy to join the people of Israel in the new age of peace, justice, and righteousness.

But when would this day come? The Jews believed that first, as God's servants, they would have to be purified through suffering. Then, at "the end of days," when conditions became completely unbearable and the Jews had been thoroughly tested, God would send the Messiah, His "anointed one." The wicked would be destroyed, and God's Kingdom established forever. So the Jewish masses thought, and they found certain statements in the Books of Isaiah, Hosea, and Daniel which seemed to bear out their hopes. One such passage put it this way:

> I saw visions in the night,
> And behold, with the clouds of heaven,
> There came one like a son of man,
> And he came to the Ancient of Days
>   [God]
> And was presented before Him.
> And to him was given dominion, glory
>   and a kingdom,
> That all peoples, nations and languages
> Should serve him;
> His dominion is an everlasting dominion,
> Which shall not pass away,
> And his kingdom one
> That shall not be destroyed.
> —Daniel 7:13-14

Though such ideas probably had originated earlier in the Persian period, they found wide acceptance during the later troubled times of Roman rule. Thus many writings dealing with "the end of days" come from this period, and some present strange visions of what was to happen before and after the establishment of God's Kingdom. Some even attempted to predict when the great event would take place.

These writings are called "apocalypses," from the Greek word meaning to "lay bare" or "reveal," and an example is the book named "Revelation" found in the Christian Bible, but based upon originally Jewish material. Here, among many other visions of "the end of days," the writer pictures a war in heaven between the angels who are supporters of Jesus, and the dragon Satan and his followers.

What Do We Really Know about Jesus?
Jesus, the person about whom the Book of Revelation spoke, was born around the year 4 B.C.E., and died sometime during the early 30's of the Common Era. Beyond his general teaching that the Kingdom of God was at hand, and various statements and actions attributed to him by later generations, we have little information about him personally.

This is strange, since Jesus lived during a period from which we have a great number of records. We know that in Palestine at the beginning of the Common Era, rabbinic writings and Roman records were carefully compiled and scrupulously preserved. Yet, other than what we find in the Christian Bible, there is practically no contemporary evidence of his life and activities. The few references to him in rabbinic writings are very late and their meaning is questionable. Nothing is said of him in the Roman records, and comments about him in other writings, such as those by Josephus, are plainly later Christian insertions. No wonder, then, that at one time certain Christian scholars questioned whether Jesus actually existed.

Yet the lack of historical information about him is understandable. One reason, certainly, is that the period of his ministry was quite brief and his association with the people extremely limited. Then, too, during his lifetime Jesus was hardly an important figure, even in tiny Palestine. Actually, his life became significant only in the years after his death, when Christianity finally became a religion.

So whatever real knowledge of Jesus we have must come from the New Testament, a collection of traditions, letters, and other material gathered and edited some 20 to 125 years after his death. Even here the details of his life are frequently vague and sometimes contradictory. Hence, it is often difficult to determine the facts about exactly what Jesus did, what he said, and where he went. For example, the New Testament gives us three different reports of Jesus'

OLD TESTAMENT

NEW TESTAMENT

THE CHRISTIAN BIBLE. It includes both the Hebrew Scriptures, called the "Old Testament," and the much smaller collection of Christian writings, known as the "New Testament."

last words. The Gospels of Matthew and Mark quote him as having said just before he died, "My Father, my Father, why have You forsaken me?" The Gospel of Luke reports his final words as, "Father, into Your hand I commend my spirit." And the Gospel of John states that Jesus' last utterance was, "It is finished."

Nevertheless, the New Testament does contain valuable historical information. In fact, it is the indispensable source for an understanding of the development of early Christianity.

About the New Testament   What exactly is the New Testament?

To begin with, it is a collection of twenty-seven writings gathered into a single book about one-fourth as large as the Hebrew Bible. The title really means "New Covenant," because at one time the English word "testament" was used where we today would prefer "covenant." It was named the "New Testament" since the Christians believed that it was the record of God's "new covenant" with mankind in place of the Hebrew Scriptures, which they now called the "Old Testament."

In the main, the writings of the New Testament contain information about the life and teachings of Jesus, the development of early Christianity, and the faith and regulations of the newly-formed religion. These were produced by people associated with the early Church, and they lived in various centers of the Mediterranean world, such as Rome, Athens, Corinth, Ephesus, Antioch, and elsewhere. Like the Hebrew Scriptures, the New Testament is the product of the gathering and editing of mate-

rials coming from various periods, and its twenty-seven different books, written in Greek, were produced during the years between approximately 50 and 150 C.E. Some of them are very brief, like the Second and Third Letters of John and the Letter of Jude, which are simply one chapter apiece. Most of the others are considerably longer.

The writings of the New Testament fall into five main categories. The first consists of the Gospels, four books that deal primarily with the life and teachings of Jesus. The word "gospel" means "good tidings," and it comes from the Old English "good spiel," which became shortened to "gospel." Because the first three—Matthew, Mark, and Luke—are quite similar to one another and contain a great deal of information in common, they are known as the "Synoptic Gospels." The last, the Gospel of John, is very different from the others, and many scholars believe it was written considerably later.

The second type of material in the New Testament is contained in the Acts of the Apostles. This material relates the story of the work of the Apostles, or "those sent forth" to teach Christianity during its early days. As such, it deals with the activities of Peter and Paul and those associated with them in spreading the message of Jesus among first-century Jews and Gentiles of the Mediterranean area.

The third category of New Testament material is represented by the fourteen Epistles, or "letters" of Paul. Many scholars believe that some of them were not originally written by Paul but ascribed to him by later tradition. However, they all contain information about the problems faced by the early Christians, such as, whether they should carry on the Jewish rite of circumcision, and the various regulations and practices developed by the young movement.

The fourth group of New Testament writings represents material similar to that appearing in the Epistles, for it, too, contains "letters." However, these letters were written not by Paul but by other leaders of early Christianity to help their followers meet various new problems that arose. Among the more serious problems was "heresy," or teachings about Jesus, Christianity, and church practice that differed from those sanctioned by the movement's leaders. For instance, there were certain people who wanted to exclude all Jewish writings, even the "Old Testament," from Christianity. The writers of these epistles strongly opposed this.

The Book of Revelation represents the final type of material found in the New Testament. As we have already observed, it is an apocalypse, a "revelation" concerning the events leading to the messianic age. It tells of the glorious future which the followers of Christianity will enjoy once their persecutors and other evil forces are destroyed and the Kingdom of God is established. The Book of Revelation contains many strange visions, including the well-known one of the "four horsemen of the Apocalypse" who, before the coming of the Messiah, will devastate the earth with sword, famine, plague, and wild beasts.

This collection of material, together with the books of the "Old Testament" arranged in somewhat different order from that in the Jewish Bible, comprises the Protestant Bible. The Roman Catholic Bible contains, in addition, seven books from the Apocrypha, the collection of writings that the Jews had not considered sufficiently sacred to include within the Hebrew Scriptures.

The Earlier Life of Jesus   It is almost wholly from the first three Gospels, then, that we learn about the life of Jesus. Yet the varying accounts they offer and the legends they incorporate about a Jesus whom later generations regarded as the literal "son of God," make many details of his life somewhat uncertain. The following seems to be a reasonably accurate account.

Jesus was born of Jewish parents, Mary and Joseph, about the year 4 B.C.E. Though the family's home was the village of Nazareth in northern Palestine, two of the Gospels tell us that his birthplace was Bethlehem, south of Jerusalem. He seems to have had a number of brothers and sisters, and the Gospels mention the names of James, Joseph, Simon, and Judas. Roman Catholics, however, prefer to consider them merely near relatives.

His childhood was spent in the typical surroundings of the poorer Jews who lived in Galilee, and undoubtedly he learned something of the Bible and rabbinic use of parables and stories. He spoke Aramaic, a Semitic language similar to Hebrew, which was used in Palestine during that time.

The Gospel of Luke reports that when Jesus was twelve, he astonished the sages at the Jerusalem Temple with his knowledge. Beyond this, the details of his first thirty years are practically unreported. However, we can assume that he followed the usual pattern of Jewish life in northern Palestine, receiving the usual limited Jewish education, carrying out the various Jewish observances, and attending the synagogue. Apparently he followed his father's occupation as a carpenter.

In about his thirtieth year, Jesus met John the Baptist, a Jew who made his home in the desert regions of Palestine. John preached that the Messiah was coming. As preparation for the coming, John practiced baptism, or immersion in water, which was supposed to wash away the sins of all who submitted to it. Immersion in water is mentioned numerous times in the Hebrew Scriptures and rabbinic literature as a means of cleansing oneself, as, for example, after touching unclean animals, or before participating in various religious rituals.

Jesus was one of those baptized by John in the Jordan River and he was profoundly affected by this experience. He thought deeply about it, and after intense self-searching, he came to believe that he was the Messiah, the one who would usher in the Kingdom of God. He viewed John the Baptist as the forerunner of the Messiah, somewhat as the Jews of his time pictured the prophet Elijah.

Jesus now felt called upon to spread the word. He gathered to himself a few men who believed in his message and they became his disciples. Together they set out to proclaim the approaching great day to the masses of the Jewish people.

The Ministry of Jesus   For one to three years—estimates vary—Jesus wandered about

THE BIRTH OF CHRISTIANITY

Palestine preaching the coming of the Kingdom of God. He began to build up a following among the poor people of Galilee. Before long the report went out that he was able to perform cures and miracles, which naturally brought the ailing and the curious.

Evidently he was a persuasive teacher who attracted people to him by the simplicity of his life, the sincerity of his words, and his manner of speaking. Especially appealing were his parables, simple stories, and pithy similes that served to illustrate some moral. For example, when the people asked him why he insisted on being in the company of sinners, he answered, "Those who are well have no need of a physician; only those who are sick," implying that his mission was to help people overcome their sins. In another story, Jesus compared the world of his day to a fig tree that was beginning to sprout leaves. As the appearance of the leaves on the tree indicated that summer was near, so all the signs of the times pointed to the approaching "end of days."

Especially well-known, though somewhat anti-Jewish because it does not present a fair picture of Jewish practice, is his parable of the Good Samaritan as told in the Gospel of Luke:

> And behold, a man learned in the Law stood up and put him [Jesus] to the test, saying, "Teacher, what shall I do to inherit eternal Life?"
>
> He said to him, "What is written in the Law? How does it read?"
>
> And he answered, "You shall love the Lord your God with all your heart, and with all your soul, and with all your strength, and with all your mind; and your neighbor as yourself."
>
> And he said to him, "You have answered right; do this and you will live."
>
> But he, desiring to justify himself, said to Jesus, "And who is my neighbor?"
>
> Jesus replied, "A man was going down from Jerusalem to Jericho and he fell among robbers who stripped him and beat him and departed, leaving him half-dead. Now, by chance, a priest was going down that road, and when he saw him he passed by on the other side. So likewise,

JOHN THE BAPTIST. A well-known painting of John baptizing Jesus in the Jordan River, a significant event in the life of Christ.

> a Levite, when he came to the place and saw him, passed by on the other side. But a Samaritan, as he journeyed, came to where he was, and when he saw him he had compassion. And he went to him and bound up his wounds, pouring on oil and wine; then he set him on his own beast and brought him to an inn and took care of him. And the next day he took out two denarii [coins] and gave them to the innkeeper saying, 'Take care of him, and whatever more you spend, I will repay you when I come back.' Which of these three do you think proved neighbor to the man who fell among the robbers?"
>
> He said, "The one who showed mercy on him."
>
> And Jesus said to him, "Go and do likewise."
>
> —Luke 10:25-37

By and large, the form and substance of Jesus' message were completely within the spirit of the biblical writers, prophets, and rabbis. In fact, there are parallels to most of Jesus' teachings in Jewish literature. For example, the statement about "loving the Lord" in the parable of the Good Samaritan is taken almost word for word from the Book of Deuteronomy.

But Jesus' emphasis upon the approaching end of the world and the coming of God's Kingdom led him to certain conclusions that sometimes differed from the accepted Jewish ways of thinking. For instance, he was indifferent

HEALING THE SICK. In this painting, young children are being brought to Jesus, while numbers of sick people gather around him, seeking to be cured.

to the practical needs of life, such as food, shelter, and clothing; he even taught that people should give up their wealth. He was not concerned with the need for positive action to wipe out social evils. He did not feel the family was important, as emphasized in his own failure to marry and beget children. He was also impatient with certain Jewish observances, such as restrictions against performing various acts on the Sabbath.

This is understandable in view of the fact that he was convinced that the "end of days" was at hand. After all, in God's Kingdom such things would be considered minor indeed!

Jesus Goes to Jerusalem   Meanwhile, opposition to Jesus was developing among various groups of people. The more observant Jews looked upon him as one who encouraged breaking the laws of the Torah. Those who sought to overthrow the Romans objected to his warning that "all who take the sword will perish by the sword." Nor did the priests and other Jewish officials look favorably upon this man who seemed to be disputing their authority.

It was at this time that Jesus chose to reveal himself to his disciples as the Messiah. The news excited them greatly. Seeing the effect upon them, evidently Jesus decided that all of the people must know who he was, and he prepared to announce himself as the Messiah in the holy city of Jerusalem.

He was not unaware, of course, of the danger to himself. He knew that John the Baptist had been beheaded because he was regarded as a threat to the reign of Herod, the puppet ruler of Palestine under the Romans. As the self-announced Messiah he, too, might suffer the same fate. Yet he was impelled to carry out his mission.

Shortly before Passover, Jesus made his way to Jerusalem. The city was crowded with thousands of Jewish pilgrims who had come to participate in the Passover observances of the Temple. Aware of the traditions about the Messiah, Jesus attracted attention to himself by riding an ass into Jerusalem, thus fulfilling this statement of the prophet Zechariah:

> Rejoice greatly, O daughter of Zion!
> Shout aloud, O daughter of Jerusalem!
> Lo, your king comes to you;
> Triumphant and victorious is he,
> Humble and riding on an ass,
> On a colt, the foal of an ass.
> —Zechariah 9:9

Jesus even went to the Temple and created a disturbance there by driving away the men who changed the people's money into the proper currency for the purchase of birds for sacrifices.

But his mission ended in failure. By refusing to denounce the Romans, he antagonized the people whom he addressed. For they expected a Messiah who would put an end to the injustices of Roman rule. Instead, he insisted that the people should continue to submit to Roman authority and pay their taxes. Reports were also circulated that he advocated the destruction of the Temple itself, which incurred the anger especially of the priestly class whose religion centered around the Temple and its worship.

The Death of Jesus   Discouraged and disheartened, Jesus retired with his disciples to participate in the Seder, the Passover evening meal, or as some believe, to usher in the Sabbath. This is what has come to be known as the "Last Supper," for shortly thereafter Jesus was

ΗΒΑΗΦΩΡΟC

PONTIUS PILATE. A Flemish tapestry pictures the Roman governor turning Jesus over to the crowd so that they may make the final decision about his fate.

THE BIRTH OF CHRISTIANITY

arrested by Roman soldiers while his disciples fled in panic.

Naturally, word of Jesus' activities had come to the attention of the Roman authorities. It was a critical time for them. Jerusalem was overcrowded with Jewish pilgrims from all over Palestine, and their discontent with Roman rule ran high. The Romans knew from previous experience how easily the Jews could be stirred up into a riotous mob that might destroy their garrison in Jerusalem. From their point of view, then, anyone around whom the Jews might rally—especially one who spoke of himself as the Messiah or, as the Romans understood it, "king of the Jews"—could serve to spark a mighty explosion. Therefore, Jesus was promptly arrested and charged with treason.

He was brought before Pontius Pilate, the Roman procurator or governor, who heard the charges against him. The official promptly condemned him to death as a revolutionary, self-styled "king of the Jews." According to the Roman practice of the times, Jesus was taken out and crucified. After his death, sympathetic Jews removed his body from the cross and buried it in a tomb.

Jesus' Crucifixion and the Jews Such, in brief, is the life-story of the Jesus who lived during the early years of the Common Era.

Throughout, we observe that, though somewhat of a mystic, Jesus was nonetheless a loyal Jew whose most intimate disciples and followers were also Jewish. His message that the Messianic age was approaching was directed only to his fellow Jews, for whose welfare he was deeply concerned. True, many of the Jews did not agree with him. But it is plain that he represented a threat chiefly to the Romans, who feared any Jewish leader that might turn the masses against them.

Yet the New Testament would have us believe that it was the Jews, and especially their leaders, who hated Jesus and deliberately arranged for his execution. For, according to the Gospels, he was betrayed by Judas, a Jewish disciple. Then he was willfully condemned to death and turned over to the Roman governor by a sanhedrin, or court of Jewish elders, presided over by the high priest.

Moreover, the Gospels attempt to absolve the Romans of all responsibility for his death. They describe Pontius Pilate as being moved by pity for Jesus and offering to spare his life. However, as they tell it, the Jewish people insisted that he be put to death. Having no other choice, the Roman official was forced to have him taken out and crucified.

It is this account of the Jews' responsibility for the death of Jesus that has caused so much mischief and heartache over the centuries. However, today many reputable Christian scholars recognize that much of the material about the life of Jesus and the development of the early Church found in the New Testament cannot be regarded as historical fact. It represents, rather, the response of the early followers of Christianity to situations that they encountered several decades or more after the events they describe.

We must remember that Mark, the oldest of the Gospels, did not appear in final form until about 60 C.E. at the very earliest, and more probably sometime after 70 C.E. By this time, the author undoubtedly read into the life of Jesus the circumstances that existed some thirty to fifty years later. In the years between Jesus' death and the appearance of the first Gospel, relations between the early Christians and the

Jews had become strained. Eventually, as we know, the two religious groups parted and became bitter rivals. Thus, on the one hand, the writers of the Gospels were moved by hostility toward Judaism and the Jews. And, on the other hand, because they wished to win over the people of the Roman Empire to their faith, they sought to absolve the Romans of any real guilt in connection with the killing of Jesus.

That this is the case is borne out by the various discrepancies that appear in the Gospel accounts. From reliable Jewish sources of the times, we note that, as described in the New Testament, the trial of Jesus by the sanhedrin, or Jewish court, is not in keeping with prescribed Jewish court procedure. Furthermore, the trial of a Jew would scarcely be allowed to take place on the eve of a major holiday like Passover. As a matter of fact, the sentence of death by any Jewish court during this period was a rarity indeed, and in view of the nature of the charges brought against Jesus, it would have been practically impossible. We also know that Pontius Pilate was scarcely the kind of sympathetic individual pictured by the Gospels. Roman records tell us that he was later removed from his position by the Roman government itself because of his excessive cruelty.

What the role of the Jews was in the death of Jesus we can only guess, but it was hardly a major one. Perhaps one of his disciples did betray him. Perhaps certain Jewish officials connected with the Temple did complain about Jesus' activities. But the final authority for his execution rested solely with the Romans, and they were the only ones who had sufficient reason to fear him as the leader of a possible Jewish uprising. Hence their haste in taking him prisoner, finding him guilty and binding him to the cross.

To many religious Christians, however, a discussion of who was guilty of Jesus' crucifixion is unnecessary, since they believe that Jesus willed his own death as a sacrifice for man's sins. Viewed from this religious belief, then, all those involved in the crucifixion were unconscious agents of God's will in carrying out His plan of salvation for man.

After Jesus' Death   With the death of Jesus, the cause for which he gave his life seemed at an end. With unbelieving eyes, the disciples who fled when Jesus was taken prisoner saw their leader crucified like a common criminal. This was not at all in keeping with their belief that the Messiah would triumph over the Romans and restore freedom to the Jews.

However, the disciples continued to think of Jesus and wonder about the events of his ministry and the various things he had said. Undoubtedly, they also felt guilty about having abandoned him to his fate. Then, the Gospels report, on the morning of the third day after his crucifixion, some women, including Mary Magdalene, a follower whom he had healed, went to the tomb where Jesus' body had been taken. It was empty! As they turned to leave, they saw angels and heard voices that told them that Jesus had risen from the dead. Some of his

VISIONS OF ANGELS. Women returning to the tomb where the body of Jesus was taken find no trace of it. According to tradition angels appeared.

60

THE BIRTH OF CHRISTIANITY

disciples also saw him. In fact, they reported that later in Galilee, Jesus told them that he was indeed the Messiah and urged them to spread the word that he would return soon to usher in his Father's Kingdom.

To the disciples this was all the proof they needed that Jesus was truly the Messiah. For according to popular belief, were not the dead to be resurrected in Messianic times? And had not Jesus himself returned to life? Surely, then, he had come to earth to prepare the world for the Kingdom of God, and would soon return to usher it in.

Moved by such beliefs and overcoming their fears of the Romans, the disciples began attending the Temple and various synagogues, spreading the word that the Messiah for whom the Jews were praying had already arrived. Most of the people disputed the claims of these Nazarenes, as the followers of Jesus of Nazareth came to be called. They saw no reason to accept the account of Jesus' miraculous resurrection. Where, they asked, was proof that this had really happened? And why, if Jesus was the Messiah, were the Jews still oppressed by the Romans? The Nazarenes urged them to be patient and wait for his promised return. They would then see ample evidence of God's deliverance.

A few Jews were persuaded by them, but most regarded the Nazarenes as simple-minded folk, given to visions about their dead leader. Yet the Jewish authorities did nothing to prevent them from worshipping in the synagogue and carrying on their Jewish observances. For, at the time, the Nazarenes were only one of a number of sects within Judaism, and there was no reason for the people to bar them, simply because they happened to hold different views on the subject of the Messiah.

From a Jewish Sect to a New Religion   With the death of Jesus, then, his closest followers continued to remain loyal to his memory and formed a tiny sect of their own within the larger body of the Jewish people.

However, their belief in the resurrection of their leader and in his ultimate return marks

A MIRACLE. This tapestry by Raphael shows Peter, the chief disciple of Jesus, summoning a cripple to rise up and walk.

the great turning point in the development of Christianity. For during Jesus' lifetime, it was his essentially Jewish message of the coming of God's Kingdom that was central. Now, with his death and his reported resurrection, it was faith in Jesus himself that was to become the dominant element in the belief of his followers. And it was precisely this that gave birth to Christianity as a new religion.

For a period of several decades, the Nazarenes continued to remain a Jewish sect. Yet during these years their belief in Jesus and his eventual return grew more intense. Soon it became a point of serious dispute between themselves and their fellow Jews. Still, whether they would ever have broken completely away from Judaism is questionable. After all, they were thoroughly faithful to Jewish observance and still considered themselves loyal Jews.

What was it, then, that led to the creation of a new and separate religion?

The answer lies not with the intimate disciples of Jesus, but with one who never knew him during his lifetime. This was a man called Paul. . . .

61

TOPICS TO DISCUSS

1. To what extent was the message of Jesus Jewish?
2. How would you reply to someone who accuses the Jews of having killed Jesus?
3. In what ways does the Bible of the Christians differ from that of the Jews?
4. How might Judaism today have differed if the Jews had agreed with the Nazarenes?

THINGS TO DO

1. As a student of religion, compare the accounts about Jesus as found in the following Gospel passages: Matthew 2 and Luke 2:1-21; Matthew 7:28-29 and Mark 1:21-28; Matthew 5:3-12 and Luke 6:20-23; Matthew 5:31-32 and Mark 10:11-12; and Matthew 27:11-14 and Luke 23:2-5. What conclusions do you reach?
2. Prepare a newspaper article of the times describing the crucifixion of Jesus and the events leading up to it.
3. Stage a debate between the leaders of the Jews and the Nazarenes over the matter of the Messiahship of Jesus.

OTHER THINGS TO READ

BALLOU, ROBERT O., *The Portable World Bible*, Viking, "The New Testament: The Life of Christ," pp. 346-385; "Sermons and Sayings of Jesus," pp. 385-411.

BAMBERGER, BERNARD J., *The Story of Judaism*, UAHC, Chapter 16, "The Birth of a New Religion," pp. 94-100.

GAER, JOSEPH, *How the Great Religions Began*, Signet, "Christianity," pp. 166-186.

NOSS, JOHN B., *Man's Religions*, Macmillan, Chapter 14, "Christianity in Its Opening Phase: The Religion of Jesus," pp. 555-581; pp. 583-585.

PIKE, E. ROYSTON, *Encyclopaedia of Religion and Religions*, Meridian, "Apostle," p. 25; "Jesus Christ," pp. 209-211; "Jesus Myth Theory," p. 211; "John the Baptist," p. 214.

SANDMEL, SAMUEL, *A Jewish Understanding of the New Testament*, HUC, Chapter 1, "A Description of the New Testament," pp. 3-6; Chapter 2, "The Historian's Approach," pp. 7-17; Chapter 3, "The Jewish Background," pp. 18-31; Chapter 11, "The Gospel Process," pp. 107-114.

7
CHRISTIANITY BECOMES A SEPARATE RELIGION

Saul of Tarsus Is Converted   The road to Damascus was rough and difficult to travel, but the man walking along the rocky path plodded on.

He was known as Saul of Tarsus, a tent-maker by profession, and a staunch defender of Judaism against the growing influence of the Nazarene sect. He came originally from Tarsus, an important city of Asia Minor, and was the son of a man who had been granted Roman citizenship, quite an honor for someone who did not live in Italy.

Saul, better known by his Greek name Paul, seems to have been well-acquainted with the Hellenistic, Greek dominated, culture of the times. He spoke the Greek language and appears to have been familiar with philosophy and various works of Greek literature. At the same time, he also had some knowledge of Judaism, especially of the Hebrew Scriptures in Greek translation, and possessed a certain skill in interpreting the Bible. He regarded himself as a devout Jew and an opponent of the teachings about Jesus that the Nazarenes were spreading. In fact, he seems to have taken it upon himself to combat their doctrine in Jerusalem where he first learned of it.

The Book of Acts in the New Testament tells us that when word reached him that Nazarene missionaries were active among the Jews of Damascus, he felt compelled to fight against

them there. So he set off for Damascus, determined to force them to return to Jerusalem.

However, we are told that on the way Paul had a vision. In a brilliant flash of light, he seemed to hear the voice of the resurrected Jesus saying, "Paul, Paul, why do you persecute me?" For three days he was blinded. Then a follower of Jesus came to him and his sight was restored.

Deeply stirred by this experience, Paul not only abandoned his attempts to stop the missionaries, but actually became a convert to the new group. With the same zeal with which he had once attacked it, Paul now began to serve as an apostle, a "messenger," or missionary, of the Nazarene faith among the peoples of Asia Minor.

Such is the account of Paul's conversion given by the author of the Books of Acts. However, many scholars believe it to be a dramatized version of what happened. Some are even convinced that Paul was subject to visions as a result of epilepsy. But, whatever the explanation, the fact remains that in some way Saul of Tarsus was moved to become an active worker for the Nazarene cause.

And it was this man, more than any other, who succeeded in transforming a tiny Jewish sect into a religion that ultimately became one of the most wide-spread and influential on earth.

Religious Rivalry in the Roman World As Paul commenced his missionary work, he found himself in the midst of the tumultuous religious rivalry of the Roman world. For the great spiritual unrest that had started with the Greek conquest had gone on unchecked. As we have already seen, many of the beliefs of the old national religions had broken down, and the masses of people were in search of more satisfying forms of faith. Gradually, too, certain new and different religious ideas had made their way into the Roman world, and each attracted a following.

One popular approach was that of Greek philosophy. The ideas taught by the philosophers had great appeal to the more intelligent who had outgrown the childish myths about gods scarcely better than humans. In philosophy they also discovered sound moral principles for living, based upon clear and logical reasoning, and a great many were attracted by Stoic philosophy in particular.

The name comes from the Greek word *"stoa,"* "porch," the place in Athens from which its founder, Zeno, taught. There was, he declared, but one great universal Force that permeates everything in the world, shaped it, and established the laws by which it operates. To respect this Force and aspire to be in harmony with it is man's highest good. Therefore, he must strive to live a virtuous life; that is, one consistent with the laws of nature.

For years, Stoic missionaries in threadbare garments moved among the cities of the Mediterranean world preaching this doctrine. In a world filled with turmoil such teachings that stressed self-control and self-discipline seemed most welcome. Persuaded by them, many adopted Stoicism.

Judaism, too, made its bid for the support of people seeking a more advanced religious way of life. In addition to high ethical and intellectual principles, Judaism penetrated to the depths of men's souls and offered a rich and stirring life of faith expressed in special acts, such as the observance of religious holidays, ceremonies, and rituals of worship.

Considerable numbers of non-Jews were attracted to Judaism, and many became converts. Its teachings of a world based upon truth and justice and guided by the one great, unseen God who insisted upon righteousness and brotherliness had great appeal. Moreover, people were moved by the uncompromising devotion of the Jews to their faith, their sense of group kinship, and their zeal for carrying out religious duties. No doubt, Temple and synagogue worship, the Bible, and the various Jewish observances also impressed them.

But for the great majority of people, Greek philosophy did not possess sufficient emotional appeal, and Judaism seemed either too intellectual a religion or too demanding. Many non-Jews of the times looked with particular disfavor upon the practice of circumcision and the dietary laws, since these seemed contrary to everything they considered civilized and modern.

Consequently, the masses of the Roman world turned instead to the various "mystery" religions, so called because only those who joined them knew of their rites and teachings. They made none of Judaism's strict demands. Yet, at the same time, they offered emotional warmth, divine support in everyday life, and the promise of personal survival after death.

Two of the more popular mystery religions involved the worship of Cybele, the great Mother-goddess of Asia Minor, and Isis, the Mother-goddess of Egypt. Both were rooted in ancient beliefs about the "death" and "rebirth" of nature. In both, the individual believed that he could be reborn to new life through the power of the Mother-goddess. They taught that, having lost her son by death, she was able eventually to restore him to life. So, by appealing to her and participating in the ritual of the god's death and resurrection, the worshipper could win her support and achieve his own immortality. To some extent, the veneration of Mary, the mother of Jesus, especially among the Roman Catholics and Eastern Orthodox, can be traced back to these beliefs.

Undoubtedly, the most influential of all of the mystery religions was the worship of the Persian deity, Mithra, since it had special appeal to Roman soldiers. Mithra was believed to be the god who sprang to life from a rock and performed many brave deeds. He was said to have conquered the sun-god and killed a great bull that sought to destroy mankind. Later, Mithra was thought to have gone to live in the heavens, where he sat in judgment upon the souls of the dead. It was promised that at the end of the world those who had been faithful would live on with him forever, but the wicked would be utterly destroyed.

Mithraism appeared on the scene at least half a century before Jesus was born. Interestingly, it offered certain features that later found their way into Christianity, its greatest rival in the Roman world. The followers of Mithraism observed sacraments of bread and wine and of baptism. They employed the sign of the cross and conducted a Last Supper, symbolic of one which Mithra was said to have held with the sun-god and other divinities. They also observed the twenty-fifth day of December as a holiday of gift-giving. To them it commemorated the birth of the sun, since it was noted that around this time the days began to grow longer.

Paul's Missionary Work The Gentiles, the "common people" of the Roman world, were influenced far more by the mystery cults than by Judaism or the various Greek philosophies, and it was among them that Paul carried on his missionary work. Scholars have tried to piece together an orderly account of his activities. However, all we can be sure of is that, beginning around the late 40's or early 50's of the Common Era, Paul carried on his missionary activities in various communities of the Mediterranean world. His work consisted mainly of helping to organize small Christian groups and guiding others that had already come into existence.

Our most reliable information about his activities comes from his various epistles, or "letters," that appear in the New Testament. From these we learn that he had contact with a number of small groups of early Christians, such as those in Philippi, Thessalonia, and Corinth—

all located in Greece, and the one in Galatia, in Asia Minor, which he himself founded. Apparently, the city of Antioch, in Syria, was his central base of operation. From here he journeyed to the various other communities where he would usually stay for long periods of time, preaching his message, making converts, and organizing them into functioning Christian groups.

Although not a well person, Paul appears to have been a man of tremendous energy, natively bright, and full of enthusiasm for his cause. He seems to have understood the thinking and needs of the early Christians with whom he worked. Even his fiery temper helped him, for he succeeded in overwhelming those who offered him any opposition. Undoubtedly, people were also impressed with the man's self-sacrifice. He received nothing in the way of support for his missionary work, but all his life continued to earn his living as a tent-maker.

By and large, Paul's efforts met with success. He established a number of new Christian groups. He also helped strengthen those that had already been formed by apostles who came first from Jerusalem, and later from other centers of Asia Minor. All of these he supervised personally, either on the scene or by letter, and he was able to settle many of the controversies that arose among the early Christians, especially over questions of leadership, teachings, and practices. In addition, Paul also raised funds for the "mother church," the original band of Nazarenes, or Jewish Christians, in Jerusalem. Under the leadership of Peter, Jesus' chief disciple, and James, the brother of Jesus, this group still continued its activities.

In his work Paul encountered considerable opposition. Leaders of various Christian groups disputed with him over matters of authority, observance, and belief. His fellow Jews took issue with him, too, and in one instance his overzealousness seems to have earned him a lashing. He was probably also imprisoned by the Roman authorities, who, as we shall see, regarded Paul and the early Christians not only as trouble-makers but as a decided threat to the empire.

PAUL AT ATHENS. In this tapestry by Raphael, now displayed in the Vatican in Rome, the Apostle Paul is preaching his message about Christ before some of the leading citizens of Greece.

However, much of his early opposition came from the Jewish Christians, the Nazarenes, in Jerusalem, who considered themselves the real leaders of the movement. All during the early years of his ministry they seem to have opposed him, even to the point of sending out rival apostles to refute his teachings. For there were important differences between the kind of religion they and Paul were teaching.

The Source of the Conflict   The basic issue had to do with the acceptance of Judaism by the Gentile Christians.

Paul always maintained that he was a loyal Jew. But in his role as apostle to the Gentiles, he did not insist, as did the leaders of the Jerusalem group, that all Jewish practices be kept. Instead, Paul freed the Gentile Christians from the observance of Jewish laws, and he taught religious beliefs that were very different from those of Judaism.

Whether Paul took this position because of his own religious convictions or whether it grew out of his awareness of the needs of the Gentiles is something that cannot be determined. Most probably he was influenced by both factors.

As a Jew born outside of Palestine, Paul's thinking had been strongly colored by the atmosphere of Hellenistic culture and religion in which he had grown up. He was attracted by some of the features of the mystery religions as well as by certain ideas that he found in Greek philosophy. For instance, the more intimate, mystical form of approach to the deity which the mystery religions offered appealed to him, and he was especially impressed by their initiation rites through which the individual came to identify himself with the resurrected god.

He also adopted the belief held by certain Greek philosophers that the world and everything in it were composed of two elements— "spirit," which was pure and everlasting, and "matter," which was evil and subject to decay and death. These ideas found their way into Paul's teachings about man and God. Thus he viewed man as consisting chiefly of "matter," full of sin and doomed to destruction. But God was pure "spirit" and hence eternal.

At the same time, as a practical missionary, Paul realized the disadvantages of requiring Gentiles to carry on all the Jewish observances. He was undoubtedly aware of the resistance that Jewish missionary efforts encountered over circumcision, with the result that considerably fewer men were converted than women. He also knew to what extent the dietary laws, and especially the prohibition against eating pork, had deterred others from accepting Judaism.

Influenced by such considerations, as well as by his changing attitude toward Judaism in general, Paul freed converts from the requirements of circumcision, the dietary laws, and virtually all of the other Jewish practices. But, in so doing, he was opposing the very teachings of the mother group in Jerusalem. The Jewish Christians insisted that, to be followers of Jesus, all Gentiles must first become Jews and thereafter adhere strictly to Jewish observance.

Conflict now arose between Paul and the Jerusalem group. It flared up whenever missionaries sent by Peter or the other Jerusalem leaders journeyed to the outlying groups supervised by Paul. Such an instance is reported in Paul's Epistle to the Galatians where he sharply rebukes Cephas, a fellow apostle. Originally Cephas had completely shared Paul's point of

view about the dietary laws, but when messengers from the Jerusalem group appeared, he sided with them by refusing to eat the forbidden foods.

Eventually a compromise was worked out. The leaders in Jerusalem agreed that, in dealing with the Gentiles, Paul did not first have to convert them to Judaism or require them to practice circumcision and the dietary laws. However, those who worked primarily among the Jews would continue to demand Jewish observance of all converts. Harmony now reigned once more among the early Christians.

The Religious Beliefs of Paul   Actually, the differences between the teachings of Paul and the Jerusalem leaders went far beyond the question of Jewish practices. They also involved Paul's religious beliefs, which in most respects no longer resembled the teachings of Judaism. While his Epistles provide us with adequate information about his ideas, they are rather involved, and Christians themselves often differ on their exact meaning. However, here is a liberal view that seems reasonably correct.

To Paul, Jesus had ceased to be a human figure. He was not even the Jewish Messiah who called upon people to repent before the coming of God's Kingdom. Now he had become the literal "son of God." God had caused Mary to bear His son so that He, God, might appear in human form to save mankind. Jesus, therefore, was not just a man, but God Himself, as a man. At the will of God, his Father, Jesus had gladly accepted death, only to be restored through resurrection to his divine state. To Paul, the very example of Jesus' resurrection proved that not only had he been God's own son, but that all who believed in him would share the promise of everlasting life.

Thus Paul's view of Jesus was totally different from the Jewish conception of the Messiah, or even the beliefs held by the followers of Jesus in Jerusalem. True, Paul and his Gentile Christians called Jesus the "Christ," the Greek word for "Messiah." But by the term they meant the actual "son of God," not a human descendant of King David.

Paul taught that only through personal identification with Jesus the Christ, the son of God, could people achieve "salvation," that is, be saved from everlasting destruction. For all human beings were unclean, "sinful." They inherited this condition simply by being born as humans, since "matter," of which they are formed, contains the very essence of sinfulness. In contrast, the nature of God and His son Jesus was pure and everlasting "spirit."

Judaism, Paul insisted, was no longer able to remove this condition of sinfulness. Neither the Day of Atonement nor adherence to the teachings of the Torah could successfully cleanse the individual. Rather, it required the transformation of "matter" into "spirit" by means of a union with the Christ.

This could only be achieved in two ways. First, by a continual personal reliving of Jesus' death and resurrection through intense and mystical belief in him as the son of God. Second, by participation in the various rites that served to unite the individual with the Christ. Among these were Baptism and partaking of the bread and wine, symbolizing the experience of the Last Supper, often referred to today as "Communion," literally, "union with" Christ. By faith and sacraments, this was the only way, Paul declared, that men and women could be purified from their state of sinfulness and earn everlasting salvation.

Here is an essential part of that teaching as Paul himself expressed it in his Epistle to the Romans:

> ... Do you not know that all of us who have been baptized into Christ Jesus were baptized into his death? We were buried therefore with him by baptism into death, so that as Christ was raised from the dead by the glory of the Father, we too might walk in newness of life.
>
> For if we have been united with him in a death like his, we shall certainly be united with him in a resurrection like his. We know that our old self was crucified with him so that the sinful body might be destroyed, and we might no longer be enslaved to sin. ... But if we have died with Christ, we believe that we shall also live with him. For we know that Christ being raised from the dead will never die again; death no longer has dominion over him. ... So you must also consider yourselves dead to sin and alive to God in Christ Jesus.
> —Romans 6:3-11

Paul believed there was no time to be lost. Human beings must accept the Christ before the rapidly approaching end of the world arrived. Only those who were cleansed of their sins would be saved from the dreadful destruction that would precede the return of Jesus Christ to earth. They alone would receive everlasting life.

THE LAST SUPPER. In this famous painting, Jesus is seen with his disciples as they gather together for the last time. This meal is commemorated by Christians with the rite of Communion.

CHRISTIANITY BECOMES A SEPARATE RELIGION

Although the ideas of Paul as they are found in his Epistles are sometimes very difficult to understand, these seem to be his most important teachings. As interpreted and enlarged over the years, his belief in "salvation through faith in Jesus Christ, crucified and resurrected" has remained the fundamental message of Christianity to this day.

The Growth of Early Christianity Scholars, generally, maintain that Paul's teachings were based upon religious beliefs current in the Roman world, principally those connected with the mystery cults, for they share a great deal in common. The central belief of both Christianity and the mystery religions was grounded in the death of the god and his resurrection. Both required rites of initiation and identification with the life and death of the god. Both promised salvation in the form of forgiveness of sin and life-after-death. And, as we have already noted in connection with Mithraism, they often carried on similar practices.

It was these elements, plus the moral teachings which Christianity took from Judaism, that had the greatest appeal to the Gentiles of the Mediterranean world. Unlike the beliefs and practices of the Jewish Christians of Jerusalem, which often conflicted with the people's accustomed ways of life, Paul's message seemed familiar and quite acceptable. As a result, the Gentile wing of the movement forged rapidly ahead.

In contrast, the Jerusalem group made little headway. It attracted comparatively few Jews, while Gentile Christianity continued to make numerous converts among the various communities of Asia Minor, Greece, and Italy. Slowly, therefore, the Jewish Christians lost their influence in the total movement, and with the destruction of Jerusalem by the Romans in 70 C.E., they ultimately disappeared.

Over the years, the new Christianity had also introduced certain distinct rites about which we learn from the New Testament. Two of the most important were Baptism and the "Eucharist," or "thanksgiving," commemorating the Last Supper of Jesus. Both were intense inner experiences of identification with the "son of God."

In Baptism, the individual was initiated into Christianity. His going into the water symbolized that his former sinful self had died with Christ's crucifixion. His coming out represented his resurrection as a cleansed individual, who had been reborn through his new belief in the "son of God."

The ceremony of the Eucharist, involving the eating of bread and drinking of wine, also symbolized the mystical identification of the Christian with Christ. The bread represented Christ's body; the wine, his blood. By eating the bread and drinking the wine, the participant and the Christ became one, and the worshipper could personally go through the inner experience of Jesus' death on the cross.

The New Testament tells us something of the activities of the early Christians. We hear of the care of poorer members and widows, the common sharing of food, and visits by traveling preachers. Undoubtedly, the early groups also adopted some form of prayer service. Here, too, we observe the beginning of church organization with the mention of "elders," "bishops," "deacons," and other leaders.

However, the development of Christianity was far from complete. The observance of Easter, for instance, is not mentioned at all in the New Testament. Neither is Christmas. Actually, it was not until several centuries later that Christianity became a well-organized religion, with an established calendar of holidays, carefully prescribed regulations, fixed worship procedures, and a full set of church officials.

The Break between Judaism and Christianity As a result of Paul's teachings, the growth of Gentile Christianity, and the disappearance of the Jerusalem group, Judaism and Christianity eventually parted company. While the Jews had been content to allow the Jewish Christians to remain within the synagogue, they could scarcely be as tolerant of Pauline Christianity. By now it had become quite clear to them on many counts that Paul's Christianity was no longer a Jewish sect, but a religion of its own.

CALVARY. Suspected for being the potential leader of a revolt against Rome, Jesus, along with common criminals, was crucified on this rocky hilltop called Golgotha, "skull," in Hebrew. Calvary has the same meaning in Latin.

In the first place, the Gentile Christians had discontinued the practice of all Jewish ceremonial, ritual, and holiday observances. According to Paul, salvation could no longer be achieved by fulfilling the requirements of the "Law of Moses," but only through faith in Jesus Christ.

Even the Jewish Sabbath as such was abandoned. It was a bit later, when some definite time was needed for Christian worship, that Sunday was chosen, since Jesus' resurrection was believed to have occurred on that day. By so doing the Christians took advantage of the fact that, in Asia Minor, Sunday was already known as "the Emperor's Day," a title which they promptly proceeded to change to "the Lord's Day" in honor of Jesus.

Nor did the Gentile Christians seem to identify themselves at all with the Jewish people. They denied that Israel still had a covenant with God. Generally, they showed little sense of kinship with the people of Israel, and even refused to support them in their life-and-death struggle against the Romans, especially in the war of 68-70 C.E.

Furthermore, many of the basic beliefs of the Gentile Christians were opposed by Judaism. One, certainly, was Paul's teaching that Jesus was God's own son. This was something that the Jewish concept of God could not tolerate. For centuries the Jews had insisted that there was only *one* God. There could be no "God the Father" and "God the Son," as Paul maintained. Nor could He be represented in human form or seen by man.

Judaism also rejected Paul's teaching that man was fundamentally sinful and therefore needed to be "saved" through identification with Jesus. The Jews insisted that man was born sinless, and that within himself he had the capacity for righteousness. To overcome sin he needed no mystical union with a crucified god. Instead, he had only to obey God's moral and ethical laws as revealed through the teachings of Judaism. Moreover, should he sin, he had the capacity to secure forgiveness for his sins through sincere repentance, making amends for wrong-doing, and earnestly seeking to live a more righteous life. God had created human beings with human failings and human limitations; He would not reject a man's sincere efforts to grow more like Him.

Finally, under Paul's influence the Christians claimed that their religion was the "new" revelation, destined to supplant Judaism, which was the "old." The Jewish religion, they declared, was simply the forerunner of Christianity. With the appearance of Jesus, the Christians maintained, the earlier religion of Moses had lost its whole purpose for existence.

This the Jews strenuously denied, for they regarded the observance of God's laws as part of an everlasting covenant between Him and the people of Israel. The death of any man, including Jesus, in no way changed the truth of God's commandments nor modified that covenant. No Jew living by the Torah felt that his good deeds, his prayers, his rituals, were now no longer acceptable to God. On the contrary, the very way in which the Gentiles had come to accept God made the Jews feel it was more important than ever for them to be loyal to their God and their covenant.

By now, both religions were competing vigorously with one another. The followers of each claimed that only they possessed the true faith, that the others' religion was in error. Eventually, the relations between the Jews and Christians worsened. The various accusations which the first three Gospels level against the Pharisees and the Jews in general, indicate the growing antagonism of early Christianity to Judaism. By the time the Gospel of John, the latest of the Gospels, was written, bitterness against the Jews had become intense.

Undoubtedly, the Jews responded to this bitterness by defending Judaism, attacking the ideas of the early Christians, ridiculing their claims that the Messiah had already come, taunting them about his failure to reappear, and refusing them entry into the synagogue. It is also very likely that in the interests of maintaining order, Jewish authorities even administered the lash to overzealous Christian leaders, like Paul and others. Strange to say, however, there are only hints of these feelings in early Jewish literature, and no important Jewish writings on this subject at all.

We cannot be certain when the complete separation of the two religions finally took place. We can be sure, however, that the process was well under way by the time Jerusalem was destroyed by the Romans in 70 C.E.

Christianity's Debt to Judaism Despite the growing rivalry and antagonism, the early Christians drew heavily upon Judaism for many essentials of their faith.

At the very outset, they emphasized the Jewish background of their movement. The writers of the Gospels, for instance, pictured Jesus as an observant Jew and even traced his ancestry back to King David. They pointed out that John the Baptist and all of Jesus' disciples were Jews. They boasted of the considerable Jewish knowledge which Jesus possessed, and laid the scene of many of his activities in the synagogue. They linked him with the Jewish concept of the Messiah who would usher in the glorious King-

dom of God. They even quoted from the Jewish Scriptures, especially from the prophetic portions, to justify many of their beliefs about Jesus.

However, early Christianity borrowed much more. It adopted practically all of Jewish ethics for its own standard of conduct. Thus the Christians also subscribed to the Ten Commandments, the love of one's fellow man, and the practice of justice and righteousness.

Christianity's belief in monotheism originated, of course, with Judaism. Although the Christians looked upon Jesus as the son of God, and hence divine, they nevertheless insisted that Jesus and his Father were actually one and the same God—a definition of monotheism Jews have never been able to understand.

Again basing itself on Judaism, Christianity insisted upon the exclusive allegiance of its followers. For in those days it was not unusual for people to be associated with more than one religion at the same time. Thus many who were identified with the official religion of the Roman Empire were likewise followers of one or more of the mystery faiths. However, imitating the example of the Jews, early Christianity maintained that it alone possessed the true faith and that those who wished to be Christians must give up all other beliefs and observances.

For centuries Judaism regarded all of its followers, no matter where they dwelt, as belonging to one united people. Similarly, Christianity also came to view all of its adherents as members of one great universal Christian brotherhood or "church."

The institution of the church itself as the meeting place for regular prayer and observance was patterned after the synagogue. So, too, was early church music. Gradually, the Christians, like the Jews before them, produced their own liturgy and prayer book, and as we have already seen, adopted the Jewish idea of a book of sacred literature. In addition to creating their own "New Testament," they also incorporated into their Bible the existing Hebrew Scriptures, as well as other Jewish writings found in the Apocrypha.

And, though drawing here chiefly upon pagan

practice, Christianity was even influenced by Judaism to provide a number of observances that paralleled those carried on by Jews. One was the Lord's Day, observed on Sunday, that came to represent the Christian Sabbath. Easter, commemorating the resurrection of Jesus, became the spring holiday in place of Passover. Christmas, observing Jesus' birth, replaced Chanuko as the mid-winter festival.

Thus the early Christians borrowed much from Judaism. But they did not hesitate to modify it in keeping with their own teachings and the needs of the developing movement.

Early Christianity Faces a Crisis   The missionary efforts of Christianity grew more vigorous, and its number of followers steadily increased. Gradually, too, their beliefs, practices, and institutions began to take distinctive shape. But now, early in its history, Christianity faced a serious crisis.

The crisis had to do with the matter of Jesus' return. As we know, early Christianity confidently expected Jesus to reappear shortly and usher in the glorious Kingdom of God. In fact, in anticipation of the approaching moment when the son of God would return, the followers of Christianity lived together in a cooperative kind of settlement, sharing their food and other necessities.

But as time passed, many grew impatient. Special problems arose with those who ceased to work and simply lived off the labors of others. Questions were also raised about the fate of those Christians who had already died and therefore would not be present when Jesus returned.

The longer Jesus' absence continued, the more difficult the situation became. In this the Jews saw confirmation of their wisdom in rejecting Christianity and publicly said so. Some of the early Christians, too, were beginning to lose faith in the promises of Paul. Others were so eager for Jesus' return that they believed every rumor that arose. The result was a movement in constant turmoil, with disillusionment setting in each time these rumors proved to be unfounded.

Only after a number of years did the leaders of Christianity find a solution, and it was one that was suggested by certain earlier Jewish writings which dealt with the coming of the Messiah. The delay in Jesus' return, the Christians now explained, was due to various events that had not as yet occurred. Before he could reappear, the world must first undergo a period of intense violence and wickedness created by a powerful evil being called the "Antichrist." Only after the "Antichrist" had been vanquished by Jesus would he appear.

However, for some unexplainable reason the visit of the Antichrist had been delayed. Therefore, the early Christians were advised to continue working and supporting themselves because the delay might indeed be a long one. And as for those who died in the meanwhile, they would certainly receive the reward of eternal life when Jesus finally appeared.

Naturally this explanation failed to satisfy the Jews and others who were skeptical about Jesus' return. But apparently it settled the problem for the early Christians, though in later years it gave rise to various Christian movements that predicted his early reappearance. Even today the traveler on American highways constantly passes signs promising "Jesus is coming soon."

With this explanation of Jesus' delay, the new religion proceeded to organize itself on a more permanent basis. Now it began to establish the kind of religious life that could be carried on no matter how long his coming was postponed.

Conflict with Rome   Even as the early Christians were in the process of developing their religion, they came face-to-face with extinction. For the Romans were bent on destroying the new faith.

Almost from the start, as we shall shortly see, the Roman authorities regarded Christianity as a threat to the Empire. Consequently, they tried to stamp out the new religion by beating, imprisoning, and even executing its followers. Many early Christians were martyred, and among them, according to church tradition,

72

CHRISTIANITY BECOMES A SEPARATE RELIGION

were Peter, the leader of the Jewish Christians, and the Apostle Paul.

For nearly three centuries, Roman persecution continued. Yet not only did the Christian religion manage to survive, but it grew even stronger. In the process, the Catholic Church came into existence, and it was through its efforts that Christianity overcame its enemies and eventually became the official religion of the Roman Empire.

With this, the foundations were laid for Christianity to become the faith with the largest following in the present-day world. . . .

TOPICS TO DISCUSS

1. In what ways is modern Christianity the product of Paul's teachings, rather than those of Jesus?
2. What are some of the major differences between the beliefs of the Christian and those of the Jew?
3. In what respect is modern Christianity indebted to Judaism?
4. What answer would you give to the proposal that at long last Judaism should accept Jesus?

THINGS TO DO

1. Prepare a dictionary of religious terms indicating the position of both Christianity and Judaism with regard to each.
2. Construct a picture-chart showing the sources from which Christianity drew its beliefs and practices.

3. As a student of religion, investigate the meaning of the following to Paul: (1) Baptism—see Romans 6:1-4; (2) the Eucharist—see I Corinthians 11:23-26; (3) Original Sin—see Romans 6:12-14; (4) Circumcision—see Romans 2:25-29; (5) the Commands of the Torah—see Romans 4:13-15; 7:4-10.

OTHER THINGS TO READ

BALLOU, ROBERT O., *The Portable World Bible*, Viking, "New Testament: From the Acts of the Apostles," pp. 412-419; "From the Epistles," pp. 419-434.

BAMBERGER, BERNARD J., *The Story of Judaism*, UAHC, Chapter 16, "Birth of a New Religion," pp. 94-100.

NOSS, JOHN B., *Man's Religions*, Macmillan, pp. 583-599.

PIKE, E. ROYSTON, *Encyclopaedia of Religion and Religions*, Meridian, "Christ," p. 93; "Lord's Day," p. 234; "Mithraism," pp. 257-258; "Mystery Religions," pp. 267-268; "Paul," p. 294; "Peter," pp. 297-298; "Stoicism," pp. 361-362.

SANDMEL, SAMUEL, *A Jewish Understanding of the New Testament*, HUC, Chapter 5, "The Background of Paulinism," pp. 37-43; Chapter 6, "Paul," pp. 44-51; Chapter 7, "Paul's Doctrine of Christ," pp. 52-60; Chapter 8, "The Church and the Law of Moses," pp. 61-77; Chapter 9, "The Epistles of Paul," pp. 78-96; Chapter 10, "Pauline Christianity and Greek Religion," pp. 97-104.

SILVER, ABBA HILLEL, *Where Judaism Differed*, Macmillan, Chapter 6, "On Rejecting Treasures," pp. 85-107; Chapter 10, "That Men Need to Be Saved," pp. 158-181.

SMITH, HUSTON, *The Religions of Man*, Mentor, pp. 282-301.

8
THE RISE OF THE CATHOLIC CHURCH

The Christians Face Martyrdom   A ragged band of people stood huddled in the arena of the giant Colosseum of Rome. They watched anxiously as attendants moved to the opposite side of the stadium.

A shout went up from the crowd. *Christiani ad leones!* "Throw the Christians to the lions!"

Now Emperor Nero gave the signal. He and his court sat forward with mounting interest as the attendants moved quickly to the task.

A series of roars rent the air as several huge lions sprang into view. "Attack the Christians!" the spectators began shouting.

The lions looked about nervously. They had been kept without food and tormented for nearly a week, and they were in a vicious mood.

Suddenly, they spotted the group of people in the middle of the arena. For just a moment they eyed them; then they sprang forward. The victims dropped on their knees in prayer as the lions tore at them.

A wild, exultant shout from the crowd drowned out the snarling of the beasts below.

Why the Romans Persecuted the Christians
Many such scenes occurred during the first three centuries of Christianity. According to church records nearly twenty thousand Christians were martyred in Rome alone. The most severe of the persecutions took place around 65 C.E. during the reign of Emperor Nero, who

accused the Christians of having burned Rome. During the next two centuries other outbursts against them occurred. Finally, in the period following 270 C.E., and especially under Diocletian, who ruled at the start of the fourth century, persecution once more became intense.

We may wonder why the Romans were so hostile to Christianity since they were generally tolerant of other religions. The answer is that they looked upon Christianity as a subversive, traitorous religion because its followers refused to take part in certain official rites of the Empire. While by Roman law the Jews had long been declared exempt as a nation, all other peoples were expected to place a pinch of incense or offer a sacrifice in honor of the emperor. But, like the Jews before them, the Christians viewed this as a form of idolatry since the Roman emperors were also considered gods. They even refused to take the Roman oath in the name of the "divine" emperor. As a consequence, the Romans looked upon them not only as unpatriotic but downright disloyal. And because the number of Christians was increasing so rapidly, the new religious movement seemed to pose a threat to the very security of the Empire.

Ugly rumors now circulated about the Christians. It was said that none of them would serve in the Roman army or accept public office. They were believed to worship a king other than the

74

emperor, and it was rumored that in offering the Eucharist they practiced cannibalism. The result was that Christians became all the more suspect, and they suffered punishment, imprisonment, and martyrdom at the hands of the Romans.

The followers of Christianity identified their suffering with that of Jesus. In fact, they pointed out that this had been predicted in the Gospels. Therefore, to endure martyrdom bravely became an act of the highest faith. Though some Christians did give up their religion, most remained fiercely loyal. And the more they endured persecution, the more the people were impressed with their faith and courage. The result was that Christianity began to attract even more converts.

The Church of Rome Becomes Dominant   By now the Church was already calling itself "Catholic." This was a term first employed by Ignatius of Antioch, one of the early Church "fathers," or leaders, who lived during the beginning of the second century C.E. He used the word in its original meaning of "universal," "world-wide," to describe the whole of the Christian movement, as contrasted with a local body of worshippers or "church." Eventually it was applied to the overwhelming number of Christians found in the one strongly united Church, in contrast to those who subscribed to the teachings of certain smaller sects.

Recognition of a "Catholic Church" encouraged the development of a highly organized leadership, or "hierarchy." The word "hierarchy" comes from two Greek words, *hieros*, "sacred," and *arkes*, "ruler." Hence it means "sacred rulers," or Church officials.

In earlier times, the movement had been led by men called "apostles," such as Peter and Paul, and "disciples," like Barnabas and Timothy, the fellow workers of Paul. Local churches came to have their own officials, too, known in the ascending order of their importance as deacons, elders, and bishops.

With the death of the apostles and disciples, an ordained clergy gradually succeeded them. In local churches, the *episcopoi*, a word meaning

"overseers" or "superintendents," but later called "bishops," became the chief members of the clergy. Each local church came to have its own bishop, and he in turn ordained the deacons and elders by "laying hands upon them," a practice followed by the Jews in ordaining their rabbis. Now all the officials of each church, clergy as well as laymen, were held responsible to its bishop.

Eventually, certain bishops began to assume control over all the churches in their area. Each important locality had its own bishop. There was a bishop of Antioch, a bishop of Corinth, a bishop of Rome, and so forth. By the third century C.E., Christians were generally described as being under the leadership of the bishop of an area. All bishops were considered to have equal authority, although the decisions of individual ones were subject to review by various councils of bishops.

The bishop of Rome gradually was turned to as one of the more important leaders of the Church. Rome was not only the capital and most influential city of the Empire, but beginning about 100 C.E., it had the largest community of Christians. Moreover, Church tradition contributed much to his authority. It was believed that Peter, the chief disciple of Jesus and the person who led the original Christians, was the founder of the Church of Rome and hence its first "bishop." Later bishops viewed themselves as Peter's direct successors and, therefore, responsible for the well-being of Christianity as a whole. Thus, during the second and third centuries C.E., it was the bishop of Rome who led the fight against those who deviated from the official doctrines of the Church. During one of these disputes he even ousted a number of churches in Asia Minor.

Sometime in the early part of the fourth century the title of "pope" came into being to describe the Bishop of Rome. The word is taken from the Greek, *pappas*, and Late Latin, *papa*, meaning "father," a term originally applied to all bishops but increasingly used for the Bishop of Rome. Julius (337-352 C.E.) and Innocent I (402-417), both Bishops of Rome, wrote letters to bishops in Antioch and northern Africa re-

ST. PETER. The chief disciple of Jesus is looked upon by Catholics as the founder and first bishop of the Church of Rome.

CONSTANTINE THE GREAT. Having helped establish the supremacy of Christianity within the Roman Empire, he was later made a saint.

minding them of the authority of the Roman church over all the Christian churches. Succeeding bishops in the East and West came to look upon the papacy as the chief religious office of the Catholic Church; local bishops were considered subject to its sacred authority. Thus the Roman Church gradually became dominant.

Christianity Becomes the Official Religion
Strengthened by the determination of its followers, Christianity had been able to withstand even the most intense persecutions. Now, a growing and well-organized Church was prepared to meet the final assault.

Though for about a half-century there had been practical toleration of Christianity, one last attempt to root it out was made at the beginning of the fourth century C.E. Ruthlessly, the emperor Diocletian, spurred on by his son-in-law Galerius, burned its churches, confiscated its literature, and executed thousands of

its followers. But he failed in his efforts to destroy Christianity, and with this, Roman leadership finally realized that it could not defeat the "enemy." Instead, it decided to make the Church its ally.

In 311 C.E., therefore, the Roman leaders who came after Diocletian, chiefly the Emperor Galerius, now a sick man, issued an "edict of toleration to Christians" which permitted them to practice their religion so long as they did nothing contrary to the welfare of the Empire. A year or so later, Constantine and his co-emperor, Licinius, published a decree that gave Christianity full legal equality with all other religions of the Roman world and ordered confiscated Church property to be returned.

Gradually, thereafter, other edicts issued by Constantine gave Christianity a preferred position in the Empire. An early act of his, for example, was a prohibition of all conversions to Judaism, which had the effect of limiting the growth of a rival religion. Slowly the Jews and other religious groups found themselves subject to the authority of the Church, and ultimately, in 380, Theodosius I made Christianity the official religion of the Roman Empire.

Constantine had not been particularly interested in the Christian religion; rather, he was concerned with uniting his Empire. With this in mind, he summoned the Council of Nicea in 325 to compel the Christians to settle a dispute that was threatening to split the Church, and hence to split the Empire.

As it had developed from the earliest days of the Church, the accepted doctrine of Christianity was that God was not just two aspects or "persons," but three, and, at the same time, still only one God. To God the Father and God the Son (Jesus Christ), had been added the belief in God the Holy Ghost (the Spirit of God through which He appears to men). Christians believed that all the aspects of God found in the Trinity—Father, Son, and Holy Ghost—were one, the same, and equal.

But Arius, an official in the church of Alexandria in Egypt, was teaching that Jesus Christ was not one and the same as God, his Father. The Father was truly the Supreme Being; Jesus was a lesser Being created by the Father before the beginning of the world. Arianism, as this belief was called, quickly spread throughout Christianity. Especially in the eastern part of the Roman Empire did the Church find itself badly divided over the issue.

At Nicea, where the bishops and other clergy gathered, the Church decided against Arius. His teachings were declared a "heresy," an opinion held in opposition to the accepted doctrine of the Church. For this heresy, he and the two bishops who supported him were promptly banished from the Empire. Thereby, Constantine was successful in restoring the unity of the Catholic Church and through it, of course, that of his own Empire.

The Need for Systematic Church Doctrine
The issue over Arianism and other "heresies" that various sects were spreading made the Church realize the necessity for defining its teachings. Unlike Judaism, which was based upon a way of life prescribed by its Law, Christianity centered about its beliefs. Although these in general had been well established by the time of Paul's death, their precise meaning remained open to interpretation. So, as different individuals and churches came forward with their own views about the nature of God, Jesus, Christian practice, and the like, confusion set in.

There was already precedent for systematizing Christian doctrine. During the middle of the second century C.E., there had appeared the so-called Apostles' Creed, the first official statement of Christian belief. Emended somewhat later on, it now reads as follows:

> I believe in God the Father, Almighty Creator of heaven and earth;
>
> And in Jesus Christ, His only Son, Our Lord, who was conceived by the Holy Ghost, born of the Virgin Mary, suffered under Pontius Pilate, was crucified, died, and was buried. He descended into hell; the third day He arose again from the dead; He ascended into heaven; and sits at the right hand of God the Father Almighty; from whence He shall come to judge the living and the dead.
>
> I believe in the Holy Ghost, the Holy Catholic Church, the communion of saints, the forgiveness of sins, the resurrection of the body, and life everlasting. Amen.

However, even the Apostles' Creed was open to further interpretation, and various meanings were given to such terms as "Catholic Church," "the forgiveness of sins," "His only Son," "the Holy Ghost," and others. The result was so many conflicting opinions, so-called "heresies," that the Catholic Church seemed in danger of being torn apart by fierce disputes over doctrine.

The Work of Augustine
It was Augustine, one of Christianity's greatest minds, who helped preserve the unity of the Church. Born in North Africa about 354 C.E. to a Christian mother and a pagan father, he led a wild, riotous life throughout early manhood. However, when he

THE DEVELOPMENT OF CHRISTIANITY
TO CONSTANTINE

IMPORTANT WORLD EVENTS	DATE	DEVELOPMENTS IN CHRISTIANITY
	About 4 B.C.E.	Birth of Jesus.
26 Pontius Pilate becomes Procurator of Judea. 	About 29 C.E.	Jesus baptized by John the Baptist.
	About 30	Jesus crucified.
	About 40	Start of Paul's ministry and writing of his Epistles. Gradual development of Christianity.
54 Nero becomes Roman Emperor, to **68.**		
Fire destroys Rome.	About 64	Intense persecution of Christians begins. Death of Peter and Paul.
Fall of Jerusalem. 	About 70	Break between Christianity and Judaism. First of Gospels (Mark) completed.
	About 100	Rome becomes largest Christian community. Importance of Bishop of Rome grows.
	117	Ignatius, who first used the term "catholic," dies.
135 Final destruction of Jerusalem.	About 150	Apostles' Creed appears.
	About 154	Celebration of Easter first mentioned.
	About 190	Asia Minor churches excommunicated by Bishop of Rome.
	About 250	The Church develops basic organization of clergy.
	270	Intense persecution renewed, especially with Emperor Diocletian, from **303** on.
	311	Edict of Toleration issued by Romans.
306 Constantine the Great becomes one of the rulers of Rome.	About 312	Christianity given legal equality. Church gradually wins preferred position in Roman Empire.

ceased to find satisfaction from this kind of living, he turned to the study of various Greek philosophies. Then, for nine years, he followed Manicheism, the popular Persian faith that emphasized the conflict between the two great forces of good and evil. However, nothing seemed to satisfy his inner needs.

In 383, Augustine left Carthage for Rome and then for Milan. There after long but unconvincing study of Christianity he underwent an unusual experience that led to his conversion. One day, he tells us in his *Confessions*, he was terribly upset by his inability to resist temptation. He fled from a companion into the garden. Suddenly, he heard the voice of a child from a nearby house say in a singsong voice, "Take up and read, take up and read."

Augustine could not think of any child's game that went this way. Puzzled, he opened the copy of the Epistle to the Romans that he had been holding. His eyes fell upon a passage that called upon people to give up riotous living and drunkenness and take upon themselves the Lord Jesus Christ. The passage struck home. A sense of the power of Christianity overcame him; he felt inwardly converted. Suddenly, he felt a calmness that he had not known before.

Augustine then started to study Christianity in earnest, and a few years later, both he and his illegitimate son underwent baptism. Not long after, he returned to North Africa where he was ordained a priest. Ultimately he became the Bishop of Hippo, an important North African city.

Before his death in 429, he produced many important works, including his *Confessions*, the story of his life up to his conversion, and *The City of God*. In the latter he defended Christianity against the pagan charge that neglect of the old gods had caused the downfall of Rome. Rather, said Augustine, Christianity made possible a better kingdom, a heavenly reign through which people can be saved from sin. The Church, which is the "City of God," must eventually replace all states and nations and come to rule the world so that mankind may find salvation. It was this teaching which gave the Christians purpose for living during

the trying period following the fall of the Roman Empire. Later it gave rise to those political concepts under which the Church established its authority over kings and princes in the medieval world.

But Augustine's greatest work was his interpretation of the Church and its doctrines. Here he was engaged in combating the teachings of various "heretics." For instance, there were those who questioned the whole place of the Church in Christianity. It was their contention that simply by faith in Christ alone, and without the ministry of the Church, man had the power within himself to keep God's law and overcome sin. Augustine branded this as untrue. Man at birth, he said, has the tendency to evil through "original sin," the result of Adam's disobedience to God. He cannot overcome his sinfulness without the intervention of Christ through the cleansing rite of Baptism. But even then he is incapable by himself of living without sin, and he requires the saving gift of God's intervention to insure his salvation. This, known as God's "grace," is made possible to man through the Church.

Augustine also defended the Church against those who believed that the sinfulness of the clergy rendered its sacraments worthless. No, he declared, the sacraments are not human ceremonies, they are God's. As performed in the

ST. AUGUSTINE TEACHING. One of the great minds of Catholicism, he defined and interpreted most of its major doctrines during the early days of the Church.

Church they are merely outward, visible symbols of God's activity. Hence, their capacity to provide salvation in no way depends upon the character of the person who administers them, and no matter what the conduct of the priest, the sacraments given in the name of the Church are always completely valid.

The Church, he maintained, is the true embodiment of Christ on earth. As such, it automatically enjoys four qualities: unity, holiness, apostolicity (claiming true descent from Peter, the chief disciple of Jesus), and catholicity (world-wide in nature and possessing the true doctrine of Christianity).

So, by defining Christian belief and practice, Augustine succeeded in strengthening the Church. By doing so, he prepared it for a still more prominent role in the affairs of the world. Yet in the process the Church was converted into something vastly different from the synagogue. Where the synagogue sought to serve God, the Church claimed to be the living body of Christ in the world and hence to represent him. The human and humble character of the synagogue in the mother faith had given way to the divinity and authority of the Church itself.

The Church and the Fall of Rome Throughout the fourth and fifth centuries, the Roman Empire was threatened by various European tribes, such as the Goths and Vandals, and by a people of central Asia known as the Huns. In 455, the city of Rome was sacked by the Vandals, and twenty-one years later the rule of all Italy passed into the hands of the "barbarians."

As the Roman Empire came to an end, the Church was in tremendous turmoil. Libraries hundreds of years old lay in ashes. Church schools and colleges were destroyed. The learning that had been part of Roman culture died out, and a period which historians call the "Dark Ages" set in.

Slowly the Church rallied, and to a great extent it was aided by its monastic movement, the various communities of monks and nuns.

Almost from the start, Christianity's emphasis upon the approaching Kingdom of God created the urge in certain of its followers to practice asceticism; that is, to turn their backs upon normal ways of living. Paul's stress upon the sinfulness of man encouraged this even more. If by its very nature, as Paul maintained, human life was prone to sin, then as much of it

THE HUNS TURN BACK. In 452 C.E., Pope Leo I succeeded in persuading Attila, leader of the German tribes invading Italy, not to attack the city of Rome.

80

as possible should be avoided. To deny the "desire of the flesh" was a high religious act. The result was that, even in Paul's day, many followed his suggestion to refrain if at all possible from marriage. This, of course, was in sharp contrast to Judaism with its stress upon family life as a supreme command of God.

Though the Church never taught that marriage was evil or that abstaining from it was required of everyone, by the end of the third century the trend toward intense asceticism had grown. Now there were numbers of individuals leaving their communities and going to isolated places where in absolute solitude they could meditate, fast, and afflict themselves. All forms of "mortification of the flesh," acts designed to destroy the vigor of the body, were practiced. Some of these hermits lived in deserts, some in caves or even trees. One, the famous Simeon Stylites, dwelt atop a pillar in a ruined city for thirty years. These so-called "pillar-saints" flourished in the East to the tenth century C.E.

Some went mad out of loneliness. Others died from their rigors. Many found it impossible to carry on their disciplines by themselves, and soon a group-type of ascetic life emerged. Monasteries with all sorts of religious disciplines and prescribed work, such as farming, writing, carpentry, were organized, and nunneries were also established for the women. Special vows were required of all who entered. In most instances they included vows of chastity (refraining from marriage and any act involving sex), poverty (not being permitted to have possessions of one's own), and obedience. Eventually these became the vows demanded of all the regular clergy as well.

With the fall of Rome, these monasteries and convents became the refuge of culture in the Western world. However, instead of Greek and Roman knowledge, its members concentrated on intense study of sacred Church literature and Christian traditions and beliefs. In contrast, Judaism required no monasteries to perpetuate learning. It was part of normal Jewish living for all Jews to study and to learn. Hence, the Jews had no period when culture and education nearly ceased. Nor did Judaism ever feel the need to create a monastic movement, since "denial of the flesh" meant a denial of God's command to live fully and "be fruitful and multiply."

Meanwhile, the Church had also succeeded in converting the "barbarians," and now counted the peoples of the British Isles, France, and Germany among its followers. The result was that, even with the overthrow of the Roman Empire, the ruling powers continued to be supporters of the Church.

The Church Becomes a Political Force   The power of the Church grew steadily throughout the centuries that followed. Greatly enriched by gifts of land and money, Roman Catholicism became a major political force in the Middle Ages. In the year 800, Pope Leo III helped establish Charlemagne as the first emperor of what came to be known as the Holy Roman Empire, and eventually the popes became extremely influential in approving or disapproving the candidacies of particular rulers.

The climax of the Church's rise to power took place in the eleventh century in a clash between Pope Gregory VII and King Henry IV, emperor of the Holy Roman Empire. It illustrates well the tremendous power which the Church came to wield.

In 1075, Pope Gregory VII declared the Church supreme in political, as well as religious matters and denied the right of any layman, even a king, to appoint bishops to their offices. Henry challenged him by appointing three bishops in Italy and two in Germany without his consent. The Pope refused to accept his appointees. Henry then "deposed the pope" in 1076, demanding that Gregory surrender his papal office as a "false monk." The Pope in turn claimed that he was responsible only to God and refused to resign. He went on to excommunicate the King and deny him authority over his subjects.

The power of excommunication was a potent weapon. It denied the sacraments of the Church to the excommunicant and thereby put his soul in danger of everlasting torment after death.

Moreover, he was branded an outcast for the rest of his life. No Christian was supposed to have anything to do with him or even speak to him.

Henry's rule began to crumble. To preserve his reign, he had only one choice: exercise the privilege of all penitents by begging the forgiveness of the Pope. So, in the midst of winter, after four weeks of great hardship in crossing the frozen Alps, Henry arrived in Canossa, in northern Italy, where Gregory was on his way to a Church council. Henry asked forgiveness, but the Pope refused it. Then, clad only in a coarse woolen shirt, barefooted and bareheaded, Henry walked through the deep snow to the cas-

ICON. The Virgin Mary with the infant Jesus, surrounded by scenes of Christ's later life, make up this icon which appears in a Russian Orthodox church.

tle where the Pope was staying. He was kept standing in bitter cold outside the gate for three days before he was permitted to enter. When he was admitted at last, Henry prostrated himself before the Pope. But now the Pope could not deny him. Gregory removed the excommunication and blessed him.

Such was the recognized authority of the Church during the eleventh through the fourteenth centuries! But it was the abuse of this very power which, as we shall see later, corrupted the Church, earned the hostility of the ruling classes as well as the peasantry, and eventually destroyed the unity of Christianity.

The Division between East and West   As if a warning, this very period was the one in which the Catholic Church suffered its most serious setback since the days of the Arian heresy. This was a split between the Western and Eastern branches of Christianity.

Even in early times, there had always been conflict between the Christians of the Western part of the Roman Empire and those in the East, especially in Constantinople and Asia Minor. In large part the cause was political. In fact, the Roman Empire itself eventually broke in two at the end of the fourth century C.E. with the result that there were now two capitals, Rome and Constantinople.

But there were other reasons as well. For example, deep-seated differences in belief and practice existed between East and West. The churches in the East centered their attention much more upon worship and devotional rites and far less upon the doctrinal concerns of the West. Specifying one's beliefs, they felt, was secondary to enriching the inner experience of the Christian. The Eastern Church also used icons (religious pictures and statues) in worship to an extent that was not nearly so common in the Roman Church. And there was a major language barrier between the two Churches. Those in the East used Greek in worship; those in the West, Latin. Their Bibles were also in the different languages.

For a long time there had been a great deal of rivalry between the bishops of Rome and

Constantinople. The supreme authority of the papacy was also challenged by the antiquity of the position of the bishop in Antioch as well as by the new importance of the Eastern Empire. Although eventually the Eastern churches came to acknowledge the overlordship of the pope, distance led them generally to ignore him. The breach was widened by the establishment of the Holy Roman Empire, for now the bishop, or "Patriarch," of Constantinople and the Eastern churches were part of a rival empire.

The final break came in 1054 with a dispute over the West's use of unleavened bread in the Eucharist and the Latinization of the liturgy in Bulgaria. A more basic issue, however, was the role of the Holy Ghost in the Trinity, a dispute that had erupted two centuries earlier. The West insisted that the Holy Ghost proceeded from both the Father and the Son, and hence all were to be glorified equally. The East insisted that the Holy Ghost proceeded from the Father only, and therefore glory was to be given to the Father, through the Son, with both united in the Holy Ghost.

The dispute was marked by intense bitterness, with the result that Pope Leo IX proceeded to excommunicate Michael Cerularius, the Patriarch of Constantinople, and his Church. The latter, in turn, excommunicated the Pope and the Western Church for being in error. The rupture between East and West was now complete. Henceforth, in contrast to the Catholics of the East, who called themselves "Orthodox" (that is, "correct in faith"), the followers of the Western Church became known as *Roman* Catholics.

The Eastern Orthodox Faith Though there were several attempts to heal the rupture, ever since then the Eastern Church has maintained its separate existence. In addition to the points already mentioned, Eastern Orthodoxy differs from Roman Catholicism in the following principal ways:

1. In Eastern Orthodoxy the Father is considered to be the sole begetter of the Holy Spirit in the Trinity.

2. The Eastern Orthodox Church rejects the absolute authority of the pope.

3. Married men may be ordained as priests and deacons in Eastern Orthodoxy. However, its bishops are selected from the ranks of monastic or other celibate (unmarried) clergy.

4. The Eastern Church uses leavened rather than unleavened bread for the ceremony of the Eucharist, and there is a somewhat different interpretation of the sacrament.

5. The date of Easter is set differently so that it often does not coincide with that of the other forms of Christianity.

Though the Patriarch of Constantinople (now Istanbul, Turkey) claims authority over the entire Eastern Church, it is really divided between himself and the patriarchs of four other major cities: Alexandria, Antioch, Jerusalem, and Moscow. In each case, the patriarch is appointed by the Church. But in Greece and Russia, he is invested in office by his particular government, which may also depose him.

The Russian and Greek Orthodox Churches are the major branches of the Eastern Church. Today Eastern Orthodoxy has a total of about 137 million followers in the world. Unlike the Roman Catholic Church, it cooperates with the various Protestant churches in interpreting Christianity through its membership in the World Council of the Churches of Christ. Today, too, the Eastern Orthodox churches are also engaged in discussions with Roman Catholicism, seeking ways to bridge the gap between their faiths.

Numbering about two and three-quarter million adherents in the United States, Eastern Orthodoxy is divided into 23 different groups, based upon the different countries of origin. The largest is the Greek Orthodox Church, with the next largest ones, the Russian, Serbian, and Ukranian Churches. Each Church convention, attended by both priests and laymen, appoints its bishops, and some local parishes even select their own priests.

The first Greek Orthodox settlement in the United States took place during the Colonial period in Florida. Russian Orthodoxy came in when Alaska, originally a part of Russia, was purchased by the United States. It was then that the Bishop of Alaska moved his headquarters to San Francisco.

Originally the various Orthodox Churches in America conducted their worship—always the same liturgy—in the particular tongue of the old country, but slowly, in all but the Greek Church, some English has come into the service. The worship, centering around the Eucharist, is marked by colorful ceremonial, and is chanted by priests wearing striking robes. They are answered by lay cantors or highly trained choirs. The service is always sung, and a layman must always be present to respond.

Everywhere in the church there are richly decorated murals and icons. Even the candle-lighted altar is seen through a golden screen upon which there are depictions of Christ, the

Virgin Mary, Apostles, and Saints. Adding to the brilliance of the church are golden vessels and jeweled copies of the Gospels, and the smell of incense pervades all.

In the home, too, there is usually a family sanctuary, a portion of a room with an icon of Christ illuminated by a hanging lamp. It is here that Eastern Orthodox parents and children carry on regular private worship.

The Crusades   Despite the rivalry of Eastern Orthodoxy, Roman Catholicism continued to be the most powerful religious force in the then known world. But by now a new and more serious competitor, Islam, had arisen to challenge it.

The Moslem faith already enjoyed the support of millions in the Middle East and had the allegiance of a large empire. By the end of the eleventh century, the forces of Islam were once

RUSSIAN ORTHODOX WORSHIP. Colorful rites, performed by participants in striking vestments and conducted against a background of vivid imagery, contribute to the pageantry of worship in the Eastern Orthodox faith.

more on the move, this time under the leadership of the aggressive Seljuk Turks. They were bent on the conquest of Constantinople, which was the capital of the Byzantine Empire and center of Eastern Orthodoxy, as well as the gateway to Europe.

Consequently, when the Byzantine ruler appealed to Pope Urban II for aid, the latter was eager to lend his assistance because he recognized that the Moslems represented a serious danger to the West. If the Byzantine Empire fell, all Europe and the Roman Church itself would be sure to come under attack. But Pope Urban also saw this as a golden opportunity to reunite the Eastern Church with his own.

Urban promised help, and in November of 1095, he issued a call for Christians to help rescue the holy places of the East from the Moslems. There was an enthusiastic response. The masses were fired by the idea of freeing the Holy Land, as well as by the papal promise of spiritual rewards to volunteers, including the suspension of some of the earthly punishments for sin. But love of adventure, hope of plunder, and religious prejudice also played an important part in spurring thousands of recruits to answer the call.

A mixed horde gathered. They became known as "Crusaders," a term taken from the Latin, *cruciata*, meaning "marked with a cross," because of the symbol they wore on their garments. On the way to the Holy Land, they stopped to pillage and massacre scores of Jewish and other non-Christian communities. Soon the mob was joined by skilled soldiers from nations all over Europe. Finally, in 1099, after a long, hard siege, the Crusaders captured Jerusalem and slaughtered all the Jews and Moslems in the city.

Within a century, Jerusalem was reconquered by the Moslems, this time under their great leader Saladin. Though further crusades were called for—the last took place in 1271—the Christians were unable to retain the Holy Land for long.

Effects of the Crusades   While the Crusades stirred up new interest in the Church, they also produced great unrest in the medieval world. After the excitement it was hard for the people to get back to ordinary, everyday living. The Crusades, too, brought tragedy to the Jews. In addition to murdering and uprooting thousands, the Crusades stirred up religious hatred that set off many centuries of Jewish persecution.

But there were other far-reaching effects. The Crusades brought the peoples of Europe into communication with the culture of the Moslem world, a culture that had preserved and interpreted much of Greek philosophic, scientific, and political thought. After the long period of the "Dark Ages," this communication reawakened a love of secular learning in the West. Now, slowly, painfully, Europeans began to lay the foundations of modern knowledge, including the various sciences.

The Crusades also stimulated new trade with the East, with the result that European port cities grew enormously and a new commercial class came into being. This, in turn, threatened to disrupt the feudal system under which European society was then organized and in which the Church enjoyed a privileged position. Feudalism, quite understandably, made no provision for the growing group of wealthy shipowners and merchants who sought their legitimate role in the political and economic life of the times.

All this created problems for the Church. Though the revival of Greek thought stimulated the intellectual life of the Church itself, it also produced conflicts over certain of the teachings of classical philosophy which some wanted the Church to accept. The rise of the new commercial class competed with the power of the Church and challenged its authority within the feudal system. And the general restlessness of the times encouraged attacks upon the privileged position of the Church and its clergy, as well as upon some of their practices.

For some time now the Church had been suffering from the usual ills of an organization whose powers were abused. Corruption was wide-spread. Priests perverted the teachings of the Church and traded on religious ignorance, even to the extent of selling "tickets of admission" to heaven. All sorts of fees were charged for baptisms, weddings, and funerals, and there was trafficking in church offices. Monks, who were vowed to live lives of poverty, ate and drank like nobles; and clergy, who were consecrated to purity, behaved scandalously.

These scandals were widely known, especially since some of the greatest writers of the Middle Ages, men like Dante, Chaucer, and Boccaccio, all Catholics, described the glaring abuses of churchmen. In protest, certain Christians, notably the Cathari and Waldensians of southern France and northern Italy, had already broken away from the Church. They established sects of their own in which they sought to purify the teachings and practices of Christianity.

The Church promptly met this threat with force and established the Inquisition, which was designed to discover and suppress heresy among Catholics. Torture and secret trials were used to gain information. In most cases the punishment was penance or imprisonment, but as time passed, death sentences became more common. The Inquisition was especially cruel on the Marranos, Jews who had been forced to convert to Catholicism by Spanish and Portuguese rulers during the thirteenth through the fifteenth centuries. Although outwardly Catholics, the Marranos had continued to practice Judaism secretly and were, therefore, guilty of heresy in the eyes of the Church.

Eventually, with the rise of Protestantism in the early sixteenth century, the effectiveness of the Inquisition came to an end. For the loss of political authority in many countries made it impossible any longer for the Church to execute heretics. It now had to depend on spiritual punishment, excommunication, to enforce its will.

Attempts at Church Reform   Meanwhile, within the Church, some were not at all convinced that the use of force would succeed. Agencies like the Inquisition, they felt, did not touch the real problem. In their judgment what was needed was Church reform. Among them were four individuals who, because of their holiness in the eyes of the Church as well as their important contributions to Catholicism, were later canonized as saints.

The first was *Dominic of Castile.* Born in Castile in 1170, he was a pious man who saw that the Church was suffering from ills that suppression could not cure. Above all, he was convinced that Catholicism had to face up to the challenge of the new thought that was sweeping through Europe as the result of the revival of Greek and Roman culture. Hence churchmen needed to rethink and reinterpret the doctrines of the Church in the light of the intellectual climate of the day.

With the approval of the pope, he founded an "Order of Preachers," more popularly known as Dominicans, dedicated principally to religious study and preaching. Dressed in white habits (a form of gown) and black cloaks, he and his followers first preached against the Albigensian heretics in southern France. Later they went to the various cities of Europe, the

DANTE. Greatest of the Italian poets, he exposed many of the short-comings of the Roman Catholic Church of the fourteenth century.

THE DEVELOPMENT OF ROMAN CATHOLICISM

FROM CONSTANTINE TO THE CRUSADES

IMPORTANT WORLD EVENTS	DATE	DEVELOPMENTS IN ROMAN CATHOLICISM
Constantine the Great becomes Emperor of Rome.	324	
	325	Council of Nicea decides against Arianism.
328 Constantine establishes Constantinople as capital of Eastern Empire. Beginnings of the Byzantine Empire.		
	About 354	Augustine born. Celebration of Christmas first appears in Rome.
	380	Emperor Theodosius I makes Christianity the official Roman religion.
	402	Innocent I becomes Bishop of Rome and claims authority over all churches.
	About 426	Augustine completes *The City of God*.
	440	Growth of the power of the papacy under Pope Leo the Great.
455 Rome sacked by the Vandals.		
476 Fall of Rome.		
622 Mohammed's flight from Mecca to Medina.		
	800	Pope Leo III crowns Charlemagne Emperor of the Holy Roman Empire.
From **1037** Rise of the Seljuk Turks.		
	1054	Eastern Orthodoxy breaks with the Roman Catholic Church.
	1077	Pope Gregory VII removes excommunication of Henry IV.
	1095	Pope Urban II calls for a Crusade against the Turks.
1099 Crusaders capture Jerusalem.		

DOMINICANS. Wearing their traditional white habits, members of this order have dedicated themselves to study and preaching.

a life of penance (repentance for sin), poverty, and service to his fellow man. The virtues of simple Christian living modeled after Jesus— "imitation of Christ," he called it—became his ideal.

He gathered together a group whom he called his "little brothers." Wearing coarse grey habits with hoods, and beggar's ropes around their waists, Francis and his followers lived solely by begging and sought to aid the poor, the lepers, and other outcasts of society. Stories arose of his love for birds and animals as an expression of his own love for God the Creator.

The movement of love and compassion grew. Francis' writings—chiefly regulations for his followers and some letters that are considered

university towns especially, to preach the teachings of the Church and explain the reasons for Christian belief. They set an example to the people by leading lives of strict poverty, living only upon charity, and spending long hours seeking to discover sound arguments to support the doctrines of Christianity. By the time Dominic died, he had established more than sixty Dominican centers in Spain, Italy, Germany, and England.

Another young man who was affected by the unrest in the Europe of his day was Giovanni Bernadone, better known as *Francis of Assisi*. Born in 1182, he was taken into the textile business of his father when he was only 14. But Giovanni showed by his extravagance and recklessness that he was ill-suited for this kind of life, so he became a soldier. In the army his vanity in dress earned him the nickname Francesco, "the Frenchman."

Shortly after he entered the army, he was taken prisoner and underwent a long period of illness. While he was convalescing, he experienced a powerful religious conversion which expressed itself in a strong love for his fellow human beings and all of God's creatures. At the age of 24, he abandoned his military career for

A FRANCISCAN BROTHER. This order of the Church is noted for its assistance to the poor and its work in the foreign-mission field.

gems of humility and simplicity—became treasured works. After a considerable time, the pope recognized the Franciscan order. By 1226, the year Francis died, there were some five hundred Franciscan friars all over Europe.

Thomas Aquinas, perhaps the greatest scholar the Catholic Church ever produced, also lived during these critical days. Born of a noble family in Italy about 1225, he eventually joined the Dominican order, much to the disappointment of his parents. In his early years, he applied himself so earnestly to his study of the teachings of the Church that his fellow students in Cologne, weary of his silence, called him the "Dumb Ox." Still he persisted, and throughout his entire life continued to study, lecture, and write. As a professor of theology in Paris, and then as an adviser to the pope, he defended the teachings of the Church and produced such outstanding writings as the three-part work called *Summa Theologiae*, "A Summary of Theology."

During his day there were many in the Church who condemned the revival of Greek learning and especially the study of Aristotle's philosophy. They feared that the latter particularly would destroy the faith of Catholics, but Thomas Aquinas defended such study. He pointed out that there were two kinds of human knowledge. One, like philosophy and science, which was based upon man's power to reason, could provide a great deal of useful information, even about the existence and nature of God. The second kind, an even higher form of knowledge, came to man through faith. Revealed by God, it dealt with things that human reason alone could not discover, such as man's awareness of the Trinity, bodily resurrection, original sin, and the like. Yet one should not believe anything that appears contrary to fact, and doctrines based upon faith should be tested by reason. In so doing, said Thomas Aquinas, Christianity will show itself to be in complete harmony with philosophy and science.

Thus in his writings Thomas Aquinas tried to prove that the Church's doctrines were capable of being taught with the aid of reason, and that there was sound, logical evidence for faith in God as revealed through Jesus Christ. He

THOMAS AQUINAS. Distinguished for his intellectual brilliance, he succeeded in harmonizing Catholic doctrine and philosophic thought. The Church later made him a saint.

went even further, and his work in Catholicism became somewhat like that of Maimonides in Judaism. In fact, he knew of Maimonides' work and refers to him affectionately in his *Summa* as "Rabbi Moses."

Now, as Maimonides had done for Judaism nearly a century before, Aquinas took the great mass of Catholic teachings and organized them into a system of thought which he attempted to harmonize with the principles of Greek philosophy. So brilliant was the result that it has remained the basis of Catholic theology to this day. Moreover, within recent times there has been a great revival of his teachings in an intellectual movement known as Neo- (new) Thomism.

The last of this distinguished quartet was *Ignatius of Loyola*, who lived several centuries after Dominic, Francis, and Aquinas, in the stormy Renaissance period, when the crisis in the Catholic Church had deepened still further. During Ignatius' own lifetime, the English monarchy as well as large segments of the German Church broke away from the papacy as part of the Protestant movement.

Born in 1491, Ignatius, a Basque (Spanish) nobleman, spent his first thirty years as the typical gay young man of the times, drinking, fighting, and leading a life of pleasure. As a captain in the army of the Duke of Najera, he was seriously wounded. During his convalescence, he began reading books about Jesus and the lives of St. Francis and St. Dominic. Deeply influenced, he decided to serve as a "knight of the Virgin." In order to become a priest, he devoted himself for ten years to study, a discipline at which he was not skilled. Then, moved in part by the growing Protestant revolt, Ignatius determined to come to the aid of the Church in some more vigorous way.

With nine companions he organized the "Company of Jesus," which he placed at the command of the pope. The best-known of his early followers was his Basque countryman, Francis Xavier. As general of the order, Ignatius applied the principles of military discipline and obedience that he had learned as a soldier. He sent members to posts of duty wherever they were needed. Eventually this came to include a wide variety of activities, from combating heresy, thereby helping the pope maintain the spiritual power of the

THE LATE POPE JOHN XXIII. Carried on his portable throne, he blesses those who line the streets as he travels to the cathedral that he occupies as Bishop of Rome.

Church, to preaching, educational work, and carrying on missionary activities in the Americas and the Far East.

The Society of Jesus, or "Jesuits," as the order came to be known, was recognized by the pope in 1540, and spread rapidly throughout Italy, Germany, Spain, and Portugal. By the end of the sixteenth century, it had become one of the most active agencies within the Church.

The Catholic Church Today   The end of the fifteenth century was the high watermark of political power for the Catholic Church. After that it declined rapidly as the result of the break-up of feudalism, the rise of Protestantism, the growth of independent nations, and the appearance of democracy with the French Revolution and Napoleonic wars. In the nineteenth century, the old Papal States were compelled to become part of the new Italian nation. By a treaty with the Italian government in 1929, Vatican City, a tiny "city-within-a-city" in

MODERN JESUITS. Here fellow-Jesuits greet Father Charles McCarthy, a missionary in China, who has just been released from a Communist prison.

90

THE RISE OF THE CATHOLIC CHURCH

Rome, became the last piece of land to fly the papal flag.

Consequently, the Catholic Church was forced more and more to rely upon its spiritual influence, and it is here that the pope and the bishops have retained great powers. For over the years, Roman Catholicism has continued to maintain itself as a vast, world-wide church, carefully disciplined and tightly controlled. Its priests, bishops, and the members of its various religious orders are highly responsive to the will of the pope. So, too, are the Catholic people, who look upon him in spiritual matters as the supreme teacher of their religion. His position was further reinforced and strengthened by the "doctrine of papal infallibility," officially proclaimed by the Church in 1870. It declares that when the pope speaks with the full authority of his office on the subject of Catholic belief, and not just a speech or message, he voices the absolute truth. To disagree with what he has thus declared is heresy. However, in 1964, the bishops were empowered to share authority with the pope in the governing of the Church.

It is interesting to compare this with the fierce individualism of Judaism, in which no rabbi has any spiritual authority over any other. In fact, any learned and pious layman has the right to differ with a rabbi on the interpretation of Judaism.

Familiarity with the long history of the Church may help to explain why, of all the religions today, Roman Catholicism has the largest number of followers. There are some 537 million Roman Catholics in the world and nearly 41 million in the United States.

And through the loyalty and devotion of its followers, the spiritual influence of the Catholic Church has continued to be great. The reason for this may become plainer after we examine the Church's beliefs, its forms of worship, and system of organization. . . .

TOPICS TO DISCUSS

1. In what ways does Roman Catholicism still embody the teachings of Paul? How does it differ from those of Jesus?
2. In what fundamental ways is Roman Catholicism different from Judaism?
3. How do the beliefs and practices of a member of the Eastern (Greek) Orthodox Church differ from those of a Roman Catholic?
4. How do you explain the fact that, despite their different interpretations, Reform Jews are not classified as "heretics" by Judaism?

THINGS TO DO

1. Commence a book of Christian biographies, compiling information about the leading figures of early Christianity, the Roman Catholic Church, and the Eastern Orthodox Church.
2. Prepare a chart comparing the most important beliefs and practices of Roman Catholicism with those of modern Judaism.
3. Invite a priest or informed layman of a Greek Orthodox Church in your community to explain his beliefs and practices.

OTHER THINGS TO READ

ARCHER, JOHN CLARK, and CARL E. PURINTON, *Faiths Men Live By*, Ronald Press, pp. 421-444.

MANWELL, REGINALD D., and SOPHIA L. FAHS, *The Church Across the Street*, Beacon Press, Chapter 5, "Ignatius Loyola, 1491-1556," pp. 70-94.

NOSS, JOHN B., *Man's Religions*, Macmillan, pp. 593-637; 662-669.

PIKE, E. ROYSTON, *Encyclopaedia of Religion and Religions*, Meridian, "Christmas," pp. 99-100; "Easter," pp. 132-133; "Eastern Orthodox Church," pp. 133-135; "Excommunication," p. 149; "Inquisition," pp. 193-194; "Papacy," pp. 289-290.

SMITH, HUSTON, *The World's Great Religions*, Mentor, pp. 290-310.

SPENCE, HARTZELL, *The Story of America's Religions*, Holt, Rinehart, Winston, Chapter 7, "The Eastern Orthodox," pp. 115-129.

The World's Great Religions, Time, "The Eastern Orthodox," pp. 244-247.

9
THE RELIGION OF THE ROMAN CATHOLIC

The Wider Influence of Catholicism The great audience in the concert hall applauded long and enthusiastically after the distinguished artist had finished singing the *Ave Maria*. In the London Museum, a hushed group filed past Michelangelo's painting, "Entombment of Christ." A score of tourists were ushered into the Sistine Chapel of the Vatican at Rome and gazed in awe at its magnificence. At Cambridge, in England, visitors looked admiringly upon the rich colors of an illuminated manuscript of the New Testament, and in the stillness of the vast Cathedral of Notre Dame in Paris, onlookers marvelled at the delicate coloring of its huge round stained-glass windows.

At the same time, in America, a university class in English literature was studying *Piers Plowman*, a religious allegory by William Langland; a group of school children in the Metropolitan Museum of Art in New York was being shown a sculpture of "Madonna and Child"; a crowd of visitors was viewing a giant mural based upon the Apostles' Creed which decorated the altar of a new St. Louis church.

These and countless other works of art illustrate the wide influence of Roman Catholicism on Western culture. Over the centuries, the Catholic religion has inspired thousands of artists everywhere to render various aspects of the faith into painting, sculpture, architecture, music, and literature.

Behind all of these lie the teachings of Catholicism and the ways of worship by which it seeks to express and implement them.

The Core of Catholic Belief The Catholic believes that he possesses the true religion and that his Church alone is the valid interpreter of Christianity. This is why Catholics are generally not permitted to attend the services of other religions or participate in joint worship. To do so would, in the eyes of the Church, be a denial of the gifts and teachings God gave through Christ.

For this reason, it is also held that no one outside the Church can be "saved," except the "invincibly ignorant." This refers to those who have not been able to know that it is the true Church; that is, people who lived in pre-Christian times or those of any age for whom the message of Catholicism has been so badly distorted that its acceptance is impossible.

To redeem man, Catholics believe, God in His mercy sent to earth His divine son, Jesus, in human form. This is known as the "Incarnation," the process by which, as Catholics explain, the son of God took on human nature, retaining, however, the nature of true God while becoming true man. His mother was the Virgin

Mary. According to the doctrine of the "Immaculate Conception," proclaimed as official belief by the Church in 1854, she did not receive the guilt of original sin when she was conceived by her mother, as all people do. Thus she was fit to be the mother of the Christ. Through the power of the Holy Ghost, the infant Jesus was conceived by her in the great miracle called the "Virgin Birth." And according to Catholic belief, Mary remained a virgin throughout her entire life.

God is viewed in His threefold nature as the Trinity of "persons." He is the Father, the Son, and the Holy Ghost or Spirit, all three equal and of one nature. In Christ the union of his godly and human natures became uniquely one, though still preserving the properties of each.

Through Jesus' sacrificial death on the cross, God made it possible for all human beings to be redeemed from sin. Cleansing from "original sin" is achieved through baptism, but throughout his life man continues to be vulnerable to sin. Salvation, redemption from sin which assures a blissful supernatural life in heaven, comes as the gift of God through the Church, the permanent body of Christ, which is always here on earth and always available to man. The individual achieves salvation by mystical identification with the life of Jesus, by obedience to the truths of the Roman Catholic Church, and by partaking of its sacraments. The sacraments—the word comes from the Latin translation of the Greek word for "mystery"—are sacred rites which are believed to confer God's grace or favor upon the soul of the believer so that he may be "saved" from sin and enjoy eternal life.

After death, once the faithful Catholic's soul has been purified if need be in purgatory (a place designed to "purge" or cleanse the soul by inflicting punishment for his sins), he will be granted entry to heaven. However, those who have committed grave crimes that have not been forgiven can expect to suffer eternal torment in hell. Those who have not been redeemed from original sin, it is commonly assumed, will not see God. Ultimately, there will be a second coming of Christ. All of the dead will then be resurrected and judged by him. The "saved" will reap eternal reward; the rest will be condemned to eternal punishment.

In the worship of the Church, we observe how these beliefs are transformed into practice.

Inside the Sanctuary The Roman Catholic cathedral or church is designed to instruct and inspire the worshipper. In medieval Europe the larger cathedrals took scores of years and even centuries to complete. At a later period, the best-known artists of the world, men like Michelangelo, Raphael, Da Vinci, and others, were employed to decorate and beautify the Church.

In keeping with medieval practice, many Roman Catholic churches are built in the shape of a cross. In such churches the service is conducted at the place of the crossing of the bars, where the altar is located. The worshippers are seated in the longer section of the "cross," usually called the "nave." Except for the Mass-servers (altar boys), laymen rarely enter the area of the altar, as they do in a synagogue, where they are often seated on the pulpit, or called to it. At most, lay participants may stand only near the communion rail.

We may notice that when worshippers first come into the church and catch sight of the altar in front of the sanctuary, they genuflect (bend the knee) out of reverence for Jesus. He is thought to be present by virtue of the consecrated bread kept from previous Masses in a "tabernacle," the locked and decorated safe found at the level of the altar table.

Meanwhile, the worshippers make the sign of the cross on their body with their right hand, dipped in holy water, to remind themselves of their baptism. In certain ceremonies a censer will be burning incense, a practice derived from Temple worship in ancient times when incense was regarded as "sweet savor to the Lord."

Sometimes there are niches in the wall with statues of saints. Prominently displayed also is usually a statue of the Virgin Mary. The statues generally have in front of them burning candles which have been placed there by worshippers.

In the eyes of the Church the saints are men

THE VIRGIN MARY. Prominent in many Catholic churches is a statue of the Mother of Christ. Worshippers often light candles and recite prayers before it.

and women—individuals like Mary Magdalene, Paul, and Peter, or, in later times, Thomas Aquinas and Francis of Assisi—who have performed great deeds for God and are certain to have gone to heaven. Hence, they have been "canonized," or officially declared to be saints. People burn candles to them as a mark of reverence and respect. They meditate upon their lives and works in the hope that they may follow their example and share in their merits. They also pray to the saints to intercede for them with God. Since each of the saints had special interests and concerns in life, prayers are addressed to the particular one whose aid is sought.

The statue of the Virgin Mary may be especially impressive, and in some churches many candles burn before it. From the earliest days of the Church, Mary, the Mother of Christ, has been venerated by Catholics. As the virgin who miraculously begot Jesus, she is believed to be particularly close to God, so that prayers addressed to her carry with them the special influence of her compassion and love. A recently announced doctrine (1950) also declares that she dwells in heaven in complete bodily form. While the Church has carefully insisted that neither the images nor the veneration of Mary and the saints is in any way a substitute for God, most non-Catholics seriously question such practice. They consider it an infringement upon the worship of God alone.

In the church we notice, too, various containers of holy water blessed by the priest. This is used at different times in the ritual and is supposed to have the power of warding off evil.

The Mass If we have entered the church during a solemn high Mass, we will find that most of the service is sung and chanted by a choir while the ministers conduct the Mass. When the priest is not assisted by other ministers, it is simply called a "high" or "sung" Mass; but when other priests participate, it becomes a "solemn high Mass." If the service is not chanted at all, then we are attending what is known as a "low" Mass.

The Mass is the service of the Church that embodies the sacrament of the Eucharist. Commemorating the Last Supper of Jesus, it employs the symbols of wine and bread. According to Catholic doctrine, during the Last Supper when Jesus raised the bread and wine and said "This is my body" and "This is my blood," a marvelous event occurred. The bread became the actual body of Jesus; the wine, his blood.

This is believed to recur during the Mass. In physical appearance the wine and bread remain unchanged, but beneath their outward form, Catholics believe, their real substance has been transformed into the blood and body of Christ. This is called "transubstantiation."

The Church maintains that the sacrifice of Jesus on the cross for mankind recurs every time this transubstantiation takes place, and that it has the power to remove the sins of the people, provided they are truly repentant. This is the deepest "mystery" of the Church and one which even many Christians cannot fully understand. Hence, the Eucharist reflects

94

THE DEVELOPMENT OF ROMAN CATHOLICISM

FROM THE BIRTH OF DOMINIC TO THE PRESENT

IMPORTANT WORLD EVENTS	DATE	DEVELOPMENTS IN ROMAN CATHOLICISM
	1170	Dominic born.
	1182	Francis of Assisi born.
1215 Magna Carta issued in England.	1216	Dominican order recognized by the pope.
	1220	Franciscan order recognized by the pope.
	About **1225**	Thomas Aquinas born.
	1229	Establishment of the Inquisition.
	1271	Ninth and final Crusade.
1290 Jews expelled from England.	1378	Papacy split into rival popes, to **1417.**
	1491	Ignatius of Loyola born.
1492 Columbus discovers America. Jews expelled from Spain. Luther's 95 Theses starts the Protestant Reformation.	1517	German churches begin revolt against the Church. Start of Protestantism.
	1534	England officially breaks with the Church.
	1540	Pope recognizes Society of Jesus (Jesuit Order) founded by Ignatius of Loyola.
	1545	Council of Trent begins reforms of Church, to **1563.** Steady decline of the political power of the Church, to **twentieth century.**
	1634	First Catholic church in America.
1775 American Revolution.		
1789 French Revolution.	1845	Beginning of Irish Catholic migration to the U.S.
	1854	Doctrine of Immaculate Conception proclaimed by Pope Pius IX.
	1860	Loss of Papal States to Italy.
Franco-Prussian War.	1870	Doctrine of Papal Infallibility proclaimed.
	1929	Vatican City made a Papal State.
	1962	Second Vatican Ecumenical Council introduces changes in Catholic ritual and doctrine.

MONASTERY CHURCH. This sanctuary is housed within a Catholic monastery. At the altar in front, the sacrament of the Eucharist is celebrated with the consecrated wine and wafer. Surrounding the altar area are paintings of scenes in Christ's life and portraits of important saints.

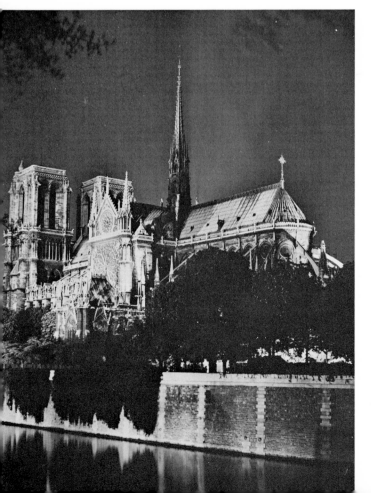

NOTRE DAME. The name of this famous cathedral in Paris refers to the Virgin Mary, to whom it is dedicated. Its construction was begun in 1163 and took nearly 70 years to complete. Gothic in style, it features enormous decorated circular or "rose" windows.

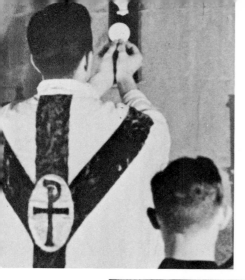

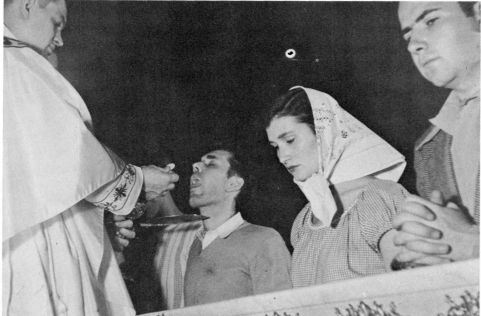

THE MASS. On the left, the Host, or bread-wafer of the Eucharist, is raised by the celebrant. On the right, the Chalice containing the consecrated wine is held aloft. Below, Catholics kneel at the altar rail as they receive the bread of Communion.

the original meaning of the word "sacrament," "mystery."

All eyes are upon the altar, which is made of stone and contains relics of the martyrs, usually small pieces of bone. Two candles are burning there. The priest officiating at the Mass is known as the "celebrant," and he follows a strict ritual in approaching the altar.

The celebrant wears a number of long flowing robes, known as "vestments," derived from the garments worn in Rome in early times. Each symbolizes an act of spiritual preparation for his participation. Different colors are worn at different seasons by the celebrant and are also hung over the tabernacle and before the altar. White is the most usual, while black is

used on Good Friday when the Church is in mourning for the crucifixion of Jesus. Certain colors are always worn for special occasions, like weddings or funerals. If we consult the "missal," or book containing all of the directions and texts necessary for the Mass, we can discover why a particular color is being worn on the day we attend.

The Mass is divided into two main sections. The first is the Mass of the Catechumens, from a Greek word meaning "to instruct." In early days, those who were taking instruction to become Christians were dismissed at this point, prior to the Eucharist. This portion of the service is modeled after the worship of the synagogue and contains preparatory prayers, readings from the New Testament and, at times, the Old Testament, and sometimes a short sermon. Then comes the second section, the Mass of the Faithful, created originally by the early Christian Church. The language is taken directly from the Old and New Testaments, and includes the famous "Holy, Holy, Holy" from the Book of Isaiah, and the *Pater Noster*, or Lord's Prayer, from the Gospel of Matthew.

Now the climax of the Mass is reached with the sacrament of the Eucharist. Having pronounced the words of Jesus from the supper table, the priest lifts up the "Chalice," a cup made of silver or gold and containing a mixture of water with the now transubstantiated wine. Similarly, he takes a rounded bread wafer, called the "Host." Having held both high above his head (the wafer first, the cup afterwards) for all to see and adore, he then proceeds with the Mass. Subsequently, he breaks the Host, which has come to be a symbol for the "breaking" or suffering of the body of Christ, and puts a piece in the cup. In the rites of the West, the words consecrating the bread and wine are spoken silently. In the East, they are often sung aloud while the wafer and the cup are held aloft.

The celebrant partakes of both the wine and the wafer, but he distributes only the wafer to the people, since the whole of Christ is believed to be contained in it. The worshipper, who has fasted for four hours before this, now receives the Host upon his tongue while he kneels at the altar rail. This is known as "receiving Communion." Every Catholic must receive Communion at Easter time, and he is expected to do so every Sunday. Those who desire may even receive Communion daily.

Following Communion, the celebrant washes, reads a verse of Scripture, and offers certain prayers. Shortly before the close of the service, the deacon at a solemn Mass was accustomed to call out *"Ite, missa est,"* which was the Latin for "Go, it is the dismissal!" It is from the word *missa* that our English word "Mass" comes, and the passage is now rendered, "Go, the Mass is ended!"

The concluding prayers include the well-known *Ave Maria,* "Hail Mary," which reads:

Hail Mary, full of grace, the Lord is with you; blessed are you amongst women, and blessed is the fruit of your womb, Jesus. Holy Mary, Mother of God, pray for us sinners now and at the hour of our death. Amen.

Thus, while some elements of the worship may be traced back to synagogue practices, it is clear that the Catholic Mass is organized around a radically different idea of what a service is supposed to do.

Some Significant Features of the Worship As we leave the church we may have a number of questions. One that generally interests non-Catholics is the use of Latin in important parts of the Mass. We must remember that up until 1963 virtually the entire service was conducted in Latin. The only exceptions were an occasional brief sermon in English (or any one of nine other languages, such as Polish and Italian, following the national origins of the members) and a single short response in Greek at the beginning of the Mass. However, by decision of the Second Vatican Ecumenical Council which began in 1962, certain reforms were introduced into Catholic worship. The use of Latin for most of the service was replaced with the language of the country, and greater participation of laymen in the worship, and regular sermons by the clergy were also introduced.

Originally Latin was used in the Mass because it was the language spoken by the people during the time of the Roman Empire, and some Latin has been part of the service ever since. In a similar way, Jews use Hebrew; Moslems, classic Arabic; and Hindus, Sanskrit. The Church feels that by preserving portions of the service and various sacraments in Latin, the continuity of its worship with the past is preserved, greater accuracy in the liturgy is maintained, and a wider sense of Catholic unity is fostered among the worshippers.

We may also wonder about the more restricted role of the layman in the conduct of the service. For, with the exception of the "commentator," a layman who may lead certain responses or read from the Scriptures, we observe that the Mass itself is carried on almost entirely by the priesthood, assisted by the "servers," or altar boys. The answer is that from earliest times the Church entrusted the conducting of the Mass only to those consecrated as priests, and it is only recently that it has permitted laymen even to lead the congregation in certain limited portions of the ritual.

In the last fifty years, the Church has been encouraging the worshipper more and more to participate in the Mass through congregational song and prayer, as historically he once did. Starting in the 1930's, it became increasingly popular for worshippers to follow the Mass in a specially prepared "missal," a book that originally contained not only the Latin text but also pictures to explain the stages of the service. Today, most portions of this missal, like the service itself, have been translated into English.

Moreover, as a result of the decisions of the Second Vatican Ecumenical Council, Catholic worshippers are now called upon to read sections of the service aloud and sing various church hymns in unison. Throughout, the worshipper is also encouraged to meditate on the mysteries of salvation that are contained within the ritual, and he may dedicate Mass prayers to a particular purpose of his choosing.

Whereas the Mass is devoted almost exclusively to communal worship, the use of the rosary, a set of small and large beads attached to the cross, is mainly associated with private prayer. It symbolizes special cycles of meditation and prayer from the life and work of Christ, and the devotion carried on with these beads is itself called the "Rosary."

The beads are used as counters for the recitation of particular prayers, such as the "Hail Mary," the Lord's Prayer, and others, in a certain prescribed manner, while the individual meditates upon a series of fifteen great "mysteries" in connection with Christ, such as the announcement of his birth, his appearance at the Temple, his crucifixion, and resurrection. In so doing one commemorates the five "joyful mysteries," the five "sorrowful mysteries," and the five "glorious mysteries" of events in the

life of Christ and Mary. Depending upon the spirit of the worshipper, such prayer is considered to be especially well received by God because it is said to prepare the individual for fullest participation in the Church's public worship.

The Other Sacraments   In addition to the Eucharist of the Mass, the Catholic Church provides six other sacraments designed to remove sin and confer salvation upon the soul of the individual. Unlike Judaism, whose observances remain "ceremonies," the performance of sacraments is essential to salvation according to the Catholic view. Thus, withholding the sacraments through excommunication is the severest punishment that the Church can administer to one of its communicants.

Originally, scholars believe, Christianity possessed only two sacraments: Baptism and the Lord's Supper, or Eucharist. However, as the religion developed, the Church instituted five more. They cover the full life-span of the individual, and are believed to convey God's grace

BAPTISM. The priest administers the first of the holy sacraments by pouring water upon the infant's head, thereby washing away original sin and uniting him with the Church.

for daily living through the consecration of significant occasions from birth to death. The seven sacraments are: (1) Baptism, (2) Confirmation, (3) Penance, (4) The Eucharist, (5) Holy Orders, (6) Holy Matrimony, (7) Extreme Unction.

The first, *Baptism,* is considered essential for salvation. On this occasion the infant receives his Christian name. However, this sacrament can take place at any time in life—as, for instance, when an adult converts to Catholicism. In all but the most extraordinary cases, it is performed by a priest. The act of baptism consists of pouring water on the head of the individual three times in the name of the Father, and of the Son, and of the Holy Ghost. This symbolizes burial with Christ and resurrected life, the washing away of original sin in Adam, and the union of the individual with the Church, the Body of Christ. Now he has received the grace of God, and is entitled to continue in this life of grace.

Confirmation is a supplement to Baptism. While not absolutely necessary for salvation, it confers spiritual maturity upon the individ-

CONFESSION. In preparation for Communion, a Catholic confesses his sins. The priest on the other side of the grille hears him and then prescribes acts of penance.

ual and strengthens him for the practice of his faith. Confirmation is generally received sometime in childhood, usually around twelve years of age when the young person is able to understand and affirm the teachings of his faith. It is usually preceded by a period of instruction in the doctrines of the Church and becomes an occasion for special dress to be worn by the confirmand and for family celebration. In most instances a bishop performs the ceremony, which consists of making the sign of the cross on the forehead of the individual with oil while he kneels before him.

Penance involves the confession of sins in the presence of a priest and his granting of "absolution," or forgiveness. Before the Catholic may receive Holy Communion, he must first have examined himself to determine whether he is free of the guilt of serious sin. If he is not free, only then must he prepare for Communion by receiving the sacrament of Penance.

Although Baptism removes original sin from man, it is recognized that human beings continue to commit sins. Some are "venial" sins, less serious offenses against God's will; others are "mortal," or mighty transgressions against the moral law which can condemn the individual to eternal punishment in hell. Both types of sins must find forgiveness if temporary or everlasting punishment is to be avoided. Hence, the individual must confess his sins and receive forgiveness, which only the Church, as the representative of Christ, has the power to grant.

Confession is usually heard in box-like confessionals found in every Catholic church. The box is dark inside to mask the penitent's identity. Sometimes one can see the priest dimly, but often a white cloth is tacked to the grille separating priest and penitent. The individual confesses the sins he has committed since his last confession, and he is expected to be genuinely sorry for them. The priest, who must observe absolute secrecy about whatever he has heard, usually says a few words of spiritual encouragement. Then he will prescribe certain religious acts, usually prayers, called "a penance," for the person to engage in as a sign of his repentance. On condition that these will be performed, the priest absolves the individual of his sins with the words, "May our Lord Jesus Christ absolve you; and I absolve you from your sins in the name of the Father and of the Son and of the Holy Ghost. Amen."

The sacrament of *Holy Orders* is not necessary for the individual's salvation but is required for those who wish to enter the clergy. It is the rite by which priests are ordained for the Catholic ministry and receive the spiritual power of the Church. The sacrament consists essentially of the laying on of the bishop's hands upon the head of the candidate.

Holy Matrimony is the sacrament of marriage by which two baptized persons are wed, and it is usually performed in conjunction with a Wedding Mass. Because of its solemn nature marriage is a sacred contract to be maintained till death and it cannot be terminated by divorce. Hence, even where couples may receive a civil divorce, the Church refuses to permit remarriage (though in certain rare cases an "annulment" may be granted, signifying that a marriage never really existed). In the event of a marriage between a Catholic and non-Catholic, the latter must promise not to interfere with his mate's religion and to baptize and rear all children in the Roman Catholic faith. Only then will the ceremony be performed by a priest. The Church also opposes all measures of birth control since it regards artificial limitations upon the number of children in a family as immoral and a violation of God's law.

Extreme Unction is the sacrament that is administered when a person is seriously ill and on the verge of death. It is believed by the Church to prepare the individual for the hereafter. It usually involves the anointing of the five senses of the dying person with oil, and is accompanied by confession and a last Communion. Because of its importance Catholics are most eager to make certain the dying receive this sacrament. However, it may also be administered shortly after death, on the assumption that the person is still somehow alive.

The Church Calendar   The whole Catholic service and ritual are fixed by the annual calendar cycle, much like the Jewish religious calendar. The vestments of the priests, and, as in Judaism, the prayers that are chanted and the very mode and tone of the service, are regulated by the particular holiday or saint's day being celebrated.

The dates of most of the holidays are set according to the ordinary calendar. However, those related to Easter follow the lunar calendar in a manner similar to the Jewish holiday cycle. This is because its date was originally based on the occurrence of Passover, when Jesus' last supper was believed to have taken place. Later on, however, the Council of Nicea divorced the date from Passover, and eventually the Church established Easter as the first Sunday following the full moon occurring on or after March 21.

In order of importance, the Church year is highlighted by the feasts of Easter, Pentecost, and Christmas. In order of time, Christmas comes first. "Advent," from the Latin word *adventus*, "the coming" (of Christ), begins on the fourth Sunday before Christmas. It is a time for sober reflection and preparation, and

EXTREME UNCTION. On his death-bed, a Catholic receives the final sacrament of the Church from a priest. It prepares him for life in the hereafter.

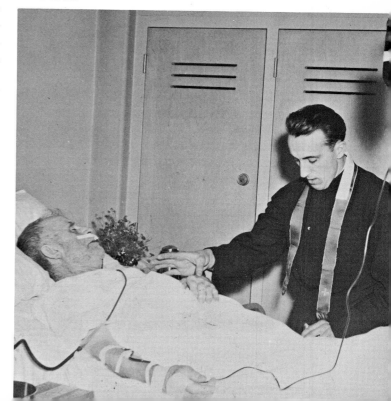

all celebrations and weddings are avoided. Christmas, commemorating Jesus' birth and anticipating his return, halts the period of mourning and changes it to joy. New Year's Day, occurring on the eighth day after Christmas, celebrates the Feast of Jesus' circumcision.

"Lent," so called because of the "lengthening" of the days of spring, begins forty days before Easter. It is connected with Jesus' forty-day fast in the wilderness, where, according to Christian belief, he was led by the Holy Spirit to undergo physical and worldly temptations in preparation for his ministry. With the growth of Christianity the observance of Easter was marked by the practice of baptizing adult converts on this day.

In the Middle Ages the day before Lent was known as *Mardi Gras*, "Fat Tuesday," and became the occasion for great merrymaking. Today in New Orleans, Munich, and elsewhere, Mardi Gras is celebrated for a period of a week or more with carnivals, masked balls, street dancing, parades, and other festivities.

The first day of Lent is Ash Wednesday, a reminder of the fact that man is dust. It is commemorated with the sign of the cross made by the priest with ashes on each person's forehead. During the Lenten period, Catholics abstain through choice from certain pleasures and foods. By church law those in good health, and between the ages of 21 and 59, are allowed only one full meal each day, although two other light, meatless meals are permitted.

During the final week of the forty-day period, the religious services begin to mount in solemnity. Palm Sunday, a week before Easter, commemorates the triumphal entry of Jesus into Jerusalem. Palm branches are carried by the worshippers just as, it is told, they were by people who came to greet Jesus as he entered the Holy City on his pilgrimage. Holy Thursday commemorates the Last Supper, and in remembrance, white vestments are worn at the Mass. On Good Friday, the day on which Jesus was crucified, the Mass is not celebrated, but a special Communion service, with scripture reading and veneration of the cross, is held. The clergy appear in black robes out of mourning, and the crucifix is removed from the altar to the steps below where the worshippers kneel and kiss it.

Holy Saturday begins to partake of the joy of Easter. Easter Sunday is the day that Jesus is believed to have risen from the dead. The cry, "Christ is risen!" dispels the gloom from the Lenten season and changes it to the joy of the Easter service with its triumphant Mass.

Pentecost, from a Greek word meaning "fifty," occurs seven weeks, or approximately fifty days, after Easter. It commemorates the descent of the Holy Spirit upon the apostles and marks the traditional beginning of the Catholic Church. Interestingly, the Jewish holiday of Shovuos is sometimes also called Pentecost because it occurs seven weeks and one day from the start of Passover.

In connection with both the Advent and Lent, scholars have pointed out the similarity with ancient pagan observances connected with the coming of the winter and spring seasons. Some of the terms used in English, including the very word "Easter," which was the name of the Anglo-Saxon goddess of Spring, come from old pagan rituals. Naturally, as we have seen, the holidays and rites marking both periods have been thoroughly reinterpreted by Christianity.

Priests and Nuns   One of the most important elements in the Roman Catholic religion is its clergy. Living and dying unmarried, going wherever the Church sends them, and most serving for no more than their food and lodging in reasonable comfort, the Catholic clergy has been a great source of strength to the Church.

Priests who serve a particular church are likely to be "secular" clergy; that is, men ordained to assist the bishop in church duties, but who do not live in monasteries or take the vow of poverty.

However, within the Church there are also the "regular" clergy, so named because they are priests who belong to a particular order and live according to its established "regulations." Among the various orders are the Benedictine, Franciscan, Dominican, Jesuit, and many others, that perform specific functions. One-fourth of all Jesuits, for example, are in

DOMINICAN MONKS. Members of this Order of Preachers, founded in 1215 by St. Dominic, are bound by vows of poverty, chastity, and obedience, and are forbidden to eat any meat.

TRAPPISTS. With only a few exceptions, perpetual silence is the rule for these monks of the Cistercian Order. Trappist regimen began some 550 years after the order was founded.

ABBEY. Trappist monks live together in this monastery presided over by an abbot. Their name comes from La Trappe in France, where their rule was first established.

CATHOLIC BROTHERS AND NUNS

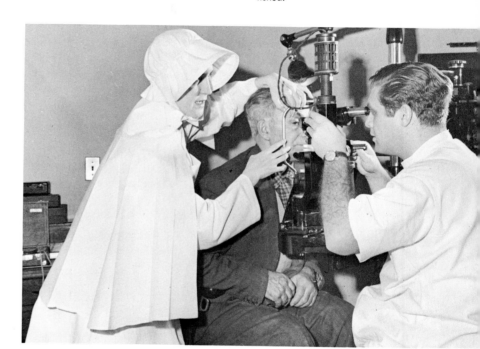

SISTERS. Nuns belonging to different orders engage in a variety of duties. Some tend the sick and poor; others assist in the training of nurses in Catholic hospitals. Many teach in Catholic colleges and parochial schools. But there are also numerous nuns that belong to orders whose members remain strictly within the convent and engage in prayer and other religious activities.

foreign mission work; many others serve as teachers and administrators of universities, colleges, and high schools. The Benedictines, of which a well-known branch is the Trappists, devote themselves to prayer and meditation, and so on.

The education of a priest is long and arduous. Normally, it consists of pursuing a Bachelor of Arts degree program at a university, college, or seminary, where the student generally majors in philosophy. The undergraduate course in a theological college, a "major seminary," takes an additional four years.

The regular clergy have a noviceship (probationary period) of one or two years, usually after two years of college study in the humanities and sciences. This time is devoted to religious development in accordance with the spiritual ideals of the particular order or group with which the novice is connected. At the end of it, the candidate for the priesthood takes simple vows of poverty, chastity, and obedience.

The Jesuits have the custom of requiring the candidate to interrupt the normal program by serving an additional three years of teaching in a college or high school, or pursuing further graduate study. Jesuits, Passionists, and certain secular candidates likewise take a longer course in philosophy than others.

At ordination, the priest is given the opportunity for work connected with a church or school, or other spiritual employment. After a few years in the ministry, some regular clergy must return for final spiritual training.

The minimum age for priestly ordination is twenty-four. Some, such as the Jesuits, will be in their early thirties at ordination because of the various kinds of religious employment they must undertake during their training.

Nuns are members of different orders patterned after those of the men: Benedictine, Cistercian, Franciscan, and others, and they are mainly concerned with meditative prayer. Those occupied with active charitable work among the poor, the sick, and the ignorant, are normally called "sisters," not "nuns." Most wear distinctive medieval dress, and take vows of poverty, chastity, and obedience. The climax of the sister's period of probation is her symbolic marriage to Jesus. Hospital work, college and lower school teaching, religious instruction, and home visitation keep the sister busy, but her first obligation from the standpoint of the Church is a life of prayer.

The Organization of the Church   In addition to its clergy, the strength of the Roman Catholic religion lies in its well-knit church organization.

The spiritual head of Roman Catholicism is, of course, the pope, and he presides over the College of Cardinals, who are presently over one hundred in number. Cardinals are principally bishops and archbishops, though there are some who are simply priests, and they are appointed by the pope, largely for the tasks of Church administration in Rome. When a pope dies, it is the College of Cardinals which selects his successor.

CARDINAL CUSHING. The Archbishop of Boston wears his Cardinal's robe, ring, and scarlet biretta (cap). As a cardinal, he is one of the governing body of the Roman Catholic Church.

THE RELIGION OF THE ROMAN CATHOLIC

For administrative purposes the Church as a whole is divided into dioceses, a term that comes from a Greek word meaning "administrative districts." At the head of each diocese is a bishop, or, if in the judgment of the Church it is a particularly important area, an archbishop. In this instance, the district is then called an "archdiocese." All bishops and archbishops are required to report to the pope personally every five years about the spiritual welfare of their diocese.

The diocese is then subdivided into parishes, the smallest administrative unit of the Church. Each has its own priests and churches, responsible to the bishop or archbishop of the diocese. A priest who has rendered distinguished service to the Church may be honored with the additional title of Canon or Monsignor.

Taking the United States as an example, we find that in 1960 there were six cardinals—one each in New York, Boston, St. Louis, Chicago, and Los Angeles—and an additional one appointed to the Vatican. The same year the *Official Catholic Directory* reported that there were thirty archbishops, 185 bishops, and about 55,000 priests. In addition, there were about one hundred religious communities of priests and unordained brothers, and nearly three hundred communities of religious women. Generally, a priest known as an "abbot" is in charge of a male monastic community. The Mother Superior serves in the same capacity for sisters. Both are ordinarily responsible to the local bishop.

This form of organization enables the Catholic Church in the United States to supervise closely its nearly 17,000 parishes, some 270 Catholic colleges and universities, over 500 seminaries, 12,000 parochial schools, 1,600 hospitals and homes, and numerous convents, monasteries, etc.

Still, the Church in the United States is also marked by a number of internal differences, due chiefly to the contrasting national origins of its membership. Though the history of Roman Catholicism in America goes back to the 1600's with the establishment of the colony of Maryland, its numbers remained small and

Catholics were very often badly persecuted by those who were fearful of the power or doctrines of the Church. Then, when the potato blight struck Ireland in the mid-1840's, over a million Irish Catholics began making their way to the United States. Shortly after, large numbers of German Catholics joined them, and these were followed in turn in the 1880's by millions of Italians and East Europeans. Each group brought with them their own particular national form of Catholic life, and to a varying extent their churches still reflect this in their practices, use of language, and outlook of the membership. Nevertheless, the overall unity of common faith and doctrine, as well as Church organization, distinguishes Roman Catholicism even in America.

How Judaism Differs   A comparison of Judaism and Catholicism reveals many basic differences in beliefs, practices, and organization.

In terms of belief, Judaism has never accepted Jesus as either the Messiah or the "son of God." For, in Judaism, God remains one, without any notion of plurality, and to Jews, those who follow the Catholic doctrine of the Trinity would be in conflict with the Jewish conception of monotheism.

There is also no place in Judaism for such teachings as the Virgin Birth, Immaculate Conception, the Incarnation of the "son of God," and all the other "mysteries" associated with Jesus as one of the persons of the Trinity. Nor do Jews look upon the New Testament as Scripture since, as they view it, the ancient covenant between God and the Jewish people has in no way been altered by the coming of Jesus.

With its staunch adherence to monotheism, Judaism insists that each individual stands in direct relationship to God. No coming of a "son of God" is needed to "save" mankind; nor is intercession by the Church through saints or clergy necessary. By obedience to God's moral and ethical Law as it has been revealed through the great Jewish teachers beginning with the patriarchs, Moses, and the prophets, each individual may find favor in the sight of his Creator.

COMPARISON BETWEEN KEY BELIEFS OF CATHOLICS AND JEWS

ROMAN CATHOLICS		JEWS
Possesses the true religion since the Church is the embodiment of Christ.	**TRUE RELIGION**	Regards Judaism as only religion for Jews. Other faiths, in so far as they promote righteousness, possess some truth.
One universal God in the form of the Trinity. Christ, as embodied in the Church, as well as Mary and the saints intervene for man.	**DEITY**	One universal God with whom man stands in direct relationship.
The Christ. He is the son of God and incarnation of God, born of the Holy Ghost and Virgin Mary.	**JESUS**	A Jew who taught many already-existing Jewish ideals. However, his emphasis upon the approaching Kingdom of God led him to somewhat different interpretations.
At birth man inherits original sin and throughout life continues to sin because it is his nature.	**MAN**	Man has the capacity to live righteously, and sin can be avoided and overcome by man.
Being "saved" from sin so that the soul may achieve a blissful hereafter. Made possible only through the Church and available only to its members.	**SALVATION**	The establishment of God's Kingdom of universal and everlasting righteousness, justice, peace upon earth. Achieved with God's aid through righteous living according to His Law and as part of the Mission of Israel. Salvation possible for all righteous people.
Accomplished by God's grace only through the agency of the Church and the sacraments it confers.	**REMOVAL OF SIN**	Accomplished by repentance, prayer, making amends, and determination to lead a righteous life.
Heaven and hell for souls of the dead. Purgatory for the removal of unabsolved sins. Resurrection and final judgment at the second coming of Christ.	**HEREAFTER**	Perfected society of mankind in the Kingdom of God. The Orthodox believe in a heavenly "Garden of Eden" and a place of punishment. Reform Jews believe that man's soul returns to God.
Old and New Testaments, including some Apocryphal books, as interpreted by the Church, as well as Church tradition.	**AUTHORITY**	The Written Law (Hebrew Scriptures) and Oral Law (rabbinic interpretation and tradition). Individual freedom of interpretation.

THE RELIGION OF THE ROMAN CATHOLIC

All of this stems from the strikingly different Jewish conception of the nature of man and the purpose of life. According to Judaism, man has within himself the capacity for living righteously. Though he is liable to sin, he does not inherit "original sin," as Catholicism maintains. Rather, all sin is the consequence of the individual's own doing. With the help of God and His Law, he can avoid it and even overcome it through repentance.

Though Catholicism agrees with the Jew's belief that life is fundamentally good, it is Judaism which alone insists that life is meant to be lived fully in this world by everyone. This is one of the reasons why Judaism, with but rare exceptions, has rejected monasticism, mortification of the flesh, celibacy, and every form of denying life. Judaism follows God's commandments in the Torah to marry, have children, and partake of all of the joys of human existence. Facing life realistically, the Jew recognizes that divorce may sometimes be justified in God's sight and that birth control may contribute to the well-being of the family as God would have us mold it.

The Jewish religion affirms that living within society is an essential part of God's plan for man. Unlike Catholicism, which focuses its attention upon saving the individual's soul for the bliss of a supernatural hereafter at the return of Christ, Judaism centers its concern upon the eventual establishment on earth of God's Kingdom of everlasting and universal peace, justice, righteousness, and brotherliness. This can be achieved only through righteous living according to the Law of God and through fulfilling the Mission of Israel to bring to all mankind the truth of God and His ways. Whatever hereafter awaits man—here Orthodoxy accepts a heavenly "Garden of Eden" as well as a place of punishment, while Reform Judaism speaks only of the immortality of the soul—comes directly through the merit earned by the kind of life one has lived upon earth.

These beliefs, in turn, make the character of Jewish observance different from that of the Church, which is based largely upon the life and work of Christ. Judaism has no sacraments by which the individual may gain God's grace and remission of sin. Even the holiday of Yom Kippur is simply a time set apart to review one's acts, to repent and make amends for misdeeds, and to renew one's dedication to the principles of righteousness as commanded by God. In general, then, Jewish observances are designed to strengthen the individual in the ideals of his religion and the practices of righteous living. Passover, for instance, becomes a time for reaffirming one's dedication to the ideal of freedom for all mankind, through reliving Israel's exodus from Egypt and renewing the Jewish promise to live by God's Law.

Nor does the synagogue represent an exclusive agency for salvation, as does the church in Roman Catholicism. As a house of worship, study, and assembly, the synagogue serves merely to strengthen and intensify the Jewish people in their reverence for God, in their commitment to His commandments, and in their will to live by them in order to help bring about His Kingdom on earth.

Finally, one notes sharp differences in terms of religious organization. The priest in Catholicism is the agent of Christ as embodied in the Church. As such, he has religious powers that no layman possesses, as, for instance, forgiveness of sin; and he may perform rites that the people may not, such as performing the sacrament of Mass. The rabbi has no such powers, and no such role. He has no spiritual powers beyond that of the ordinary Jew, and he differs from him only in so far as he possesses greater knowledge of Judaism. In fact, because in Judaism the layman stands in direct relationship to God, he may perform virtually all religious functions.

Since there is no such thing as "apostolic succession" within Judaism, or the view that the synagogue is the embodiment of God, Jews have no hierarchical organization. Hence, there are no superior authorities to control the individual rabbi or synagogue; each is independent. Nor, in view of Judaism's general attitude to life which applies to its rabbinate as well, does it permit orders of monks and nuns, brothers and sisters.

NUMBER OF CATHOLICS

The largest religious body in the world, with 537 million; second largest in the United States, with nearly 41 million.

ORGANIZATION OF THE CHURCH

The parish, composed of one or more churches, is the smallest unit, and each has its own priests. A number of parishes are combined to form a diocese under a bishop; or, if an important area, an archdiocese with an archbishop. The bishops report to the pope, head of the Church. He is selected by the College of Cardinals which has 85 members, mainly bishops and archbishops, and some priests. In addition, there are many separate orders of monks and nuns, priests, brothers and sisters, responsible ultimately to bishops.

THE CLERGY

The basic clergy is the priests, all of whom are dedicated to chastity and obedience, and most also to poverty. Abbots, monsignors, bishops, archbishops, cardinals (usually), and the pope are priests. Some monks are, too, but many are unordained clergy. Women cannot receive priestly ordination.

PRINCIPAL BELIEFS

Roman Catholicism is the true religion. Man can be redeemed from original sin only through Christ's death and resurrection, the benefits of which are available through the Church. The Church offers salvation in the form of forgiveness of sins through God's grace.

Through the motherhood of the Virgin Mary and by the power of the Holy Spirit, God the Father sent His son to earth in human form. By mystical identification with the crucified and risen Christ, and through the faith and sacraments of the Church, man achieves salvation in the form of eternal life in heaven, as well as bodily resurrection with Jesus' second coming.

A DIGEST OF ROMAN CATHOLICISM

CHIEF PRACTICES

Seven sacraments: (1) Baptism, (2) Confirmation, (3) Penance, (4) the Eucharist, (5) Holy Matrimony, (6) Holy Orders, (7) Extreme Unction. The first sacrament is essential to salvation; the fourth is central to all the sacraments. The Mass involves previous confession if there has been serious sin (Penance), and then partaking of the body and blood of Christ under the appearance of bread and wine (Eucharist).

Specific private devotions like meditation, the rosary, and other prayers of intercession to Mary and the saints are considered to be very effective because they prepare the individual for fullest participation in the Church's public worship.

MAJOR HOLY DAYS

(1) Advent, beginning the fourth Sunday before Christmas, a time of sober reflection; (2) Christmas, commemorating the birth of Jesus and the promise of his return; (3) New Year's Day, celebrating Jesus' circumcision; (4) Lent, beginning 40 days before Easter and continuing through Good Friday, the period during which Catholics abstain from certain pleasures and foods; (5) Palm Sunday, a week before Easter; (6) Holy Thursday, commemorating the Last Supper; (7) Good Friday, observing Jesus' crucifixion; (8) Easter Sunday, celebrating the resurrection of Christ; (9) Ascension Day, 40 days after Easter, when Jesus returned to God's right hand; (10) Pentecost, 50 days (7 weeks) after Easter, commemorating the descent of the Holy Spirit upon the apostles and the beginning of the Church.

THE RELIGION OF THE ROMAN CATHOLIC

Another Type of Christianity Appears But Judaism is not the only Western religion to differ with Roman Catholicism on matters of belief, practice, and organization. We have already noted certain distinctions between Eastern Orthodoxy and the Roman Church. Far greater, however, are the differences between Catholicism and Protestantism, the other major branch of Christianity.

All of this has come about only during the last 450 years, for at the end of the fifteenth century, Roman Catholicism was at the very peak of its power. As such, it was the sole spokesman for the overwhelming majority of Christians in the Western world.

Yet at the turn of the century, the Church was fighting for its very existence. Beginning in the early sixteenth century, many Christians of Germany broke away from Roman Catholicism. Other secessions followed in Switzerland, England, and the Scandinavian countries.

Now new forms of Christianity challenged the Church in matters of doctrine, observance, and authority. And they have continued to do so ever since. . . .

TOPICS TO DISCUSS

1. How does Judaism differ from Roman Catholicism in its conception of worship and religious practice? Why?
2. What elements of Judaism do we still find within Roman Catholicism?
3. How do their particular views of man and his salvation affect the Roman Catholic and the Jew?
4. Why do many people take issue with the position of the Roman Catholic Church on such questions as birth control, parochial schools, divorce, the restrictions on interreligious services, and the proscription of certain books, plays, or movies?

THINGS TO DO

1. Attend a Catholic Mass and prepare a list of all the distinctive ceremonial items and elements of worship that you observe.
2. Prepare a dictionary of doctrinal terms used by the Roman Catholic Church.
3. Invite a member of the Catholic clergy or an informed layman to explain basic Catholic views and some of the more recent trends in Church policy.

OTHER THINGS TO READ

FITCH, FLORENCE M., *One God*, Lothrop, "The Catholic Way," pp. 59-96.

HUTCHINSON, JOHN A., and JAMES A. MARTIN, JR., *Ways of Faith*, Ronald Press, pp. 324-344.

MANWELL, REGINALD D., and SOPHIA L. FAHS, *The Church Across the Street*, Beacon Press, pp. 81-90.

ROSTEN, LEO, *A Guide to the Religions of America*, Simon and Schuster, "What Is a Catholic?" by John Cogley, pp. 9-20.

SILVER, ABBA HILLEL, *Where Judaism Differed*, Macmillan, Chapter 10, "That Men Need to Be Saved," pp. 158-181; Chapter 11, "That Men Should Not Enjoy Life," pp. 182-223; Chapter 15, "That Death Is Better Than Life," pp. 265-284.

SMITH, HUSTON, *The Religions of Man*, Mentor, pp. 301-306.

SPENCE, HARTZELL, *The Story of America's Religions*, Holt, Rinehart, Winston, Chapter 6, "The Roman Catholics," pp. 94-114.

The World's Great Religions, Time, "Pathways to God's Grace," pp. 292-305.

10

REVOLT OF THE PROTESTANTS

Martin Luther Challenges the Church   The church of Juterborg, Germany, was crowded. It was a spring morning in the year 1517, and the people had gathered for worship. But the crowd was larger this day because the great Dominican preacher, Friar Tetzel, was going to speak.

The time came for the sermon and the friar arose. He brought word that the pope had authorized him to offer the people special "indulgences." An indulgence was a certificate bearing the seal of the Church which guaranteed the purchaser "absolution," forgiveness of his sins, provided he confessed them to the priest. Or it might secure forgiveness for those who had already died, some loved one whose soul was suffering in purgatory, seeking to rid itself of sin in order to find entry to heaven. These indulgences were being offered to help defray the cost of building a magnificent cathedral in Rome.

Moved by the friar's words, many came forward and purchased indulgences. A large number were sold in Juterborg that morning and all over Germany in the days that followed. As a result, funds for the building of St. Peter's Cathedral in Rome poured in, and Friar Tetzel and his superiors were quite satisfied.

But there was at least one person who was not. This was Martin Luther. Originally he had intended to become a lawyer, but midway in his studies his deep religious needs prompted him to enter a monastery. Here he plunged himself eagerly into all the rigors of its discipline. But somehow, he had no confidence that he was achieving his salvation.

In 1507, he was ordained a priest in the Augustinian order. However, his faith in the Church was shaken by a journey to Rome. There Luther observed the pride, worldliness, and misconduct of the clergy, and more and more he found himself turning to the Bible from whose words he seemed to derive inner peace.

Now thirty-four years old and a lecturer at the University of Wittenberg, he heard about the preachings of Friar Tetzel and was greatly angered by them. He considered the sale of indulgences an abuse of the teachings of the Church, and he spoke out openly against it. But his words had little effect.

As Luther's anger grew, he determined to take more drastic steps. On October 31, he made his way to the castle church of Wittenberg. There on the door, where all could see, he nailed three sheets of parchment. These contained 95 statements objecting to the sale of indulgences and calling for a public debate on the subject. They argued that indulgences were designed only to get money for the Church and that forgiveness of sin could not be secured this way. Here, for example, were two of his statements:

5. The pope has neither the will nor the power to remit any penalties except those which he has imposed by his own authority or by that of other authorities in the Church.

32. Those who believe that through indulgences they are made sure of their own salvation, will be eternally damned along with their teachers.

Rather, declared Luther, sin must be overcome through personal repentance, because forgiveness is something that only God alone can grant.

His attitude made it clear that he had been strongly influenced by his study of the Bible and especially by some of the writings of Paul. One thing in particular that impressed him was Paul's emphasis upon the words of the Hebrew prophet Habakkuk, "The righteous shall live by his faith" (Habakkuk 2:4). What Paul taught, Luther felt, was that forgiveness of sins was obtained directly through one's personal faith in a saving God as revealed in Christ. Consequently, to Luther, Paul was saying that Christian salvation was to be found through belief in Christ, and not necessarily through the institution of the Roman Catholic Church. It was this doctrine, known as "justification by faith," that was to become the basic teaching of Protestantism.

Word of Luther's act spread like wildfire. Copies of his "Ninety-five Theses," as the statement was called, were circulated throughout Germany. Excitement mounted, for Luther had done more than merely protest against the sale of indulgences. In questioning its capacity to forgive sins, he was actually challenging the whole authority of the Catholic Church itself. For, in claiming to be the embodiment of Christ on earth, the Church had long maintained that it alone had the power of forgiving sins.

Luther Leads the Reformation Naturally, the Church reacted. At first, the pope merely appealed to the other members of the Augustinian order to silence the rebel, but Luther stood his ground. In fact, he attacked indulgences from the pulpit of the Wittenberg church with

even greater vigor, and some of his university students publicly burned copies of the charges Friar Tetzel had prepared against his "Theses."

Luther was promptly summoned to Rome to stand trial for heresy. However, when the pope learned of his great popularity in Germany, he decided instead to try to win him over, even offering him a bishop's title. But Luther would not budge from his position that salvation could only be attained through a "right personal relationship with God," and the situation remained unchanged.

Then, in the winter of 1519, John Eck, a famous Catholic theologian of Leipzig, challenged Luther to a public debate. Eck was a skillful debater. He forced Luther to admit that John Hus, a Bohemian "heretic" whom the Church had burned at the stake, was justified in some of the things he had taught. Luther agreed that Hus was right when he both condemned the greed of the Church and insisted upon the individual's right to interpret the Bible for himself. This in turn led Luther to deny the supremacy of the pope. He stated, moreover, that the Bible had greater authority than the Church, and that the Eastern Orthodox could not be considered outside the Christian fold.

No Roman Catholic could hold such a position. Luther had now broken with the Church, and, in May of 1520, the pope ordered Luther's writings burned and his statements withdrawn. When Luther refused to recant, he was excommunicated and subsequently commanded to defend himself before the Emperor and Council of the Holy Roman Empire.

Luther made his appearance. A representative of the pope placed a pile of his writings before him, demanding that he retract what he had written. Luther asked time to think it over. He knew what the consequence of refusal would be. No doubt he would be burned at the stake. However, he finally announced that his conscience made it impossible for him to recant. "Here I stand," he is supposed to have asserted. "My conscience is bound by what I find in the Scriptures. I cannot do otherwise. God help me. Amen."

MARTIN
LUTHER

Four scenes from a motion picture about Luther's life. Above, he stands firm in his statements about the Church before the Emperor and his Council. In the middle scene, Luther confirms his religious position in a debate with John Eck, a leading Catholic theologian. At the lower left, Philip Melanchthon, a Protestant scholar and Luther's friend, presents the official statement of Lutheran faith and practice before the Emperor. The picture at the lower right shows Luther's protector, the Elector Frederick.

To his great surprise he was not immediately taken off to be executed, but granted permission to return home. Evidently his popularity among the masses of Germany compelled the Emperor and his Council to move slowly.

Eventually came the order for his arrest as a "heretic" and an "outcast of the empire." But by then he was safely in hiding under the protection of his prince and powerful friend, the Elector Frederick. Now Luther began writing pamphlets and books to disseminate his ideas, and later he prepared a German translation of the Bible. He was sure that once the people were able to read the Bible for themselves they would see the rightness of his teachings. He was not wrong because gradually certain other princes of Germany came to support him, and the movement he led grew rapidly.

Thus did the Protestant Reformation begin and once it started, it spread throughou Europe. In country after country, variou groups broke with the Catholic Church and formed "reform" movements of their own. No longer were the Christians of the West united in a single Church.

Why the Reformation Spread   Luther's opposition to the sale of indulgences was simply the spark that set off the Reformation. Without important underlying causes, however, it is doubtful whether the Reformation would have come into being.

The situation within the Catholic Church itself was one of these factors, with the sale of indulgences only a symptom of the deeper corruption that plagued the Church. Many churchmen themselves had long been aware of the immorality of some of the clergy and the greed of certain Church officials. In the eyes of a great many, the Church appeared far more interested in collecting funds through heavy papal taxation and such things as indulgences than in the welfare of the ordinary people. Unfortunately, those who objected too strenuously often suffered imprisonment, exile, or even burning at the stake. Meanwhile, criticism of the Church's conduct was mounting, and an explosion seemed inevitable. In fact, already

in the fifteenth century, John Hus' complaints against the abuses of the clergy had led to a break with the Church in Bohemia.

But apart from these internal dissensions, the times gave rise to fresh thinking and questioning of old values. The sixteenth century marked the flowering of the "Renaissance," that rebirth of culture stimulated by the rediscovery of the Greek and Roman classics in the wake of the Crusades. Now, as a consequence of studying the classics, scholars began to develop various types of philosophy, systems of thought that were independent of the teachings of the Church and based almost entirely upon human reason and observations of nature. Some ran directly counter to the Church's position. Thus, in the growing field of science, Nicholas Copernicus was already challenging the Church's interpretation of the story of Creation by setting

COPERNICUS. The famous Polish astronomer of the sixteenth century who, contrary to the teachings of the Church, insisted that the earth was merely one of the planets revolving around the sun.

WYCLIFFE BIBLE. The first Bible translated into English. Though suppressed by the Church, it was circulated secretly and became widely read.

forth the theory that, instead of the earth being the center of the universe, it was merely one of the planets revolving around the sun. Others, like Tycho Brahe and Johann Kepler, were soon to confirm his findings beyond all doubt.

An awakened interest in the Bible, too, was a by-product of the new scholarship, and it was stimulated by the development of printing by Gutenberg, who built his first press about 1450. For centuries Christians had been prevented from reading the Bible because the Scriptures of the Church were in Latin. But now translation into languages that the masses understood began to appear. In fact, by the late fourteenth century, John Wycliffe had already produced one in English. And as individuals more and more were able to obtain printed copies, and to read and interpret the meaning of the Bible for themselves, differences with the teachings of the Church were bound to arise. For instance, Wycliffe himself reached the conclusion that worship depended neither upon priests nor rites.

Even in political and economic life, the privileged position of the Church was threatened. The rise of the merchant class was undermining the whole feudal system and, with it, the dominant role of the Church within the system. Now, too, new forms of nationhood with a great thirst for independence, including freedom from the interference of the pope and the Holy Roman Empire, were beginning to appear.

All these factors had their effect upon the Church. Kings, princes, and barons who had once jumped to do the pope's bidding now complained about the amount of money they had to send to Rome, which prevented them from building up their own countries. The new merchant class looked upon the great tracts of Church land, which produced no taxes, as a drain upon their country's economy, and rulers in the process of creating nations of their own resented the political control which the pope exercised. The limitations which the Church imposed upon thought, religious expression, and interpretation of the Bible, antagonized the more independent-minded. Even the Church itself was torn with inner dissension, so that in the early fifteenth century there were three rival popes occupying the papacy at the same time.

With this background of unrest and even active opposition to the Church, it is little wonder that, once Luther lit the match, the Reformation spread like wildfire throughout much of Central and Western Europe.

Where Luther Differed with Catholicism

Luther continued to study and preach, and before his death in 1546, many had turned to his interpretation of Christianity, which his followers called Lutheranism. In the general atmosphere of the religious intolerance of his time, his own dogmatism and impetuosity often caused him to be harsh with those who opposed him. All his life he fought dissenting Protestant groups with almost the same vigor that he directed against Catholics. And though originally friendly to the Jews, because he hoped they would come over to his faith, in his later years he also lashed out against them in bitterness over their refusal to convert.

As his religious ideas developed, they went considerably beyond the mere issue of indulgences. Actually they served to redefine Christian belief and practice in the following five areas:

PROTESTANT HYMN. This is a replica of the original manuscript of "A Mighty Fortress Is Our God," composed by Martin Luther.

REVOLT OF THE PROTESTANTS

1. *Salvation:* Roman Catholicism, said Luther, gives man a false sense of confidence because it leads him to believe that by fulfilling the demands of the Church he can achieve salvation. This, however, is not so. Salvation comes only as a gift from God. The Church cannot grant it, and all efforts of sinful man to save himself simply serve to increase his sinfulness. The only answer for him is to recognize his own utter helplessness in the face of sin and to put his complete trust in God through Christ. For only by faith in Christ can man become reconciled to God and cleansed of sin. Those who are so "justified through their faith" will gratefully live lives of good deeds.

While this sounds somewhat like the Jewish idea of repentance, there is a vast difference here. Where the Jew believes that God will respond to man's acts, Luther feels that man can only have faith and God *may* forgive him. To Luther, man's acts of atonement are purely the result, not the cause, of forgiveness.

2. *Authority:* The true Church is not any particular religious body, declared Luther. Rather, it comprises all believing Christians over whom Christ is head. The authority for the truth of what they believe comes not from the Catholic Church, the pope, or any priest, but from the Christian Bible. This is the "guide to the word of God in Christ." Thus, as interpreted by individuals of faith with the guidance of the Holy Spirit, the Bible is the final authority in matters of religion.

3. *Clergy:* In contrast to the Church, Luther permitted each congregation to select its own clergymen, and he abolished monastic vows and priestly celibacy. He also allowed the clergy to marry; in fact, he himself married an ex-nun. In this area, and in the matter of authority, Jews stand closer to Luther than to the Roman Catholic Church.

4. *Worship:* Stressing the faith of the individual, Luther insisted that believers should fully participate in the worship, in contrast with the custom of the Church. Hence, he called for the simplification of worship and translation of the rites and ceremonials into German. He also stressed congregational singing, and

wrote a number of church hymns himself. His best-known is "A Mighty Fortress Is Our God," which has become an anthem of Protestantism generally. Moreover, Luther declared that five of the sacraments of the Catholic Church need not be observed, thus reducing the number to only two: Baptism, and the Lord's Supper or Communion, both of which he interpreted symbolically. He differed from the Catholic doctrine of transubstantiation, in insisting that in the Eucharist the wine and bread *were* the actual physical body and blood of Christ, and not, as the Church held, *converted* by a miraculous change into his body and blood.

5. *Religion and the State:* The church and state, Luther maintained, are both ordained by God and each has its separate functions. Therefore, the church should refrain from interfering in political affairs and confine itself to the spiritual welfare of the individual. Hence, in contrast to the Catholic Church of his time, Luther accepted political situations as he found them and ordered his followers to be obedient to their rulers. In fact, in upholding various princes, he even turned against the peasants who were seeking redress from abuses by these princes. Only when the basic rights to preach and carry on the rites of their church were denied, said he, should Lutherans resist. Subsequently, many Protestants, like most Jews, found this too great a denial of the prophetic demand that the state be righteous.

From a modern viewpoint, Luther's teachings may seem rather conservative. In many ways, especially in ritual, he did not depart too widely from Catholic practice since originally he had no intention of breaking with the Church. So, for instance, he continued the use of candles, the crucifix, and religious pictures in worship. However, his doctrine did represent a major departure from Catholicism because he denied its cardinal teaching that salvation could come only through the Church.

The Church fought hard to stamp out Luther's "heresy." In the face of Church hostility, the Lutherans in turn reacted just as violently against the Catholics. By 1525, there were two bitterly competing groups of German princes, Protestants and Catholics, each seeking to destroy the other, and open warfare between them finally broke out. It was not ended until the Peace of Augsburg in 1555, with the adoption of the principle that "the ruler determines the religion of his state," with equal rights for both religions. It now became possible for Lutherans and Roman Catholics to live side by side in relative peace.

The Lutheran Church Today Today, the movement that developed under Luther's leadership has become the largest Protestant denomination in the world. Its followers number about 75 million, with state churches in Germany, Finland, Sweden, Norway, and Iceland. In the United States, where the Dutch who first settled Manhattan Island were Lutherans, there are today about 8 million.

In comparison with other Protestant denominations, Lutheranism is a very conservative group. To a large extent, it has retained in modified form many of the Catholic forms of worship, such as the altar, cross, candles and vestments, and it observes the festivals and seasons of the historic Church year. Its worship generally is in the language of the people, although here in the United States there are some churches originally founded by immigrants that still use German, Swedish, and other European languages.

Lutheranism observes only the sacraments of Baptism by sprinkling, and Communion, in which Christ is believed to be truly present in the wafer and wine in some unexplainable way. Communion is preceded by public rather than private confession, and communicants receive both the bread and wine as they kneel at the altar rail. Confirmation is simply a ritual, not a sacrament, and is held annually on Palm Sunday.

The basic belief of Lutheranism is that mankind, sinful in its disobedience to the will of God, can obtain divine salvation only through faith in Christ. This is the doctrine known as "justification by faith," which maintains that salvation comes through belief in God, through Christ, and without trust in reason, rites, sac-

LUTHERAN PRACTICE. (top) Children are reminded of the meaning of their Baptism in this ritual of Confirmation, held on Palm Sunday. (center) A Communion service. (bottom) Music is an important element in Lutheran worship.

EDUCATIONAL EMPHASIS. At the top, Lutheran school children display pamphlets urging their parents to listen to the "Lutheran Hour" broadcasts. Below are two modern Lutheran parochial-school buildings in the West.

raments, or righteous deeds. Lutheranism holds that every person can approach God directly, and in this sense, all believers are the "priests" of God. Eventually, Christ will come to judge all souls. The good will live on with him forever; the sinful will be punished. Thus, in the end, the faithful will achieve victory over death.

Lutherans believe in the Trinity, and for them the Bible is the only guide to religious truth. They maintain that all Christians are bound together in one great "invisible" Church. Hence, though they regard their faith as the only true religion, they recognize that there are good Christians in many other churches.

Lutheran churches in the United States are organized into various "synods," or church councils, with which each church must be affiliated. Of the sixteen synods at present (becoming ten by 1965), the largest is the Missouri Synod, which is also the most conservative. The synods determine the general policy of the movement. However, the churches are free to choose their own ministers and decide in what way they will conduct their affairs. Lutheran pastors may marry, and in Europe, though not in the United States, they may become bishops.

Growing rapidly in the United States, the Lutheran Church has made wide use of radio, advertising, and house-to-house appeals to attract members. In this country in particular, the Church has shown great concern for the welfare of the family. It was one of the first groups in America to promote foster homes for orphans, and establish agencies and institutions providing health and welfare services for the individual. Its concern for the education of its young has also made it the largest Protestant supporter of parochial schools.

The Spread of Protestantism—John Calvin

The new rector of the University of Paris, Nicholas Cop, stood in the pulpit delivering his inaugural sermon. It is likely that it had been written for him by John Calvin, a close friend. Calvin was a young Frenchman who had originally planned to enter the priesthood, but, influenced by the teachings of Luther, turned instead to Protestantism.

The people who came to hear Cop that day in 1533 were shocked by the new rector's address. It was an attack on the Catholic Church and gave approval to many of the doctrines of the "heretic," Martin Luther. When word reached the authorities, Calvin and Cop were compelled to flee.

Now, Calvin traveled throughout Europe developing his views on Christianity. He was only 25 years old when he published what has been called "the masterpiece of Protestant religious thought," his *Institutes of the Christian Religion*. These Institutes—another word for "textbooks"—dealt with the subjects of God, Christ, and the Holy Spirit, and Church organization and practice.

Man's sinfulness, Calvin said, dims his understanding of God, but through the Bible he receives a revelation of His ways. Here he learns that God freely determines whatever He wants to happen in the world. Consequently, through the work of Christ in man's behalf, God selects for salvation whatever persons He chooses, as though they were completely without sin. Since all men are rightfully deserving of damnation because of their utter sinfulness, God's choice is simply a gift on His part and "predestined," determined by Him beforehand.

The "election" of an individual is then reflected in the person by his conduct, his good deeds, industriousness, sense of duty, and self-discipline. Those given to worldly pleasures, the lazy, irresponsible, and frivolous, show every evidence of having been damned. Therefore, each individual should do his best to appear as though he were one of God's "elect," predestined for salvation, and his life should be lived seriously, soberly, and industriously.

During one of his travels, Calvin happened to pass through Geneva, Switzerland. A friend of his, an ardent Protestant leader named William Farel, asked his assistance with the people of that city. Calvin, now only twenty-seven, began to organize Geneva into a model Protestant community, or as he called it, a "City of God," as Augustine's book a thousand years earlier had termed such a community. He promptly introduced stern rules of conduct that prohibited card-playing, drinking, dancing, and all "frivolity," and required attendance in church every Sunday. He even made the city council enforce these laws.

His strict rule began to wear on the people, and after two years, following a dispute over whether leavened or unleavened bread was to be used in Communion, Calvin was exiled. But realizing that he had brought peace and stability to their community, the people of Geneva soon regretted their decision, and several years later they begged him to return. So for the remaining twenty-three years of his life, Calvin dominated the city of Geneva with his attempts to make it a true "City of God," and his form of Protestantism took deep root in Switzerland.

Where Calvin Differed from Luther Calvin's ideas of Christianity won him friends and followers far beyond the small city of Geneva. Those who supported Calvin's ideas were called "Presbyterians," a name derived from the Greek word for "elder" and used because of Calvin's insistence upon having elected elders govern the church. One of Calvin's followers in Scotland was John Knox. It was the followers of Knox who later brought Presbyterianism to the New World.

In the main, Calvin shared the basic Protestant point of view of Martin Luther, especially in his attitude toward the Catholic Church and in his emphasis upon the Scriptures, individually interpreted, as being the highest authority in Christianity. He also stressed the sinfulness of man, perhaps to an even greater degree than Luther.

But Calvin differed from Luther in three important respects. First, he was much more extreme in his reforms of church worship. Though he retained Baptism and Communion as uniting man into the fellowship of Christ, he held that Christ was present only spiritually in the Eucharist, not physically, as Luther believed. Moreover, he centered the service about preaching, prayer, and congregational singing, and insisted that churches be plain and even austere. Hence, he removed all works of art and imagery, and even banned instrumental

CALVIN. Most of his life was spent in seeking to transform the city of Geneva into a model Christian community. He is shown here meeting with the City Council.

music. All this was quite in contrast with Luther's practices which, in many respects, still resembled those of Catholicism.

Second, Calvin stressed control of the church by the people themselves to a much greater extent than Luther. Calvin's church was ruled entirely by elders, laymen selected by the people, and the minister was made directly responsible to them. This emphasis upon control by the people carried into political life as well. Whereas Luther believed in absolute obedience to the hereditary rulers of the country, Calvin argued for greater power in the hands of the people. Since a considerable number of Presbyterians were influential in Colonial America, many modern historians regard this as an important element in the founding of American democracy.

Finally, Calvin's belief in "election" and "predestination" was quite different from that of Luther and his followers. For Lutherans, the individual had an important part to play in achieving salvation by personally reaching out for faith in the Christ which, in turn, prompted God's gift of salvation. For Calvin, God's grace was bestowed only upon those He selected; even man's faith was His gift.

Presbyterianism Today The Presbyterian Church, called the "Reformed Church" in Switzerland, Holland, France, Germany, and Hungary, has some 43 million members throughout the world, with more than 4 million in the United States.

The movement has remained faithful to the principle of elected officials. Each church selects its own ministers, as well as its elders, who are the authority in religious matters, the deacons, who handle the details of all charities, and the trustees, who conduct its business affairs. The body of elders constitutes what is called a "Session," and the various churches within a particular area comprise a "Presbytery." Three or more Presbyteries form a "Synod." Representatives of all the Synods make up the national ruling body of the Presbyterian Church, the General Assembly, whose elected head is called the "Moderator." In every stage of the

organization, half of those participating must be laymen.

The Church believes in the Trinity. It sees God as having complete control over the universe and, through Christ, over the salvation of man. However, "predestination" is no longer taught. Man attains salvation by complete commitment to God through faith in Christ and his sacrificial death. The Bible is still considered the chief source of religious authority, but its interpretation remains a matter for the conscience of the individual.

Over the years the Presbyterians have become less radical in their forms of worship, and a greater emphasis upon symbolism has come into the Church. Today, Presbyterians make use of Gothic cathedrals, organs and choirs, candles and the cross. The cross, however, is always the empty cross, never a crucifix with the body of Christ. The Church continues to observe Baptism and Communion, with Christ present only spiritually in the Eucharist.

Presbyterianism came to America with the Puritans, and by 1640 there were several thousand in New England. However, when state churches were established in the region, Presbyterians were compelled to settle in the Middle-Atlantic colonies, from New York to Maryland. Here they prospered and became the greatest supporters of the Revolution.

Throughout the years, the Presbyterian Church has emphasized education. This has been due in large measure to its insistence upon each person's right to interpret the Bible, which

each symbol represents 5 million members

8½%

METHODISTS 18 Million

11½%

BAPTISTS 25 Million

COMPARATIVE SIZE OF PROTESTANT DENOMINATIONS IN THE WORLD *

TOTAL PROTESTANTS: 214 MILLION

15%

EPISCOPALIANS 32 Million

Technically speaking, the Episcopalians and other branches of the Anglican Communion regard themselves as "Catholic," though not *Roman* Catholic. For the sake of convenience, however, they and all other Christian movements that originated as part of the Reformation are designated in this volume as "Protestant."

20%

PRESBYTERIANS 43 Million

LUTHERANS 75 Million

35%

10%

ALL OTHER DENOMINATIONS 21 Million

*Figures are for 1960

in turn requires a highly educated clergy and laity. Hence, it is not surprising that Presbyterianism has been responsible for establishing many fine American colleges and universities. Princeton University, for instance, was originally begun as a Presbyterian seminary.

Presbyterians have always been leaders in social welfare, and were among the first to engage in efforts to abolish child labor and establish better living and working conditions for the American workingman. They are likewise active in various interchurch movements, like the World Council of the Churches of Christ and the Y.M.C.A., and have contributed much to the growing harmony among the Protestants.

Among some of the more prominent Presbyterians have been six Presidents of the United States, of whom Dwight D. Eisenhower is the most recent.

The Spread of Protestantism Protestantism, unlike Roman Catholicism, tended to encourage the growth of many different religious groups.

To what extent this has taken place can be seen from the chart on the previous page showing the membership of the major Protestant denominations in the world today.

While Protestantism has only five major denominations in the world today, it actually is made up of as many as 350 different sects. From its start, Protestantism, by its very nature, gave birth to a wide variety of groups, and for good reason.

First, numerous conceptions of Christianity became inevitable when the Bible was recognized as the highest authority in religion, and each individual was given the right to interpret it. So, as people of different backgrounds, education, and nationality pored over the New Testament, they were bound to give differing emphases to one or another concept of Christian belief or practice. Some, for example, insisted upon going back to the original form of baptism, with complete immersion instead of pouring or sprinkling. Others felt that Christianity had gotten too far away from the early Church as pictured in the New Testament and demanded less elaborate worship and church or-

ZWINGLI. Originally a Catholic priest, this Swiss Protestant leader called for return to the actual teachings of the New Testament.

ganization. Such views could be readily supported by their own interpretation of Scripture.

Second, personality clashes and doctrinal disputes between the leaders of the young Protestant movement stimulated the growth of different sects. Martin Luther had violent disputes with Calvin and with many others, including Ulrich Zwingli, a Swiss reformer who had come to the conclusion that Christian beliefs and practices should conform strictly to what appeared in the New Testament. Luther promptly branded Zwingli's teachings as "the inspiration of the devil," and Zwingli replied in kind. Calvin himself was guilty of persecuting and imprisoning other Protestants who differed with him. Such hostility between the early Protestant leaders, and their attempts to suppress dissenting views, tended to multiply the number of rival sects.

Third, special national circumstances also prompted the growth of separate denominations. Particularly was this true in England where many of Protestantism's most influential churches developed. For arising out of the Reformation in that country were the Episcopalians, Unitarians, Congregationalists, Quakers, and Methodists. Today these comprise about a quarter of all the Protestants in the world.

How and why these different interpretations of Christianity came into being, and the nature of their teachings are of real importance in understanding present-day Protestantism. . . .

TOPICS TO DISCUSS

1. In what respects do Lutherans and Roman Catholics agree and disagree on religious beliefs, practices, and church organization?
2. How does Judaism differ from the teachings of the present-day Lutheran and Presbyterian churches?
3. How do you account for the great number of different Protestant sects in your community?
4. What possible effects has the existence of Protestantism had upon the Jews?

THINGS TO DO

1. Invite a member of the clergy or an informed layman from both the Lutheran and Presbyterian churches to discuss their beliefs and practices. On the basis of their visit prepare a dictionary of Protestant terminology as distinct from that of Roman Catholicism.
2. Prepare a report on Protestantism in your

own community. How many different denominations are there and what is the membership of each? What are the distinctive teachings of each, and what beliefs and practices do they share in common?
3. Construct a chart comparing the teachings and practices of Lutheranism and Presbyterianism with those of modern Judaism.

OTHER THINGS TO READ

LANDIS, BENSON Y., *World Religions*, Dutton, "Lutherans," pp. 83-87; "Presbyterians," pp. 100-103; "Reformed Churches," pp. 108-110.

MANWELL, REGINALD D., and SOPHIA L. FAHS, *The Church Across the Street*, Beacon Press, Chapter 3, "John Calvin, 1509-1564," pp. 36-50.

NOSS, JOHN B., *Man's Religions*, Macmillan, pp. 637-650.

PIKE, E. ROYSTON, *Encyclopaedia of Religion and Religions*, Meridian, "Calvin," p. 77; "Calvinism," pp. 77-78; "Faith," p. 150; "Knox," p. 224; "Luther," p. 237; "Lutheranism," p. 238; "Presbyterians," pp. 306-307; "Zwingli," p. 404.

ROSTEN, LEO, *A Guide to the Religions of America*, Simon and Schuster, "What Is a Lutheran?" by G. Elson Ruff, pp. 73-81; "What Is a Presbyterian?" by John S. Bonnell, pp. 101-110.

SMITH, HUSTON, *The Religions of Man*, Mentor, pp. 310-316.

SPENCE, HARTZELL, *The Story of America's Religions*, Holt, Rinehart, Winston, Chapter 3, "The Lutherans," pp. 39-58; Chapter 4, "The Presbyterians," pp. 59-75.

11

THE REFORMATION COMES TO ENGLAND

Henry VIII Establishes a National Church

The Reformation came to England because of some very unusual circumstances.

True, there had been discontent with Roman Catholicism in England going as far back as the days of Wycliffe, a dissenting priest who died in 1384. Not only had he protested against papal taxes, and declared the Church's doctrine of transubstantiation contrary to the teachings of Scripture, but he also translated the Bible into English for the first time so that the people might know the "real" teachings of Christianity. Another Englishman who differed with the Church over the interpretation of the Scriptures was William Tyndale, finally put to death in 1536. He produced such a splendid translation of the Bible that it later became the basis for the official Scriptures of the Church of England, the King James Version.

Thus, when the Reformation finally came to England, some groundwork had already been laid. Other men soon followed after Wycliffe and Tyndale to challenge Roman Catholicism. Some Englishmen were impressed by the revolt of Luther in Germany, and by Calvin's work in Geneva. Others were increasingly opposed to the interference of the Church in England's national affairs, and the kings were envious of its lands and riches. And still other English people had been strongly influenced by the new learning of the Renaissance, which often ran counter to the official teachings of the Church.

The immediate cause of the Reformation, however, was the romance of an English king. Around 1527, King Henry VIII fell in love with a beautiful girl named Anne Boleyn. Henry, already married to Catherine of Aragon, had grown tired of her because of her constant loyalty to Spain and her failure to produce a male heir. Since the Church did not permit divorce, Henry's real problem was how to be rid of Catherine and marry Anne.

For more than five years, Henry tried unsuccessfully to have the Church annul his marriage; that is, declare that it had never really existed, something that was possible in Catholicism. He even applied pressure to the pope by cutting off all payments to the Church, but to no avail.

Meanwhile, in 1529, Henry met Thomas Cranmer, a young professor from Oxford, who gave him some useful advice. He proposed that the King appeal to the university faculties, composed of prominent clergymen, to give him permission to obtain a divorce. Henry considered this a brilliant suggestion. He had Cranmer prepare the case and present it to the faculties of Oxford and Cambridge. They promptly ruled in the King's favor, and so did the Parliament. Then, in 1533, Thomas Cranmer, now the Archbishop of Canterbury, performed the marriage of the King to Anne. The pope promptly excommunicated Henry, and the following year Parliament retaliated by declaring the King head of the English Church.

From that day to the present—except for six years during the reign of Mary, the daughter of Henry and Catherine—the Church of England has remained outside the Roman Catholic fold.

The Work of Cranmer Apart from winning his divorce, what really interested Henry VIII was having the Crown control the English Church and its property. But other than freedom from Roman Catholic control, he wanted no changes in the beliefs and practices of his new Church of England. Cranmer, obeying the King as head of the Church, followed his wishes.

However, when Henry died and was succeeded by a sickly young boy, Cranmer introduced many Protestant reforms. He prepared a series of services in English to replace the Latin. He produced a statement of beliefs for

SECOND EDITION. The title-page of the 1552 version of **The Book of Common Prayer,** prepared by Archbishop Cranmer for use in the Church of England. The initial edition was published about three years earlier.

the new Church and a system by which it was to be governed. Now, too, priests were allowed to marry.

Most important of all was his creation of a new prayer book, called *The Book of Common Prayer,* which provided for many changes in the ritual and in the form of the prayers themselves. For instance, the idea of transubstantiation in the Eucharist was removed, and the symbols of Communion became merely a remembrance of Jesus' death. The whole congregation was also permitted to partake of both the bread and wine.

Henry's son died at the age of fifteen and he was succeeded on the throne by Mary, the eldest child of Henry and Catherine. Mary was a zealous Roman Catholic, and she immediately returned the Church of England to the Catholic fold. Those who had supported the Reformation were imprisoned, and many Protestants were burned at the stake for their "heresy." In fact, two of England's most powerful bishops were soon among the victims.

Eventually, Cranmer himself was stripped of his office as Archbishop and thrown into prison. Fearful for his life, he publicly admitted his "errors" in six separate letters and asked the forgiveness of the Queen. But it was no use, because Mary had already decided that he was to be executed.

The man who had begged for his life now overcame his panic. He announced that he had recanted only out of fear, and then he denounced the pope and the Roman Catholic Church for their false doctrines. He was led to the stake and the fire was kindled. It is reported that he cried out that the hand which had written his recantations should be burned first, and he held it directly in the flames until he himself was consumed.

Much of Cranmer's work lived on after him. In 1558, after six years of "Bloody" Mary's reign, Elizabeth, daughter of Henry and Anne, was made Queen. Imprisoned at one time by Mary, Elizabeth had become the favorite of the persecuted Protestants, and a year after she became Queen, the Church of England was once more established under the control of the

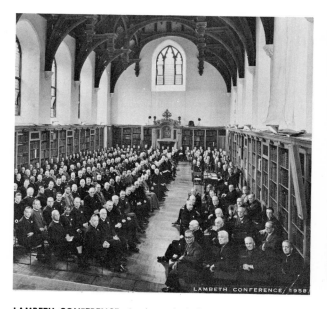

LAMBETH CONFERENCE. At the cathedral of the Archbishop of Canterbury in London, all of the bishops of the Anglican Communion gather every ten years to discuss matters of Church concern. Shown here are scenes from the 1958 Conference.

Crown. *The Book of Common Prayer* was made the official prayer book, and the English Church was placed under the authority of its own bishops. However, some of the more extreme reforms of Cranmer were abolished, and in many respects the Church of England still resembled that of Rome. It even had a hierarchical organization similar to it. Consequently, the English or "Anglican" Church came to regard itself as a form of Christianity standing midway between Roman Catholicism and Protestantism.

The Episcopal Church Today With a membership of some 32 million in the world today, the Anglican Church or Communion, as it prefers to call itself, has many branches. One, of course, is the Church of England itself, regarded as the mother Church. Although the others are removed from its control and are self-governing, they all recognize the nominal leadership of the Archbishop of Canterbury.

The first to be established outside of England was the Scottish Episcopal Church, and one of the most influential today is the Protestant Episcopal Church of the United States, with a membership of over three million. The term "Episcopal" is used because it comes from the Greek word meaning "bishop," and describes the organizational form of the Anglican Communion in which the bishops are the governing ministers. Like the Catholic Church, it too claims that its bishops are the successors of the apostles. There are also priests as well as deacons who assist them, and all of the clergymen may marry if they wish.

The organization of the Anglican Church differs in each country. Here in the United States, the Protestant Episcopal Church is organized around the individual church, or "parish," which is governed by priests and elected laymen. Parishes are then combined into dioceses under the jurisdiction of the bishop and laymen. Once every three years the entire Church holds what it calls its "General Convention," which legislates for the movement as a whole. It is organized into a House of Deputies, made up of laymen and priests, and a House of Bishops, in which only bishops sit.

Every ten years, the entire Anglican Communion conducts its Lambeth Conference in England, which is attended by all 300 bishops of the Church, under the presidency of the

125

TAKING COMMUNION. Unlike the Catholics, Episcopalians partake of both the wine and the bread of the Eucharist.

BAPTISM. A child is baptized by the Episcopalian priest. This rite and Communion are the two sacraments recognized by the entire Church, though all seven are practiced by many.

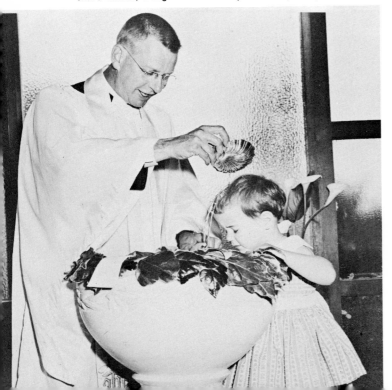

OUR RELIGION AND OUR NEIGHBORS

Archbishop of Canterbury. The Conference has no legislative authority but may recommend measures for the guidance of the Church.

In general, the whole of the Anglican Communion follows *The Book of Common Prayer.* However, wide variations of belief are possible through interpretation of its creed, essentially the Apostles' Creed, which reads as follows:

I believe in God the Father Almighty, Maker of Heaven and earth;

And in Jesus Christ, His only Son, Our Lord;

Who was conceived by the Holy Ghost, born of the Virgin Mary, suffered under Pontius Pilate, was crucified, dead, and buried; He descended into hell; the third day He rose again from the dead; He ascended into heaven, and sits on the right hand of God the Father Almighty; from thence He shall come to judge the quick [living] and the dead.

I believe in the Holy Ghost; the Holy Catholic Church; the Communion of Saints; the forgiveness of sins; the resurrection of the body; and the life everlasting. Amen.

The Church of England, and the various branches of the Anglican Communion as well, are divided into two groups, "high church" and "low church," based upon differences in practice. In the low church, services are simpler, with less emphasis upon Catholic-like ritual. Thus it does not consider confession of sins a sacrament, and recognizes only two true sacraments, Baptism and Communion. Its members do not pray to Mary or the saints. The high church, often called "Anglo-Catholic" because of the resemblance of its worship to Roman Catholicism, calls its service of Communion "Mass," and its ministers, who are permitted to hold confession, "priests."

As we see from its creed, the Anglican Communion continues to regard itself as "Catholic," but this word is used in the original sense of "universal" and not *Roman* Catholic. In its effort to reflect the universal nature of its Christianity, it regards all who are baptized into the Christian faith as members of one

126

individual "Church of Christ." Consequently, it cooperates fully with other Protestant groups in matters of common religious concern.

In general, the faith and the practices of the Anglican Communion represent a compromise between Roman Catholicism and the mainstream of Protestantism. The Church of England traces the authority of its bishops back to Christ and his apostles, sponsors orders of monks and nuns who take vows of poverty, chastity, and obedience, and firmly believes in the Trinity, the Virgin Birth, and, in the high church, the seven sacraments. But like the Protestants, it rejects the supreme authority of the pope, and accepts the Bible as the chief standard of Christian faith and conduct. It holds its services in the English language, provides considerable congregational participation in worship, and permits its worshippers to partake in both the bread and wine at Communion. It offers only symbolic interpretations of the Eucharist and does not regard either heaven or hell as actual places. Furthermore, it permits divorce and endorses birth control.

Generally reflecting a middle and upper class membership, the Episcopal Church has played a very prominent role in the history of America. Beginning with its first service in Jamestown in 1607, it soon established itself as the state religion in most of the English Colonies.

However, the Revolution caused the Church special difficulties because of its close connection with the mother Church of England, and the membership was looked upon with suspicion. Nevertheless, the majority of the founders of the nation, including George Washington, Alexander Hamilton, James Madison, and many others, were Episcopalians. Significantly, Paul Revere's lantern was hung in one of the Episcopalian churches in Boston, and Patrick Henry delivered his famous "liberty or death" speech in an Episcopalian church in Richmond. At war's end, the Church was completely divorced from the control of the Crown.

Historically, because of their strong belief in a common Church of all Christians, American Episcopalians have been leaders in the movement to unite all Protestants, and have helped create both the National and World Council of the Churches of Christ, comprising most Protestant and Eastern Orthodox bodies.

The Congregationalists   When Queen Elizabeth came to power in 1558, she inherited many difficulties. England was in the midst of war with France, and within the country itself, various plots were brewing against the Queen. The six years of Mary's reign had brought turmoil to the nation over the issue of Roman Catholicism, which she had restored. Naturally, when Elizabeth reestablished the Anglican Church, she encountered the hostility of the Catholics.

But she faced opposition from many Protestants, too. The Anglican Church, as we have

HISTORIC CHURCH. The Episcopalian "Old North Church" of Boston, made famous by Paul Revere's ride.

noted, was essentially a compromise with Catholicism. Though its beliefs were mainly of the Protestant variety, its organization and worship were basically Catholic. As a result, there were numerous "dissenters" or "nonconformists" who objected to these so-called Catholic influences. The Puritans wished to "purify" the Church of England of these influences by making it more Protestant. The Presbyterians sought to have the Church organized under presbyters and synods instead of bishops. The Unitarians denied belief in the Trinity. And the Congregationalists insisted upon simple forms of worship, the abolition of all so-called Catholic ceremonies and organization, and the complete independence of each local congregation.

Although Elizabeth granted "toleration" to many groups who differed with the Anglican Church, she would not compromise with either the Roman Catholics, or the more radical nonconformists, like the Unitarians and Congregationalists. Against these dissenters in particular she directed the most rigorous kind of persecution.

At the time, the Congregationalists were led by Robert Browne, a student at Cambridge University. When a favorite professor was re-moved from his post, and others were imprisoned for being dissenters, Browne took up their cause and began preaching reform of the state-controlled Church. Finally, in 1581, he formed what became the first Congregationalist Church in England. It was so named because the congregation determined the ritual according to its own interpretation of the Bible, and not the rules of the Anglican Church. There the members worshipped simply, without instrumental music, and with readings from the Bible, free prayer, and open discussion after the sermon.

Eventually, Browne and his group were threatened with imprisonment and they fled to Holland. As time passed, other Congregationalists also escaped England. In 1620, the members of one of these groups who had settled in Leyden, Holland, crossed the Atlantic in the "Mayflower" under the leadership of "elder"

PILGRIM LANDING. Arriving from Holland, the Pilgrims went ashore on the snowbound coast of New England. Less than a month later, they were at work building a house for common shelter.

William Brewster. There they founded the Pilgrim colony of Plymouth.

It was in America that Congregationalism made some of its most important contributions. These have included the introduction of the holiday of Thanksgiving, the creation of public schools, and the founding of such great universities and colleges as Harvard and Yale. More than this, however, as champions of freedom, the Pilgrims and Puritans brought civil rights to the New World and helped establish the system of free enterprise. As Minute Men, they set off the War of Independence, and they led the

FIRST SERVICE. The Puritans join in worship as they observe their first Sunday in the New World.

fight against slavery in the pre-Civil War period.

At the same time, in its early history Congregationalism, with its emphasis on strictness, introduced the blue laws prohibiting a great number of activities on Sunday. Though it has long since abandoned this position and has, in fact, become quite liberal, various other conservative Protestant churches today ardently support them.

Back in England, despite the persecution by Elizabeth and her successors, Congregationalism continued to grow. With the overthrow of the Crown in 1653 by Oliver Cromwell—practically a Congregationalist himself—the movement flourished. However, after Charles II regained the throne in 1660, he insisted upon absolute conformity to *The Book of Common Prayer* and the various practices of the Church of England. As a result, two years later the Congregationalists broke completely with the Anglican Church.

With other denominations, Congregationalists draw their authority from the teachings of Christ as they appear in the New Testament. But what distinguishes them from other denominations is the independence of each church. Though there are county, state, and national associations of Congregationalist churches, and Congregationalists participate in the work of the various larger Christian bodies, they do not permit them to have any control over the internal affairs of the local church. In this respect they share the sense of independence enjoyed by each Jewish congregation.

But unlike Judaism, which enjoys a high degree of unity of belief and practice within its different interpretations, strong emphasis upon congregational independence among Congregationalists has caused their worship to vary widely from church to church. By and large, however, the ritual remains simple, and emphasis is placed upon the minister's sermon. Congregationalists observe Baptism and believe in the Trinity. They regard the Bible, which may be freely interpreted by the individual, as the chief source of their knowledge of God and His ways.

In its social and political outlook and to some extent religiously, American Congregationalism is considered one of the more liberal Protestant denominations. It ordains women for the ministry, cooperates fully with other Protestant groups to achieve interdenominational harmony, and even accepts ministers from other Christian denominations without reordaining them.

In 1957, the Congregationalists merged with the Evangelical and Reformed Church. The United Church of Christ, as the denomination is now known, has a total membership of over two million in the United States and about another million in the rest of the world.

The Unitarians   Another dissenting group whom Elizabeth refused to tolerate was the Unitarians. They denied all belief in the Trinity and regarded Jesus, not as God, but simply as a

FIRST UNITARIAN. Michael Servetus, a noted sixteenth century physician, was ultimately executed for his Unitarian "heresy."

MICHAEL SERVETVS HIS... DE ARAGONIA

129

great religious and ethical teacher. Even today, because of this, the Unitarians are often not regarded as Protestants by other Protestants, and are excluded from membership in the National Council of the Churches of Christ, the organization comprising most of the Protestant denominations in the United States.

The Unitarian Church traces its origin back to the early days of Christianity when certain sects held similar beliefs. However, the modern movement, as such, began with a great sixteenth century physician, Michael Servetus, who is believed to have discovered the circulation of blood some 75 years before Harvey.

As a young man, Servetus came to the conclusion that the doctrine of the three-Gods-in-one of the Trinity was wrong. There was only one God, he declared, and Christ was simply a manifestation of God and the Holy Spirit, His form of communication with man. He published these views in his work, *The Errors of the Trinity,* and was attacked for them not only by the Catholics, who unsuccessfully tried to put him to death, but also by the leaders of the young Protestant movement. Luther called his writings "wicked," and Calvin was ultimately responsible in 1553 for having him burned at the stake in Geneva for his Unitarian "heresy."

Faustus Socinus, son of a distinguished Italian family, next took up the cause. To him Jesus was only a man, but so filled with God's wisdom that he was resurrected and placed at God's right hand. Therefore, one could pray to him.

Under Socinus' leadership, King John Sigismund, the ruler of Hungary, became a Unitarian, and by 1600 there were some 425 Unitarian churches in that country. Despite the hostility of Catholicism, which sought to destroy it, Unitarianism spread to Poland, then to Western Europe and England. Though the Unitarians were persecuted by the English Crown, the movement persisted there.

Later, Unitarianism came to New England. The First American Unitarian Church was King's Chapel in Boston, which had previously been Episcopalian but removed all references to the Trinity in 1787. In 1819, Dr. William Ellery Channing, a liberal Congregationalist minister of Boston, preached a sermon in Baltimore which contrasted Unitarianism and Calvinism. In it he voiced his objections to the doctrines of the Trinity, predestination, and original sin being preached by the conservative wing of Congregationalism. Word of his remarks quickly spread, and his views were so well received among the more liberal Congregationalists that nearly 150 of their churches in New England affiliated with the Unitarian movement.

Nonetheless, its membership has remained relatively small. Even today, Unitarianism numbers only some half-million in the world, and has just about 200,000 members in the United States. This includes those affiliated with the Universalist Church now merged with it.

Yet Unitarianism has had tremendous influence upon American thought and life, particularly because it supports social justice, peace, and intellectual freedom. Its membership has included a great many noted Americans in various fields. Among them have been Presidents Thomas Jefferson, John Quincy Adams, Millard Fillmore, and William Howard Taft, and distinguished writers like Henry W. Longfellow, Nathaniel Hawthorne, James Russell Lowell, Ralph Waldo Emerson, Julia Ward Howe, and Louisa May Alcott.

Unitarians assert that Christianity has forgotten the real Jesus, and substituted for him a mystical Christ based upon the beliefs of the old mystery religions. Instead, the Unitarian faith is rooted in a belief in one God and in a human Jesus, whom the members regard as their beloved teacher of religious values designed to help one's fellow man. Unitarians stress the goodness and dignity of man, and the necessity to carry on social reform and philanthropy to improve mankind's lot. For in their eyes, salvation can come only through the efforts of human beings inspired by the principles taught by Jesus. The Unitarian "Covenant" that is in general use today puts it this way: "In the love of truth and in the spirit of Jesus, we unite for the worship of God and the service of man."

NOTED AMERICAN UNITARIANS. (left to right) Ralph Waldo Emerson, distinguished poet and essayist; Frank Lloyd Wright, pioneer of modern architecture; Horace Mann, a champion of public education; Louisa May Alcott, popular novelist; Horace Greeley, famed newspaper publisher; and Thomas Jefferson, third president of the United States.

Contrary to Protestantism in general, the Unitarians do not believe in the Virgin Birth, in original sin, or that man is basically evil. Yet they are Christians in their observance of the Christian holidays and a number of Christian rites. Since each of the local churches determines its own practices, the religious service varies from place to place. Where Baptism is practiced, it is considered simply an act of dedication to the ethics of Jesus, and Communion is observed in the original sense of the "Lord's Supper," as a rite of remembrance and fellowship.

It should also be pointed out that among the more liberal Unitarians there are those who would place even less emphasis upon formal worship and belief, and more upon concern with the religious development of man in general. At times it almost seems as if the center of their concern is man rather than God.

Jews have found the Unitarians very close to the universal teachings of Judaism. They see in the Unitarian movement the first organized signs of the success of the Mission to which they have dedicated themselves as Jews.

The Methodists While other Protestant denominations such as the Lutherans, Presbyterians, and Baptists found their way into England from the Continent, two other denominations originated in England itself. One was the Quakers, which have remained a small group. The other, however, was destined to become one of the larger Protestant denominations. This was Methodism.

Interestingly, during his lifetime, John Wesley, its founder, never believed that he was establishing a new denomination. Actually, he remained a minister of the Church of England all his life, even though he did not always agree with its practices. But Wesley's fervent preaching, his emphasis upon spirit rather than form, his great organizational ability, and the use he and his brother made of tuneful, stirring hymns, all contributed to the birth of a separate Protestant denomination.

John and Charles Wesley were sons of an Anglican minister who lived in Epworth, England, in the eighteenth century. While attending Oxford University, they founded a club that sponsored a program of intensive religious activity. It included visiting the sick, educating the poor, praying aloud three times a day and silently every hour. The members' strict and methodical rules of conduct earned for them the nickname "Methodists."

After a brief, unhappy ministry in the Episcopal Church in Savannah, Georgia, the Wesley brothers returned to England. There a friend told them that, though they were ministers of the Church of England, they would not be true Christians until they experienced inner conversion. Shortly thereafter, and within a few days of each other, both underwent a profound spiritual conversion. "I felt my heart strangely warmed," John describes it. "I felt I could trust in Christ alone for my salvation . . . and that he had taken away my sins. . . ."

Enthusiastically, they began trying to awaken in unchurched people the feeling of God's presence in their lives through Christ. They went throughout the whole of England leading religious "revivals," particularly among the miners and factory workmen. They preached indoors and out, and organized the masses into "societies" for prayer and strict religious living. Many thousands joined these societies, and leaders were assigned to super-

131

DEVELOPMENT OF PROTESTANT DENOMINATIONS

LUTHERAN
BAPTIST
EPISCOPALIAN
UNITARIAN

LUTHERAN	BAPTIST	WORLD EVENTS	EPISCOPALIAN	UNITARIAN
1517 Luther's "95 Theses."				
1521 Luther defends himself before Emperor.				
		1519 Magellan sails around the world.		
	1525 Appearance of Anabaptists.			
	1528 Hubmeier executed for "heresy."			
			1529 Cranmer and Henry VIII meet.	
			1533 Henry VIII weds Anne Boleyn. Break with pope, and **1534** Church of England established.	**1531** Servetus publishes his *Errors of the Trinity*.
		From **1545** Council of Trent seeks to remedy Church ills, to **1563**.	**1546** Cranmer begins wide reforms.	
1555 Peace of Augsburg and end of war between Lutherans and Catholics.			**1555** Cranmer executed by Mary.	**1553** Servetus executed by Calvin.
			1559 Queen Elizabeth reestablishes Church of England.	**1559** Unitarian King of Hungary begins reign.
				1578 Socinus goes to Poland.
				1604 Socinus dies.
1624 Dutch Lutherans settle New Amsterdam.	**1611** First Baptist Church formed in England.	**1607** First permanent settlement in North America at Jamestown.	**1607** First Episcopalian service in America at Jamestown.	
1638 First Lutheran Church formed at Wilmington, Delaware by Swedes.	**1636** Roger Williams founds Providence, leading to organization of first Baptist Church, **1639**.			
		1653 Cromwell takes over control of England.		
				1787 First American Unitarian Church established in Boston.

vise them. All of this, of course, was quite in contrast to the practices of the very formal Church of England.

Meanwhile, John preached a gospel of social justice, asking his followers to give generously to the poor and hungry, and to fight slavery in England. He also developed specific rules, called the "Methodist Discipline," for the guidance of the ministers and members of the societies. Smoking, drinking, theater-going, and dancing were all barred. While today many Methodists still believe all drinking of alcoholic beverages is sinful, the other bans have gradually been disappearing.

The movement spread to Ireland and America. In 1784, the first Methodist Episcopal Church was organized in Baltimore, and in the same year Methodists created the first Sunday school in the United States. Circuit-riding preachers carried the faith all over the West, and the movement attracted thousands of pioneers in rural and frontier settlements.

By the time Charles Wesley died in 1788, and his brother John, in 1791, they left behind a movement that continued to grow in numbers and influence. Not long afterward, when the Anglican Church refused the right of taking Communion to Methodists, the movement became a separate denomination. Actually, the Wesleys themselves had paved the way for this by ordaining their own clergymen for the various societies in America, Scotland, Newfoundland, and even England itself.

Today, there are some 18 million Methodists in the world, with 12 million in the United States. They place their chief emphasis upon the inner experience of faith and its application to social needs and problems. Thus, on the one hand, the Methodists lay great stress on missionaries, revivals, and testimonies of religious experience, and on the other, seek to better the conditions of the poor and disabled by carrying on a variety of activities. Though the denomination was divided for a great number of years as a result of the slavery issue, the Northern and Southern churches were reunited in 1939. However, despite efforts to break down segregation within the church, most Negro con-

gregations are not affiliated with the national body.

At the same time, Methodists have been among the most active Protestants seeking to make our society more just and righteous. On both a national and international level, they have worked hard for peace, economic betterment, and numerous causes designed to improve the lives of all men. One of their best-known projects is the Goodwill Industries, founded by one of their churches in Boston. It employs hundreds of unfortunates who earn a living by reconditioning used articles of clothing and furniture for resale. While Judaism differs sharply with Methodism in matters of belief, it finds the Methodist emphasis on positive social action very much like its own stress on doing the commandments.

There is wide variation in Methodist practice and belief. Its churches range from those whose worship is highly formal, dignified, and near-Episcopalian, to those where great emotionalism prevails, with the congregation interrupting the sermon with shouts of "Amen" and "Hallelujah."

Though the Methodist Church requires only belief in God and in Jesus Christ as His son and savior of man, most Methodists believe in the Trinity, the Virgin Birth, and divine judgment

AROUSED MOB. With their emphasis upon the Methodist Discipline, the Wesley brothers frequently faced angry mobs as they preached in the streets of English cities.

after death. All of them maintain the two sacraments of Baptism and the Lord's Supper. They regard the Bible, which may be freely interpreted by the individual, as the source of salvation. Though their "Discipline" has been modified over the years, Methodists remain the chief supporters of "prohibition," outlawing the sale of intoxicating beverages.

The Methodist Church is strictly controlled by its governing bodies, the Districts and Conferences. The District comprises a group of local churches under a District Supervisor, and the various Annual Conferences are made up of representatives of the clergy and laymen from a number of Districts, under the supervision of the bishop. Each minister is appointed to his church by the bishop, who holds him responsible for the activity of his church and to whom he must report regularly. Once in four years, representatives of all the Annual Conferences meet in a world-wide convention, which seeks to give guidance to the Methodist movement as a whole.

With the Wesleys' historic emphasis upon teaching, Methodism has given to America some of its important institutions of higher learning. Among them are Boston University, the University of Southern California, Duke University, and Vanderbilt University.

The Quakers The other denomination which originated in England is the Quakers, more properly known as the Society of Friends, or "Friends." Its members were nicknamed "Quakers," some say, because its leader, George Fox, on trial in England, was contemptuously told by the judge to "quake before the Lord." The term "Quaker" was then applied to all of his followers. Others maintain that the name was given to them because of their trembling, or "quaking" with emotion, at the word of God as preached by Fox.

Fox founded a Quaker community in northern England in 1652, after a long period of self-searching. As a young man he had been disturbed by the seeming unconcern of many Christians for the poor, by their drinking, their failure to speak the truth at all times, and their cruelty to others, especially in time of war. For long years he searched for answers to these problems, talking to ministers, reading the Bible, and meditating in the woods by himself. Finally, he heard a voice telling him that he must carry on a mission for "pure" religion, as distinguished from formal religion with its many rites and procedures of worship. And just as he himself had received the "inner light," so he felt that everyone else should come to experience it.

Many joined him. They pledged themselves to be thoroughly honest, to cultivate the "inner light" within themselves, and to maintain brotherliness toward all of their fellow men. They refused to fight, even in war, or to take an oath, since they believed that the Bible forbade such things. While the Quakers came to be viewed as "queer," their great honesty earned them universal respect. Yet, because of their beliefs, and especially their refusal to serve in the English army, George Fox and many of his followers suffered imprisonment and flogging.

In 1681, William Penn, a gifted Quaker preacher himself, founded the colony of Pennsylvania. It was to be a place of refuge for Friends who were also being persecuted by the Puritans of New England. The Charter of Pennsylvania promised freedom for all religious sects, and the colony soon became the center of American Quakerism.

Though today there are differences between various groups of Friends, most of them believe that God can be experienced through the "inner light," similar to the Holy Spirit, and without the aid of ministers or strictly formal worship. In this sense, every Friend is considered a minister, and elders are appointed merely to supervise the meetings on Sunday mornings at the very simple and unpretentious "Meeting-Houses."

Unlike the forms of worship in Judaism, in Catholicism, and in most denominations of Protestantism with their set services, the fundamental form of Quaker worship consists essentially of sitting quietly until a member feels moved to stand and speak. He may present

DEVELOPMENT OF PROTESTANT DENOMINATIONS

PRESBYTERIAN
CONGREGATIONALIST
QUAKER
METHODIST

PRESBYTERIAN	CONGREGATIONALIST	WORLD EVENTS	QUAKER	METHODIST
1533 Calvin and Cop flee Paris.				
1536 Calvin organizes religious life in Geneva.		From **1545** Council of Trent seeks to remedy Church ills, to **1563**.		
1560 Knox founds Presbyterianism in Scotland.	**1563** Persecution of dissenters begins.			
1564 Calvin dies.	**1581** Browne forms first Congregationalist Church in England.			
		1607 First permanent settlement in North America at Jamestown.		
	1620 Pilgrims land at Plymouth.			
			1646 Fox receives the "inner light."	
			1652 Fox founds Quaker Church in England.	
	1662 Congregationalists leave Church of England.		**1681** William Penn establishes Pennsylvania.	
1706 First Presbytery formed at Philadelphia.				
				1738 John Wesley's conversion.
		1754 French and Indian War.		
		1776 American Revolution.		
				1784 First Methodist Episcopal Church organized in Baltimore.
				1791 John Wesley dies; Methodists break with the Church of England.

QUAKER WORSHIP. Conspicuously missing from this service held in a Friends' meeting house are religious symbols and even a clergyman.

religious thoughts, pray, or read from the Bible. Sometimes the group remains silent for the entire hour. Afterwards, everyone shakes hands with his neighbor. Yet there are probably as many Quakers whose services resemble those of the Congregationalists or other religiously-liberal denominations.

The Quakers have no sacraments of any kind, nor have they any formal creed. They subscribe to absolute equality for all peoples, personal honesty, and complete sincerity. Matters of belief about the Trinity, the Virgin Birth, heaven and hell, and the like, are left up to the individual. They believe, as do all liberal groups, that though there are truths in the Bible, not everything in the Bible is necessarily true. The Bible is not even their basic guide or standard for deciding religious issues and problems. It is the "inner light"—that part of God in everyone, expressed through Jesus, God's unique gift to man—that guides the Quaker.

Although they are a very small group, with less than 100,000 members in the United States and only about 200,000 in the whole world, the Friends have exerted an influence out of all proportion to their numbers. They are famous for their spirit of service to all peoples, and carry on a great many humanitarian activities throughout the world. Quakers are found in the forefront of those who work to help the oppressed, the hungry, and the needy everywhere. For instance, in 1938 a committee of three negotiated with the Nazi Gestapo in Berlin to rescue and resettle many Jews abroad.

Above all, the Quakers are recognized as leaders in the effort to put an end to war. In fact, the Friends were awarded the Nobel Peace Prize in 1947 for their activities in behalf of peace. Still, though pacifism remains strong among them, many today no longer refuse to serve in the armed forces.

Throughout the years, many distinguished Americans have been Quakers, including President Herbert Hoover and the poet John Greenleaf Whittier.

Protestantism Moves Westward   Over the years, these and other forms of Protestantism continued to grow in England. Eventually, too, all of them were transplanted to the New World, and nowhere did they prosper more. For not only has Protestantism become the majority faith in the United States, but there are more Protestants in this country than in any other part of the world.

Today, Lutheranism, Presbyterianism, Episcopalianism, Congregationalism, Unitarianism, Methodism, and Quakerism are all represented on the American scene. The United States has a great many other Protestant denominations as well. While most are only tiny sects, at least fourteen of them have a hundred thousand or more members, and several have more than a million. In fact, the Baptist faith, an import from Europe, is the largest Protestant denomination in this country. And four others, with a total membership of more than five million, are products of America itself.

Thus, to follow the further developments in Protestantism, we move westward to the United States. . . .

THE REFORMATION COMES TO ENGLAND

TOPICS TO DISCUSS

1. Why, in contrast to Judaism, does Protestantism have so many different denominations?
2. What does modern Judaism seem to share in common with various Protestant denominations? Where and why do they differ?
3. In what ways have the various Protestant denominations affected your own life as an American Jew?
4. What are some of the most important elements that most Protestants appear to share in common? What is it, then, that seems to divide them?

THINGS TO DO

1. Arrange to visit a Methodist or Congregationalist church and compare its service with that of the Roman Catholic mass. In what ways are they similar and how do they differ?
2. Prepare a report on the following Protestant denominations in your own community: the Episcopalians, Congregationalists, Unitarians, Methodists, and Quakers. What is the local membership of each, and how does each compare in size with the membership of your own interpretation of Judaism? What are the distinctive teachings and practices of each? What contribution does each make to your community?
3. Construct a chart comparing the teachings and practices of the Episcopalians, Congregationalists, Unitarians, Methodists, and Quakers, with those of modern Judaism.

OTHER THINGS TO READ

FITCH, FLORENCE M., *One God*, Lothrop, Lee, and Shepard, "The Protestant Way," pp. 99-136.

LANDIS, BENSON Y., *World Religions*, Dutton, "Anglicans," pp. 18-24; "Congregational Christian Churches," pp. 49-51; "Friends," pp. 57-59; "Methodists," pp. 91-94; "Unitarians," pp. 121-122.

MANWELL, REGINALD D., and SOPHIA L. FAHS, *The Church Across the Street*, Beacon Press, Chapter 4, "Michael Servetus, 1511-1553," pp. 52-68; Chapter 6, "Thomas Cranmer, 1489-1556," pp. 96-113; Chapter 7, "Robert Browne, 1550-1631," pp. 116-130; Chapter 9, "George Fox, 1624-1691," pp. 156-174; Chapter 10, "John Wesley, 1703-1791," pp. 176-196; Chapter 11, "Hosea Ballou, 1771-1852," pp. 198-210.

NOSS, JOHN B., *Man's Religions*, Macmillan, pp. 648-652; 656-660; 669-681.

ROSTEN, LEO, *A Guide to the Religions of America*, Simon and Schuster, "What Is a Congregationalist?" by Douglas Horton, pp. 31-37; "What Is an Episcopalian?" by W. Norman Pittenger, pp. 48-57; "What Is a Methodist?" by Ralph W. Sockman, pp. 82-90; "What Is a Quaker?" by Richmond P. Miller, pp. 121-132; "What Is a Unitarian?" by Karl M. Chworowsky, pp. 141-148.

SPENCE, HARTZELL, *The Story of America's Religions*, Holt, Rinehart, Winston, Chapter 1, "The Methodists," pp. 1-22; Chapter 5, "The Congregationalists," pp. 76-93; Chapter 8, "The Episcopalians," pp. 130-145; Chapter 14, "The Quakers," pp. 235-250.

12

PROTESTANTISM IN AMERICA

Effects of the Reformation   Although some criticisms of the Roman Catholic Church had been voiced earlier, Martin Luther's revolt signalled the real beginning of the Reformation. Once it began, a variety of factors—differences of belief and practice, conflicts between personalities, and peculiar national circumstances—led to the formation of the various Protestant denominations.

The Reformation also led to two other far-reaching developments. One was the movement within the Roman Catholic Church itself, generally called the "Counter-Reformation." Through this movement, the Church fought the spread of Protestantism—chiefly through the work of the Society of Jesus founded by Loyola—and it actually halted it in Hungary, Poland, and elsewhere. The second was a process of self-reform undertaken by the Church through various actions taken by the Council of Trent.

This Church Council opened its first session in December, 1545, with the reading of the following decree:

> Does it please you, for the praise and glory of the holy and undivided Trinity, Father, Son, and Holy Ghost, for the advance and exaltation of the Christian faith and religion, for the extirpation [rooting out] of heresies, for the peace and unity of the Church, for the reform

of the clergy and Christian people, for the suppression and destruction of the enemies of the Christian name, to decree and declare that the holy and general Council of Trent begins and has begun?

To which those present answered, "It pleases us."

Meeting on and off down to the year 1563, the Council of Trent succeeded in laying down fundamental Catholic doctrine and ending most of the abuses within the Church. Naturally, it rejected the Protestant belief in "justification by faith," and reaffirmed the authority of the Latin Scriptures, as interpreted by the Church, and the teachings of Catholic tradition as the basic sources of Christian truth. The priests and bishops were now instructed to preach regularly and provide public interpretation of the Bible. Regulations were also adopted for more careful supervision of the clergy, and certain former Church practices, such as the sale of indulgences, were deemed undesirable and ordered discontinued. These reforms produced a new zeal and enthusiasm for Catholicism among its followers.

However, an even more important result of the Protestant Reformation was the adoption of a different kind of relationship between religion and the state. Up until then, the rulers of most European countries considered themselves protectors of the Catholic faith. But, once other interpretations of Christianity became permanent, most states were forced to face problems of adjustment. One solution came about after numerous wars in Germany between Catholics and Protestants. Here, it was finally agreed that, though the ruler determined the official religion of the state, both religious groups were to enjoy equal rights. Consequently, it now became possible for German Catholics and Protestants to live together in relative peace.

A different solution was worked out in America. This was the doctrine of "the separation of church and state," which not only prohibited the adoption of a national religion, but barred all interference by the government in religious affairs.

This development had come about gradually, since originally most of the thirteen colonies had given a preferred position to some particular religion. As time passed, however, and the number of different religious groups in the New World multiplied, the colonies slowly found themselves forced to extend a greater measure of tolerance to settlers of other faiths. Eventually, several weeks before the Declaration of Independence, the people of Virginia issued a "Declaration of Rights" in which they asserted that "all men are equally entitled to the free exercise of religion." Later, the First Amendment to the newly-ratified Federal Constitution applied this principle to the nation as a whole with the statement, "Congress shall make no law respecting an establishment of religion." Thus, in the United States, religion was free to develop as it wished, and eventually, with the liberalization of various state constitutions, equal rights for all religious groups became universal.

This principle of "separation of church and state" contributed to the remarkable growth of Protestantism in America.

Protestantism in the United States　　In the United States today, there are approximately 62½ million Protestants, representing about a third of all Protestants in the world. As we have noted, slightly more than half the population of America associated with organized religion is Protestant, and, as the majority faith, it exerts a powerful influence upon the religious life of this country.

The chart on the following page shows the comparative size of the leading Protestant denominations in the United States. There we see that only eight different denominations with a membership of one million or more comprise some 55 million, or 86 per cent, of America's 62½ million Protestants. The remaining Protestants are found in about 300 separate denominations, most of which, however, have only a few thousand members or less.

And we also discover that the Baptists, with 21 million followers, comprise one-third of all Protestants in the United States. As such, it is America's largest denomination.

The Baptists　　How did the Baptist Church begin?

Its origins go back to the year 1525, when the Protestant authorities of Zurich, Switzerland, ordered all Christian children to be baptized.

BAPTIST RITE. Performed with complete immersion in the baptistry of the church, Baptism is never administered to a young child, since it requires a more mature acceptance of Christianity.

COMPARATIVE SIZE OF PROTESTANT DENOMINATIONS IN THE UNITED STATES *

 represents 500,000 members

TOTAL PROTESTANTS: 62½ MILLION

½% — CHRISTIAN SCIENTISTS about 300,000

½% — SEVENTH DAY ADVENTISTS 330,000

2% — MORMONS ** 1,500,000

4% — UNITED CHURCH OF CHRIST (Congregationalist) 2,250,000

5% — DISCIPLES OF CHRIST 3,000,000

5% — EPISCOPALIANS ** 3,250,000

7% — PRESBYTERIANS 4,250,000

13% — LUTHERANS 8,000,000

19% — METHODISTS 12,000,000

33½% — BAPTISTS 21,000,000

10½% — ALL OTHER DENOMINATIONS about 6,750,000

** Technically, neither group considers itself Protestant. However, since most people regard them as part of Protestantism and for the sake of convenience, we include them here in this category.

*Figures are for 1960

A number of parents refused because they believed that Baptism should be performed only at an age when one was capable of understanding its significance, generally in youth or young adulthood.

To them, unlike the Catholics, Baptism had no connection with the washing away of original sin, but represented the public acceptance of Christian faith. One could not just be born or brought into Christianity. It was something one had to accept with the full responsibility of one's mind and heart. Therefore, one simply could not be ready for Baptism and entry into Christianity until, as a grown person, he had personally come to believe in Christ.

These people had been nicknamed "Anabaptists," or "those baptized again." For, though they had originally been baptized as Catholic babies, they now insisted upon being rebaptized as adults in keeping with their new beliefs. Continuing to meet stubborn resistance to its decree, the Zurich government a year later ordered all Anabaptists to be imprisoned or drowned.

One of them was a man named Balthasar Hubmeier, a Swiss preacher who attracted a large following. Imprisoned and tortured in Zurich, he fled to Germany where he and others organized an Anabaptist movement in which each congregation had control of its own affairs. There they were opposed by both the Catholics and Lutherans, who could not bear the idea of not baptizing children and waiting for people to decide to be Christians. As a result, many of the Anabaptists were banished and their leaders martyred. In 1528, Hubmeier himself was burned to death in Vienna, and his wife drowned.

Yet the movement continued to spread. In the Netherlands, its supporters were known as "Mennonites," after the name of their leader, Menno Simons. Here a group of Englishmen, who had broken with the Church of England and had fled to Holland, first came into contact with their teachings. When some returned to London around 1611, they established the first permanent Baptist congregation in England.

The movement grew very slowly until the

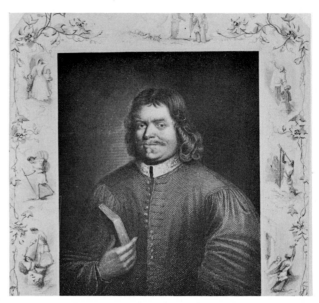

JOHN BUNYAN. Recognized as the leader of the young Baptist Church in England, he gained his chief fame as the writer of **Pilgrim's Progress.**

cause was taken up by two men in different lands. One was John Bunyan, the great writer of *Pilgrim's Progress,* an allegorical tale of how Christian, its hero, made his way from the City of Destruction to the Heavenly City of God. A mender of pots and pans by occupation, Bunyan became the minister of the Bedford Church in 1672 and eventually became recognized as leader of the Baptists in England. Throughout his life he endured the most severe poverty and was imprisoned for nearly fifteen years for the "unlicensed preaching" of his dissenting beliefs. Though he founded no organized movement, his wide-spread popularity as a writer gave new prestige to the Baptist cause.

Across the ocean, in far-away America, another man who broke with the Church of England was Roger Williams, organizer of the colony of Rhode Island. There, for the first time, the Church was free from control by the state. In the town of Providence, to which he fled from arrest in Massachusetts as a religious dissenter, he and eleven other colonists were rebaptized in 1639. It is from this date that the Baptists trace the beginnings of their movement in America.

The Baptist faith has enjoyed an amazing

growth in the United States, so much so that only 4 million of its 25 million followers live outside of this country. Instrumental in getting the First Amendment to the Constitution adopted, Baptists still insist upon complete religious liberty for everyone and remain the great champions of the separation of church and state in America. Significantly, it was the Baptists who were also the leaders in fighting for the independence of Texas when Mexico refused them religious freedom.

Among Baptists each church is sovereign and governs its own affairs, although there are some regional associations which carry on certain common tasks. Appealing mainly to the masses, the Baptist faith has no fixed creed, and there are wide variations in belief and practice. However, virtually all members believe in the Trinity, the majority in the Virgin Birth, and some in an actual heaven and hell. Communion is widely observed on the first Sunday of each month. Central in the church, in addition to the pulpit, is the baptistry, a water-tank several feet deep, where baptism through total immersion is performed, but only for those old enough to understand its meaning.

One activity that involves most Baptists is their missionary work. It is vigorously carried on, and, hence, it is not surprising that the famous evangelist, Billy Graham, should have come out of this Church. As Baptists conceive of their faith, it requires them to "spread the Gospel message" to everyone, and they carry on all types of missions both here and abroad. Particularly noteworthy have been their activities among the American Indians, Negroes, and Spanish-speaking peoples of the Southwest.

With their devotion to the free expression of their faith, it was inevitable that American Baptists should produce all sorts of congregations, subscribing to innumerable doctrines and forms of worship. As a result, the Baptists today represent a "family" of denominations, each with somewhat different emphases, rather than a single, common Church. They are organized within as many as 29 different loose federations, some practically all-white, and others Negro. The largest and most aggressive is the Southern Baptist Convention, which often refuses to cooperate with other Protestant groups.

The Disciples of Christ   Four other denominations deserve mention, not only because of their influence in the United States, but because they all originated in this country. One of them is the Disciples of Christ with a total world membership of about 3½ million. It is also known in various parts of America as the "Christian Church" or "Churches of Christ."

Though its origins go back earlier, the Disciples Church was officially organized as the result of two separate efforts. One was begun in 1803 in Kentucky under the leadership of Barton W. Stone, and the other, in 1809 in western Pennsylvania and western Virginia, with Thomas Campbell. Both were well-educated Presbyterian ministers who advocated a form of Christianity that followed the practices and organization of the early Church as pictured by the New Testament. They also believed that there should be one movement which would cut across denominational lines and unite all Christians. Yet, like many other movements intended to unite all sects or religions, this one quickly became another of the particular groups it set out to replace.

During these early years of the nineteenth century, large numbers of Americans were moving westward. Many of the pioneers were religious folk who had been affiliated with some church back home, but there were also a great number who did not belong to any. Both Stone and Campbell saw this as a real opportunity for bringing all the pioneers into one church, without denominational differences and subscribing to the practices of New Testament times. Winning the unchurched and overcoming denominational loyalties was difficult, but each succeeded in attracting a substantial following. Finally, in 1832, they merged their separate groups to form the Disciples of Christ.

Among the Disciples today, each church is completely independent; hence the forms of organization and worship vary. Some churches, for instance, do not permit the use of instrumental music. However, most do, and usually the church of the Disciples has a pastor, elders who concern themselves with religious matters, and deacons who handle the business affairs. At their services, the Disciples carry on Communion every Sunday, and Baptism by complete immersion of those who have reached the age of understanding.

Many Christians have been attracted to the Disciples precisely because the Church maintains complete liberty of conscience and each person's right to interpret the Scriptures according to his own understanding. There is no official creed, and the Disciples enjoy a wide latitude of belief. Consequently, though most of the members believe in the Trinity, the Virgin Birth, and the sinfulness of man who can only be redeemed through the sacrifice of Christ, others do not.

The Disciples continue to regard themselves, not as a separate denomination, but as the movement designed to bring all Protestants into one united Christian Church.

The Mormons   Mormonism is another faith native to the United States. Technically, its followers claim that they are not Protestants since they hold that their religion grew directly out of a divine revelation to their founder. Yet, in terms of many of its beliefs and practices, Mormonism shares most of the elements of Protestantism.

"Mormon" is the usual term for a member of the Church of Jesus Christ of the Latter-Day Saints. Numbering about a million and a half, the movement is divided into six separate groups. The largest is in Utah, with headquarters in Salt Lake City.

Mormonism was founded by Joseph Smith, a farmer who lived in New York State. In 1820, he received a vision of two angels urging him to prepare mankind for the second coming of Jesus Christ by restoring the teachings of the Gospels. In another vision, an angel entrusted to Smith's care a series of golden plates written in a strange language and a set of prism-like eyeglasses to help him translate them. These plates, transcribed by Smith, his wife, and a friend, were published as *The Book of Mormon* in 1829.

The Book claims to be a series of prophetic

MORMONISM. On the left, Joseph Smith, a New York farmer, who claimed a revelation calling upon him to prepare the world for Christ's return. Years later, his followers fled to Utah where they built Salt Lake City. On the right are pictures of that city's great religious structures: (above) the interior of the Mormon Tabernacle; (below) the white-domed Tabernacle, with the Salt Lake Temple to its right.

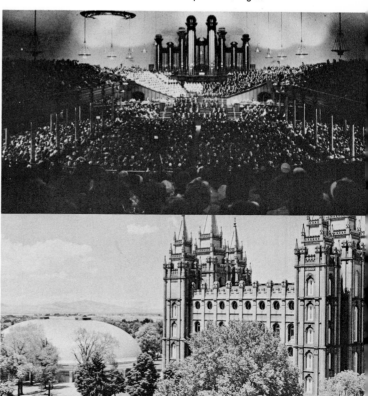

writings which, among many other things, predicts their own revelation to Smith and his co-workers. For one of the passages in *The Book of Mormon* states:

> And it shall come to pass that the Lord God shall bring forth unto you a book. . . . A revelation from God from the beginning of the world to the ending thereof . . . shall be delivered unto the man of whom I have spoken. The book shall be hid from the eyes of the world that the eyes of none shall behold it, save it be that three witnesses shall behold it by the power of God.

The Book of Mormon contains revelations said to be compiled by the prophet Mormon, a descendant of the lost tribes of Israel. Hence, the Mormons believe that they are the modern descendants of God's "Chosen People." The book relates the history of two migrations of Israelites. One began during the period of the Tower of Babel. The second occurred some time after the destruction of the Kingdoms of Israel and Judah, when Israelites occupied the North American continent, and a portion of the group became the ancestors of the American Indians. Christ, after his resurrection, visited these Israelites and bestowed "pure" Christianity upon them. He promised to return in the "latter days."

Smith and five other men believed that they were living in this period of the "latter days," just prior to the second appearance of Jesus, and they organized their own church in 1830. As it grew, it produced a number of strong communities in the Midwest, but the separatism of the Mormons and their attacks upon the teachings of other churches aroused people against them.

Eventually, the bitterness toward them exploded into mob violence. Smith and others were martyred. The rest of the people were driven out of their Missouri settlements. Now, under the leadership of Brigham Young, they were forced to begin a long, sad trek westward during which six thousand perished. Finally, in 1847, the group came to the desert-like region around the Great Salt Lake in Utah, "a land that nobody wanted." With much suffering and hard work, the people gradually built Salt Lake City with its magnificent Mormon Tabernacle and Temple, and established their permanent headquarters there.

The Mormons believe in the second coming of Jesus, who is the son of God and the intermediary between man and God. Then, if worthy, the followers of Mormonism will be resurrected and live a divine life in God's Kingdom, which will be located on the American continent. They accept belief in the Trinity, the Virgin Birth, and a physical heaven and hell. They also practice Communion and Baptism, immersing only those over eight years of age and following it with a simple Confirmation. At the age of twelve, all males are expected to be ordained to the "priesthood," a ministry of laymen.

The Mormon Church operates under a strong central organization consisting of a "First Presidency" of three presiding "high priests." Below them are a Council of Twelve Apostles and other officials. There is no professional clergy, and laymen take turns in filling the positions of bishops and priests for a term. Young adults may even be drafted as missionaries for a two-year period at their own expense.

The group is known for its many distinctive beliefs and practices, which are incorporated into a close-knit Mormon fellowship and way of life. It regards *The Book of Mormon* as having equal authority with the Bible, and Joseph Smith, Brigham Young, and others of its leaders, as prophets. It believes that people still receive divine revelations and that the presiding officials of the Church hold the keys to the Kingdom of God.

Mormons give ten per cent of their income to the Church, a practice derived from the "tithing" carried on by the Jews in Bible times, and anyone in need is promptly cared for. The group does not believe in divorce or intermarriage with others, and the members are prohibited from drinking, smoking, and using tea or coffee. Non-Mormons are called "Gentiles"; hence according to their terminology, Jews are likewise known as "Gentiles." At one time the Mormons practiced polygamy, but it was abolished by the Church nearly seventy years ago.

The Seventh Day Adventists   Seventh Day Adventism is another Protestant sect that arose in the United States. Its roots go back to the period beginning around the 1820's, when there was a strong feeling among certain Protestants in England as well as the United States that the second coming of Jesus was rapidly approaching. Clergymen were openly preaching the "advent," or reappearance of Christ, and enthusiasm among the masses began to run high.

One who was stirred by the idea was an American farmer named William Miller. He had served as a captain in the War of 1812, and then about 1818, after two years of studying the Bible carefully, Miller became convinced that Christ was coming quite soon. On the basis of a verse in the Book of Daniel, he began preaching that Jesus would appear in 1843. Thousands of people flocked to him, awaiting the return of Christ.

When 1843 passed without the expected event, Miller announced that he had made an error in his calculations, and that Jesus would come on October 22 of the following year. There was a revival of excitement among his followers. Many sold their businesses and gathered on housetops and hills to welcome Jesus, only to be disappointed once more. Now most of his following melted away. But there were still some who believed in him, especially since it was now said that the second coming of Christ was not at hand but only the "final stage of

SEVENTH DAY ADVENTISTS. (upper left) An Adventist church. (below) A conference of the membership held in 1958 in Cleveland. The Church stresses the immanent return of Christ, the literal truth of the Bible, and the strict observance of Friday night and Saturday as the true Sabbath.

prophecy," prior to the end of the world. Christ, they said, had now entered the heavenly sanctuary to minister there as priest, and he had already commenced his investigation of mankind in anticipation of the final judgment. With this reinterpretation a group known as the Adventists was formed in 1845.

Since then the movement has split into four different sects, the largest of which is the Seventh Day Adventists. It has a membership of more than 300,000 in the United States, and about a million in the world-at-large. The group derives its name from its observance of Saturday, instead of Sunday, as the Sabbath. The members point out that both the calendar itself as well as the traditions of the Jews confirm the fact that Saturday is the seventh day. Hence, to them it is the real Sabbath to be kept free of all work and observed with services which even young babies are expected to attend.

Seventh Day Adventists still maintain that Jesus is coming soon. First, however, the end of the world must take place with great upheaval and destruction. When Jesus returns, the earth will be purified by fire, and he and his followers will live together forever.

The movement is organized under a General Conference, which appoints the clergy and establishes the religious policy of the Church. The members believe in the Virgin Birth and salvation through Jesus Christ; they practice Baptism and Communion, and accept the Bible literally. All Adventists tithe, and some of them also observe certain of the Jewish dietary laws.

Adventists have long been dedicated to the promotion of sound health measures, emphasizing sunshine, fresh air, and simple diet. Many also advocate vegetarianism. From all of this has sprung the creation of many Adventist health institutions and medical schools. Interestingly, it also led one of its members, John Kellogg, to produce the first corn flakes, from which has come the present-day American practice of eating dry breakfast cereals.

The Christian Scientists   The youngest of the four American-born Christian religious movements is Christian Science, which originated with Mrs. Mary Baker Eddy in the second half of the nineteenth century. Sickly most of her life, she ultimately found recovery through her religious experiences, and this prompted her to organize a movement based upon healing through faith.

The daughter of a New Hampshire land-owner, Mary Baker Eddy had her first experience with religious healing at the age of 12. At her mother's recommendation, she prayed during an illness and her fever promptly disappeared. Then, at the age of 45, she had a similar experience. Severely injured by a fall on an icy street, she lay for three days in critical condition. However, upon opening the Bible and reading an account of Jesus' healing, she immediately recovered.

She began to study the Bible intensively. Then she became a practitioner of "Christian science," helping to heal people and training others to carry on the work. In 1876, she and several of her students formed the Christian Science Association, and three years later in Boston, they founded the First Church of Christ, Scientist, the Mother Church of the movement.

Since then, the movement has grown to more than 3,000 churches throughout the world, with an estimated membership of a half-million members, of whom more than 300,000 live in the United States. (The Church does not permit a census of its members.) In addition to many books, the movement also publishes an excellent daily newspaper, *The Christian Science Monitor*, which supplies its readers with outstanding coverage of world events, without, however, scandalous or sensational stories. Interestingly, too, in line with the views of the movement, it rarely mentions the word "death."

Briefly, Christian Science believes that, since God is good, He cannot have created the evil in the world, like sickness, sorrow, sin, or death. All of these have to do only with our material existence and are truly unreal. What is real are the things of the spirit. Therefore, if man is able to develop genuine religious faith, if he can learn to live the life of the spirit, he can overcome the illusions of illness and pain. Thus, released from pain and suffering, he remains well. In fact, this is the only form of healing that the Church recognizes, and it emphatically rejects the need for medicines, doctors, or hospitals.

Consequently, its teachings maintain that through study and prayer under its guidance, and without medical aid, the individual can overcome disease. As proof, the Church points to the many cases of healing by Jesus, who is considered the first teacher of Christian Science. Particularly do Christian Scientists cite this passage from the Gospel of Mark in which Jesus says:

> And these signs will accompany those who believe: In My name they will cast out demons; they will speak in new tongues; they will pick up serpents, and if they drink any deadly thing, it will not hurt them; they will lay their hands on the sick, and they will recover.
> —Mark 16:17-18

Christian Scientists consider themselves part of Protestantism, although many Protestants

MOTHER CHURCH. The Christian Science Church of Boston maintains strict control over the movement. Pictured here is a service being conducted in the Mother Church.

do not accept them. Hence, they are not members of the National Council of the Churches of Christ in America.

Christian Scientists believe in the Virgin Birth and their own form of the Trinity in which Jesus is not the Deity, but the divine son of God. They do not practice either Baptism or Communion. The Church holds its service on Sunday morning, and conducts a gathering during midweek in which people give testimonials of cures they have had. Indeed, Christian Science claims for itself many remarkable cures.

All local churches are under the strict control of the Mother Church in Boston, which is managed by a permanent Board of Directors. Christian Science has no ordained clergymen or pastors. The first and second readers in the church function as ministers and read from the Bible, with the aid of Mrs. Eddy's *Science and Health with Key to the Scriptures*, a basic

FOUNDER. Mary Baker Eddy, born in 1821 in New Hampshire, developed the practice of religious healing that led to the creation of the Christian Science Church.

DEVELOPMENT OF PROTESTANT DENOMINATIONS

DISCIPLES OF CHRIST
MORMON
SEVENTH DAY ADVENTIST
CHRISTIAN SCIENCE

DISCIPLES OF CHRIST	MORMON	WORLD EVENTS	SEVENTH DAY ADVENTIST	CHRISTIAN SCIENCE
1803 Barton Stone organizes churches in Kentucky.				
1809 Thomas Campbell organizes churches in Pennsylvania and Virginia.				
		1815 Napoleon finally defeated.		
			1818 William Miller becomes convinced of approaching advent of Christ.	
	1820 Joseph Smith receives vision of two angels.		**1820's** Beginning of general feeling among some Protestants of Jesus' second coming.	**1821** Mary Baker Eddy born.
	1829 *The Book of Mormon* translated.			
	1830 First church established.			
1832 Disciples movement united.		**1833** Britain outlaws slavery.		
			1843 Christ due to appear, according to Miller, also **1844**.	
			1845 Organized Adventist movement formed.	
	1847 Brigham Young leads Mormons to Utah.			
		1854 Crimean War.		
		1861 Civil War in America.		
				1866 Mrs. Eddy recovers from fall.
				1876 Christian Science Association formed.
				1879 Mother Church established in Boston.

text in the movement. There are also trained practitioners, paid like physicians on a fee basis, who counsel and pray with those who seek help.

Variations Without End   We have now dealt with twelve of the most influential and representative churches within the broad mainstream of the Protestant faith. Though they comprise nearly 90 per cent of all Protestants in the United States, by no means do they exhaust all of the varieties of Protestantism found on the American scene. Often, from signs along the highways, literature received through the mail, radio broadcasts, house-to-house appeals, and newspaper reports of their activities, we hear of a great many other groups.

The truth is that within American Protestantism there are probably more than 300 different sects. Some are represented by only a single congregation, while others may have as many as several hundred thousand members. And because of the similarities of their names— sometimes a new sect may adopt the name of an already-existing one—it is quite confusing even to Christians to distinguish between them. For instance, there are many different sects that bear the name of "Church of God" and "Church of Christ."

Historically, these sects have come into being mainly among the less educated and poorer classes. Many are offshoots of larger denominations, like the Primitive Baptists and Freewill Baptists, who broke away from the established Baptist Church, or the Nazarene and Holiness Churches, which left the ranks of Methodism. Some, however, such as the House of David or Father Divine's Peace Mission, have developed spontaneously within the ranks of Protestantism.

Whatever their origins, these sects offer an endless variety of practices and beliefs. Most, however, seem to fall into four main categories, though elements of each may be found within a single sect.

One type, generally an offshoot of some larger denomination, is characterized by either its opposition to a certain practice or belief of the parent group, or by its insistence upon something it deems essential to "genuine" faith. Often this is traced back to the New Testament and, therefore, viewed as "true to the nature of original Christianity."

So there are Seventh Day Baptists who observe Saturday as the Sabbath instead of Sunday, and certain Churches of Christ which forbid all instrumental music in worship since it is unauthorized by the New Testament. The adoption of all sorts of practices, such as footwashing, anointing with oil, special kinds of baptism, and particular forms of dress, have repeatedly given rise to new church groups.

The second type, of which Jehovah's Witnesses is a good example, can be classified as "Adventists"; that is, sects which foresee the approaching end of the world through some great catastrophe, and the ultimate reappearance of Christ. They offer escape to their followers from the fiery hell and promise them a glorious hereafter. Because of the urgency of their message, these sects are generally quite forceful in trying to persuade and convert all who seem unaware of the coming cataclysm.

A third type of sect is one that forms a separate community of its own. In this category we find such groups as the House of David and the United Society of Believers, more commonly known as the Shakers. Because the members of such sects generally believe that it is society which is responsible for much of man's sinfulness, they will band together to create a "new society" and thereby protect themselves from the evils of the outside world. Usually the community shares everything in common. Some, like the Shakers, believe in complete celibacy; others, like the now extinct Oneida Community of New York State, have practiced multiple marriage. Such communities present a great many other differences in belief and practice.

The last, but undoubtedly the most common type of these Protestant sects, is one which places its chief stress upon having the Holy Spirit take possession of the individual with a great rebirth of "faith." This is most often marked by some kind of intense emotionalism, such as falling into a trance, a seizure, or

PENTECOSTAL WORSHIP. Springing up in vacant stores and private homes, Pentecostal sects of all types conduct services that stress the inspiration of the Holy Spirit. Instrumental music and singing, accompanied by vigorous evangelistic preaching, contribute to the high degree of emotionalism that characterizes these sects.

"speaking with tongues," babbling in some strange language or unintelligible jargon.

The name usually given to such sects is "Pentecostal," after the term describing the fiftieth day following the resurrection of Christ. For, as stated by the New Testament:

> When the day of Pentecost had come, they [the apostles] were all together in one place. And suddenly a sound came from heaven like the rush of a mighty wind and it filled all the house where they were sitting. And there appeared to them tongues as of fire, distributed and resting on each one of them. And they were all filled with the Holy Spirit and began to speak in other tongues, as the Spirit gave them utterance.
> —Acts 2:1-4

Hence, Pentecostal sects are those given to the inspiration of the Holy Spirit as manifested by acts of emotion. The so-called Holy Rollers, who throw themselves on the ground and roll with great ecstasy when the Spirit stirs them, represent one form. More extreme are the various snake cults, where individuals, moved by the Spirit and believing themselves under its protection, will freely handle rattlesnakes and other poisonous reptiles.

The most common variety, however, is that represented by the numerous branches of the Church of God. Their form of worship is marked by repeated revivals that feature singing, Scripture-reading, fiery evangelistic preaching, and "testimonials" by the worshippers to their finding "faith." During these

150

services the people often display a high degree of emotionalism involving trances or seizures of various kinds. The high point is reached when the worshippers are called upon to be "saved" by coming forward, confessing their sins and experiencing God's forgiveness. It is then that individuals often "see the light" and are moved to even greater ecstasy.

The Protestants Strive for Greater Unity

With the existence of so many sects, each interpreting Christianity somewhat differently, it becomes extremely difficult to define Protestantism. But this is true even if one only considers the major denominations. For instance, the Unitarians, who are usually classified as Protestants, are not regarded as such by most of the other denominations. The Christian Scientists, who call themselves Protestants, do not carry on two of its most common rites, Baptism and Communion. The Episcopalians insist that they are really not Protestants but "Catholics," though not part of the *Roman* Catholic Church.

Many Protestant leaders today deplore the movement's lack of unity, and have tried to find common bases upon which all Protestants can agree. Beyond the fact that its followers are Christians who do not accept the authority of the Roman Catholic or Eastern Orthodox Churches, they cite the following six elements that seem to be shared by most denominations: (1) belief in salvation through faith in Jesus Christ; (2) belief in the Trinity or in some special relationship of Jesus to God; (3) belief in the Bible as the highest source of religious authority; (4) belief in the Church as an instrument of Christian faith; (5) acceptance of a code of desirable Christian behavior; (6) certain distinctively Christian practices, such as Baptism and Communion.

Yet, within each of these categories, we find differences of interpretation, both between and among the various denominations. Some Protestants regard the Bible as literally true, others view it as containing truth which must be sifted from legend and tradition. Most Protestants associate salvation with the hereafter, but some view it principally in connection with this world. And, among the various denominations, there are many different meanings given to particular Christian beliefs such as "original sin," "heaven," "hell," and the like.

Nevertheless, in recent years Protestants have been earnestly seeking greater unity through several means. One is the merger of various denominations, and it is reported that during the past century more than a hundred have taken place all over the world. An example is the recent union between the Congregationalists and the Evangelical and Reformed Church. This was achieved in 1957 after some twenty years of negotiations.

A second force working for greater unity among Christians is the "ecumenical" or worldwide movement of cooperation between all denominations, both nationally and internationally. In 1908, the Federal Council of the Churches of Christ in America was organized. Known today as the National Council of the Churches of Christ in the United States of America, it comprises some 25 different Protestant denominations and seven Eastern Orthodox bodies. All told, it represents nearly 40 million church members.

In 1948, the World Council of the Churches of Christ was established in Amsterdam. Its membership in 1961 comprised 185 different denominations located in more than 60 countries, and included most of the Eastern Orthodox churches as well as practically all of the largest Protestant groups in the United States. All told, this represents some 350 million Christians engaged in promoting greater cooperation between the various denominations. The World Council and other movements are also contributing to the enlargement of Protestant thinking in line with the needs and developments in modern life. The Vatican Ecumenical Council that began in 1962 sought to promote understanding between Catholics and Protestants.

From all indications, therefore, it appears likely that the trend toward greater harmony within Christianity will continue. But because of the many differences that do exist, it is improbable that all Protestants will ever be part of one single, united Church.

DENOMINATIONS AND MEMBERSHIP	CHURCH ORGANIZATION	CHIEF PRACTICES	MAJOR BELIEFS
BAPTIST U.S. — 21 million World — 25 million	Each church independent. Twenty-nine loose federations in the U.S.	2 sacraments: Communion (once a month) and Baptism (by immersion and only for those old enough to understand its meaning).	No fixed creed and wid variations in doctrine Belief in Trinity, Virgi Birth (many), actua heaven and hell (some Fundamentalists believe in literal truth of th Bible; liberals do no Stresses separation o church and state and re ligious liberty.
CHRISTIAN SCIENCE U. S. — About 300,000 World — ½ million	All churches controlled by Mother Church. No ordained clergy, but lay readers and practitioners.	No sacraments. Sunday service of readings; midweek meeting for testimonials of cures.	Trinity (as reinterprete with Jesus as divine so of God), Virgin Birth. Il ness and evil are unrea and can be overcome b faith and prayer. Reject medical aid.
UNITED CHURCH OF CHRIST (Congregationalist) U.S. — 2¼ million World — 3¼ million	Each church independent. Ordained ministers, including women. Accepts ministers of other denominations.	2 sacraments: Communion and Baptism. Simple worship with emphasis on sermon.	Wide variations in doc trine. Belief in Trinity Virgin Birth (some). Em phasizes independence o each congregation, free in terpretation of the Bibl and interdenominationa cooperation.
DISCIPLES OF CHRIST U.S. — 3 million World — 3½ million	Each church independent. Ordained ministers.	2 sacraments: Communion and Baptism (by immersion and only for those old enough to understand its meaning).	No official creed and wid variations in doctrine Belief in Trinity, Virgi Birth, actual heaven an hell (many), basic sinful ness of man (some). At tempts to adhere to Chris tianity of New Testamen times. Seeks to unite al Christians in a singl Church.
EPISCOPALIAN U.S. — 3¼ million World — 32 million	All churches under supervision of dioceses and General Convention. Ordained clergy: bishops, priests and deacons. Monks and nuns.	In high church, all 7 sacraments and semi-Catholic ritual. In low church, only 2 sacraments (Communion and Baptism) and less formal worship.	Trinity, Virgin Birth, doe not call self "Protestant. Regards all Christians a united in one indivisibl Church. Represents com promise between Protes tanism and Catholicism
LUTHERAN U.S. — 8 million World — 75 million	All churches under supervision of Synods. Ordained clergy selected by individual churches.	2 sacraments: Baptism and Communion. Carries on modified forms of Catholic worship.	Trinity, Virgin Birth Eventually Christ wil come and judge all souls Salvation comes throug belief alone. Requires onl belief in God and Christ

PROTESTANT DENOMINATIONS

DENOMINATIONS AND MEMBERSHIP	CHURCH ORGANIZATION	CHIEF PRACTICES	MAJOR BELIEFS
PRESBYTERIAN U.S.—4¼ million World —43 million	All churches under supervision of Presbyteries, Synods and General Assembly. Ordained ministers elected by each church. Emphasis upon elected officials.	2 sacraments: Communion and Baptism. Originally plain bare churches, but increasing use of symbolism in worship.	Trinity, Virgin Birth (many), heaven and hell (many). No longer teaches predestination. God has complete control over the universe. It is man's responsibility to receive salvation through his faith in Christ. "Priesthood of all believers."
METHODIST U.S.—12 million World—18 million	All churches under supervision of Annual Conference and General Conference. Ordained clergy: bishops, superintendents, ministers.	2 sacraments: Baptism and Communion. Variations in type of service between near Episcopal and less formal.	Trinity (most), Virgin Birth (most), and judgment after death. Emphasizes inner experiences of religion and its application to the needs of society.
MORMON **(Church of the Latter-Day Saints)** U.S.—1½ million World—1½ million	All churches under control of presidency of 3 "high priests." No ordained clergy.	2 sacraments: Baptism (by immersion and only for those 8 years and older) followed by Confirmation and Communion.	Trinity, Virgin Birth, actual heaven and hell. Belief in second coming of Jesus. Book of Mormon considered sacred. Do not consider themselves Protestants.
QUAKER **(Society of Friends)** U.S. — 125,000 World — 300,000	Each "church" independent. Many have no ministers.	No sacraments. Wide variety of service, though basic form is Sunday meeting of silence interrupted only by those wishing to speak, pray or read from the Bible.	No official creed and wide freedom of personal opinion on Trinity, Virgin Birth. Man is essentially good, and with guidance of God's spirit (the "inner light") he can overcome evil in the world. Belief in service to fellow man, peace, and absolute honesty.
UNITARIAN AND UNIVERSALIST U.S. — 200,000 World — ½ million	Each church independent. Ordained ministers.	Practice varies. Where observed, the sacraments of Baptism and Communion are reinterpreted.	One God (not Trinity). Jesus regarded as human teacher of great religious values. Man is basically good and finds salvation through his efforts to help his fellow man.
SEVENTH DAY ADVENTISTS U.S. — 330,000 World — 1 million	All churches under supervision of General Conference. Ordained ministers.	2 sacraments: Baptism and Communion. Observance of Saturday as the Sabbath. Some practice certain Jewish dietary laws.	Trinity, Virgin Birth, actual heaven and hell. Believe in second coming of Jesus soon, to be preceded by end of the world and its purification by fire.

Judaism and Protestantism Comparisons between Judaism and Protestantism as a whole are difficult because of the different interpretations found among the latter's many denominations. Yet, as we have observed, there are certain elements that may be considered characteristic of Protestantism in general. Among them is belief in the doctrines of original sin, personal salvation through faith in Jesus Christ, and some form of the Trinity. In addition, at least two observances, Baptism and Communion, are carried on by most Protestants.

In general, Judaism differs just as fundamentally with the Protestant form of Christianity as it does with the Roman Catholic. It cannot view Jesus as either the "son of God" or "divine," since to the Jew, God remains strictly one, never a Trinity.

Nor can it accept the basic Christian beliefs in the doctrine of original sin and salvation through Jesus Christ. And despite certain reinterpretations of original sin, connecting it more with man's inner compulsion to sin rather than tracing his sinfulness back to the fall of Adam, Jews continue to regard this as limiting the real freedom of man. Judaism maintains that man enters life fully without sin and has complete freedom within himself to resist and overcome evil.

Moreover, salvation in Jewish terms is achieved through faithfulness to the ancient covenant between God and Israel, and this involves righteous conduct in accordance with God's Law as part of the Mission of the Jewish people to bring about His Kingdom upon earth. Consequently, Judaism rejects the central Protestant teaching of "justification through faith in Jesus Christ."

There are, of course, many other significant differences between Judaism and Protestantism. For instance, neither Baptism nor Communion, connected as they are with the life and death of Jesus, can have any place in the synagogue. And, whereas Protestantism regards the Old and New Testaments as the chief source of its religious authority, Judaism rejects the New Testament and relies exclusively upon its Hebrew Scriptures and the long centuries of rabbinical interpretation as embodied in the Oral Law.

So much, then, for some of the principal distinctions between Judaism and Protestantism as a whole. But Judaism finds important differences even with those faiths, such as Unitarianism and Christian Science, whose connection with Protestantism is disputed. For we must remember that Unitarianism, despite its abandonment of the Trinity, is still deeply rooted in the Christian tradition and derives its beliefs and observances chiefly from the message and activities of Jesus. Moreover, it lacks those concepts which lie at the very heart of Judaism, such as its belief in the ancient covenant between God and Israel and the historic Mission of the Jewish people.

Similarly, Christian Science is also grounded in the teachings and deeds of Jesus, and its central beliefs grow out of the traditions of Christianity. More than this, however, Judaism opposes the Christian Scientist's denial of the real existence of the body and his belief in healing strictly through faith. Judaism has always insisted that pain and suffering are realities and that the employment of medical aid in illness is a religious duty. In fact, the Talmud actually prohibits a scholar from living in any community that does not have a physician.

All of this does not mean that there are not certain concerns that Judaism and Protestantism share in common. For example, with Protestantism as a whole, Judaism insists upon the highest standards of moral and ethical conduct. With the Unitarians and Methodists, the Jew is vitally interested in the welfare of his fellow man and society in general, and with the Baptists, he champions religious liberty and the separation of church and state. With the Congregationalists, the Jew insists upon the independence of the individual congregation, and with the Quakers, he has a deep commitment to advance the cause of brotherliness and peace.

Nevertheless, we should remember that these have always been concerns of Judaism. To a large extent, Protestantism has emphasized them because it has drawn so heavily from the

COMPARISON BETWEEN KEY BELIEFS OF PROTESTANTS AND JEWS

(Because Protestantism offers so many different interpretations of Christian teachings, the statement of Protestant beliefs here can be true only in the most general sense. They are presented here simply for purposes of comparison with the teachings of Judaism.)

PROTESTANTS		JEWS
Belief in Christ is the only true religion. No one true Church, but a fellowship of all Christians.	**TRUE RELIGION**	Regards Judaism as the truest of all faiths and the only religion for Jews. Other faiths, in so far as they promote righteousness, possess some truth.
One universal God in the form of the Trinity composed of the Father, Son, and Holy Spirit. God is approached through Christ.	**DEITY**	One universal God with whom man stands in direct relationship.
The Christ, the divine Son of God. Most accept Virgin Birth.	**JESUS**	A Jew who taught many already-existing Jewish ideals. However, his emphasis upon the approaching Kingdom of God led him to somewhat different interpretations.
Belief in original sin of man (variously interpreted) accepted by most. Therefore man requires redemption.	**MAN**	Man, born without sin, has the capacity to live righteously, and sin can be avoided and overcome by man.
Being "saved" from sin which brings deliverance in the hereafter and (for some) in this world.	**SALVATION**	The establishment of God's Kingdom of universal and everlasting righteousness, justice, peace upon earth. Achieved with God's aid through righteous living according to His Law and as part of the Mission of Israel. Salvation possible for all righteous people.
Granted directly by Christ through the faith of the individual.	**REMOVAL OF SIN**	Accomplished by repentance, prayer, making amends, and determination to lead a righteous life.
Heaven and hell for most, although variously interpreted. General belief in punishment and reward after death.	**HEREAFTER**	Perfected society of mankind in a Kingdom of God. Liberal Jews do not believe in a literal heaven or hell but maintain that all men's souls return to God.
Old and New Testaments as interpreted by the individual.	**AUTHORITY**	The Written Law (Hebrew Scriptures) and Oral Law (rabbinic interpretation and tradition). Individual freedom of interpretation.

"Old Testament" and the accounts of the life of Jesus, rooted as it was in the Judaism of his times. It is our strong conviction that the more fervently Jews remain true to their own religious ideals, the more they strengthen their Protestant brothers in those areas which both hold in common. Thus the work of bringing all men to know God and live by His law is furthered.

What Happened to Judaism? Christianity has long held the belief that, with the coming of Jesus, Judaism's task was completed. For, according to Paul and others, faith in Christ replaced the older laws of Moses and the teachings of the prophets. Thus, many, if not the majority of Christians today, believe that once Christianity appeared, Judaism ceased to progress. Undoubtedly influenced by this concept, even the noted English historian Arnold Toynbee once classified the modern Jew as a "fossil."

Yet the world is slowly coming to know better. More and more Christian scholars today have discovered that, far from remaining as it was some 1900 years ago, Judaism continued to develop. A number, including George Foot Moore, R. Travers Herford, and others, have written glowingly of the achievements of Judaism in the centuries following the death of Jesus. Many more have begun to recognize the contributions of Judaism in the medieval and modern world. For instance, in a recent book dealing with the relationship between modern Judaism and Christianity, the well-known Anglican clergyman James Parkes included a chapter that had to be called "The Rediscovery That Jews Are a Living People and Judaism a Living Religion."

To the Jew, of course, the fact that Judaism has continued to develop over the past two thousand years comes as no surprise. Jews have always felt that their covenant with God meant that He will preserve them even as they try to live by His law. As a matter of historical fact, the existence of a vast literature including the Mishnah, Talmud, Midrash, Codes, and many other important religious works, proves to the Jew that far from being "fossils," the Jewish people have remained highly creative.

Indeed, we can safely say that much of Judaism as we know it today is the product of those developments. . . .

TOPICS TO DISCUSS

1. What particular contributions have the various American Protestant denominations made to your own life as an American Jew? How, in turn, have they been influenced by Judaism?
2. How do you account for the fact that, unlike the situation within Judaism, so many different sects exist within Protestantism?
3. In what ways does modern Judaism differ from the more religiously-liberal Protestant faiths, such as the Congregationalists and Unitarians? What do they appear to share in common?
4. What trends do you observe among the Protestants in the United States, and how do you account for them?

THINGS TO DO

1. Construct a chart comparing the teachings and practices of the Baptists, Disciples of Christ, Mormons, Seventh Day Adventists, and Christian Scientists with those of modern Judaism.
2. Securing the necessary information from your local Council of Churches, prepare a report on the kinds of activities presently carried on in your community through cooperation between the different Protestant denominations.
3. Attend the worship service of one of the more religiously-liberal Protestant faiths and prepare a report on the similarities and differences with your own Sabbath service.

OTHER THINGS TO READ

CLARK, ELMER T., *The Small Sects in America*, Abingdon-Cokesbury.
LANDIS, BENSON Y., *World Religions*, Dutton, "Adventists," pp. 15-18; "Baptists," pp. 25-30; "Brethren Churches," pp. 30-31; "Christian

Science," pp. 44-46; "Churches of Christ," pp. 46-47; "Churches of God," pp. 47-49; "Disciples of Christ," pp. 52-53; "Evangelistic Associations," p. 57; "International Church of the Foursquare Gospel," p. 66; "Jehovah's Witnesses," pp. 72-74; "Latter-Day Saints," pp. 79-83; "Mennonites," pp. 87-91; "Moravians," pp. 95-96; "Nazarene, Church of," pp. 96-97; "New Jerusalem, Churches of," pp. 97-98; "Old Catholic Churches," pp. 98-99; "Pentecostal Churches," pp. 99-100; "Reformed Churches," pp. 108-110; "Salvation Army," pp. 115-116.

MANWELL, REGINALD D., and SOPHIA L. FAHS, *The Church Across the Street*, Beacon Press, Chapter 8, "John Bunyan, 1628-1688," pp. 132-154; Chapter 12, "Joseph Smith, 1805-1844," pp. 212-228; Chapter 13, "Mary Baker Eddy, 1821-1910," pp. 230-242.

NOSS, JOHN B., *Man's Religions*, Macmillan, pp. 652-656; 674-681.

ROSTEN, LEO, *A Guide to the Religions of America*, Simon and Schuster, "What Is a Baptist?" by William B. Lipphard, pp. 1-8; "What Is a Christian Scientist?" by George Channing, pp. 21-30; "Who Are the Disciples of Christ?" by James E. Craig, pp. 38-47; "Who Are Jehovah's Witnesses?" by Milton G. Henschel, pp. 58-64; "What Is a 'Mormon'?" by Richard L. Evans, pp. 91-100; "What Is a Protestant?" by Henry P. Van Dusen, pp. 111-120; "What Is a Seventh-Day Adventist?" by Arthur S. Maxwell, pp. 133-140; "Doctrines and Beliefs," pp. 175-195.

SPENCE, HARTZELL, *The Story of America's Religions*, Holt, Rinehart, Winston, pp. x-xii; Chapter 2, "The Baptists," pp. 23-38; Chapter 10, "The Seventh-Day Adventists," pp. 165-182; Chapter 11, "The Disciples of Christ," pp. 183-197; Chapter 12, "The Mormons," pp. 198-219; Chapter 13, "The Christian Scientists," pp. 220-234.

13

WHAT HAPPENED TO JUDAISM

The Siege of Jerusalem   A cheer went up from the Roman soldiers when they saw the huge battering rams move into position against the walls of Jerusalem. For nearly four years, the people and the land had been bitterly ravaged by continual fighting. But now, in August of 70 C.E., the end was in sight at last.

Overhead the giant catapults began hurling rocks into the heart of the city, and the soldiers let loose round after round of flaming arrows. Soon smoke, then flames, appeared in various sections of the besieged city.

Slowly, one of the smaller gates of the city opened, and out came a group of Jews carrying a casket. "Cease shooting," a Roman officer commanded. "It's one of their teachers; a 'rabbi,' they call him," he explained to the soldiers. "They asked permission to bury him in the cemetery outside the walls."

The procession slowly made its way past the battering rams into the Roman lines. "Who has died?" one of the soldiers called out.

"Our teacher, Yochanan ben Zakkai, the beloved pupil of Hillel," a member of the party answered sadly.

"He's lucky," muttered a soldier. "When we finish with Jerusalem, all the other people will wish they had died too."

The men carrying the casket said nothing but moved on slowly. When the procession reached the rear of the Roman lines, it stopped and the coffin was set down. One of the men opened it, and out crawled Rabbi Yochanan very much alive but stiff from his long confinement. "Wait here," he told the others. "I want to see General Vespasian."

Yochanan made his way directly to the general's tent. "Greetings, Emperor," he said. "I am Yochanan ben Zakkai. . . ."

"Emperor?" Vespasian asked in surprise, "You mean, 'general'. . . ."

Yochanan shook his head. "No, I meant 'emperor,' for you are to be the next emperor of Rome."

At that moment a messenger rushed in breathlessly. "Hail Emperor!" he greeted Vespasian. The general read the message.

"You were right, Yochanan. I've just been made emperor." Vespasian poured some wine. "Come now, I'm in a mood to celebrate. Though you're a Jew, ask a favor of me, and I'll grant it. Anything. . . ."

"Only a little thing, Emperor. Let me open a school for my students in the small port-city of Yavneh."

"Request granted!" declared Vespasian. "Though I wonder why you did not ask for something more important. . . ."

"It is enough," answered Yochanan softly, "more than enough. . . ."

WHAT HAPPENED TO JUDAISM

The Work at Yavneh   Such is the story told by the Talmud. And it was the labors of the rabbis of that school at Yavneh which insured the preservation of Judaism after the Romans destroyed Jerusalem in 70 C.E.

All during the period following Jesus' death, the Jews had been building up to a final struggle against the Romans. True, the Romans had not pressed the Jews to worship the emperor, but tensions between them continued to mount. Roman rule was stern, taxes were extremely high, and many of the governors of Judea were more concerned with becoming wealthy than administering the country wisely. Some were needlessly cruel and tried to provoke the people by profaning the holy city of Jerusalem with images on the banners of their legions. And, on the other side, there were many Jews who yearned for the restoration of their own nation and freedom from the yoke of Rome.

The result was a number of revolts, climaxed by a major war beginning in 66 C.E., which taxed the fighting skill of the Romans to its utmost. Only after four desperate years of battle were their legions able to capture the stronghold of Jerusalem. They burned the Temple, slaughtered those who resisted, and carried off thousands into slavery. Once more Judaism faced the situation of 586 B.C.E. when the Babylonians had triumphed.

But now there were three important differences. First, the concept of a universal God enabled Judaism to carry on no matter where Jews might live. Thanks to the teachings of Jeremiah, Second Isaiah, Ezekiel, and the other prophets, the Jews' belief in a national Deity had been replaced by a God who could be worshipped everywhere.

Second, the Jews were well-experienced in living in foreign lands. In fact, at the time of the destruction of Jerusalem, there were probably more Jews living outside of Palestine than in it. For more than 600 years, a large and flourishing settlement had existed in Babylonia, since only a few of the exiles of 586 B.C.E. ever returned to Palestine. There were also large Jewish communities in Alexandria and elsewhere in Egypt, and even in Rome itself. By now the pattern of Jewish life for the "Diaspora"—that is, the areas outside of Palestine—was already well-established. With the development of the synagogue, the Temple was no longer needed; and the rabbis, the successors of the scribes, were more than an adequate replacement for the priesthood.

Third, Judaism had by this time perfected the process of interpreting its Law, begun by the scribes in Babylonia. Reinterpretation of the regulations contained in its sacred literature enabled the Jewish religion to cope with the changing patterns of life in the Diaspora as well as in Palestine. Thus, for example, with the advance of society, the earlier law of "an eye for an eye and a tooth for a tooth," found in the Torah, had been redefined to mean monetary compensation for damages.

Yochanan and his students at Yavneh merely carried on this process, this time for people living principally in the Diaspora. In the course of their work they created precise rules for synagogue observance, ceremonial practice, personal conduct, and civil and criminal procedures for Jewish courts. They also made provisions for Jewish education and the training of new generations of rabbis equipped with a thorough knowledge of Judaism. The successful example of Yavneh ultimately led to the establishment of other schools, chiefly in Babylonia.

The Jews Develop an "Oral Law"   Over the course of many years, the scholars at Yavneh continued to interpret the Bible, and thousands of decisions cited in the names of the hundreds of different rabbis responsible for them were accumulated. Now, in training new generations of scholars, each rabbi transmitted to his students not only the biblical law but also its various interpretations. All of this, in turn, was expanded and passed on to succeeding generations.

Since writing was laborious and books were few, the process of transmission was carried on entirely by word of mouth. Moreover, there was strong objection to putting this material into more permanent form lest it come to rival the great "Written Law" of the Bible. So, learned

צורת הכמים מסוכין בבני ברקומספרים ביציאת מצרים כל הלילה

AT YAVNEH. In this small Palestinian port-city, beginning around 70 C.E., the rabbis labored to reinterpret the Torah for the changed circumstances of post-biblical times. Here, a medieval picture shows the scholars engaged in discussion during their meal.

through repetition and memorization, this body of information became known as the "Oral Law." Each separate interpretation cited in the name of the author was called a *mishnah*, from the Hebrew verb meaning to "teach" or "repeat." Torah now came to be spoken of in this wider sense, embracing both the written and oral Jewish religious tradition.

With the passing of time, the "Oral Law" came to be regarded as sacred as the "Written Law" itself, and the tradition grew up that both had really been given to Moses at Sinai. However, in the case of the "Oral Law," it had not been transmitted all at once but passed on from generation to generation through the God-directed process of tradition.

Gradually, beginning in the early part of the second century of the Common Era, some of the rabbis recognized the necessity of organizing the Oral Law in more permanent form. As the number of mishnayos (plural of *mishnah*) multiplied, to memorize all of them had become an almost impossible task. Furthermore, since there were rival schools of interpretation, the decisions found in the mishnayos did not always agree, and the result was confusion about the law. For instance, there was a continuing controversy over the teachings of Hillel and Shammai, two scholars who lived shortly before the Common Era and whose decisions often reflected opposite points of view.

But it was the great Jewish uprising against the Romans which took place shortly before 135 C.E. that finally made some permanent collection of the mishnayos imperative. Under the leadership of Bar Kochba, "Son of the Star," and with the encouragement of the renowned Rabbi Akiba, the Jews again revolted. To put down the rebellion the Romans were forced to send their finest legions, and Palestine was once more drenched in Jewish blood.

The Romans were now determined to destroy the Jews once and for all. To accomplish this they sought to prevent the Jews from observing such essential religious practices as circumcision and from educating students in the Torah. When rabbis like Akiba and others persisted in teaching, they were promptly executed, joining the long line of Jewish martyrs to their faith.

This critical situation compelled the people to realize that they could delay no longer in converting the Oral Law into written form.

The Appearance of the Mishnah and Talmud

A number of rabbis engaged in the task of compiling the mishnayos into some orderly arrangement. However, it was Rabbi Judah Ha-Nasi (literally, "the Prince," but actually the title he bore as head of the Sanhedrin, the supreme Jewish court), who lived from approximately 135 to 220 C.E., whom tradition recognizes as having produced the final work, called *the* Mishnah.

Written in a Hebrew dialect which includes a large number of Aramaic words from the language of the times, as well as numerous Latin and Greek expressions, his Mishnah was divided into six sections. One dealt with agriculture, another with the holidays, and the others with laws regarding women, lawsuits for damages, worship procedures, and ritual cleanliness. Judah Ha-Nasi also declared which of the rabbis' decisions were binding upon the people.

The appearance of his Mishnah around 200 C.E. did not, however, put an end to the process of interpreting Jewish law. Not only did the rabbis continue to produce other laws that were once more transmitted orally to their students, but they undertook to discover the reasoning that lay behind the earlier decisions which appeared in the Mishnah. These discussions were called the *G'moro*, another word for "study."

At first they, too, were committed to memory, but after about two centuries, new disturbances

in Palestine prompted the rabbis also to collect this material in writing. Thus, about 425 C.E., the Palestinian or "Jerusalem" Talmud was produced. The word *talmud* likewise means "study."

Another Talmud appeared about seventy-five years later, this time in Babylonia. For, beginning more than two centuries earlier, the Jews of Babylonia had developed a number of schools of their own, including important ones at Nehardea, Pumbedita, Mechuza, and Sura. Here the Babylonian Jewish scholars also discussed the origins of the Mishnaic laws, and added to the oral traditions which they received from the rabbis of Palestine. Around 367 C.E., when Rab Ashi became head of the great school at Sura, he devoted his life to putting this material into written form. Others finally finished the work around 500.

This Babylonian Talmud, rather than the smaller Palestinian work, became *the* Talmud, the authoritative guide for the religious life of the Jews. It is arranged according to the order of Judah Ha-Nasi's Mishnah. Published in many thick volumes, it contains the various mishnayos (the earlier rabbinic decisions) and the G'moro (the later rabbis' discussions of the reasoning that lay back of them).

Though written tersely, which makes it difficult to follow, the Talmud is nonetheless one of the most amazing collections of religious literature in the world. Within its pages one finds all sorts of material—legends, personal anecdotes, legal arguments, technical discussions, biographies, information about nature, historical incidents, etc. However, it is its emphasis upon clear, logical interpretation of Jewish law that enabled the Jews to maintain a high level of intellectual activity despite the intense persecution of later centuries.

The Achievements of the Rabbis

Thanks to the work originally begun at Yabneh, the compilation of the Mishnah and the Talmud, and continuing interpretations by rabbis for centuries after, Judaism progressed far beyond the biblical stage.

One of the early accomplishments of the rab-

THE TALMUD. The reinterpretation of Jewish Law, contained in the Mishnah and G'moro, was transmitted orally until conditions made it necessary to preserve it on scrolls. Today, this work appears in as many as 20 large printed volumes.

bis was to establish the "canon" of the Bible. The word "canon" comes from the Greek and means "rule." As applied to the Bible, it refers to the "approved contents of the Scriptures," or those books which Judaism considered to be inspired by God and therefore sacred literature. By the end of the second century C.E., after the rabbis finally gave their sanction to several questionable books—chiefly Ecclesiastes and Song of Songs—they declared the Bible "closed." In the process they rejected other Jewish writings, including the Books of Maccabees, which now became part of the Apocrypha, the "hidden," or unapproved volumes. Naturally, as Christian works, the "New Testament" had long before been ruled out.

Another of their great achievements was the arrangement of the synagogue service. This centered about the Sh'ma and the so-called "Eighteen Benedictions," the series of blessings beginning with the prayer "God of our fathers, Abraham, Isaac, and Jacob." However, the rabbis also provided special prayers for each of the Jewish holidays, and prescribed Torah and Prophetic readings for each Sabbath. They made provision for "sermons," too, discussions of particular subjects based upon interpretations of the Written and Oral Law. Many collections of these formed new works known by the name of *midrash*, "interpretation."

OUR RELIGION AND OUR NEIGHBORS

Undoubtedly the rabbis' greatest accomplishment was their maintenance of Judaism as a practical religious way of life for its followers. Man, the rabbis taught, had the capacity to be righteous and avoid sin. By virtue of their ancient covenant with God, the Jews had received His Torah which, if followed, would make for righteous living and ultimately the creation of a just, moral, peaceful society here upon earth. Moreover, after death the righteous would enjoy eternal life in a heavenly "Garden of Eden" and bodily resurrection with the coming of the Messiah and the establishment of God's Kingdom.

The "good life" for the Jew demanded the highest standards of conduct in family affairs, business dealings, and his relationships with others. It included kindness to animals, help to the needy and the stranger, and a host of other merciful acts prescribed by the *mitzvos*, commandments of God as revealed through His Written and Oral Law. Required, too, were proper worship, diligent study of Judaism's sacred literature, a useful occupation, marriage and children, and good manners, called *derech eretz*.

A life lived according to these prescriptions was designated as *Kiddush Ha-Shem*, "sanctification of God's name." In this manner, the Jew demonstrated to the world that he was consecrated to the one, universal, and holy God. Thereby, he also participated in the Mission of his people to help bring about God's Kingdom upon earth for all mankind.

Those who failed in their efforts to live according to God's Law always had the opportunity for repentance. "God," the rabbis taught, "is ever ready to receive the repentance of the individual." Thus *t'shuvo*, "repentance," is the antidote to sin. If anyone is genuinely sorry for his misdeeds, seeks God's forgiveness, and makes amends for his wrong-doing, and if he sincerely resolves not to repeat his acts, he can be restored to God's favor. And, though repentance is possible at all times, the Day of Atonement serves as the great annual reminder of the necessity to seek forgiveness for all of one's sins.

Reaction Against the Oral Law   Even while the Oral Law was first being created, there had been those who disagreed with the process. We recall that prior to 70 C.E., the Sadducees, the representatives of the priesthood and the upper classes of Palestine, objected to the very notion of an Oral Law. For them the literal prescriptions of the Bible were sufficient. Hence, they protested against many of the interpretations of the scribes and rabbis, especially those having to do with belief in the ultimate resurrection of the body. They found no justification in the Bible, they said, for such beliefs.

However, the masses supported the rabbis who were the leaders of the Pharisees. And, with the waning power of the Sadducees after the destruction of Jerusalem in 70 C.E., the institution of the Oral Law went unchallenged for almost seven centuries.

Then, about the middle of the eighth century, there arose once more a group who spoke out vigorously against the Oral Law. They were known as the Karaites, "Scripturalists," and one of their chief spokesmen was a Babylonian scholar named Anan ben David. Legend, colored by the prejudices of his opponents, tells us that jealousy moved him to attack the rabbinate on the issue of the Oral Law because he was not chosen head of the Babylonian Jewish community.

However, it seems more reasonable to believe that Anan ben David was sincere in his views that rabbinical interpretation and the demands of its innumerable laws had complicated the practice of Judaism. "Let us reject the authority of the Mishnah and Talmud," he argued in essence, "and return to the more simple, original source of Judaism, the Hebrew Scriptures as interpreted by the individual." Hence the name of the movement, Karaism, "Scripturalism."

Now, wherever possible, the Karaites reorganized Jewish practice on the basis of biblical law. Yet, because of the vastly different circumstances of the times, they themselves were frequently forced to reinterpret the Bible. In some instances they even had to adopt the very rabbinical decisions to which they had objected.

Often, too, in attempting to return to the regulations of the Bible, they made the observance of Judaism more strict and even impractical. Thus, while the rabbis permitted a fire to be kindled before the Sabbath for light and warmth, the Karaites prohibited all fire on the Sabbath and their homes remained cold and dark.

Naturally, the rise of Karaism provoked heated controversies among the Jews. For several centuries the conflict raged between the rabbis and Karaites. Then, nearly two centuries after Anan ben David's death, a superbly-equipped rabbinical scholar succeeded in turning the tide against them. This was Saadia ben Joseph, born to a noble family in Egypt about the year 882, and one of Judaism's most brilliant scholars.

Saadia Strikes Back   A colorful, strong-willed person, Saadia spent a good deal of his life fighting those with whom he disagreed. As head of the important rabbinical school at Sura, he battled the political leader of the Babylonian Jewish community who expected him to obey his wishes without question. Though Saadia was forced to flee for his safety, he was eventually asked to return to Sura and head the school once more.

But there were others with whom he fought. One was a prominent individual who questioned the miracles and morals of the Bible; another was a distinguished Palestinian scholar who objected to the way in which Babylonian Jews established the dates of the holidays.

However, Saadia's most devastating attacks were leveled against the Karaites. Already, at the age of twenty, he had begun to lay the groundwork for their defeat. He issued a Hebrew dictionary that explained the words found in the Bible and proved that the interpretations of the rabbis were correct, and not fictitious, as the followers of Karaism maintained.

Then, three years later, Saadia led a major campaign against them. He challenged many of their statements regarding the Bible. Through his knowledge of Hebrew grammar and the language itself, he showed how the Bible was designed to be interpreted, and that the rabbis were simply carrying out the intentions of the founders of Judaism. He had beaten the Karaites on their own ground—knowledge of the Bible.

Though Saadia's work helped turn the tide against Karaism, to a large extent the movement itself was responsible for its own decline. The return to pure biblical Judaism proved itself well-nigh impossible. It became increasingly clear that if the Jewish religion was to function at all in the Diaspora, continual reinterpretation was essential. However, it was Saadia who gave the defenders of the Oral Law their strongest weapons by proving that the Bible itself demanded the continuing development of Judaism through new explanation and application. Ony in this way could it grow and maintain its vitality.

The Golden Age of Judaism   From the time shortly after the completion of the Mishnah to about 1000 C.E., Babylonia remained the center of rabbinical scholarship. There the practices and beliefs of a full Jewish religious life that could be lived outside of Palestine were hammered out. In their various schools, the rabbis occupied themselves with further interpretations of the Oral Law by responding to numerous questions posed by Jewish communities all over the world. They likewise trained students in the Law who could serve in the Diaspora. By now, they had also completed the structure of the Hebrew prayer book and laid down the regulations for most of the Jewish observances.

Then, shortly thereafter, the center of Jewish life shifted to the West, and specifically to Spain. This was one of the few sections of Europe controlled, not by the Christians, but by the more tolerant Moslems.

The Jews of Spain were greatly influenced by Arabic culture, which contained much of the old Greek and Roman thought. For when Rome fell and the Christians abandoned Greek and Roman culture to study their own sacred traditions, the Moslem teachers had preserved most of the old classics in Arabic. It was through the Arabs, then, that the Jews were re-introduced to the thinking of the Greek philosophers. Now the greatest of the Jewish scholars found themselves seeking to harmonize the doctrines of Judaism with the teachings of philosophy.

Actually, the process had already begun in the tenth century with Saadia's great work, *The Book of Beliefs and Opinions*. In it he had dealt with some of the teachings of Greek philosophy and Saadia concluded that Judaism was thoroughly in harmony with sound, logical thought.

But a century or so later, some of the most brilliant minds in Judaism again came to grapple seriously with this subject. It was during this period, lasting from approximately 1000 to 1400 C.E., that we encounter such distinguished Jewish thinkers as Solomon Ibn Gabirol, Bachya Ibn Pakuda, Judah Halevi, Moses Maimonides, and many others. Since this was also a period of great poets, grammarians, mathematicians, statesmen, and the like, it has often been called "The Golden Age" of Jewish history.

Some of the Jewish thinkers of this period, like the great poet Judah Halevi, found serious shortcomings in Greek philosophy. He conceded that the use of reason in religion was important, but he noted that reason alone could easily lead people astray. Therefore, he concluded, revelation through the Written and Oral Law was more reliable as the authority for Judaism than Greek philosophy. But others insisted that though Judaism had indeed been revealed by God to man, it was nevertheless based upon sound reasoning and in harmony with the thought of the greatest Greek philosophers, such as Aristotle and Plato.

Differences of opinion on this subject continued, but in the process, by the time the Golden Age was over, the beliefs and teachings of Judaism had been thoroughly explored. By then, too, a series of logical and systematic works explaining Jewish doctrines and practices had been produced.

The one individual who contributed most to this development, and undoubtedly the outstanding representative of the Golden Age, was Maimonides.

The Work of Maimonides   The city of Cordova, Spain, had fallen into the hands of a fanatic group of Moslems who gave the inhabitants the choice between accepting Islam or death. Among the Jews who fled the city disguised as Arabs was the family of Moses ben Maimon, better known as Maimonides. Born in 1135 and only a young boy at the time, Maimonides was taken by his family to North Africa. Even here they were not safe, and they finally settled in Fostat, a suburb of Cairo, Egypt.

As Maimonides grew up, he became an excellent student of Judaism as well as the sciences of his day. He learned a great deal of the knowledge of the times, which included astronomy, philosophy, theology, medicine, and many other fields. He finally chose medicine as his life's work, and he proved such an outstanding physician that he was appointed to serve as doctor to Saladin's chief official.

His was a busy practice. Writes Maimonides himself:

> I reside in Fostat; the king lives in Cairo, a considerable distance away. My duties to the king are very heavy. I am obliged to visit him every day, early in the morning. When he or any of his children or the inmates of his harem are ill, I dare not leave Cairo but must stay during the greater part of the day in the palace. . . .
>
> As a rule, I go to Cairo very early in the day, and even if nothing unusual happens, I do not return before the afternoon, when I am almost dying with hunger. But then I find my office at home filled with Jews and Gentiles, with nobles and common people, awaiting my return. . . .

Nevertheless, whatever spare time he was able to find he devoted to the pursuit of Jewish learning.

To begin with, he was distressed over the state in which he found the Oral Law. He noted, for instance, that the contents of the Talmud had no satisfactory scheme of organization. Thus it was possible for a discussion about

MAIMONIDES. Known also as the Rambam, this great twelfth century scholar and philosopher succeeded in systematizing Jewish law and harmonizing Judaism with Greek philosophy.

Passover to include references to the slaughter of animals, the observance of other holidays, and even questions having to do with business matters. Moreover, there were countless rabbinical decisions scattered about in many later works, and it was frequently a matter of considerable searching to discover the requirements of the Jewish law in a particular matter. Even then, with the difficulties of understanding the Talmud, a definite decision was not always possible.

Maimonides determined to prepare a master code of all Jewish law. It took him ten years to arrange it in separate, logical categories in a volume which he called the *Mishneh Torah,* "Repetition of the Torah." However, when he finished, the rules regarding Passover, for instance, were under one heading, those involv-

Title page of the *Mishneh Torah* of Maimonides
by Nathan Ben Simeon Ha-levi. Cologne, 1296

MISHNEH TORAH. Title page of an illuminated manuscript of the
thirteenth century. Maimonides labored 10 years to organize Jewish
laws into 14 systematic categories.

ing business matters were under another, and
so on. His work also eliminated conflicting opinions and stated each decision in easy-to-read
Hebrew. So valuable was this volume that it is
used to this very day.

"The Guide of the Perplexed"   But it was for
a special and beloved pupil of his that Maimonides was moved to write his most important
work, The *Moreh Nevuchim*, "The Guide of the
Perplexed."

This was Joseph Aknin, a forced convert to
Islam. He was a gifted student of the sciences
as well as of Judaism, who had secretly remained a Jew. When he was about 30 he heard
of Maimonides and hastened to him so he might
study with him. Maimonides, in turn, became

so fond of him that he came to look upon Joseph
as a son.

Because Aknin and others like him found so
many conflicts between the teachings of Judaism and the philosophical thought of the day,
Maimonides determined to prepare a volume
that would deal with these questions. As he
notes in the introduction, the object of his
work was:

> . . . to enlighten a religious man who
> has been trained to believe in the truth
> of our holy Law, who conscientiously
> fulfills his moral and religious duties,
> and at the same time has been success-
> ful in his philosophical studies. Human
> reason has moved him to abide within
> its sphere; and on the other hand, he is
> disturbed by the literal interpretation
> of the Law. . . . Hence he is lost in per-
> plexity and anxiety.

Now, chapter by chapter, he sent off his "Guide
of the Perplexed," as lessons to Joseph by which
he might learn the truth.

Actually, Maimonides had long been interested in Greek philosophy, which he learned
through his study of Arabic culture. Like most
scholars of his day, he was impressed with the
reasoning of Aristotle. Though there appeared
to be vast differences between the principles of
the philosopher and the teachings of Judaism,
Maimonides felt that beneath the surface there
was a basic harmony. In fact, he stated that in
his opinion no Jewish teachings were in conflict
with Aristotle, and this he set out to prove in
his work.

To begin with, he utilized Aristotle's reasoning to prove the existence of God, and then reinterpreted the philosopher's conception of God
so that it coincided with that of Judaism. Man
knows God, said Aristotle, through the highest
processes of thinking. To this Maimonides
added that the best thinkers were the prophets
since it was God Himself who guided their
thinking. Thus Israel's Torah is the best that
human reason can attain.

Thereafter, step by step, Maimonides demonstrated that everything in Judaism was in harmony with the teachings of Aristotle. Many

confusing biblical expressions, like "the hand of God," or "the anger of God," were shown to be figures of speech, since "the Bible speaks in the language of men." However, when properly understood, these were seen to embody the highest philosophical truths. Analyzing the pertinent passages of the Bible dealing with the soul, he showed through interpretation that, in keeping with Aristotle's views, it was the source of man's greatest knowledge and related to the Highest Intelligence, God.

Maimonides also proved that there was sound logic behind all of Judaism's ceremonial practices. Even the dietary laws and those connected with Temple sacrifices, he said, had been designed to help the Jew remain faithful to the worship of the one God.

Though everyone respected Maimonides' enormous knowledge, many Jews did not agree with his "Guide of the Perplexed." Some felt that his teachings were far too liberal and that he relied too much upon Greek philosophy rather than the teachings of Judaism. Some were fearful that the study of Greek philosophy might prove harmful to Judaism. Others found serious fault with the fundamental reasoning of Aristotle upon which Maimonides drew so heavily.

And so, after his death in 1204, conflict over his "Guide of the Perplexed" raged among the rabbis for practically an entire century. Eventually, however, it became universally acclaimed, and even outstanding Christian thinkers turned to it. In fact, as we have already noted, Thomas Aquinas, in preparing his own books on Catholic theology, referred frequently to the writings of Maimonides.

The Beliefs of Judaism   As the result of the impact of classical philosophy and the thinking it stimulated, the beliefs of the Jews were thoroughly defined by the close of the Golden Age. We find them expressed most simply in Maimonides' first important writing, a commentary on the Mishnah produced during the latter part of the twelfth century. This is the "Thirteen Articles of Faith," often termed the "Maimonidean Creed," which appears in the present-day Orthodox prayer book.

While Judaism has no actual "creed," or set of beliefs to which all Jews must subscribe, Maimonides' "Thirteen Articles of Faith" do contain the central teachings of Judaism as they had developed. In fact, they have remained the basic doctrine of Orthodox Judaism to this day. Here, in brief form, are the principles stated by Maimonides:

I believe with perfect faith that:
1. God is the Creator of all.
2. He is strictly and uniquely One.
3. He is pure "spirit," and not "body."
4. He is eternal.
5. To Him alone must prayers be addressed.
6. The teachings of the Prophets are true.
7. Moses was the foremost Prophet.
8. The whole Torah was transmitted by God to Moses.
9. The Torah will not be changed; nor will there be another Torah.
10. God knows the thoughts and deeds of mankind.
11. Man is rewarded or punished by God according to his actions.
12. The Messiah will come.
13. The dead will be resurrected.

We observe how, in part, these principles reflect Maimonides' reaction to some of the major teachings of both Christianity and Islam. As opposed to Christianity, in Judaism, he pointed out, God has no bodily form, and is strictly One, not a Trinity. Nor are prayers to be addressed to the Virgin Mary, saints, or Jesus, but only to God; and the Written and Oral Law given by God to Israel is unchanging and not in need of a "New" Testament or Koran. And contrary to Moslem claims about Mohammed, Maimonides declared that Judaism rejects the notion that there is any prophet or "lawgiver" greater than Moses, or that the teachings of Islam are superior to its own.

More basically, however, Maimonides was concerned with presenting the essence of Judaism. Once again we observe that the Jewish people gain "salvation" (though the term as such is not used) strictly through obedience to the will of God as revealed in the Written and Oral Law. It is the *conduct* of the people of

THE DEVELOPMENT OF JUDAISM

FROM THE BIRTH OF JESUS TO BACHYA

EVENTS AFFECTING JEWISH LIFE	DEVELOPMENTS IN JUDAISM	MAJOR HAPPENINGS IN CHRISTIANITY
	4 B.C.E. Schools of Hillel and Shammai. Sadducees oppose Oral Law.	Birth of Jesus.
		About 30 C.E. Execution of Jesus.
66 C.E. Jewish revolt in Palestine.		
70 Destruction of Jerusalem and growth of the Diaspora.	Yochanan ben Zakkai founds Yavneh School. Development of Oral Law.	Beginning of final break with Jews. Written Gospels start.
		About 100 Growth of Roman Church.
135 End of Bar Kochba's revolt. Execution of Akiba.	By now canon of Bible and basic prayers established. Beginnings of the Mishnah.	**About 150** Appearance of the Apostoles' Creed.

	200 Judah Ha-Nasi's Mishnah. Beginnings of G'moro and sermonic midrash.	
	219 School founded at Nehardia (Babylonia).	**311** Constantine's Edict of Tolerance.
		325 Council of Nicea.
		380 Christianity made official religion of Roman Empire.

	425 Palestinian Talmud is completed.	**About 426** Augustine's *The City of God*.
476 Fall of Rome.		
	500 Babylonian Talmud completed.	
622 Mohammed flees to Medina.		
760 Moslems begin conquest.	Anan ben David leads the Karaites.	
		800 Charlemagne crowned Emperor of the Holy Roman Empire.

	935 Saadia's *Beliefs and Opinions*.	
	1000 Start of "Golden Age."	
	1021 Solomon Ibn Gabirol born.	
	1040 Rashi, commentator, born.	
	1050 Bachya Ibn Pakuda born.	

168

WHAT HAPPENED TO JUDAISM

Israel that determines their merit before God and leads to the establishment of His Kingdom on earth. Hence, in contrast to Christianity with its emphasis upon faith in the sacrificial death of a "savior," Judaism holds that it is one's deeds that establish his worthiness in the sight of God.

The Decline of Judaism The work of Maimonides represented the high point of Judaism's "Golden Age." Despite important contributions by other great scholars in the thirteenth and fourteenth centuries in Spain and southern France, the Jewish religion was about to enter the period of its greatest decline.

It had already started in other sections of Europe in 1096 with the First Crusade and the massacre of thousands of Jews in Germany and elsewhere. Succeeding Crusades only added to the suffering of the Jews. Now rumors began circulating throughout Europe that they murdered Christians to use their blood for Passover. It was also said that, because of their hatred of Jesus, Jews would creep into the church and stab the Host, the wafer used in Catholic Communion and symbolizing the body of Christ. Such tales often led to the destruction of Jewish communities.

All through succeeding centuries attacks upon the Jews increased, until finally the Jews of Spain, the central force of the Golden Age, fell victim. Now all over Europe Jewish creativity was blunted, and the Jews were hard-pressed to preserve what they had produced.

We may wonder why, at this particular period in history, the Jews were singled out for such intense persecution, and what effect this had upon the development of Judaism. . . .

TOPICS TO DISCUSS

1. How do you explain the fact that in Judaism, as well as in Christianity, interpretation of the Scriptures is so necessary?
2. How do you react to the argument of historic Christianity that Judaism lost its purpose for existence with the coming of Jesus?
3. In what ways has modern Judaism been affected by the contributions of the ancient rabbis?
4. Like philosophy in former times, how does the existence of modern science compel the Jews of today to think through the position of Judaism?

THINGS TO DO

1. Conduct a debate on the subject: *Resolved*, That the rabbis of today should prepare a new Talmud.
2. Prepare a report for the class on one of the following: (a) the Mishnah, (b) the Jerusalem Talmud, (c) the Babylonian Talmud, or (d) the Midrash.
3. Prepare a chart comparing the Maimonidean Creed with the 1937 "Guiding Principles of Reform Judaism." In what respects do they agree, and how do they differ?

OTHER THINGS TO READ

BAMBERGER, BERNARD J., *The Story of Judaism*, UAHC, Chapter 17, "Judah and Rome," pp. 101-104; Chapter 18, "The World of the Rabbis," pp. 107-116; Chapter 19, "The Way of the Law," pp. 117-123; Chapter 20, "The Ideals of Rabbinic Judaism," pp. 124-129; Chapter 21, "The Torah Returns to Babylon," pp. 130-134; Chapter 22, "New Paths," pp. 135-142; Chapter 23, "New Paths (continued)," pp. 143-149; Chapter 24, "The Golden Age," pp. 153-159; Chapter 25, "An Age of Reason," pp. 160-169; Chapter 26, "An Age of Reason (continued)," pp. 170-175; Chapter 27, "War Among the Theologians," pp. 176-184.

BROWNE, LEWIS, *The Wisdom of Israel*, Modern Library, "Wisdom from the Mishna," pp. 179-186; "Wisdom from the Gemara," pp. 187-243; "Wisdom from the Midrash," pp. 244-298; "The Speculations of Saadia," pp. 303-304; "The Wisdom of Ibn Gabirol," pp. 322-344; "The Contentions of Judah Ha-Levi," pp. 369-374; "The Philosophy of Maimonides," pp. 403-440.

COHEN, A., *Everyman's Talmud*, Dent, "Introduction," pp. xv-xxxviii.

MARCUS, JACOB R., *The Jew in the Medieval World*, Jewish Publication Society, #47, "Anan and the Rise of Karaism, About 760," pp. 233-

240; #57, "Saadia, 882-942," pp. 287-292; #62, "Maimonides, 1135-1204," pp. 306-310; #75, "Maimonides on Art and Charity, 1180," pp. 364-366.

ROTH, CECIL, editor, *The Standard Jewish Encyclopedia*, Doubleday, "Karaites," pp. 1106-1108; "Law, Oral," pp. 1174-1175; "Mishnah," pp. 1329-1330; "Moses Ben Maimon," pp. 1361-1364; "Talmud," pp. 1783-1789.

SACHAR, ABRAM L., *A History of the Jews*, Knopf, Chapter 12, "The Development of the Talmud," pp. 143-154; Chapter 13, "The New Moslem World," pp. 155-167; Chapter 14, "The Golden Age in Moslem Spain," pp. 168-183.

YELLIN, DAVID, and ISRAEL ABRAHAMS, *Maimonides*, Jewish Publication Society.

14

HOW THE JEWS REACTED TO PERSECUTION

The Pope Holds a Council As they sat in the great hall of the Lateran Church in Rome, the thousand or so members of the Roman Catholic clergy were talking among themselves.

"Do you know why the pope has called us together?" an abbot asked a bishop sitting nearby.

"The spread of heresy disturbs the Holy Father," answered the bishop.

"It cannot be the Albigensians," remarked a priest who overheard them. "All the heretics of southern France were rooted out in the Crusade two years ago."

"You are right, my son," replied the bishop, "but the heresies have spread to others. Today too many speak ill of the Church."

"I believe it is the nobles who stir up the people," said the abbot. "Where I come from, the princes and barons are jealous of the Church's wealth, its lands. . . ."

The bishop interrupted. "No matter. This Holy Father is not a man to be trifled with. . . ." A hush came over the great hall as the pope entered, and those assembled promptly kneeled.

The pope took his place at the head of the assembly. Then he spoke. "It has come to my attention that heresy is continuing to infect the faithful. We have already taken certain measures to root it out, but there is more we must do. We must put a stop to the mingling of our flock with the infidels who mock our faith. Therefore, I have drawn up a decree which shall

be read." He nodded to an official who stood nearby holding a long roll of parchment. The man began to read aloud. . . .

"A confusion has grown up by which Jews and Moslems cannot be distinguished from Christians. Therefore, we decree that at all times they must be marked off in the eyes of the public by the character of their dress. Moreover, let them not go forth in public during the last three days before Easter, and especially on Good Friday, so that they may not mock the faithful and insult our Redeemer. . . . Nor shall Jews exercise authority over Christians by being appointed to any public office. . . ." The official paused. "Is it your desire that this be done?"

"So be it," the assemblage roared in approval.

The Intensification of Persecution This decree and others were issued in 1215 by the Fourth Lateran Council under the leadership of Pope Innocent III. As a result, the European Jew found himself set apart from the rest of society. Now that a distinctive garment or badge left no doubt of his identity, he could be isolated culturally, socially, and politically.

Actually, this was no new legislation, for practically all of Innocent's decrees had previously been adopted by the Church. From the earliest days of organized Christianity its followers had been hostile to the Jews, and, with

171

MEDIEVAL JEWS. Except where they were compelled by law to dress differently, Jews generally wore the same types of clothes as their neighbors.

for the power of the Church, life became increasingly more difficult for European Jewry. Now that the Church wielded greater influence within the feudal system, the Jews found themselves barred from farming and most other normal occupations of the times. The Church's political power, too, especially within the Holy Roman Empire, allied the authorities of the state against them. And as corruption among the clergy grew more wide-spread and heresies multiplied, the popes sought scapegoats for the Church's own shortcomings. Consequently the Jews and their scholarship were often held responsible for the spread of heresy.

Gradually, popular resentment against Jews mounted. By the end of the eleventh century, feelings ran so high that the Crusaders poured into one Jewish community after another and butchered their residents. In a few months during the First Crusade alone, some twelve thousand Jews perished in the Rhineland.

In 1198, when the power of the Church was at its height, Innocent III became pope. By nature he was a cruel person, and because he considered himself especially chosen to extend the authority of the Church, he tolerated no opposition. He selected and deposed kings almost at will. He put down heresy ruthlessly, drenching the soil of southern France with the blood of the Albigensians and others who revolted against the Church. He was also the first pope to refuse to protect the Jews from physical attack. And now, as a result of the enforcement of his decree compelling them to wear special dress, Jews were more easily singled out for assault and murder.

Attacks upon the Jews became more frequent. Soon they were herded into ghettos which served even more effectively to cut them off from contact with the outside world. These were usually located in the most undesirable sections of the city, sometimes alongside a river given to flooding or a garbage dump. To add to their misery, they were victimized in all sorts of ways. For one thing, special oppressive taxes were levied against them. They were expelled from various countries, from England in 1290, from France in 1306, and from Spain in 1492.

the rivalry of the two faiths during the Roman period, their bitterness grew. When Christianity finally became the official religion of the Empire during the fourth century, it decided that the Jews must be brought into the Church. Therefore, restrictions were imposed upon them to make their lot so unhappy that they would convert. It became unlawful, for instance, for Jews to employ Christians, hold public office, or engage in various occupations. And from time to time the Jews suffered other indignities, such as being compelled to listen to sermons designed to convert them.

Yet, by and large, the Church protected the Jews against physical attack, for it was not its intention to destroy them, only to win them over to Christianity. Fortunately, too, not all of the popes enforced the Church's more repressive anti-Jewish legislation. Thus the Jews were able to earn a living, organize their own communities with synagogues, schools, social and charitable facilities, and carry on the further development of Judaism.

However, as the popes grew more zealous

SPANISH DISPUTATION. In the Middle Ages, Jews were frequently compelled to engage in debates about their religion with representatives of the Church. Here, such a disputation is being conducted before King Ferdinand and Queen Isabella of Spain.

AFTERMATH OF A POGROM. Typical is this scene from an original painting, of an East European Jewish family leaving their lifelong home after the brutal devastation by a mob of hostile non-Jews.

What is more, the Jews were even held responsible for every catastrophe that occurred, including the devastating plague called the Black Death that swept through Europe in the mid-fourteenth century.

The consequence was that for many centuries life for the Jews was extremely dangerous and oppressive. Even the coming of the Reformation did little to relieve the situation because the early Protestants were generally as intolerant as the Catholics.

How the Jews Reacted   Sustained by their religion, the Jews reacted in three ways. First, they clung all the more fiercely to Judaism, which was their chief satisfaction. If anything, persecution proved how necessary the teachings of Judaism were to the world. So, within the synagogue, in their own vigorous Jewish community life, and through the study of the Oral and Written Law, they found ample personal happiness as well as forgetfulness of the hostility outside.

Under the circumstances their Judaism tended to turn inward, withdrawing from contact with the non-Jewish world. Now Jewish learning became restricted to the fairly narrow study of the Talmud, and Jewish scholarship consisted mainly of adding commentary upon commentary to the Written and Oral Law. Ultimately, with the appearance in 1567 of Joseph Karo's *Shulchan Aruch,* "The Prepared Table," a code embodying the whole of the Law,

Judaism became practically static.

The second reaction was that Jews were forced to adapt themselves to the hostile times. Jews found ways of coping with the restrictions against them. If it was necessary to become money-lenders—one of the few occupations prohibited by the Church to Christians but open to Jews—then they took up this despised profession. If governments demanded exorbitant taxes for the privilege of remaining in the country, then they raised the necessary sums by heavy self-imposed taxes. Sometimes, as in the case of Spain where the Church demanded conversion, many Jews publicly adopted Christianity. However, these "Marranos," as they were called, managed to carry on their faith secretly, despite the spying of the Inquisition. Not infrequently did self-preservation demand all sorts of humiliations and sacrifices.

The third reaction was that Jews turned, for an avenue of escape, to mysticism, called *Kabala,* "tradition." Originating in the East, it was later transmitted to Italy and Spain, and it found a warm welcome in the ghettos of Europe.

In part, Kabala involved the belief that man's soul sought to move upward from realm to realm until at last it reached God Himself. This could be achieved only by the most intense self-purification and meditation. The result was an outburst of extreme piety and fervent prayer as individuals sought to attain to the highest level of communion with God.

173

But there were far less commendable forms of Kabala that were linked with magic. These sought to discover the deep "secrets" of the Torah. Through devious interpretations of passages of the Scriptures, the use of angels' names, combinations of particular Hebrew letters, and the like, people believed that they could protect themselves against evil spirits and dangers that seemed to lurk everywhere.

Mysticism also spawned the various Jewish messianic movements that arose during the thirteenth through eighteenth centuries. In the course of their studies, kabalists sometimes attempted to predict when the Messiah would come. Thus it is not surprising that from time to time certain individuals would appear claiming to be the deliverer of the Jews or the very Messiah himself.

One who proclaimed himself the Messiah in 1665 was Sabbatai Zevi, and he aroused such tremendous fervor in the Jews that many sold their possessions in order to join him as he prepared to take over the Holy Land. In 1666, Sabbatai entered Constantinople, where many thought he would fulfil the prophecy of one of his followers, Nathan Ghazzati, that Sabbatai would place the Sultan's crown on his own head. But once there, Sabbatai was confronted by the Turkish authorities with the choice between death or conversion to Islam. He promptly chose the latter, much to the dismay of his supporters. It was a similar story with the other messianic pretenders. For a while they awakened hope in the hearts of the Jews; then came only anguish.

Suddenly, beginning around the mid-eighteenth century, the Jews began to shake themselves loose from the grip of despair. In Eastern Europe, despite persecution that was to last well into the twentieth century, the new spirit gave birth to two movements that have profoundly influenced the modern Jew. The first was Chasidism.

A Strange Revelation "This innkeeper is a very strange fellow," thought the guest who had remained overnight in the tiny Ukranian village. "Why does he keep insisting that I stay here over the Sabbath, especially since this is only Tuesday and he knows how anxious I am to return home?"

Determined to get on with his journey, the guest bade the innkeeper good-bye and set off in his carriage. But he hadn't travelled far when a wheel broke and he had to return to the inn. He supposed it would take only a short time to fix it, but one thing after another intervened and the days wore on. Now, there was no choice but to remain over the Sabbath.

"I am glad to see that you've decided to stay," said the innkeeper. "It will be good to have someone to spend the Sabbath with."

That night the guest fell into a deep sleep. Suddenly he awoke. He thought he saw a fire burning in the main room of the inn, but when he rushed out to sound the alarm, he discovered that it was a great white light which filled the room. The light was so overpowering that the guest fell into a faint.

The next morning when he sought some explanation from the innkeeper, he was nowhere to be found. His wife explained that he had gone to his cave for Sabbath morning prayers. Finally, the innkeeper returned dressed in his white Sabbath robe. Then, after the Sabbath meal, he revealed such wonderful secrets of the Torah that the guest was truly astonished.

Some days later when the guest reached his destination he reported what had happened. "A great light lives close by," he told the people. "He should be invited to dwell in this community." The people immediately set off for the inn, and when they found the innkeeper they carried him all the way back on their shoulders. And all the people marveled at the wonderful things he taught them.

So, according to Chasidic legend, did Israel ben Eliezer, better known as the Baal Shem Tov, "The Master of the Good Name" (or as we might interpret it, "The possessor of special God-given powers"), finally reveal himself in his thirty-sixth year to the Jews of Poland. And with him came the glow of a "new light" in Eastern Europe.

The Growth of Chasidism The movement

174

THE DEVELOPMENT OF JUDAISM

FROM THE BIRTH OF HALEVI TO THE REFORMATION

EVENTS AFFECTING JEWISH LIFE	DEVELOPMENTS IN JUDAISM	MAJOR HAPPENINGS IN CHRISTIANITY

EVENTS AFFECTING JEWISH LIFE

1085 Christians reconquer most of Spain.

1096 First Crusade begins. Massacre of Jewish communities.

1215 Fourth Lateran Council decrees special dress for Jews.

1271 Final Crusade.

1290 Jews expelled from England.

1306 France expels Jews.

1348 Black Death

1391 Many Spanish Jews forcibly converted to Christianity.

1421 Expulsion of German Jews starts.

1492 Spain expels Jews.

1496 Portugal expels Jews.

1516 Venice establishes a ghetto. Increasing persecution of European Jewry.

DEVELOPMENTS IN JUDAISM

Judah Halevi born.

1135 Maimonides born.

1180 Maimonides' *Mishneh Torah.*

About 1200 Kabala comes to Europe.

1275 False Messiahs begin to appear.

Ghettos introduced in Germany.

Rise of Jewish mysticism.

MAJOR HAPPENINGS IN CHRISTIANITY

1054 Eastern Orthodoxy breaks with Roman Catholic Church.

1170 Dominic born.

1182 Francis of Assisi born.

About 1225 Thomas Aquinas born.

1229 Inquisition established.

1378 Split in papacy to 1417.

1491 Ignatius of Loyola born.

1517 Luther's "95 Theses."

1533 Reformation begins in England.

led by the Baal Shem Tov was called Chasidism, a name taken from the Hebrew word for "piety" or "saintliness." To some extent it represented the reaction of eighteenth century Russian and Polish Jewry to the growing lack of warmth in a Judaism that seemed to center about long and involved Talmudic arguments.

Born around 1700, Israel Baal Shem Tov had spent half of his life, first as a clay-digger, then as an innkeeper, living among the Carpathian mountains. All the while, he kept thinking about the world and the nature of God and man. Then, sometime before 1740, he received a revelation that sent him back to spread his teachings among the people. This he did with a warm, religious spirit and by means of homely, appealing stories that delighted his hearers.

God, he pointed out, was not to be found only in the study of the Law or through intellectual exercises. He was also to be experienced by the heart through a life of inner religious fervor, joyous prayer, and intense happiness in Jewish living. Cheerfulness, music, dancing, inward enthusiasm in worship—all of these, he taught, brought man closer to God.

He did not reject rabbinic Judaism as the Karaites had done some nine centuries before, but placed less emphasis upon it. He realized that the physical and spiritual oppression of the times called for a rejuvenation of the Jewish spirit through a rekindling of the emotions. Illustrative of his message is this anecdote from Chasidic lore:

> Once the Baal Shem Tov refused to enter a synagogue. "I cannot go in," he said. "It is crowded with teachings and prayers from wall to wall and from floor to ceiling. How could there be room for me?"
> Those around him stared at him for they did not understand what he meant. He then explained, "The words from the lips of those whose teaching and praying do not come from hearts lifted to heaven cannot rise. They fill the house from wall to wall and from floor to ceiling."

To the Baal Shem Tov and his followers, the true love of God was intimate and personal,

MODERN CHASID. A youthful follower of Chasidism, the religious movement that arose in the eighteenth century in Eastern Europe.

almost like the relationship between father and child, or close friends. Interwoven with this was a warm affection for all of God's creatures, especially the common people. To help them find the joy of life, to ease their burdens and to give them sympathetic counsel through the teachings of Judaism, were all part of the Baal Shem Tov's purpose. And this he accomplished in part with his charmingly simple parables, biblical interpretations, and folk tales.

He also injected a new spirit into the worship. To attend a Chasidic service, even today, is to understand something of what the Baal Shem Tov sought to do. For the movement, though small, still exists, and one occasionally sees Chasidim who wear the heavy garments and large fur hats of fashionable eighteenth century Poland. Their services are generally filled with religious fervor, featuring enthusiastic singing by the congregation, and even dancing and handclapping in time to lively tunes.

Throughout the rest of the Baal Shem Tov's life, his humble teachings and the watchword of the movement, "Joy in the Torah," stirred the world-weary Jews of Eastern Europe. Thousands became followers of Chasidism, and after his death in 1760, various disciples carried on the movement. They were known as *tzadikim*, "holy men," and so beloved were they that their followers believed them to be endowed with special powers and even capable of performing miracles. People would travel many miles to be in the presence of a particular tzadik, to ask questions or favors of him. In time, the position of tzadik became limited to certain families. Indeed, these families adopted many of the trappings of royalty, holding court for their followers in kingly fashion.

Eventually, the opposition of the leading rabbis of Eastern Europe, the excesses and rivalries among the tzadikim themselves, and the superstitions of their followers, brought the movement into disrepute. But the charm of Chasidic teachings, its song and dance, and the spirit of its religious warmth and fellowship, have lived on to influence present-day Judaism. Many of our modern synagogue and Jewish folk tunes come directly from the Chasidim. So do a number of folk dances, as well as the spirit of the Oneg Shabbat, the Sabbath eve gathering.

Thanks to the writings of one of its leading modern disciples, Chasidism is also having a profound influence, not only upon Jewish religious thought, but upon the thinking of many Protestant theologians as well. That person is Martin Buber, whose teachings stress people's need for something more than simply a concept of God. Man, he observes, must establish an intimate relationship with Him, an "I–Thou" relationship. In a similar way, he must likewise enter into a close personal relationship with his fellow man who is not some object to be used for one's own purposes, but a "thou," a God-given personality in his own right. And through such ties each individual will then be able to approach even closer to God Himself.

Developments in the West Chasidism, in Eastern Europe, was one attempt of the Jews to overcome the atmosphere of despair produced by centuries of persecution. A second and far different effort was made in the West as a consequence of a new spirit of freedom that was in the air.

In Western Europe the growth of the middle class, the Protestant Reformation, and the rise of national states had already undermined the old feudal system. By the mid-eighteenth century, it appeared certain that important changes in political, social, and economic life were soon to occur. Moreover, the discoveries of science and developments in human thought and literature had given rise to ideas about basic human rights and the equality of all peoples. Outstanding liberals, like Rousseau and Voltaire in France, Locke in England, and many others, were advocating systems of government that promised a much larger measure of personal liberty to all.

Already the Jews were beginning to feel the effects. In England a Prime Minister tried twice to secure their citizenship, and in Germany attempts were being made to remove some of the special Jewish taxes. In 1779, Gotthold Ephraim Lessing, one of Germany's great writers, published the drama, *Nathan the Wise*, in which he advocated more humane treatment of the Jews. In Austria a number of restrictions upon Jewish occupations, commercial activities, and schooling were removed. And in America talk about a "Bill of Rights" and the actions of some of the young states gave promise of unlimited freedom to the Jews.

In this atmosphere of increasing enlightenment, certain European Jews were convinced that total emancipation was not far off. Hence, it was necessary to prepare their people for the new freedom.

One such individual was Moses Mendelssohn, born in Germany in 1729. In spite of the restrictions against Jews, his own ill-health, and the deformity of a hunch-back, he had managed to secure an excellent general as well as Jewish education. His writings on philosophy and his wide knowledge of German literature soon made him an outstanding figure of the day. In fact, it was Mendelssohn after whom the Jewish hero of Lessing's *Nathan the Wise* was patterned.

Mendelssohn was a devout Jew, who practiced Traditional Judaism all his life. Nevertheless, he felt the need for certain changes in Jewish life. The Jews, for instance, spoke mainly Judeo-German, a dialect made up of German and Hebrew, the forerunner of present-day Yiddish. Therefore, Mendelssohn advocated that, in anticipation of their freedom, Jews should learn the language of their country. To this end he established a school in Berlin where Jewish students could study secular as well as Jewish subjects in German. Then, in 1783, he translated the Five Books of Moses into German, using Hebrew characters instead of German so that Jews would be able to read it. Thereby, he succeeded in introducing many to the German language and, through it, to the culture of eighteenth century Europe.

After so many centuries of enforced isolation, the Jews hastened to catch up with the outside world. Some, like the children of Moses Mendelssohn himself, were so enchanted with non-Jewish culture that they eventually abandoned Judaism and became Christians. Others, like the poet Heinrich Heine, who chafed at the restrictions still imposed upon the Jews, underwent baptism to enjoy the privileges of a Christian. Fearful for the future of Judaism, many of the leading rabbis of Europe spoke out against the study of secular culture, and some even condemned Mendelssohn's translation of the Bible.

But Mendelssohn and others had reestablished Jewish contact with the outside world, and Judaism in the West was bound to feel its effects. However, neither Mendelssohn nor anyone else had as yet produced a form of Judaism that could meet the challenges of Jewish emancipation, which was to become a reality by the end of the eighteenth century.

Conditions Grow Worse in Eastern Europe

While the Jews of the West were beginning to win their freedom, the position of Jewry in Eastern Europe continued to deteriorate. Beginning with 1790, the Jews of Russia, Poland, and Lithuania found themselves confined to an increasingly smaller area called the "Pale of Settlement," located mainly in former Polish territory. Here various hostile measures were taken against them. In 1827, for instance, the Russians began impressing twelve-year-old Jewish boys into military service for a period of twenty-five years, all the while inducing

them by every possible means to convert to Christianity. Then, starting in the middle 1840's, the government began to campaign in earnest for the mass conversion of the Jews by promising certain benefits to those who attended specially-created Russian schools designed to wean them away from their religion.

Nonetheless, the Jews of Eastern Europe continued to hope that some of the freedoms then enjoyed by Jews in the West would penetrate Russia. Around the middle of the nineteenth century, they even organized a movement called the *Haskala*, or "Enlightenment," to acquaint themselves with modern culture. Interestingly, much of the material that was written about European history, literature, science, and thought appeared in the Hebrew language, which now began to take on new vigor.

However, despite relief provided by an occasional liberal czar, oppression of the Jews continued. It culminated in 1882 with the so-called "May Laws," designed to convert a third of the Jews, drive out a third, and exterminate the remaining third. Now "pogroms," physical attacks upon the Jews, became frequent, and Russian Jewry began to despair of ever gaining freedom. Many started to look for deliverance elsewhere. Those who could, fled to the United States in ever-increasing numbers. But many others found their answer in Zionism.

The Growth of Zionism

For centuries Jews had prayed for the coming of the Messiah and a return to the Holy Land. However, in 1862, two men proposed that the return to Palestine start at once.

One was an Orthodox rabbi, Hirsch Kalischer; the other, Moses Hess, a German Jewish Socialist who, because of the rise of anti-Semitism, became disillusioned with the promise of freedom. Stimulated by the desperate plight of the Russian Jew in the 1880's, others also began urging the immediate rebuilding of Palestine. Finally, in 1882, about 40 young men founded a colony there called *Rishon Le-Zion*, "The First in Zion."

Now Zionist activity in Eastern Europe began to mount. Despite the extreme hardships

DREYFUS REINSTATED. Twelve years after Captain Alfred Dreyfus of the French general staff was accused of treason, his name was finally cleared and he was restored to his army career. The case aroused wide-spread anti-Semitism in Europe.

of the early pioneers, other colonies were established in Palestine. The Haskala movement, originally designed to deal with European thought, rededicated itself to the stimulation of Zionism through the development of a new Hebrew culture.

It was the Dreyfus Affair in France, however, that gave new impetus to the movement and eventually enlisted the support of many Jews of the West. In 1894, Alfred Dreyfus, a Jewish captain on the French general staff, was falsely accused of selling military secrets to the Germans and put on trial. An Austrian journalist, Theodor Herzl, covered the sensational proceedings and was shocked by the anti-Semitism that they aroused throughout Europe.

As a result he became convinced that national existence for the Jews in a homeland of their own was essential. It alone, he believed, could reduce anti-Semitism and provide Jews everywhere with new inner dignity and status in the eyes of the nations.

Two years later Herzl published *The Jewish State* in which he offered a practical plan for the rebuilding of Palestine. This led to the convening of the first Zionist Congress in Basle, Switzerland, in 1897 and the formation of an official world Zionist movement, whose work profoundly affected Jewish life and thought everywhere.

There were others who saw Zionism in terms somewhat different from Herzl. One was Achad

THE DEVELOPMENT OF JUDAISM

FROM THE ENGLISH REFORMATION TO THE FRENCH REVOLUTION

EVENTS AFFECTING JEWISH LIFE	DEVELOPMENTS IN JUDAISM	MAJOR HAPPENINGS IN CHRISTIANITY

EVENTS AFFECTING JEWISH LIFE

1546 Luther expresses hostility toward Jews.

1567 Beginning of expulsion of Jews from Italian cities.

1593 Marranos arrive in Amsterdam.

1654 Jews settle in New Amsterdam.

1655 Jews readmitted to England.

1670 Jews expelled from Vienna.

1730 First public synagogue in New York.

1775 Papal edict against Rome's Jews.

1776 American Declaration of Independence.

1781 Dohm's plea for Jewish emancipation.

DEVELOPMENTS IN JUDAISM

1534 Birth of Isaac Luria, noted Kabalist, to 1562.

1567 Joseph Karo's *Shulchan Aruch* published.

1632 Birth of Baruch Spinoza, great philosopher, to 1677.

1665 Sabbatai Zevi proclaims himself the Messiah.

1700 Birth of Baal Shem Tov, founder of Chasidism, to 1760.

1720 Birth of Elijah (Vilna Gaon), great traditional scholar, to 1797.

1729 Birth of Moses Mendelssohn, leader of Jewish "Enlightenment," to 1786.

1772 Vilna rabbis oppose Chasidism.

1778 Mendelssohn's Bible translation begun, to 1783.

MAJOR HAPPENINGS IN CHRISTIANITY

1545 Council of Trent begins Catholic Church Reforms, to 1563.

1555 Peace of Augsburg grant equal rights to Protestants.

1564 Calvin, founder of Presbyterianism dies.

1604 Socinus (Unitarian) dies.

1607 First Episcopalian service i America.

1611 Baptists form church in Eng land.

1634-9 First Catholic, Lutheran Baptist Churches in America.

1662 Congregationalists break with Church of England.

1681 William Penn (Quaker) foun Pennsylvania.

1730 Conversion of John Wesle (Methodist).

1784 First Methodist church America.

HOW THE JEWS REACTED TO PERSECUTION

Ha-Am, "One of the People," the pen name of Asher Ginsberg, a noted Russian-Jewish writer of Hebrew essays. He conceived of the Homeland in Palestine as a great spiritual center for world Jewry. Jewish resettlement there, he felt, would inspire a revived Hebrew culture and a renewed sense of ethical idealism among Jews everywhere. A number of others pictured the Jewish State as the living embodiment of national justice and righteousness through the establishment of a society built upon principles of cooperative, democratic social living.

Still, there were some Jews—a minority, to be sure—who opposed the idea of a Jewish State on religious and other grounds. Some of the Orthodox declared that a return to Palestine could only follow the appearance of the Messiah; other Jews maintained that a universalistic Judaism no longer required such a return, and that the establishment of a Jewish State there would create additional problems for Jews living in the Diaspora.

It required more than a half-century of heroic struggle to realize the Zionist dream. Much of the work involved reclaiming the land, draining swamps, planting trees, creating farms, and building modern cities. But gaining the right to establish a Jewish state also taxed the energies of the Zionist movement to the extreme. It was not until 1917 that the British government issued the Balfour Declaration which promised Jews a homeland in Palestine. Even then there was bitter conflict with Great Britain, who assumed control of the country after World War I and placed innumerable restrictions upon the

Jews there, severely limiting the number of Jewish immigrants who might be admitted. Many of the neighboring Arab peoples, too, were violently hostile to the Zionist idea and periodically terrorized the country. But in the 1930's and 1940's European Jewry was undergoing terrible persecution and mass-slaughter at the hands of Hitler and the Nazis, and hundreds of thousands of Jews were clamoring to get into Palestine as a haven of refuge.

Finally, in November of 1947, in an effort to settle the problem of Palestine, the United Nations voted to partition the country into separate Arab and Jewish states. However, even as the British started to withdraw, Arab guerrillas began attacking the Jewish settlements. Soon the Jews were fighting for their very existence against a bloody invasion launched by five neighboring Arab states. In the midst of this war, in May of 1948, the Jews proclaimed the establishment of the State of Israel; however, it took almost another year of savage fighting to drive the Arabs back and make independence a reality.

In many ways, the dream of Herzl, as embodied in the State of Israel, has had a profound effect on world Jewry. The revival of Hebrew culture in Israel, the example of Jews striving to create a nation based upon Jewish ethical and moral values, and pride in the achievements of those living there, have enheartened the Jewish people everywhere. It has served to strengthen their sense of identity with one another, and the revival of spoken Hebrew in Israel, as well as the developments

ISRAEL TODAY

Scenes from the modern State of Israel reveal the progress there in many ways. (right) A pioneering settlement in the barren Negev. (center) Workers on a kibbutz in Galilee relax at their new snack-bar. (left) Tel Aviv, with the Dan Hotel in the foreground.

GREAT SANHEDRIN. At the call of Napoleon, this body of 71 Jews, two-thirds of whom were rabbis, convened in Paris in 1807. It re-affirmed Judaism's compatibility with French citizenship.

there in Jewish thought, music, dance, art, and scholarship, have had an increasing impact upon Jewish life all over the world.

Emancipation in the West   The Jews of Eastern Europe never did win their freedom. Though promises of equality were made to them following World War I, the promises were not honored. The Jews there continued to suffer until they emigrated, or were destroyed by Hitler, or submerged under the anti-religious and often anti-Semitic rule of the Soviet Union.

However, in the West the Jews were finally emancipated. In America, with the adoption of the Constitution in 1789 and the inclusion of the Bill of Rights as the first ten amendments, they became full citizens of the land, though they still had to overcome various state restrictions. In France, too, the Jews were granted complete freedom in 1791, two years after the great Revolution broke out. As the armies of Napoleon marched over Europe, equality for the Jews likewise became the law in many parts of Switzerland, Italy, Germany, and elsewhere.

As a result of the new freedom, certain Jews became conscious of the need to reinterpret Judaism in the light of the changed conditions of life. In fact, the decisions of the Assembly of Jewish Notables and Great Sanhedrin, summoned by Napoleon in 1806 and 1807, made this very plain.

Aroused by complaints against the Jews from certain prejudiced quarters, Napoleon sum-

moned prominent Jewish representatives from France, Italy, and Germany to answer a number of key questions. In general, Napoleon wanted to know about the authority of Jewish law and the relationship of the Jews to their fellow countrymen now that they had become citizens. By and large, the answer that he received was that the Jews considered themselves bound by the laws of the land and thoroughly devoted to their country and their fellow citizens. The Assembly of Jewish Notables and Great Sanhedrin admitted that Jewish civil law was no longer in force.

But to many, changes in various religious practices and beliefs also seemed needed. Economic circumstances made work on the Sabbath a necessity for most people, and now that Jews were no longer confined to the ghetto, walking to the synagogue on the Sabbath became increasingly more difficult. The new emphasis upon the language and culture of the land and the decline of knowledge of Hebrew was already making the all-Hebrew service incomprehensible to growing numbers of Jews. And many also wondered how loyal citizens could continue to pray in good faith for the coming of a Messiah who would deliver them from "exile."

How Modern Judaism Came to Be   At the time there seemed to be only two choices open to the Jew. One was the abandonment of Judaism; the other, unswerving adherence to ghetto Orthodoxy.

Already certain Jews had become discouraged by what seemed to them the unbridgeable gulf between Judaism and modern life. Many had grown indifferent to their faith; some were even converting to Christianity.

However, the majority, led by their rabbis, continued to carry on with the Judaism they were accustomed to. According to their view, the religious beliefs and practices that had been adopted in final form in the ghetto were part of the divinely ordained faith that was unchangeable by man. "Better no freedom," declared the more extreme among their leaders, "than a single change in the God-given Law."

But some Jews began to see a third possibil-

182

ity open to the emancipated Jew. This was to reinterpret Judaism in line with modern life and thought.

And so, throughout the nineteenth century, the struggle raged between those who sought once again to readjust Judaism to changed circumstances and those who insisted that the Jewish faith had to remain as it was.

Out of that conflict emerged the religion of the present-day Jew. . . .

TOPICS TO DISCUSS

1. How has modern Jewish life and thought been affected by the centuries of religious persecution?
2. To what extent is religion still the cause of modern anti-Semitism?
3. Why and how does Judaism need to be reinterpreted for life in modern America?
4. In what ways has the establishment of the State of Israel affected the life and thought of American Jewry?

THINGS TO DO

1. Prepare a report for the class on one of the following: (a) False Messiahs; (b) Kabalism; (c) the Shulchan Aruch; (d) Chasidism; (e) Haskala; (f) Zionism.
2. Create a dictionary of Jewish biography by preparing sketches of the lives and contributions of the following: Joseph Karo, Sabbatai Zevi, Israel Baal Shem Tov, Moses Mendelssohn, Theodor Herzl, Achad Ha-Am (Asher Ginsburg), and Martin Buber.
3. Utilizing the English translation of the abbreviated *Shulchan Aruch* (Golden, *Code of Jewish Law*), study the following four chapters of Volume I: Chapter 1, "Laws Relating to Conduct Upon Rising in the Morning"; Chapter 29, "Moral Laws Which a Man Should Accustom Himself to Observe"; Chapter 37, "Laws Concerning the Immersion of Utensils"; and Chapter 38, "Laws Concerning the Bread, the Cooked Food and the Milk of a Non-Jew." Then write a brief essay on your observations about the *Shulchan Aruch* and the modern Jew.

OTHER THINGS TO READ

BAMBERGER, BERNARD J., *The Story of Judaism*, UAHC, Chapter 28, "Judaism in Christian Europe," pp. 185-197; Chapter 29, "The Cabala," pp. 198-208; Chapter 30, "Darkness at Sunrise," pp. 211-217; Chapter 31, "The Ghetto Days," pp. 218-222; Chapter 33, "Dreams," pp. 233-237; Chapter 34, "Nightmares," pp. 238-242; Chapter 35, "The Rebirth of Joy," pp. 243-249; Chapter 37, "Another Dawn," pp. 257-262; Chapter 38, "Morning with Clouds," pp. 263-265; Chapter 44, "Under the Heel of the Tsars," pp. 303-311; Chapter 46, "The Era of Pogroms," pp. 324-330; Chapter 48, "The Birth of Political Zionism," pp. 341-346; Chapter 52, "The Last Glories of European Jewry," pp. 372-377.

BROWNE, LEWIS, *The Wisdom of Israel*, Modern Library, "The Shulhan Aruk of Rabbi Karo," pp. 477-484; "Sayings of the Baal Shem-Tov," pp. 546-558; "The Sayings of the Bratzlaver," pp. 559-566; "Hasidic Tales and Teachings," pp. 567-598; "Convictions of Moses Mendelssohn," pp. 603-609; "Thus Spake Asher Ginzberg," pp. 649-654.

MARCUS, JACOB R., *The Jew in the Medieval World*, Jewish Publication Society, #5, "The Expulsion of the Jews from France, 1182," pp. 24-27; #9, "The Black Death and the Jews, 1348-1349," pp. 43-48; #27, "Innocent and the Jews, 1215," pp. 137-141; #33, "Martin Luther and the Jews, 1523-1543," pp. 166-169; #52, "Isaac Luria, the Cabalist, 1534-1572," pp. 256-260; #53, "Shabbethai Zebi, False Messiah, 1666," pp. 261-269; #54, "The Rise of the Hasidim, about 1735-1740," pp. 270-275.

SACHAR, HOWARD M., *The Course of Modern Jewish History*, World, Chapter 1, "The Jew as Non-European," pp. 25-35; Chapter 2, "The Glimmering Dawn in the West," pp. 36-52; Chapter 3, "Emancipation in the West," pp. 53-71; Chapter 4, "Incarceration: The Jews of Eastern Europe," pp. 72-96; Chapter 10, "Jewish Humanism in Eastern Europe," pp. 199-220; Chapter 11, "The Emergence of Anti-Semitism," pp. 221-239; Chapter 13, "The Rise of Zionism," pp. 261-283; Chapter 18, "The Palestine Mandate," pp. 369-393; Chapter 22, "The Birth of Israel," pp. 460-488.

SCHWARTZMAN, SYLVAN D., *Reform Judaism in the Making*, UAHC, Chapter 2, "The Jew of Medieval Europe," pp. 12-19; Chapter 3, "The First Rays of Freedom," pp. 20-27; Chapter 4, "The European Jew Becomes a Citizen," pp. 28-37.

15

THE FAITH OF THE MODERN JEW

The Birth of Reform Judaism "I have the impression that the students are not responding to our worship services," Israel Jacobson was remarking to one of the teachers.

Jacobson was a well-known Jewish financier and philanthropist, and was later appointed by Napoleon's brother as head of the Jewish community of Westphalia. Now, however, he was visiting the school which he had founded in 1801 in the small town of Seesen, some seventy-five miles south of Hanover in Germany. By establishing this school Jacobson had made it possible for sixty students, most of whom were Jewish, to get a good general education.

"I've noticed it, too," the teacher replied with some sadness. "I've even spoken to the boys about it. . . . Most of them say they just don't understand the service. . . ."

"It's really too bad," declared Jacobson shaking his head, "too bad for them and for Judaism. But I know what they mean because I've often felt the same way. . . ." He thought a moment. "Certainly here at this school we should be able to do something about it. . . ."

"Do something?" the teacher looked at him. "What can anyone do about it?"

Israel Jacobson was thinking out loud. "What if we were to build an attractive synagogue here . . . and hold the kind of services that the students could understand? Perhaps we could translate some of the prayers into German;

maybe certain hymns, too. . . . And we could have a school choir. . . ." His eyes brightened with excitement. "Why not? Why not indeed?"

The teacher watched him disappear down the hall. He was impressed with Mr. Jacobson's ideas. But little did he realize that these ideas and innovations would lead to the birth of a new movement in Judaism.

Reform Judaism in Europe In 1810, Jacobson completed the sanctuary at the Seesen school, and introduced more modern forms of worship. These included a shortened ritual with a sermon, certain prayers and hymns in German, and a well-trained school choir accompanied on the organ. The following year he established a new ceremony called Confirmation at which five of the students publicly pledged themselves to remain faithful to their religion.

Friends of Jacobson were so impressed with these services that they introduced similar ones in Berlin. In 1817, others founded a liberal congregation in Hamburg. They introduced the reforms of Jacobson, and also eliminated certain prayers calling for the coming of a personal Messiah to lead the Jews back to Palestine. All of this met the immediate and vigorous opposition of the traditionalists, who ultimately came to be called "Orthodox." But despite their objection to these changes as violations of Jewish law, the reforms spread to England and other European countries.

In the main, the advocates of Reform—led by men like Abraham Geiger, the learned rabbi of the Breslau congregation—sought changes in synagogue worship that would make for a more solemn and meaningful service. They supported a more reasonable observance of the Sabbath and holidays, and certain modifications of Jewish belief, especially in connection with the Messiah, the return of the "exiles" to Palestine, and bodily resurrection. They also advocated reforms of various customs and laws, such as those involving mourning practices, Jewish marriage and divorce procedures, and the religious status of women.

In their demand for change, the reformers were aided by the new science of Judaism which they created. Now many aspects of Judaism were studied with the same scientific methods that were being used in general historical and literary research. This work, carried on by such scholars as Leopold Zunz, Isaac Marcus Jost, Abraham Geiger, and others, showed conclusively that, despite claims to the contrary by the Orthodox, Judaism had undergone many changes over the centuries. In fact, most of the needed reforms were sanctioned by the very rabbis who had helped produce the Oral Law. Thus, the regular sermon had been a common synagogue practice during Roman times, and prayer in languages other than Hebrew had been carried on even earlier. This was obvious from the fact that most of the Kaddish itself appears in the prayer book in Aramaic.

Between the years 1844 and 1871, the rabbinical leaders of Reform, later joined by interested laymen, held a number of conferences at which they discussed various religious changes. Studies were made of Jewish tradition, and on the basis of their findings, the conferences succeeded in introducing important modifications of Jewish practice and belief.

Nonetheless, the movement failed to gain a large following. The Orthodox, who held positions of authority in most Jewish communities, fought the reformers at every hand, and they were aided by the political reaction which set

in after the defeat of Napoleon in 1815. New restrictions against the Jews and a rising tide of anti-Semitism made religious reforms seem superfluous. So, failing to win mass support, the Reform movement languished in Europe.

Reform Takes Root in America   It was in the United States that Reform Judaism prospered, for the American atmosphere of religious freedom and pioneering was highly congenial to its development.

There had been Jews living in America ever since 23 refugees from the Inquisition in Brazil landed in New Amsterdam in 1654. Here, over the opposition of the governor, Peter Stuyvesant, they succeeded in gaining the right to serve in the militia, to trade and own property, and to have a cemetery of their own. In succeeding years, others, mainly Sephardim (Jews of Spanish descent), settled in a number of New England, Middle Atlantic and Southern colonies, and the first synagogues were established in Newport, Rhode Island, and New York City.

During the Revolution, there were about 2,000 Jews in America. Most sided with those fighting for independence, and they proudly contributed both their services in the militia and their resources to the cause. While most restrictions against the Jews were removed during the Revolution, a number of them still remained on the state level and were only gradually repealed. Yet, in contrast to most sections

FIRST JEWISH SETTLEMENT. In 1654, twenty-three Jewish refugees from Recife, Brazil, settled in New Amsterdam, despite the opposition of its Dutch governor.

of Europe, the Jews of America enjoyed considerable equality under the law, and great opportunity.

It was in response to this environment that American Jews, too, began seeking certain changes in their mode of worship. Starting in Charleston, South Carolina, in 1824, a small group of reformers in the Beth Elohim Congregation gradually influenced the membership to accept the use of the organ and other changes in worship.

Subsequently, beginning in the 1840's, many more Jews began emigrating to America, this time from Germany and Central Europe, to escape the intolerance there. Some undoubtedly had been associated with Reform in Europe, and they now commenced promoting the cause in this country. By 1841, groups of Jews in the United States, notably in Baltimore, New York, Philadelphia, and Chicago, began organizing Reform societies. In April of the following year, the Har Sinai Society of Baltimore became the first American congregation to be

REFORM ORGANIZER. Isaac M. Wise, who arrived from Europe in 1846, succeeded in establishing all three major American Reform institutions: a union of congregations, a rabbinical seminary, and a permanent rabbinical body.

organized as Reform right from the start. Soon other Reform societies grew into congregations and a number of former Orthodox synagogues became Reform.

Shortly thereafter, the movement began to secure the services of certain gifted liberal European rabbis who sought the freedom of America. One was Isaac M. Wise, who arrived in 1846 and converted congregations in Albany and Cincinnati to Reform. It was he who gave the movement its organizational structure with the establishment of a union of congregations in 1873, a rabbinical seminary in 1875, and a permanent rabbinical body in 1889.

Originally, Wise had hoped to unite all American Jewry and therefore agreed to a number of compromises with the Orthodox. However, not only did his plan fail, but he almost split the young Reform movement.

The leader of the opposition was David Einhorn. His religious liberalism had led to a stormy rabbinical career prior to his coming to this country at the age of forty-six. Now, as the rabbi of Baltimore's Har Sinai Congregation, he was as outspoken and unyielding as ever in behalf of Reform. He took strong exception to Wise's compromises with the Orthodox, especially his willingness to accept the provisions of the Talmud as binding upon the Liberal Jew. "Ceremonials and practices," Einhorn insisted, "are merely outer symbols of the Jewish faith that change as life itself changes. What is permanent in Judaism is its belief in the One God, the moral and ethical teachings of the Bible, faith in the equality and basic goodness of men and in the coming of a great Messianic Age, when all mankind will find lasting peace and happiness upon earth." Einhorn's views were reflected in the prayer book he prepared which ultimately became the basis for the *Union Prayerbook* used today by Reform Jews.

Meanwhile, the American movement was developing its own forms of worship. They included the use of English as well as Hebrew in prayer, the holding of a late Friday evening service, the seating of men and women together, the use of the organ and mixed choir, and the abolition of the head-covering. The reformers also eliminated the extra days of the Jewish holidays, and made many modifications in Jewish mourning, marriage, and divorce procedures. In contrast to the movement in Europe, American Reform did not hesitate to break with Jewish tradition where it seriously conflicted with the realities of modern life.

Then, in 1885, a number of Reform rabbis gathered at Pittsburgh to produce a set of principles. Generally, they agreed with the position of Einhorn, and the platform they created emphasized the following eight points:

1. Judaism's concept of God is central and man's most important religious truth.
2. Judaism is in harmony with the new discoveries of science, and recognizes that, though the Bible contains some myths and legends, it still remains the great source of religious truth.
3. Only those ceremonial practices that are meaningful to the modern Jew can be acceptable to him.
4. The modern Jew rejects all Jewish laws regulating diet and dress.
5. The modern Jew believes in a Messianic Age for all mankind, but not in the coming of a personal Messiah to lead the Jews back to Palestine.
6. It is the Mission of the Jews to help bring about the Messianic Age in which God's Kingdom of truth, justice, and peace will be established on earth.
7. The modern Jew believes in the immortality of the soul, in contrast to the belief of the Orthodox in bodily resurrection in a heavenly Garden of Eden.
8. It is the obligation of all Jews to work for the creation of a society based upon the principle of justice to all.

With the creation of the Pittsburgh Platform, harmony in the movement was gradually restored between the forces led by Wise and Einhorn. Reform continued to grow, and by the end of the 1880's, it was the majority faith of American Jewry.

REFORM WORSHIP. A daily service conducted in the chapel of the House of Living Judaism, the New York headquarters of the Union of American Hebrew Congregations.

Then, with the persecutions in Russia beginning in the 1880's, large numbers of East European Jews gradually made their way to America. Since most of them came with a background of Orthodoxy, Reform was soon reduced to a small minority of the Jews in the United States. Though the movement continued to grow during the half-century that followed, it has only been since the 1940's that Reform has once more come to represent a sizable proportion of American Jewry.

Reform Judaism Today In 1937, fifty-two years after Pittsburgh, American Reform adopted its present platform, called the "Guiding Principles of Reform Judaism." It did so primarily because of certain changes that had

FROM EASTERN EUROPE. Beginning in the 1880's, an increasing number of Jews made their way into the United States through Ellis Island, in New York harbor.

taken place since Reform's earlier days.

The Pittsburgh Platform, for example, had come into being even before the World Zionist movement was organized. Now, with the rise of Zionism as a significant force in Jewish life, the Reform movement wished to express positive support for the rebuilding of the Jewish Homeland in Palestine. Moreover, time had shown that there was need for the development of greater religious practice among Reform Jews, and the growing tragedy of Hitler's anti-Semitism in Germany called for stronger em-phasis upon the unity of the Jewish people everywhere.

So, while the "Guiding Principles" reaffirmed much of the Pittsburgh Platform, the 1937 platform added certain features that were not contained within the 1885 statement. For instance, it declared Reform's belief in the common historic and religious kinship of the Jewish people and called for the support of all Jews in the upbuilding of Palestine as a center of Jewish life. It urged the wider cultivation of prayer and ceremony, the greater use of Hebrew in worship and instruction, and full support for measures of social justice designed to protect the aged, the sick, and the unemployed.

Basically, however, Reform reasserted its faith in the One, living God who created all and to whom, as a loving Father, man turns in worship. Through the Torah and the historic tradition of Israel, it declared, He gave His moral laws by which mankind might find perfection. In His sight, all men are His children, capable of overcoming evil and establishing the good. Especially did He charge the Jewish people with responsibility for becoming His co-partners in carrying out their Mission to establish His Kingdom of brotherhood, justice, truth, and peace on earth.

In the years that have followed the adoption of the "Guiding Principles," the Reform move-

NAZI GERMANY. Adolph Hitler's accession to power in 1933 intensified Germany's attacks on the Jews until, by the end of World War II, some 6 million in Europe had been murdered. Below (left to right): Shop windows labeled with the word "Jew"; Hitler addressing the Nazi Party in 1935; prominent Jews compelled by Storm Troopers to clean the streets.

ment has grown to about a million members, or approximately a third of all American Jews affiliated with a synagogue. Under the leadership of the World Union for Progressive Judaism, founded in 1926, the movement has also begun to show real growth abroad. Today there are sizable Reform congregations, not only in England, France, and a number of other European countries, but also in Australia, South Africa, India, Israel, and elsewhere.

Perhaps the most important contribution of Reform has been its insistence that Judaism must continue to grow through the process of reinterpretation and change. Thus it has modernized synagogue worship and Jewish religious practice, established equality for women, and developed a new and more meaningful program of religious education. Other significant achievements have been its emphasis upon Social Action and the creation of a form of national organization that has become the model for the other interpretations of Judaism.

In Reform each congregation is completely independent. It selects its own rabbi, who has been ordained only after five years of postgraduate study at the Hebrew Union College–Jewish Institute of Religion, and together they determine the congregation's own policies and practices. The decisions of the Union of American Hebrew Congregations, representing the Reform temples, and the Central Conference of American Rabbis, made up of nearly 800 Liberal rabbis, are merely advisory.

The Rise of Conservative Judaism   Conservative Judaism came into being as an outgrowth of the Reform movement in Europe.

At the second conference of liberal rabbis held in Frankfort in 1845, Zacharias Frankel, a prominent German rabbi, withdrew from the sessions because he objected to the decision that the use of Hebrew in worship was not absolutely essential. His position, he claimed, was based upon the principle of "positive-historical Judaism," by which he meant the preservation of all practices and beliefs that had come down through the centuries. Changes could be made, he said, only if they were approved by the Jew-

189

REFORM INSTITUTIONS. (top) The House of Living Judaism in New York, headquarters of the Union of American Hebrew Congregations. (center) The Cincinnati school of the Hebrew Union College–Jewish Institute of Religion. (lower right) The New York school and (lower left) the California school in Los Angeles.

CONSERVATIVE SEMINARY. The training institution for American Conservative rabbis is The Jewish Theological Seminary, founded in 1886 and located in New York.

Theological Seminary in New York for the training of American Conservative rabbis. Its first president was Sabato Morais, a leading rabbi and Bible professor. He was succeeded in 1902 by Solomon Schechter, one of the great Jewish scholars of England, who made the Seminary an outstanding center of Jewish learning.

As the Conservative movement took root in America, it attracted many who had originally been Orthodox but who now desired certain changes in Jewish practice without, however, going to the full extent of Reform. The Conservative Jew felt more comfortable worshipping with covered head and carrying on many of the traditional practices. More and more, Conservatism, as a kind of compromise between Orthodoxy and Reform, won increasing support among the former East European Jews.

Over the years, however, the Conservative movement has frequently adopted the example of Reform Judaism. Gradually, it has introduced certain modifications making for greater decorum in worship. Other changes have permitted men and women to sit together in the synagogue, the holding of a late Friday evening service, and in some congregations, the use of the organ.

ish people as a whole and sanctioned by their leaders.

Thus, while Frankel no longer regarded the Written and Oral Law as literally God-given or unchangeable by man—and he did give his approval to certain modifications of synagogue practice—the position he took seemed to make any serious reforms in Judaism unlikely. As leader of the new Conservative group, Frankel became the head of a more modern rabbinical school founded in Breslau in 1854. However, like Reform, the Conservative movement also made only modest headway in Europe.

In the 1880's, a number of European Conservative rabbis came to America. While they agreed that Judaism should make certain adjustments to modern life, they objected to some of the extremes to which they felt American Reform had gone. They considered the Pittsburgh Platform "radical," and its adoption prompted them in 1886 to create the Jewish

The Conservative Movement Today Conservative Judaism in the United States today has approximately the same number of followers as Reform, and thus also represents about a third of all American Jews affiliated with a synagogue. It, too, has its own organization of congregations, called the United Synagogue of America, and a permanent rabbinical association, the Rabbinical Assembly of America.

The official position of the Conservative movement to which the great majority of its rabbis and laymen subscribe upholds the authority of the Oral and Written Law. Though the worship and prayer book have been modified, by and large the movement seeks to maintain traditional Jewish law in so far as that is possible.

DEVELOPMENTS IN REFORM, CONSERVATIVE, AND ORTHODOX JUDAISM TO 1845

EVENTS AFFECTING JEWISH LIFE

1789 Outbreak of French Revolution.

1790 Establishment of "Pale of Settlement" in Russia.

1791 Citizenship granted the Jews of France.

1806 Assembly of Jewish Notables.

1807 Great Sanhedrin.

1815 Defeat of Napoleon. Restrictions against the Jews renewed.

1840 Increased persecution of Russian Jewry.

REFORM JUDAISM

1801 Jacobson founds Seesen School; gradually introduces reforms in worship.

Reform services in Berlin.

1810 First Confirmation held.

About 1819 Science of Judaism begins.

1824 Reform starts in Charleston, S. C.

1838 Geiger leads Reform in Breslau.

1841 Charleston builds temple with organ.

1842 Har Sinai Society formed in Baltimore. Reform congregation established in England.

1844 Beginning of European Reform Conferences, to **1871**.

CONSERVATIVE AND ORTHODOX JUDAISM

Orthodox
1836 Samson Raphael Hirsch publishes his *Nineteen Letters*.

Conservative
1845 Frankel withdraws from Frankfurt Rabbinical Conference.

FINAL TOUCH. A Conservative rabbi has the privilege of lettering in the final words of a new Torah acquired by the congregation, an event calling for special celebration.

CONSERVATIVE SERVICE. Members of the congregation stand as the Torahs are carried through the synagogue in commemoration of the Festival of the Rejoicing of the Law.

However, during the past twenty-five years, another group has arisen within Conservatism. Known as the Reconstructionist movement and led by Mordecai Kaplan, a retired professor of the Jewish Theological Seminary, its supporters advocate sweeping changes in the philosophy of Conservatism. Though the Reconstructionists believe that traditional customs and practices should continue to be observed as "folkways" of the Jewish people, they do not consider them to be absolutely binding. They also reject all belief in a personal Messiah, in bodily resurrection, and in the concept of the Jews as a "Chosen People."

Reconstructionism, a name which Dr. Kaplan derived from the need for "reconstructing" Jewish life in modern times, claims that Judaism is a *civilization* in which religion is the central element. Other concepts, such as Jewish culture, the unity of the Jewish people, and the development of Jewish life in the State of Israel, are also essential. To him and his supporters, the American Jew lives not only in an American civilization, but in a Jewish one as well. To promote that civilization, they say, American Jewry should be organized in unified Jewish communities that are responsible for all phases of Jewish activity.

The movement publishes its own magazine, *The Reconstructionist*, occasional books, and its own prayer book for the use of congregations that share its point of view. Its program has had considerable influence upon Reform rabbis and laymen, and some have become actively identified with it. However, thus far, most of the adherents of Reconstructionism belong to the Conservative movement.

The Reaction of Orthodoxy By and large, Orthodoxy, which is that interpretation of Judaism based upon strict adherence to the God-given and unchangeable Written and Oral Law, strongly opposes both Reform and Conservatism.

In the earlier days of Reform in Europe, the Orthodox considered it a form of "heresy." Therefore, they sought to uproot it by every possible means. They appealed to the government to suppress it, issued public condemnations of the most violent sort, and even demanded the withdrawal of Orthodox Jews from Jewish communities that supported Reform temples.

Though the Orthodox themselves finally made certain modifications in their worship, such as introducing greater decorum in the synagogue and a weekly sermon in the language of the country, they remained unyielding toward other changes. In fact, under the leadership of Samson Raphael Hirsch, the Orthodox developed a new militancy. In his book, *The Nineteen Letters of Ben Uziel*, written anonymously in 1836, Hirsch declared that what was needed was not a reform of Judaism but a reform of Jews, so

192

RELIGIOUS AFFILIATION OF JEWS IN THE UNITED STATES *

REFORM
18%

UNAFFILIATED
46%

CONSERVATIVE
18%

ORTHODOX
18%

REFORM
about 1,000,000

CONSERVATIVE
about 1,000,000

ORTHODOX
about 1,000,000

UNAFFILIATED
about 2,500,000

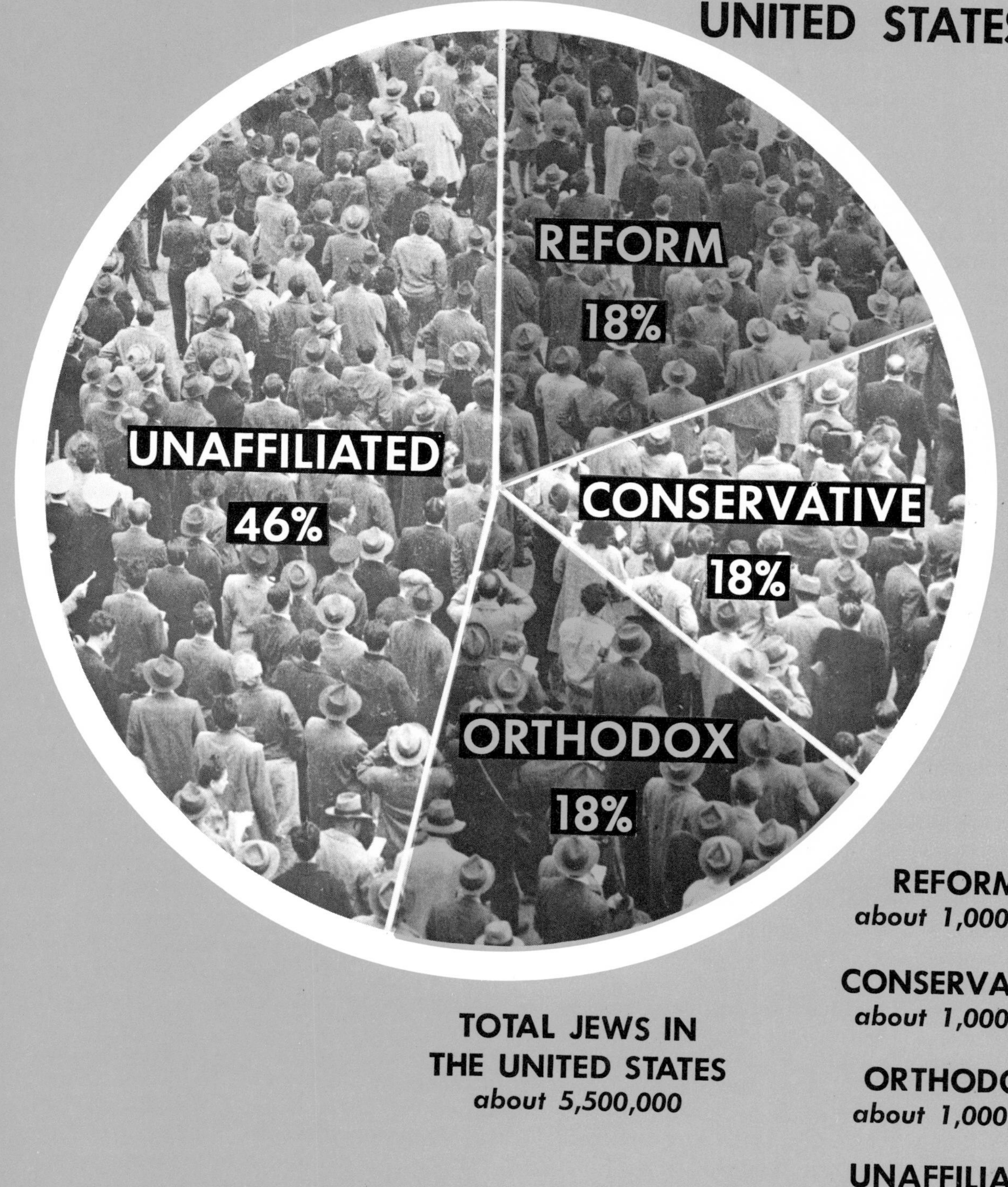

**TOTAL JEWS IN
THE UNITED STATES**
about 5,500,000

*Figures are for 1960

that their greater knowledge of the Law would develop a deeper loyalty to the tradition. His later works sought to justify its practices.

In the United States, some of the congregations founded in Colonial times had continued to remain Orthodox, though of an American variety. Upon coming to this country, the East European Jews who fled Russian persecution beginning in the 1880's found them quite different from those they had known at home. Therefore, they established synagogues of their own that were more in keeping with the customs they knew. For the education of the young, they developed, first, the *cheder* and *yeshivo* patterned after their schools in Europe, and later, the afternoon school, called the *talmud Torah*.

HISTORIC ORTHODOX CONGREGATION. Tracing its origins back to the first Jewish settlers of the city, the Shearith Israel Congregation of New York worships in this imposing synagogue.

Orthodox Judaism Today   In present-day America, one finds many varieties of Orthodoxy. It ranges from that of the old pre-Revolutionary congregation to that of the Chasidic synagogue with its bearded and quaintly-dressed followers, who worship much as did their ancestors in Poland.

However, the majority practice what is called "modern Orthodoxy," which adheres to Jewish tradition as Divine Law, but is modern in the dignity of its worship and in the introduction of certain new practices, such as the Bas Mitzvah of girls. Its followers are affiliated with the Union of Orthodox Jewish Congregations comprising some 700 synagogues, and their rabbis are members of the Rabbinical Council of America. Their rabbinate is trained by modern rabbinical seminaries, chiefly the Rabbi Isaac Elchanan Rabbinical Seminary of Yeshiva University in New York and the Hebrew Theological College of Chicago, now called the Jewish University of America.

A rival group that has preserved more of the East European pattern of Orthodoxy is led by the Yiddish-speaking rabbis of the *Agudas Horabonim*, the Union of Orthodox Rabbis. They claim complete authority over Orthodox Jewish life in America and do not cooperate with any other Jewish religious body. However, even within this interpretation of Orthodoxy, there are some factions that refuse to accept their leadership.

Though Orthodoxy has lost many of its followers to Reform and Conservatism, it still has an actual membership in the United States of around one million, though it claims about twice that number. Within recent years, and as a result of its new appeal and more vigorous leadership, the movement has enjoyed somewhat of a revival.

Continuing to adhere to Maimonides' "Thirteen Articles of Faith" with its doctrine of an unchanging Jewish Law, the Orthodox insist upon the observance of all traditional practices. These include the dietary laws, the requirement of a Jewish divorce for remarriage, and the separation of men and women in the synagogue. Instrumental music is not permitted in the worship, women do not enjoy religious equality, and many modern funeral practices are prohibited. At the same time, the Orthodox lay great stress upon a thorough Hebrew education, and today they vigorously champion a system of day schools where students carry on their general studies as well.

The Observances of the Jew   Despite their differences, the followers of the various interpretations of Judaism are linked together by many ties. Among them are their common Jewish history and identity, devotion to important Jewish causes, association in various Jewish

194

DEVELOPMENTS IN REFORM, CONSERVATIVE, AND ORTHODOX JUDAISM FROM 1845 TO 1897

EVENTS AFFECTING JEWISH LIFE

1848 Unsuccessful revolutions leading to large scale German emigration to America.

About 1850 Haskala develops in Eastern Europe.

1862 Kalischer and Hess call for rebuilding of Zion.

1882 Russian "May Laws." Start of Eastern European immigration to the U.S. First settlement of Russian pioneers in Palestine.

1894 Start of Dreyfus Affair.

1896 Herzl's *Jewish State*.

1897 First Zionist Congress. Growth of Zionist movement begins.

REFORM JUDAISM

1846 Wise comes to America.

1855 Einhorn comes to America.

1873 Union of American Hebrew Congregations formed.

1875 Hebrew Union College founded in Cincinnati.

1885 "Pittsburgh Platform" created.

1889 Central Conference of American Rabbis organized.

CONSERVATIVE AND ORTHODOX JUDAISM

Conservative
1845 Frankel withdraws from Frankfurt Rabbinical Conference.

Conservative
1854 Frankel becomes head of new Breslau Seminary.

Orthodox
Beginning in 1881 Formation of many new Orthodox congregations in America.

Conservative
1886 Jewish Theological Seminary founded in New York.

Orthodox
1896 Founding of Isaac Elchanan Seminary (now part of Yeshiva University).

INDIVIDUAL RESEARCH. Students of a Reform religious school use the temple library as part of their Jewish education.

DAY SCHOOL. At this school which they attend all day, Conservative young people receive both secular and Jewish education.

organizations, and a great many essentials of Judaism itself. For Reform, Conservative, and Orthodox Jews alike have synagogues, rabbis, Torahs, and most Jewish ceremonial items in common. All employ Hebrew in their worship, utilize many common prayers and hymns, and provide for Jewish education. They all affirm their belief in One God and His covenant with Israel, and subscribe to the same high standards of ethics and morals, and the most wholesome kind of family relationships.

But nothing is more effective in preserving the basic unity of the Jews than their religious observances. In the main, these center about the celebration of the Sabbath and holidays, and the commemoration of significant occasions in the life of the individual. True, there are differences in details. The Orthodox and Conservative Jews, for instance, observe an additional day of the major holidays, keep certain minor holidays that Reform has seen fit to abandon, and have stricter laws governing the observance of the Sabbath and holidays. Nevertheless, the various common observances serve to unify the whole of Jewish religious life.

The occurrence of the Jewish holidays is determined by the lunar calendar, not the solar one that is in general use. Hence, the dates on which they fall fluctuate from year to year. All

of them, too—including the Sabbath—start and end at sundown.

The calendar year commences with Rosh Hashono (New Year's Day) and Yom Kippur (Day of Atonement), an intense period of repentance. The remaining major holidays of Judaism are the "Pilgrim Festivals," so called because during Temple times Jews were expected to observe them in Jerusalem. These are Sukos (Festival of Booths), Passover, and Shovuos (Festival of Weeks). All of them grew out of agricultural life in ancient Palestine, but in the course of time became associated with significant events in the Jewish past. Two of the most important minor festivals are Chanuko (Festival of Rededication) commemorating the victory of the Maccabees over the Syrian Greeks in 165 B.C.E., and Purim (Festival of Lots) celebrating the deliverance of the Jews of Persia, as told by the Book of Esther. The weekly observance of the Sabbath completes the cycle of holy days.

Unquestionably, most of the Jewish holidays go back to very ancient times. Some, especially those connected with the various seasons of the year, were originally rooted in primitive beliefs. However, through reinterpretation over the centuries, they have come to symbolize the highest ideals and values in Judaism.

196

DEVELOPMENTS IN REFORM, CONSERVATIVE, AND ORTHODOX JUDAISM,
FROM 1898 TO THE PRESENT

EVENTS AFFECTING JEWISH LIFE	REFORM JUDAISM	CONSERVATIVE JUDAISM	ORTHODOX JUDAISM
			**1898** Creation of Union of Orthodox Jewish Congregations.
			Formation of Union of Orthodox Rabbis.
1914 World War I begins.		**1902** Schecter becomes head of Jewish Theological Seminary.	
		**1913** Founding of United Synagogue of America.	
		1919 Rabbinical Assembly of America organized.	**1921** Creation of Hebrew Theological College of Chicago (now the Jewish University of America).
	1922 Founding of Jewish Institute of Religion (merged with Hebrew Union College in 1950).		
1933 Hitler comes to power. Start of Jewish massacres.	**1926** Founding of World Union for Progressive Judaism.	**1934** Beginning of Reconstructionist movement.	
	1937 "Guiding Principles" adopted		**1935** Creation of Rabbinical Council of America.
1939 World War II begins.			**1938** Beginning of growth of Day Schools.
1948 State of Israel established.			

SUKOS IN ISRAEL. Jewish youth wearing the talis (prayer-shawl) are reverently holding the traditional palm-branch (lulov) and citron (esrog).

BUYING AN ESROG. In preparation for the celebration of Sukos, Israeli Jews purchase their citrons.

Rituals hallowing the life of the individual from birth to death comprise the second type of Jewish observance. Among the most important of these are: (1) the circumcision of all males, (2) the naming of children in the synagogue, (3) in Reform, the consecration of children entering the religious school, (4) Bar and Bas Mitzvah, (5) Confirmation, chiefly in Reform and Conservatism, (6) marriage, (7) the funeral and other observances connected with death. Though many of these rites, too, stem from very ancient practices, reinterpretation over the centuries has continued to keep them meaningful and inspiring in the lives of the Jewish people.

We Turn Eastward   So far, we have been concerned with the development of the beliefs and practices of the great religions of the West;

namely, Judaism and the various forms of Christianity—Roman Catholicism, Eastern Orthodoxy, and Protestantism. These are the faiths with which we have the most contact, for their followers represent considerably more than 90 per cent of all Americans associated with organized religion.

But in the entire world, the Jews and Christians combined are only about 35 per cent of all religious people. This means that the followers of other faiths represent a sizable majority in most of the remaining portions of the globe.

Those who live in the West have become increasingly more aware of this as the peoples of the East emerge from centuries of backwardness and subjugation to play a significant role in the modern world. Just as their cultures, traditions, and ways of life are being comprehended in the West, so, too, their religions are bound to become better known.

This is especially true of Islam, the chief faith of the Middle East, whose followers comprise the second largest religious body in the world. . . .

TOPICS TO DISCUSS

1. In what fundamental ways is modern Jewish religious life different from that of Roman Catholicism, Eastern Orthodoxy, and Protestantism?
2. For what reasons have Reform, Conservatism, and Reconstructionism come into being? In what basic ways do they differ from Orthodoxy?
3. Despite their different interpretations of Judaism, how are the religious Jews of your community united? What, in turn, serves to link them with the so-called "non-affiliated" Jews?
4. On what fundamental beliefs do all religious Jews agree? Wherein do they differ, and why?

THINGS TO DO

1. Prepare a report on Jewish religious affiliation in your own community. How many Jews are connected with Reform, Orthodox, and Conservative congregations? How many

are unaffiliated? How do you explain the facts as you have found them?

2. Invite an Orthodox and Conservative rabbi, or informed laymen, to present their points of view about Judaism. Then compare your own views with theirs. Where do they agree, and where do they differ?

3. Prepare a chart listing the characteristics of the "good Jew" from the points of view of Orthodoxy, Conservatism, and Reform. How, then, would you define a good Jew?

OTHER THINGS TO READ

BAMBERGER, BERNARD J., *The Story of Judaism*, UAHC, Part 6, "Era of Hope," pp. 253-330; Part 7, "The Road to the Abyss," pp. 333-403; Part 8, "Problems and Opportunities," pp. 407-450.

FITCH, FLORENCE M., *One God*, Lothrop, Lee, and Shepard, "The Jewish Way," pp. 13-55.

SACHAR, HOWARD M., *The Course of Modern Jewish History*, World, Chapter 8, "The Rise of Jewish Life in the New World," pp. 160-180; Chapter 15, "The Great Migration and Settlement in America," pp. 305-322; Chapter 18, "The Palestine Mandate," pp. 369-393; Chapter 19, "The Impact of the Jews on Western Culture," pp. 394-418; Chapter 24, "The Growth of the American-Jewish Community," pp. 520-541.

SCHWARTZMAN, SYLVAN D., *Reform Judaism in the Making*, UAHC.

SMITH, HUSTON, *The Religions of Man*, Mentor, Chapter 7, "Judaism," pp. 233-272.

SPENCE, HARTZELL, *The Story of America's Religions*, Holt, Rinehart, Winston, Chapter 9, "The Jews," pp. 146-164.

STEINBERG, MILTON, *Basic Judaism*, Harcourt, Brace.

16

ISLAM, THE GREAT RELIGION OF THE MIDDLE EAST

The Religions of Asia   More than one-half of the world's population lives on the single continent of Asia. They are peoples of great imagination and spiritual consciousness, and in the long process of their history they have given birth to practically all of the major faiths in the world today. For we must remember that even the great religions of the West were cradled in the Near Eastern portion of the Asian continent.

As we have already noted in the case of Mesopotamia and India, early in their history the peoples of Asia developed various forms of religion. These were based upon a variety of beliefs in the Supernatural, which ranged from faith in mana, animistic spirits, and totems, to deities representing many of the forces of nature, such as the sun, earth, life-giving water, and the like. From these prehistoric beliefs and practices, eventually emerged the modern religions of the Middle and Far East.

Today, there are many different religions in Asia. Some, such as Jainism (India), Shintoism (Japan), Sikhism (India), and Zoroastrianism (Iran), have a more limited number of followers. But there are four faiths, which, from the standpoint of numbers alone, are extremely influential. These are Islam, Hinduism, Buddhism, and Confucianism. Together they include almost one and a quarter billion people, and as we observe from the chart on the follow-ing page, they outnumber by more than 25 per cent the combined followers of all the major religions of the West.

Islam Appears on the Scene   In this chapter and in those to follow, we shall look briefly at the development, teachings, and practices of the four major religions of Asia. We begin with the one that has the largest following, Islam, which, as we have seen, has more than 431 million adherents.

Actually, Mohammedanism, or Islam as its followers insist it be called, more closely resembles the religions of the West than those of the East. And, like Judaism and Christianity, it, too, arose in the Middle East.

In the seventh century C.E., Islam suddenly burst upon the scene. Within several centuries, the Moslems, stirred by the frenzy of a "holy war," swept across many parts of Asia, Africa, and Europe, and came within a fraction of taking over control of the then-known world. Had it not been for their defeat at the Battle of Tours in 732, they would certainly have overrun France and brought Islam to most of the Western world.

It had been a time of relative quiet among the followers of both Judaism and Christianity. The Talmud had recently been completed, and succeeding generations of rabbis were busily occupied with explaining its teachings and fur-

COMPARATIVE SIZES
OF ASIAN AND
WESTERN RELIGIONS *

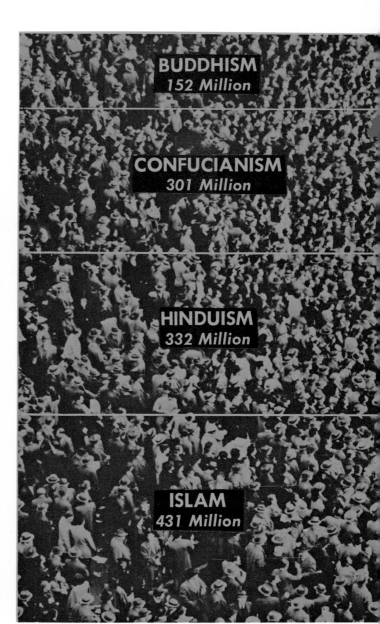

BUDDHISM
152 Million

CONFUCIANISM
301 Million

HINDUISM
332 Million

ISLAM
431 Million

JUDAISM
▼ 12¾ Million

EASTERN ORTHODOXY
137 Million

PROTESTANTISM
214 Million

ROMAN CATHOLICISM
537 Million

WESTERN

ASIAN

Total membership of major Western religions: 900 million

Total membership of major religions of Asia: 1,216 million

*Figures are for 1960

MOHAMMED. After his flight to Medina in 622 C.E., he began to attract numerous followers. They soon constituted a powerful army that succeeded in unifying the different peoples of Arabia.

ther expanding the Oral Law. As for Christianity, it was still recovering from the fall of Rome and had not as yet established itself as the great spiritual and political force of Europe.

Suddenly, the quiet of the Dark Ages was shattered by the armies of Islam that rose up to challenge the Roman, Byzantine, and Persian Empires in the name of Allah and his great Prophet, Mohammed.

Who were these people and what were their beliefs?

How the Arab Peoples Came to Be The original followers of Mohammed were Semitic peoples of the great Arabian peninsula, the area known today as Saudi Arabia. It is here, as we observe from the map on page 211, that the holy Moslem cities of Mecca and Medina are located.

According to their legends, the Arabs trace their descent from the Patriarch Abraham him-

self. Abraham, so the Bible tells us, had children with two different women. One was his wife Sarah, who had been childless for many years. The other was Hagar, Sarah's servant, whom she gave to Abraham so that he might have an heir. Hagar bore Abraham a son, Ishmael.

Then a remarkable thing occurred. In their old age, Abraham and Sarah finally had a son of their own, Isaac. Sarah now grew jealous of Hagar and Ishmael and insisted that Abraham send them away. Nothing else would satisfy her. So the next day Hagar, with Ishmael on her shoulders, was sent out into the desert.

The hot sun blazed down, and she soon became so weary and thirsty that she could go no farther. Hagar threw herself down on the ground and wept, knowing that she and her son would shortly die. Then, according to Arab legend, Ishmael kicked the sand in anger, and on that very spot a spring gushed up, the holy waters of Zemzem.

When Abraham learned what had happened, he is said to have journeyed to the spring and built a temple near it, called the Ka'aba because it was in the form of a "cube." He also brought the great black stone (actually a meteorite), which Adam had taken with him from the Garden of Eden, and placed it in the shrine. There Hagar and her son continued to dwell, and the descendants of Ishmael built a holy city around the shrine. This is the city of Mecca.

The offspring of Abraham and Hagar, through their son Ishmael, became the Arab people. The descendants of Abraham and Sarah, through their son Isaac, became the Jews.

So runs the Arab legend which Mohammed believed, and it played an important part in the development of the Moslem faith.

A Divine Revelation Comes to Mohammed
Mohammed, whose name means "the Praised One," was born in Mecca about 570 C.E. into a powerful Arabian tribe. Most of the information we have about him and his life comes from the Islamic "Wisdom," collections of traditions

that grew up among the first generation of his followers. These remained in oral form for some time and were committed to writing only at a much later period. Though they contain a great deal of legendary material, scholars have been able to sift through them and to piece together what is believed to be a reasonably accurate account of Mohammed's life.

Mohammed's father died about two months before his birth; his mother, when he was only six. So, for the remainder of his childhood he was reared by poor relatives. Early in life Mohammed became a camel driver and caravan leader. During his many travels through desert country, he came into contact with various peoples and among them were Jews and Christians, from whom he learned something about their religions. Others, slaves and relatives, added to his fund of information about Christianity and Judaism. He was especially impressed with their concept of the one universal God that could not be represented by images, and with the belief that idolators would be punished at a Last Judgment with everlasting fire.

At the same time, he knew from his associations with the masses of the Arab people that most of them were pagans. They worshipped idols and various forces of nature, certain rocks, caves, springs, and palm trees, and they had numerous local gods and goddesses. In Mecca, for instance, Hubal was the chief male deity, although the people also believed in a distant creator-god named Allah. They likewise worshipped three female deities, the so-called "daughters of Allah." One was a Mother-goddess named al-Lat, another was a goddess of destiny, and the third, a goddess quite similar to Venus. The people also believed in many lesser spirits, particularly angels and Jinn, demons or evil beings. The beliefs of the people were riddled with all sorts of superstitions, and their standards of morality were very low. Some of them even sacrificed their children, girls particularly.

In the desert Mohammed had time for thought and meditation. Undoubtedly, he was moved by what he had learned about the Bible and the teachings of Jesus as well as the legends of his own people, especially those concerning their great ancestor, Abraham. Then, as Islamic tradition tells it, Mohammed, at about the age of forty, experienced a vision of the angel Gabriel, the messenger of God, in a cave at the base of a mountain near Mecca. The angel told him in part:

> Recite! in the name of your Lord who created,
> Created man from clots of blood.
> Recite! for your Lord is the most beneficent,
> Who has taught the use of the pen,
> Has taught man that which he knew not . . .
> Truly unto the Lord is the return of all . . .
> Nay! do not obey him [the wicked]; but adore and draw near to God.

This and all of the other revelations that Mohammed received were later recorded in Islam's sacred book, the *Koran,* named after the Arabic word meaning "the reading," and somewhat smaller in size than the New Testament. Considered by orthodox Moslems to be the actual revelation of God, the *Koran* contains 114 chapters, each called a "sura." Each sura begins with the phrase "In the name of God, the Compassionate, the Merciful." Except for the opening one, the suras are arranged according to length, with the longest coming first. In addition to presenting the beliefs, laws, and practices of Islam, the *Koran* also contains numerous legends and anecdotes derived from Jewish and Christian sources.

Mohammed Establishes a Religion Mohammed now began to receive other revelations from the angel Gabriel, who called him the Messenger of Allah, a Prophet following in the tradition of Abraham, Moses, and Jesus. Contrary to general Arab belief, Mohammed was thoroughly convinced that there was only one God, "Allah," from the Arabic word meaning *"The* God." It was further revealed to Mohammed that a great Day of Judgment would take

MECCA. Located in Saudi Arabia, about 50 miles inland from the Red Sea, this holy city centers about the Ka'aba, the shrine built in the form of a large black cube. The hope of every devout Moslem is to make a pilgrimage here at least once during his lifetime.

place when all men would be resurrected and sentenced either to everlasting punishment in hell or to eternal life in heaven. The *Koran* predicted:

> On that day there shall be a blast on the trumpet, and all that are in the heavens, and all that are on earth, shall be terror-stricken, except him whom God is pleased to deliver. . . .
>
> He who shall present himself with good works, shall reap the benefit therefrom, and they shall be secure from terror on that day.
>
> And they who shall present themselves

with evil shall because of it be flung face downwards into the fire. . . .

Man could be assured of the reward of heaven through five means: (1) Surrendering to the will of Allah, as revealed by His Prophet, Mohammed. Thus, the word *Islam*, describing the faith, comes from the Arabic word *salam* (related to the Hebrew *sholom*), "peace." It refers to that "peace" which one gains by submission to God, and, therefore, comes to mean "surrender to God." The word *Moslem*, then, referring to the believer, is "one who surrenders or submits" to God. (2) Abandoning idolatry.

204

(3) Prayer and meditation. (4) Acting justly and mercifully. (5) Encouraging others to be patient and perform good deeds.

At first, Mohammed revealed his teachings only to his wife, a wealthy widow some fifteen years older than he, his cousin Ali, and Abu Bakr, a person of some stature in Mecca, who became his most loyal disciple and later his successor. Then, about the year 616, he started to preach publicly of the coming of the Day of Judgment. Gradually, he also began to speak of the unity of God and of himself as the Prophet of Allah. But over a four-year period he attracted only a following of some forty people.

His actions aroused the animosity of the authorities of Mecca. Loyal to the gods of their sacred city and even dependent for their livelihood upon the worship of them by pilgrims from neighboring areas, they feared his attacks on idolatry. For even within the Ka'aba, their sacred shrine, stood idols that were revered by the people.

Aware of their hostility, Mohammed secretly arranged with the people of Yathrib, a city some 275 miles away, to serve as their leader. They had turned to him to put an end to the civil strife that was constantly breaking out in their community. But, when the Meccans learned of his plan to leave, they determined to kill him. Consequently, Mohammed fled for his life to Yathrib, and it is this *hegira*, "flight," occurring in the year 622, that the Moslems consider the official beginning of their religion.

Mohammed received a warm welcome in Yathrib, later renamed in his honor Medina, "*The* City" (of the Prophet). Taking over control of the community, he promptly introduced sound administration and reestablished order. He also called for regular religious practice, with a weekly service on Friday, then daily prayer. Alms for the poor as well as for the cause of the new faith were likewise collected.

By now his concept of God was beginning to change, until eventually Allah became the deity who established the path to salvation for Moslems alone. Allah's ways were now beyond all questioning, and in this sense he resembled a mighty Arab sheik whose every demand had to be obeyed. Allah's people, therefore, were truly expected to be "submitters," or in Arabic, Moslems.

Shortly after Mohammed established himself in Medina, he organized his followers into raiding parties that attacked the caravans of Mecca. When he had built up his forces, he defeated the army of the Meccans, and at the age of 60 finally captured their city. He promptly ordered the destruction of the city's idols, but paid honor to the black stone of the Ka'aba by riding seven times around the shrine. Thereby, he gave his sanction to pilgrimages to the holy city.

Now, in keeping with his teaching that all Moslems were members of one mighty "Brotherhood," he began to unify the whole of Arabia. He even invited the Jews and Christians to convert to his religion, pointing out that he accepted the Mosaic Law and the Christian Gospel. But, as the *Koran* angrily relates, the Jews rejected the Moslems:

> Of old we [the Moslems] accepted the covenant of the children of Israel, and sent apostles to them. As often as an apostle came to them with that for which they had no desire, some they treated as liars, and some they slew;
> And they reckoned that no harm would come of it—so they became blind and deaf. Then was God turned unto them; then many of them again became blind and deaf! But God beheld what they did.

At first Mohammed was determined to destroy the Jews, but he finally agreed to tolerate them on condition that they pay a sizable proportion of their income to the Moslem leaders. Later, a similar decision was made regarding the Christians who also refused to convert. Generally, except for occasional persecution by fanatical sects, the Jews fared well at the hands of the Moslems.

Mohammed died in 632. By then his armies led by Abu Bakr, who promptly became the Caliph, or "successor," were well on the way to taking over Syria, Palestine, Egypt, and large portions of the Persian Empire. Within a century, the Moslems had conquered Spain and North Africa, and even threatened France.

The Principal Beliefs of Islam The early eighth century marked the period of Islam's greatest growth, though the faith of Mohammed continued to make inroads in the East, even coming into India in the eleventh century. However, rivalries between various claimants to the caliphate and disputes over interpretations of Mohammed's teachings quickly split the movement into numerous groups. Thus, today there are some 250 different sects among the 431 million followers of Islam.

The largest sect, numbering some 150 million, are the Sunnis, who believe that the caliph must be selected from among members of Mohammed's own tribe. Their name is derived from the Arabic word for "the path," for they maintain that their six collections of tradition follow the religious ways approved by Mohammed himself.

The next most numerous group are the Shi'ites, "the party of Ali," who number about 20 million. In contrast to the Sunnis, they trace the descent of their caliphs from Ali, the cousin and son-in-law of Mohammed. Subdivided into many smaller sects, the Shi'ites reject the traditions of the Sunnis and claim that their own collections represent the original teachings of Mohammed.

An especially interesting group of Moslems is the Sufis, meaning "wool-wearers," ascetics who originally wore woolen robes. They originated in the eighth century and eventually organized themselves into monastic orders. Wearing monk's robes, practicing celibacy, fasting, and meditation, they sought to unite themselves with God through mystical contemplation. Those who undertook a life of wandering from place to place and were dependent upon charity for their sustenance became known as dervishes, from a Persian word meaning "one who comes to the door" begging, and a number of such dervish orders were founded during the twelfth century. Today, the majority of dervishes remain with their orders in quiet contemplation. However, the more extreme, like the Whirling Dervishes, who whirl about in religious ecstasy to music, attract a great deal of public attention.

The religion of the Moslems is also divided between those, like the Shi'ites, who are very "orthodox" in their beliefs, and other groups who are quite liberal and find support for their teachings and practices on the basis of human reason.

Though there are considerable differences of belief among the many sects, all followers of Islam subscribe to these six fundamental doctrines:

1. "There is no God but Allah"; that is, there is only one God and He created heaven and earth.
2. Around the throne of God are the angels who serve Him and make known His will. Lower than the angels are the Jinn, male and female spirits, one of whom—the Devil—caused the fall of Adam in the Garden of Eden.
3. Allah has revealed Himself and His will through the prophets, of whom Abraham, Moses, and Jesus were the forerunners of the last and greatest prophet, Mohammed. He alone handed down the perfect revelation.
4. There are certain divinely-inspired writings, originally 104 sacred books, of which only four have survived. These are the Five Books of Moses, the Psalms, the Christian Gospel, and the *Koran*. Except for the *Koran*, which is identical with the word of God, all the others are in mutilated form and contain many errors.
5. There will be a Last Judgment when all people will be resurrected and brought to justice. Then the books that record each man's deeds will be read and judgment meted out. The righteous will enter Paradise; the wicked will go to one of the seven levels of Hell.
6. Everyone must submit completely to Allah's will since all is predetermined by Him and man cannot alter his fate.

Naturally, with as many divisions as we find

ISLAM

within Islam, these have all been subject to a great many different interpretations. For instance, some Moslems no longer view life as thoroughly predetermined by Allah, but accord the individual almost unlimited freedom of action.

Moslem Practices   The Moslem's practices consist of five main duties.

The first is prayer, "the key to Paradise." Every Moslem is required to pray five times in the span of each day, beginning at dawn and ending at darkness. Before praying, he undergoes religious purification with water or sand. During his worship, he keeps his face toward Mecca, the holy city, while assuming a series of thirteen different positions and reciting a number of exclamations and portions of the *Koran.* Usually recited is Sura 1:

> Praise be to God, the Lord of the worlds!
> The compassionate, the merciful!
> King on the day of reckoning!
> You only do we worship, and to You do
>   we cry for help.
> Guide us on the straight path,
> The path of those to whom You have
>   been gracious—with whom You are
>   not angry, and who go not astray.

On Friday, the Moslem "Sabbath" (though not a day of rest), the men must attend a mosque, usually at noon, to hear a reading from the *Koran* and the recitation of prayers by the *Imam,* the individual appointed to conduct the ritual.

The religion of Islam has no clergy in the Western sense. The *Imam,* a title taken from the Arabic word for "the one who precedes," is merely the person who stands at the head of the congregation and recites prayers. Another official is the *Cadi,* or judge, who decides cases on the basis of Moslem religious law.

The second principal duty is giving alms to the poor at least once a year. One is expected to give two and a half per cent annually of whatever he possesses, an amount set by Mohammed.

The third duty is fasting, particularly during the entire month of Ramadan, the ninth month, which, because of an uncorrected lunar calen-

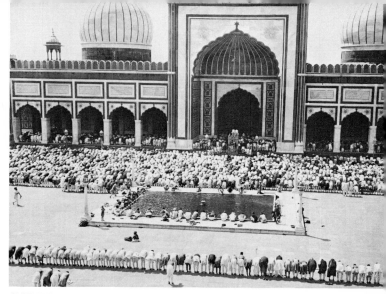

MOSLEMS AT PRAYER. Those gathered at this mosque face toward Mecca and assume various bodily positions as they recite prayers and selections from the **Koran**.

dar, may occur at all seasons of the year. This commemorates the giving of the *Koran* to Mohammed, and the Moslem observes it by scrupulously refraining from eating, drinking, and indulging in pleasures from dawn to sunset every day. After sunset, however, he may resume normal living. The end of Ramadan is an occasion for public rejoicing.

Among other Moslem holidays is the Festival of Ashura, a voluntary fast observed from sunset to sunset on the tenth day of the first month. It was adapted by Mohammed from the Jewish Day of Atonement with the purpose of having it atone for the sins of the coming year.

The fourth duty is a pilgrimage to Mecca. The Moslem is expected, if at all possible, to make at least one pilgrimage to Mecca during his lifetime. Normally, such pilgrimages take place annually from the 7th to the 10th day of the twelfth month. Upon coming near the holy city, the pilgrim puts on seamless white garments and goes without shoes. Once inside Mecca, he engages in visiting the sacred mosque, circling the Ka'aba shrine, which houses the holy black stone that the pilgrim must touch. He also is expected to visit several sacred mountains in the area. Some seventy thousand pilgrims make the visit to Mecca each year.

The Moslem carries on other practices as well. There are particular ceremonies connected with the life-cycle of the individual, including those involving the circumcision of all males, marriage, and death. Among the rites associated

THE RISE OF ISLAM

DEVELOPMENTS IN ISLAM

About 570 Birth of Mohammed

616 Mohammed's public ministry starts.

622 Flight to Medina.

632 Death of Mohammed.

638 Start of Moslem conquest in Syria, Egypt, Persia.

657 Islam splits into 3 sects.

670 Moslem conquest of North Africa.

711 Moslem conquest of Spain.

732 Moslems are defeated in France.

750 Split in the Moslem Empire.

About 1000 Moslems invade India.

About 1258 on Breakdown of caliphate by countries.

1492 Moslem kingdom ends in Spain.

KEY HAPPENINGS IN JUDAISM

Commentaries on Talmud; further growth of Oral Law.

About 760 Anan ben David leads the Karaites.

About 935 Saadia's *Beliefs and Opinions*.

Around 1000 Start of "Golden Age" with Gabirol, Halevi, and others.

1180 Maimonides' *Mishneh Torah*.

Jews expelled from Spain.

KEY HAPPENINGS IN CHRISTIANITY

Gradual recovery from fall of Rome study of Christian tradition.

800 Holy Roman Empire starts.

1054 Split between the Roman Catholic and Eastern Orthodox Churches.

1096 First Crusade begins.

1215 Fourth Lateran Council. Age of Dominic, Francis, Thomas Aquinas.

ISLAM

with death are the washing of the body, graveside prayers, and a period of mourning following the burial.

The fifth duty relates to behavior, ritual, and action. Islam prescribes an extensive code of approved conduct for the believer. This includes such ethical requirements as kindness to parents, care of orphans, and the use of honest weights and measures. The Moslem is also expected to carry on the ritual slaughter of animals, and the more orthodox require the segregation and veiling of women. Among the orthodox, too, all are prohibited from drinking wine and other intoxicating beverages, and from eating of blood, swine-flesh, or animals already dead. Traditionally, Moslems may take no more than four wives, although in practice most have only one.

Islam in the Modern World   In their thirteen hundred years of existence, the Moslems have had an important effect upon Western civilization. It was they, we must remember, who kept alive the learning of the Greeks and Romans during the period of the Dark Ages, so that the Western world was able eventually to rediscover it and enter upon the Renaissance. From the Moslems, too, have come significant

PILGRIMS. Converging on Mecca from all parts of the world, Moslems often undergo great hardships, including desert travel on foot, in order to reach the holy city.

ABLUTIONS. Before praying, Moslems must engage in religious purification. This pool near the mosque satisfies the requirement of washing the feet.

contributions of their own in literature, science, medicine, and architecture, as well as the impetus to several types of so-called "universal" religions to which some people of the West have been attracted.

One of these is Baha'i, a universalistic faith, originating as an offshoot of a Shi'ite sect in Persia with Baha'ullah (1817-1892), after whom the movement is named. Its teachings affirm the unity of God and all mankind, and incorporate many of the ethical teachings of the major religions. Baha'i predicts the coming of a day, brought about by the Spirit of God working through His "Chosen Mouthpiece" (that is, men like Moses, Jesus, Mohammed, and those like Baha'ullah, who have written its scriptures), when the whole human race will be united. There is no priesthood or ritual, but several distinctive temples are maintained, one of which is in Chicago. The headquarters of the movement is located in Haifa, Israel.

Once Islam's early period of rapid growth and conquest came to an end, it became relatively dormant. Like all religions, Islam's teachings underwent much reinterpretation during the years after the early developments. But it has only been in recent times that the Moslems have begun to show a real revival of activity.

Politically, of course, the Arab world has been experiencing a reawakening. Many Moslem nations, formerly colonies ruled by Western countries, in North Africa and the Middle East have gained their independence. With the granting of the independence of India, the new Moslem state of Pakistan has come into being, and a number of other Moslem lands, such as Turkey and Egypt, are undergoing considerable industrialization.

Of far-reaching importance, too, is Islam's reaction to other challenges of modern times. In Egypt and other countries of the Arab world, there have been concerted efforts to overcome centuries of divisiveness and to create greater unity among all Moslems. A noticeable revival of interest in the faith is now taking place in Turkey where, in 1928, Islam was disassociated from the state.

Other significant religious developments are occurring within Islam. In many parts of the world, notably Africa and India, Moslem missionaries are enjoying great success in converting the native peoples. Because there is no "color" or "class" line among the faithful, the Negroes and lower castes of India are coming over to Islam by the tens of thousands. There have also been some changes in the status of Moslem women. In the past, they were compelled to go about heavily veiled and were sharply restricted as to their activities. But today in Turkey, the Middle East, and Pakistan, many have removed the veil, and in Egypt, some have recently even begun to attend Moslem universities.

Among the intellectuals, serious thought is once more being given to the reinterpretation of Islamic teachings. To date, only a small mi-

BAHA'I HEADQUARTERS. The lofty, golden-domed building toward the right is the famous Baha'i Temple in Haifa, Israel. A nineteenth century offshoot of a Persian Moslem sect, Baha'i is one of a number of universalistic faiths currently in existence.

CENTERS OF ISLAM

TOTAL MOSLEMS
431 MILLION

EUROPE

ASIA

U.S.S.R.

MANCHURIA

MONGOLIA

JAPAN

Korea

CHINA

Tibet

TURKEY

Kashmir

Afghanistan

IRAN

Pakistan

INDIA

Burma

Pak.

Thailand

Malaya

INDONESIA

IRAQ

Medina

SAUDI ARABIA

Mecca

Ceylon

Indian Ocean

AUSTRALIA

EGYPT

AFRICA

nority has advocated a greater degree of religious liberalism and more reliance on Western thought. There are, for instance, certain liberal Moslems in Pakistan who stress the study of science as lending support to their faith and portray Islam as a religion based largely upon the moral and ethical teachings of Mohammed. Generally, however, the present trend is much more toward mysticism and religious conservatism. The result is that those theologians who call for a return to the beliefs and practices carried on during Mohammed's time are far more influential than the advocates of religious liberalism.

Despite these trends, it seems hardly likely that any major religious change will take place in the near future among the Moslem masses, most of whom are illiterate and poverty-ridden. Rather, the prospect is that the vast majority will continue to practice their religion in accustomed ways, and according to the interpretations of their particular sects.

Judaism and Islam Among the Moslem peoples there is a wide variety of beliefs and practices. Nevertheless, by studying the doctrines of Islam shared in common by the vast majority of Moslems, we can see the differences and similarities between Islam and Judaism.

Five principal differences are these:

1. Though Moslems insist that Allah is the only God, most of them still believe in the existence of other supernatural beings, such as angels and Jinn. This, certainly, is something that present-day Judaism, with its strict monotheism, does not tolerate.

2. The Jew does not share the widespread Moslem belief in the complete determination of the fate of man and the necessity for his absolute submission to the arbitrary will of God. Rather, Judaism views man as having free choice between right and wrong, and serving as the "co-partner of God" in the work of human salvation. With God's aid, and by living according to His will as revealed by His Law, the Jewish people are active agents in seeking to establish His Kingdom upon earth, not passive beings upon whom, according to Islam, God works His predetermined will.

3. Like most Christians, the Moslems center their hope for salvation upon the hereafter, with a Last Judgment and eternal life in heaven and hell. The Jew, on the other hand, is principally concerned with salvation for mankind here on earth.

4. Judaism does not view Mohammed as one of God's prophets, much less the greatest of them, nor the *Koran* as His "perfect revelation." For the Jew, the chief authority remains the Bible and the centuries of Oral Law.

5. Islam reserves salvation exclusively for Moslems, and consigns all nonbelievers to eternal damnation. In contrast, Judaism looks to the establishment of the Kingdom of God on earth for all mankind.

What both share in common is a strict belief in the unity of God and in certain ethical standards that are demanded by Him. In this respect, Islam is more closely linked with Judaism and with all the other great religions of the West, than with the religions of the East.

A Much Earlier Religion Indeed, as we shall see, Islam has far more in common with the Western faiths than with those of the Far East. Only in its original emphasis on man's utter dependency upon the will of Allah does Islam even begin to approach certain concepts underlying the Eastern religions. But even here, there is a vast difference. For God, as such, has never been central to the teachings of the Far East. Nor do their ethical standards grow out of His demands.

Islam differs from Far Eastern religions in still another respect. By comparison with these religions, Islam was really quite late in making its appearance. Actually, some fifteen hundred to two thousand years before Mohammed's birth, the peoples of India had already begun to evolve a religion whose influence was destined to spread throughout the East. And today, those beliefs and practices have influenced the faiths of more than a half-billion people living on the continent of Asia.

That religion is Hinduism. . . .

TOPICS TO DISCUSS

1. What Moslem beliefs and practices seem to be outgrowths of primitive religion? Which have been borrowed from Judaism?
2. How does the life of Mohammed differ from that of Moses? From that of Jesus?
3. What essential elements does Islam share in common with Western religion?
4. How is Islam different from modern Judaism? From Roman Catholicism and Protestantism?

THINGS TO DO

1. Prepare a chart showing the main similarities and differences between the beliefs of Islam and those of Judaism.
2. As a student of religion, secure a copy of the *Koran* and read Suras 2 and 3. From these prepare a report on the key practices and beliefs contained in them.
3. If possible, invite a Moslem exchange student, or someone else well-informed about Islam, to discuss that faith with you. What, as he observes them, are some of the more important developments presently taking place in the Moslem world? And how does he account for the position the Moslems have taken toward the State of Israel?

OTHER THINGS TO READ

BALLOU, ROBERT O., *The Portable World Bible,* Viking, "The Moslem," pp. 437-450; "Mohammedan Scriptures," pp. 451-479.

GAER, JOSEPH, *How the Great Religions Began,* Signet Key, Book 3, Part 4, "Mohammedanism," pp. 192-214.

————, *The Wisdom of the Living Religions,* Dodd, Mead, Part 7, "The Sayings of Mohammedanism," pp. 221-246.

NOSS, JOHN B., *Man's Religions,* Macmillan, Chapter 16, "Islam," pp. 682-742.

SMITH, HUSTON, *The Religions of Man,* Mentor, Chapter 6, "Islam," pp. 201-232.

The World's Great Religions, Time, "The World of Islam," pp. 99-130.

17

GREAT RELIGIONS OF THE EAST:

1. Hinduism

Religion in India Religion in India is expressed in such a multitude of different and even conflicting ways that the average Westerner is frequently bewildered.

In a modern city like New Delhi, we may attend types of Hindu worship that in many respects resemble a typical church service. Yet, in one of the more than half-million villages where 70 per cent of the Indian people live, we can expect to find a local shrine dominated by a large image.

In an office located in the city, an "untouchable" busily works away alongside a member of an upper caste. Officially, "untouchability" was outlawed by the Indian government when the country gained its independence in 1950. Yet, out in the countryside, a white-skinned member of an upper caste will often scowl simply at the sight of a black-skinned "untouchable" who is about to cast his shadow upon him.

Together with scores of university young men and women, most of them in Western dress, we may visit a modern auditorium to hear a discussion on the highest intellectual level of the philosophy of some noted Hindu sage. Or, in one of their classes, we may study the teachings of the great modern Hindu poet, Rabindranath Tagore, a world-famous opponent of war and all other forms of aggression.

Yet, outside a village only a short distance away, we will see, sitting alongside a river bank, a group of white-robed women and turbaned men listening to an aged teacher, who is explaining one of the Indian classics. Resting among them may be a large cow who looks as though she, too, is meditating on the words of the old man.

Or, at an *asrama*, or *ashram* (a hermitage or monastic community), we may listen to a learned discourse on one of the twelve major systems of Hindu religious thought. The following morning we watch the teacher standing before his own personal shrine, reciting his prayers in the presence of a small family god made of metal, stone, or wood.

Indeed, in India we find religious scenes of every description. In an ornate temple built some eight hundred years ago in the form of a huge tower, we observe the priests start the day. First, they awaken the deity, a large image with four arms and four heads, with solemn music and the recitation of prayers from the sacred writings. At sunrise, they bathe it and anoint it with sandal paste. Later on, the people come and lie prostrate before it.

Nearby, beneath a large tree, sits a man with legs crossed, lost in meditation. All the while, women in flowing robes are circling the tree while quoting from various holy books and praying that they may have a male child.

In the streets beyond, many corpses are being carried on litters to a blazing fire. Once the

214

bodies are burned, the ashes will be gathered up in sacks and taken to a holy spot on the river to be scattered with petals of flowers.

All of this, and infinitely more, is part of Hinduism as it is found among the peoples of India today. And complicating everything is the fact that their ancient society is now being transformed into a modern cooperative state. Hence, side-by-side and even intermingled with old Hindu practices are the new ways of the twentieth century.

The Nature of Hinduism

A Westerner has considerable difficulty in trying to grasp the fundamentals of Hinduism.

The truth is that this is a religion within which we can find almost every sort of belief, from the most highly intellectual to the most coarse, with hundreds of different interpretations and emphases. In fact, each village generally has its own particular folk-version.

Since it is also the nature of Hinduism to recognize truth in all faiths, over the centuries it has absorbed into itself the teachings and practices of the different peoples who at one time or another made their way into India. Therefore, one need not be surprised to find elements of Islam, Christianity, and other religions, intermingled with the Hindu beliefs of a particular region, sect, or caste.

All of this gives Hinduism the appearance of being, not a single religion, but a "collection of religions," with the features of each inseparably intertwined. Perhaps more than anything else, what allows us to speak of it as a religion is the fact that it is practiced almost entirely by the people of a single nation, India.

This is borne out by the meaning of the very word, "Hindu." It comes from the name of one of India's great rivers, the Indus, which in turn gives the whole region the name of "India." Hinduism, therefore, is essentially the "religion of the people of India," and it is a fact that of the 332 million Hindus in the world, some 310 million live in that country.

Yet Hinduism has had an important effect upon many more people beyond the borders of India. Its system of thought, which is far different from that of Islam or the religions of the West, has greatly influenced the other major Eastern faiths. Hence, to follow the religious thinking of much of the Orient, one must understand the fundamentals of Hinduism.

The Earlier Period of Hinduism

Historically, Hinduism is the product of two main stages of development. Most of its lower forms of belief and practice arose during its earlier period. The later period produced its higher forms.

Sometime around the year 1200 B.C.E.—some say it was closer to 1500 B.C.E.—India was invaded from the northwest by certain Aryan peoples of Europe. They proceeded to make the darker-skinned natives the lowest class of society, while they became the three upper classes—the priests or Brahmins, the warriors, and the workers. Over the centuries, the classes crystallized into a rigid caste system in which the dark-skinned peoples became the "outcastes," or "untouchables," since contact with them or even their shadow was believed to be defiling. Today, among the Hindus, there are more than three thousand different sub-castes into which the four major castes are divided.

The Aryans brought with them their own form of religion, which became intermingled with the beliefs and practices of the natives and developed into the worship of numerous gods, spirits of the dead, and forces of nature. Slowly, certain more important gods emerged, principally those of the Sun (Fire), Rain, and Earth, each bearing different names in different places. All sorts of myths about them as well as rituals, formulas, prayers, and guides for conduct arose. These were collected into one of the world's earliest sacred literatures, the *Vedas*, "Knowledge," of which there are four major works.

Perhaps the most important of these is the *Rig-Veda*, "The Veda of Praise," which is a collection of more than a thousand hymns or prayers to various gods. Some are directed to the older deities—Dyaus Pitar (the "Jupiter" of the Romans), a great Mother-goddess, and Mitra (corresponding to "Mithra" of the Persians), perhaps originally a sun-god. Many

TEMPLE IN INDIA. A Jainist sits in worship and contemplation before the image of one of the supernatural beings revered by his faith. Jainism is practiced by almost 2 million Indians.

more, however, are devoted to the nature deities of India, such as Indra, the storm-god; Rudra, the mountain-god; Yama, the god of the dead; and Varuna, the god of the skies, who maintains order in the physical universe.

In the *Rig-Veda*, we find this hymn to the storm-god, Indra:

> I will declare the manly deeds of Indra
> . . . the thunder-wielder.
> He slew the dragon, then disclosed the
>   waters, and cleft the channels of the
>   mountain torrents. . . .
> Indra is king of all that moves and moves
>   not, of creatures tame and horned,
>   the thunder-wielder.
> Over all living men he rules as sovereign,
>   containing all as spokes within a
>   wheel.

And to Varuna, the sky-god, we read:

> Sing forth a hymn sublime and solemn,
>   grateful to glorious Varuna, imperial
>   ruler,
> Who, like one who slays the victim, has
>   spread out earth as a skin to spread
>   in front of Surya [a sun-god].
> In the treetops the air he has extended,
>   put milk in cows and vigorous speed in
>   horses,
> Set intellect in hearts, fire in the waters,
>   Surya [a sun-god] in heaven and Soma
>   [the god of drink] on the mountain.
> Varuna lets the big cask, opening down-
>   ward, flow through the heaven and
>   earth and air's mid-region.
> Therewith the sovereign of the universe
>   waters earth as the shower of rain
>   spreads dew upon the barley. . . .

Primarily, what the worshippers sought from their gods were good fortune, victory in war, children, and the like. To obtain these, they performed sacrificial rites and provided food and drink for the deities and spirits. As time passed, the notion of gaining entry into a heaven full of the enjoyments of life became part of their religion. Gradually, too, the priesthood grew almost as important as the gods themselves, for only they possessed knowledge of the complex ways of pleasing each of them. Through regular and proper performance of sacrifices and other rites by the priests, it became possible for the individual to find not only well-being in this life, but access to heaven after death.

Thus, most of the present-day Hindu practices and rites, as well as the numerous legends about the gods, evolved during this early period.

The Development of Hindu Beliefs Beginning around 600 B.C.E., the beliefs that are now central in Hinduism started to appear. In the main they are found in a number of works, quite difficult to understand, called the *Upanishads*, meaning "sessions with a teacher."

According to their teachings, the basis of all existence—whether that of gods, men, beasts, the earth, or sky—is a single substance. It is called "Brahman," the indefinable, unknowable source of everything in the universe, an impersonal "Something." The heavens with its 330 million deities, as well as the least speck of dirt, are all believed to be aspects of Brahman. This is one way Brahman is described in the *Upanishads:*

> He [Brahman] is the sun, dwelling in the bright heaven; he is the air, dwelling in the sky; he is the fire, dwelling on the hearth. . . . He dwells in men, in gods, in the sacrifice, in heaven; he is born in the water, on earth, in the sacred fire, on the mountains. . . .

Brahman alone is the real essence of everything, and whatever man sees in the world is simply its appearance, not its genuine substance. Similarly, all human desires for wealth, food, happiness, and the like, involve things that are not basically real, and hence are doomed to frustration.

Man's objective in life is to unite his inner self, his soul, with its real essence which is Brahman. When this state of unity is reached, the individual achieves the condition of ecstasy known as "Nirvana." This term comes from two Sanskrit words meaning "not" and "wind" in the sense that something remains completely undisturbed. Hence, in this connection "Nirvana" means to be "undisturbed by any desires." To achieve this is to merge completely and eternally with Brahman.

But this is extremely difficult to accomplish. Man and everything in the universe must pass through repeated rebirths in their efforts to return finally to Brahman and end the process of reincarnation (rebirth after death). Therefore, the main hope for the individual is that his life will merit reincarnation in some higher form and thus continue his progress toward Brahman.

A life of merit means that one will be reincarnated into a higher caste the next time he appears on earth. An unworthy life may mean reincarnation as an animal, a tree, or even a vegetable. One of the Hindu writings declares, "For stealing grain, a man becomes a rat; . . . for stealing a woman, a bear; for stealing cattle, a he-goat."

VARUNA. One of the oldest of India's ancient gods, he was originally a sky-deity. Later he became the god of the sea, indicated here by the swan on which he is riding.

One's station in life, especially the caste into which he has been born, is the result of his behavior during his previous lives. If a person was born an untouchable, he must have sinned during his former existence and, therefore, merited nothing better. Those who have been born into the highest caste have obviously earned this position through their good works in former lives. The caste into which one is born remains unchangeable during his lifetime.

The Hindu, then, sees his life in vastly different terms than the religious person of the West. The latter views physical existence as concluded within a single lifetime. Though his spirit lives on (with many believing in the promise of an ultimate resurrection), no one anticipates a repeated renewal of existence on earth.

Not so the Hindu. To him each individual has a multiple existence extending over a long series of previous and future lifetimes. He begins the cycle as one of the simpler forms of life, and gradually, through repeated rebirths, attains the state of a human being. What happens thereafter in successive lifetimes will

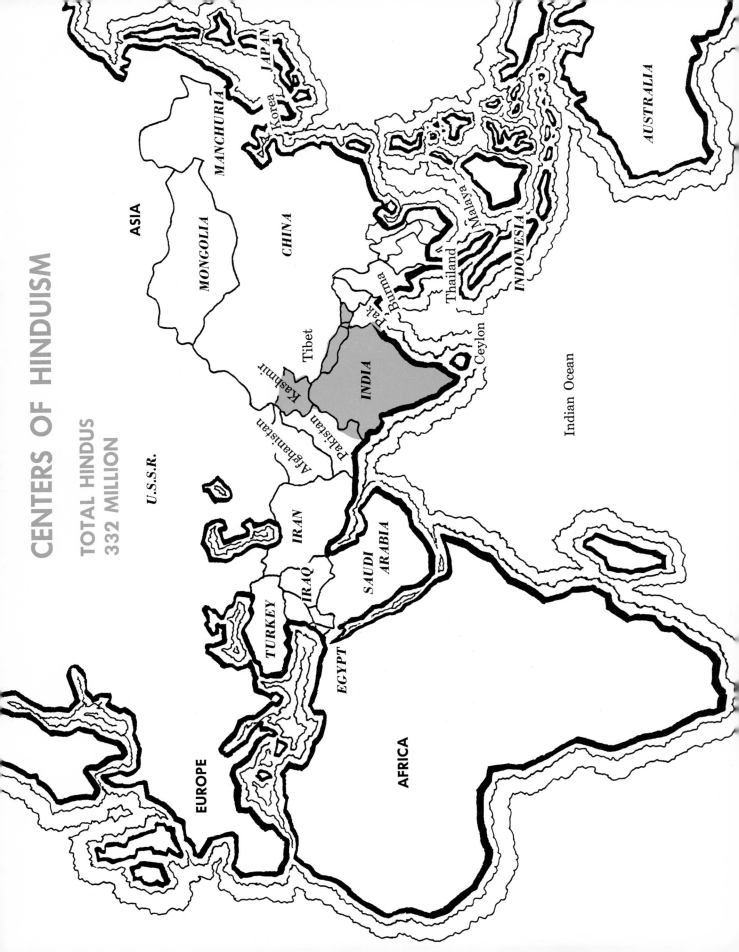

CENTERS OF HINDUISM

TOTAL HINDUS 332 MILLION

be the consequence of his actions, operating through the unchanging Law of Karma.

Karma is a word that means "deeds" or "works." In effect, it determines the consequences of one's intentions and deeds upon his next reincarnation. Operating on the basis of strict "cause and effect," the Law of Karma rewards (or punishes) the individual for his acts during his lifetime with the form of rebirth he merits.

There are a number of stages through which people may pass on their way upward to Brahman. The lowest is when one's primary interest is seeking pleasure. Above this comes the desire for wealth, power, or fame. Next, his life is dedicated to duty in behalf of others, his fellow man and the community. Finally, there is that stage when he seeks and attains Nirvana and the infinite Brahman. It is then that the cycle of lives is blissfully concluded.

The Ways of Hinduism   To achieve the final merging of oneself into Brahman within a single lifetime is possible only for those within the three upper castes. But even for them, it is most unlikely because of the extreme difficulty of performing these four demands: (1) After the appropriate rites of childhood, the young man devotes himself to the study of Hindu sacred literature, especially the *Vedas*. (2) Upon reaching manhood, he embarks upon a period of good works, including marriage, establishing a family, and carrying on his duties toward society. (3) Around middle-age, and only when one feels sincerely called, he forsakes the world. He now lives as a hermit and concentrates upon spiritual matters through the study of the Hindu sacred writings until he becomes indifferent to all desires. (4) Finally, he lives as a "holy man," reentering the world to give of his inspiration to others, but oblivious to all physical wants. He may undertake severe mental and physical discipline through the practice of *yoga*, "yoking" oneself to Brahman through intense concentration and seeking to attain the highest state of bliss. Actually, this entire program is simply an ideal, and except for the rare individual, it is not practiced.

Instead of striving for this almost impossible goal, most religious Hindus limit their objective to trying to achieve a higher form of life in their next reincarnation. This may be accomplished in four possible ways, through "The Way of Works," "The Way of Knowledge," "The Way of Devotion," and "The Way of Concentration." Each is followed by different groups of Hindus, although aspects of all four are often intermixed in the innumerable varieties of Hinduism.

The Way of Works involves the faithful performance of one's duties, particularly those of one's caste, as prescribed by the various Hindu writings. This includes properly carrying out the religious sacrifices, performing the appropriate rites at each important stage of life from birth to death, ministering to the spirits of the dead, and obeying numerous religious laws. Here, different codes of Hindu law prescribe such responsibilities as study of the *Vedas*, dietary restrictions, and hospitality; and the higher the caste, the greater the obligations.

Naturally, the Way of Works, carried on for its own sake and not for the reward, is designed to create merit for oneself, so that, according to the Law of Karma, the individual may enjoy the highest possible form of reincarnation in his next life. And if in his lifetime a Hindu succeeds in having more good deeds than bad, he will realize this objective.

For women, the Way of Works has traditionally required the faithful fulfilment of her duties to her husband, which include obedience, patience, and respect. Here, in the *Ordinances of Manu*, collected about 200 B.C.E. by the Hindu priests, are some of the prescriptions that have applied to the conduct of women:

> No act is to be done according to her own will by a young girl, a young woman, or even by an old woman, though in their own homes. In her childhood, a girl should be under the will of her father; in her youth, of her husband; her husband being dead, of her sons. A woman should never enjoy her own will. She must never wish separation of herself from her father, husband, or sons, for by separation from them a woman

would make both families contemptible. She must always be cheerful and clever in household business, with the furniture well cleaned, and without a free hand in expenditure.

The good wife of a husband, be he living or dead, if she desire the world where her husband is, must never do anything disagreeable to him. . . .

Over the centuries much of this has undergone modification. Certainly, today, in an India where equal rights for women are guaranteed, the status of women has markedly improved. All are now entitled to vote, and an increasing number, though still small, are becoming educated. A few even hold important political posts.

The Way of Knowledge is based upon the belief that the cause of evil and suffering is ignorance of the truth of Brahman. Mainly, it is the assumption that the individual and the world in which he lives are real. But, according to Hindu thought, it only "seems" real. True reality is Brahman alone, and to know Brahman is the purpose of the Way of Knowledge. Study of the sacred writings, of which there are many besides the *Vedas*, practice of Yoga disciplines, and intense contemplation of Brahman are some of the tasks involved in following the Way of Knowledge.

The Way of Devotion, the most common among the Hindus, begins with fulfilling one's personal obligations to his parents, family, community, and so on. Chiefly, however, it calls for self-dedication to a particular god or goddess. Each of these, say the Hindus, is merely a representation of Brahman in one of his many human reincarnations, and all incorporate different aspects of him. Faithful devotion to these deities—mainly Vishnu, the Preserver-god, and his associates, or Siva, the Destroyer-god, and his associates—can win their support in cleansing one from evil and attaining a meritorious reincarnation.

Vishnu is believed to represent a union with Brahman and is the creator-god who took on physical form to overcome evil. He has already passed through nine reincarnations, the most important of which are his appearances as Rama and Krishna. It is about them that two

of the great Hindu religious works are written—the *Ramayana*, "The Adventures of the God Rama," and the *Bhagavad-Gita*, "The Lord's Song," telling of the exploits of the god Krishna. To identify oneself with Vishnu or any of his reincarnations may finally unite one with Brahman. So in the *Bhagavad-Gita* the god Krishna advises his worshippers:

> Give me your whole heart,
> Love and adore me,
> Worship me always,
> Bow to me only,
> And you shall find me.
> This is a promise from me
> Who loves you dearly.
> Lay down all duties
> In me, your refuge.
> Fear no longer,
> For I will save you
> From sin and from bondage.

The other great deity, Siva, is the Destroyer. In association with other gods and goddesses, he brings about floods, earthquakes, famine, and other disasters. Yet the Hindus believe that, as the Destroyer, Siva is really a force for good since, in his destructiveness, he helps bring about the end of things and, therefore, the return of all to Brahman. Among the deities connected with Siva is a goddess who takes on different characteristics and names in various sections of India. As Durga, for instance, she is the favorite of the robber caste known as Thugs, and as Kali, she is a cruel goddess who is pictured as devouring human flesh.

Finally, there is the Way of Concentration, considered by the holy men to be the most important of all. The object here is for the individual to rid himself of all conscious and unconscious thought so that he may ultimately attain to his real self, which is identical with Brahman.

This is achieved only by the most rigorous and stringent self-discipline. It begins with the careful cultivation of certain moral behavior, such as avoiding falsehood, stealing, and the like, and practicing cleanliness, self-control, and devotion to study. To achieve the state of intense concentration necessary to advance upon this Way, one must learn to avoid all distractions. He must sit a certain way, especially in the lotus or cross-legged position, control his breathing, and overcome all sensation. Gradually, as he conquers every extraneous thought, he loses all consciousness of himself and time. It is at that point that his mind is capable of being completely absorbed into Brahman.

The Practices of Hinduism   Much of Hindu ritual is carried on by the priests who minister at the many local shrines. However, there are a number of other important religious specialists, and among them are the *yogin, swami,* and *guru.*

A *yogin,* or holy man, is one who has renounced all worldly life and is seeking to attain Nirvana through his own particular spiritual disciplines. Both he and the *swami,* a member of a religious order, serve as good influences upon the lives of the ordinary Hindu. The *swami* is vowed to chastity, poverty, and obedience, and adheres to the religious and social practices of his order. A *guru* is one's personal religious teacher. His task is to transmit to the individual knowledge of the *Vedas.*

It is impossible to describe all of the numerous rituals and holy days that play a part in the worship of the Hindu gods, because each of the countless deities has his own special rites. Except for a minority of Hindus who carry on a highly intellectual and ethical devotion to Siva and Vishnu, the masses worship the many gods and goddesses in their temples and homes with all sorts of images, symbols, and rites. Certainly as practiced by the more backward peoples of India, much of it appears to be idol-worship, combined with rituals that are magical, superstitious and, by Western standards, even immoral.

The Hindu is obliged to carry on many daily practices. These are performed in the morning, at midday, and evening, and they involve a great many different rituals. Among them are bathing, placing special marks on one's forehead, assuming certain bodily positions, precise recitation of sacred texts that may be repeated scores of times daily, study, and the like. The

221

orthodox Hindu must also carry out his "Five Daily Obligations," involving the offering of food to the god, generally at his private shrine at home, reading from the *Vedas,* a water-libation, a food-offering to animals, and care of guests, for which alms to the poor may be substituted.

The calendar of the Hindu is filled with holidays bound up with the various gods who control the cycle of nature that determines the outcome of the crops. Some, like various pilgrim festivals, are joyous. Such a one is the occasion when the sacred thread is placed upon the deity and he is transported through the streets in the presence of his happy worshippers. Others, such as the birthdays of the gods or the dark, moonless periods of the month, are more solemn. In the observance of the holidays, the rites of some are conducted by priests in the ornate temples, while those of others are performed chiefly by the individual at home.

There are also observances connected with the life-cycle of the individual. In infancy, these include the naming of the child after a god, and special ceremonies for each stage of the child's growth, as, for instance, when he first tastes rice, solid food, and so on. At a later age, and marking the beginning of their manhood, boys

HINDU HOLY MEN. The Yogin on the left wears on his forehead the sacred sign of Brahma, one of the major Hindu gods. The one on the right bears the symbol of the sun in his hands, as he stands in a sacred position.

BATHING GHATS. Along the rivers of India the people have built small piers, called "Ghats," as landing-places, but more especially for bathing. Hindus regard bathing in the 7 sacred rivers as highly meritorious, and each year millions go to Benares to immerse themselves in the Ganges.

of the upper castes receive secret names and special prayers which only they are taught. It is then, too, that they receive the sacred thread, worn diagonally across the body, as the badge of both their caste and their faith.

Marriages, arranged with the families by matchmakers, are conducted by a priest in a twilight ceremony. In India child-marriage is common. Though under the British the marriage of children younger than fourteen was banned, it is not unusual even today for youngsters of eight or nine to be married.

Finally, there are the rites associated with death. If at all possible, a person who considers himself nearing death goes to the sacred city of Benares and there bathes in the Ganges River in order to be cleansed from his sins. When he dies, his body is burned on a pyre, which is counted upon to release him from a long series of reincarnations. After death, the Hindu is believed to go either to a heaven or hell where he awaits rebirth, and his survivors offer special prayers to hasten his reincarnation.

Since in Hinduism widows are not permitted to remarry, formerly they would throw themselves upon the burning pyre of their husbands. However, with the coming of the British to India this practice was prohibited. Today, many widows shave off their hair and simply wait for an early death in order that they may be quickly reunited with their husbands.

One of the rites most widely practiced by the Hindu involves bathing away his sins in one of the seven sacred rivers of India, and especially where the Ganges joins the Jumna River. Pilgrimages to this holy spot are made every twelve years, and in the past, as many as four million Hindus have appeared there.

To the Hindu everything that exists is sacred, since Brahman is in all. Hence, he shows reverence toward trees, rivers, innumerable holy places, insects, and especially cows, which are considered very sacred. This veneration is expressed by strict vegetarianism among the more pious, and by complete non-violence toward animals as well as humans among the masses generally. It is this aspect of Hinduism

222

FOR CREMATION. Many Ghats, or piers along streams and rivers, are used for burning the bodies of the Hindu dead.

that served as the basis of the determined nation-wide campaign of non-violence and passive resistance led by Mahatma Gandhi. In 1950, the non-violent campaign finally succeeded in freeing India from British rule.

Judaism and Hinduism   Hinduism today is undergoing many changes as the result of the modernization of India. Thus, important modifications of the caste system have been introduced by the Indian government, especially to relieve the terrible situation of millions of untouchables and to give them and others greater opportunities in life. Modernists among the Hindus have also de-emphasized the religious stress on reincarnation after death, and concentrated instead on programs designed to improve social conditions for the poverty-stricken masses.

With these programs the Jew is certainly in sympathy. Basic to the Jew's faith is his concern for his fellow man everywhere and the belief that each person's dignity as a child of God requires that his essential human needs be met.

Still, it is only within comparatively recent times that any sizable number of Hindus has been concerned with such matters. This is in sharp contrast to the Jews and their faith. As a matter of fact, from what we have observed of Hinduism in general, we may certainly say that in most respects its central teachings are foreign to Judaism.

To begin with, the Hindu believes in the illusory nature of the world and everything in it. In fact, to accept the reality of what one experiences through the senses is considered to be the gravest sort of error. This, of course, is contrary to Judaism's teachings, which are based upon belief in the reality of man, the world, and all existence, summarized so simply in Genesis, "In the beginning God created the heaven and the earth . . . and God saw that it was good." And the Jew's faith in the eventual establishment of God's Kingdom upon earth is something that is inconceivable to the Hindu in view of his belief that every aspect of life itself is unreal.

Lacking in most of Hinduism, too, with its great variety of deities, including Rama, Krishna, Vishnu, Siva, and all their associates, is Judaism's concept of absolute monotheism. Nor is Brahman, the essence of everything, in any way comparable to the God of the Jews, who is deeply concerned with the acts and welfare of mankind. Though the informed Hindu views his gods as merely different manifestations of Brahman, it is difficult not to regard the Hinduism that is carried on by the masses as polytheism, accompanied by the practice of idolatry.

Moreover, we do not find in Hinduism any parallel to the Jewish view of man's existence, the purpose of life, and the function of religion. To the Hindu, a man has not one, but a multiple number of lives, and the purpose of his life is to achieve for himself a more desirable form of reincarnation after death through the operation of the Law of Karma. It is to this main end that the most popular expressions of Hinduism direct themselves.

A DIGEST OF ISLAM AND HINDUISM

ISLAM

ORGANIZATION

Many sects: the largest is the Sunnis. The Shi'ites are more orthodox.

No clergy as such, though various countries have their own Caliphs (highest official of the faith). *Imans* are leaders of prayer in mosques. The *Cadi* is the Moslem judge.

MEMBERSHIP

431 million — chiefly in north and central Africa, Turkey, the Middle East, Iran, Pakistan, Afghanistan, Siberia, and China.

PRACTICES

Sacred writings: *The Koran*, Mosaic laws, Psalms, Christian Gospel, Traditions.

Prayer 5 times daily. Worship in mosque on Friday ("Sabbath"). Alms to poor.

Chief holidays: fast of month of Ramadan, Ashura, pilgrimage to Mecca.

Life-cycle ceremonies of circumcision, marriage, and death.

DISTINCTIVE BELIEFS

Belief in one God (Allah) who created all, and angels and male and female spirits (Jinn). God revealed His will to Abraham, Moses, Jesus and His greatest prophet, Mohammed.

Last Judgment, with resurrection and sentence of the dead. The righteous will go to paradise; the wicked to hell.

Man must submit to God's will since all is predetermined by Him (most Moslems).

HINDUISM

ORGANIZATION

Innumerable sects.

Three upper castes consist of the priesthood, warriors, and workers; and the "outcastes," or untouchables. Many subcastes.

Clergy: priests, *yogins*, *swamis*. *Gurus* are personal teachers.

MEMBERSHIP

332 million — chiefly in India and Nepal.

PRACTICES

Sacred writings: The *Vedas*, *Upanishads*, *Ramayana*, *Bhagavad-Gita*, and others.

Chief holidays connected with the gods, seasons, and agricultural cycle. Daily rites both in temples and at home.

Life-cycle ceremonies of childhood, manhood, marriage and death.

Bathing away of sins in sacred rivers. Pilgrimage to the Ganges River where it joins the Jumna.

DISTINCTIVE BELIEFS

All that exists is part of Brahman, the great indefinable substance that underlies everything. Since everything is basically unreal, man's objective is to return to Brahman. But he is prevented by numerous rebirths determined by the Law of Karma, which also accounts for his station in life.

Only for a few is a return to Brahman in one lifetime possible. For the masses a higher form of reincarnation is sought through the Way of Works, Knowledge, Devotion to various gods, and Concentration. The gods worshipped are chiefly Vishnu (Creator god) or Siva (Destroyer god), and their associates.

In Judaism, on the other hand, within a single lifetime, each person is challenged to live the righteous life according to the will of God in order that he may improve society materially as well as spiritually.

The differences between the two religions can be seen most clearly in the practical effects of their teachings. Hinduism has produced a passive outlook upon life, extreme mysticism and asceticism, and a caste society rooted in the operation of the Law of Karma. Hinduism tends to place primary emphasis on the spiritual purification of the individual, rather than the improvement of society as a whole. To a great extent, much of modern Hindu thought as well as intensive efforts by the Indian government have been devoted to changing these emphases and redirecting the energies of the Hindu masses toward the improvement of their society.

Judaism, in contrast with the inwardness of Hinduism, has served to inspire its followers to ever-higher levels of moral and social achievement for the whole community.

To a large extent, as we shall shortly see, this tendency toward inwardness and social withdrawal applies as well to the other Oriental faiths.

Moving Farther Eastward   Though Hinduism, as such, is found today chiefly in India, in the period following the sixth century B.C.E., an offshoot of the Hindu faith began to make its way farther east. This was Buddhism, which in its early stages represented certain modifications of Hinduism as introduced by Buddha.

By coincidence, at almost the same time in China, another great teacher, Confucius, was gathering disciples. Many centuries after his death, his followers combined his doctrines and others with some of the practices of Buddhism to form the religion known as Confucianism. Together, the Confucianists and Buddhists now number almost half a billion people.

Thus, the beliefs and practices of Buddhism, many of which grew directly out of the Hindu religion, became the essential elements in not merely one but two great Far Eastern faiths of the modern world. . . .

TOPICS TO DISCUSS

1. Using Hinduism as an example, what fundamental differences do you find between the thinking of the Eastern and Western religions?
2. What are the chief objectives of the Hindu religion in comparison with those of Judaism, Christianity, and Islam? How do you account for the differences?
3. What similarities and differences do you find between Hinduism and Judaism?
4. In what ways have Hinduism, Christianity, Islam, and Judaism affected the societies in which they exist? How do you explain this?

THINGS TO DO

1. Prepare a picture-chart showing the historical development of the Hindu religion.
2. Create a dictionary of Hindu terms that are essential in understanding the religion.
3. Prepare a chart contrasting the basic teachings of Hinduism with those of Judaism or of Western religion in general.

OTHER THINGS TO READ

BALLOU, ROBERT O., *The Portable World Bible*, Viking, "The Hindu," pp. 17-91.

FITCH, FLORENCE MARY, *Their Search for God*, Lothrop, Lee, and Shepard, "The Hindu Way," pp. 10-51.

GAER, JOSEPH, *How the Great Religions Began*, Signet Key, Book 1, Part 3, "Hindustan," pp. 55-67.

———, *The Wisdom of the Living Religions*, Dodd, Mead, Part 4, "The Sayings of Hinduism," pp. 115-145.

KITAGAWA, JOSEPH M., *Religions of the East*, Westminster, Chapter 3, "Hinduism and the Caste System," pp. 99-154.

MORGAN, KENNETH W., editor, *The Religion of the Hindus*, Ronald Press.

NOSS, JOHN B., *Man's Religions*, Macmillan, Chapter 3, "Early Hinduism," pp. 113-140; Chapter 7, "Later Hinduism," pp. 224-273.

SMITH, HUSTON, *The Religions of Man*, Mentor, Chapter 2, "Hinduism," pp. 23-88.

The World's Great Religions, Time, "The Spirit of Hinduism," pp. 9-38.

18

GREAT RELIGIONS OF THE EAST:
2. Buddhism

The "Strangeness" of the Oriental Faiths
Knowledge of Hinduism helps us see why Westerners often find the religions of the East so mystifying. It is not merely the strange terms, or the different customs, that puzzle the Westerner. Fundamentally, the oriental conception of religion differs markedly from that of the West. The differences may be summarized in the following three ways:

First, unlike Judaism, Christianity, and Islam, the religions of the East do not demand that their adherents accept a single set of basic beliefs and practices. Eastern religions freely permit their followers to incorporate the teachings and observances of other faiths. Consequently, within Hinduism, for example, one of its more modern sects has adopted the teachings of a divine Jesus and conducts its services very much like a Protestant church. The result of such permissiveness is that each of the Oriental faiths resembles a collection of different religions, with innumerable sects whose beliefs and practices are intermixed with those of the others.

Second, the Eastern religions have their own particular perspective on life which, in the past, has made them appear almost indifferent to the material advancement of their people. Unlike Judaism with its acceptance of the reality of life and the need to establish God's Kingdom upon earth, both Hinduism and Buddhism have viewed life as illusory and, therefore, set their sights on man's finding salvation elsewhere. Indeed, they have encouraged the individual to seek Nirvana, and put before him the ideal of attaining it through the "enlightenment" that comes chiefly from curbing his worldly desires. This, in turn, has led him to turn his gaze away from social problems. And, to a large extent, Confucianism shares this quality because of the influence of Buddhism and Taoism, as well as its own concern with preserving the ways of the past rather than striving for the material advancement of society.

Third, the Eastern religions differ from those of the West in their attitude to the matter of God. We have already seen that originally and fundamentally the Hindu conception of Brahman was really not that of deity but of the underlying substance of everything in the universe. Similarly, the teachings of both Buddha and Confucius had virtually nothing to do with a concept of God. Consequently, as desirable human virtues first came to be defined by the Eastern faiths, they were not at all related, as in Judaism, to the holiness of God and the acts that He demanded of His worshippers. Rather, they were designed simply as patterns of conduct enabling the individual to become more in harmony with the essence of life as each faith conceived it. In Hinduism, man sought to escape the illusion that life is real; in Buddhism, he endeavored to overcome self-centered desire; and in Confucianism, he labored to re-establish harmonious relationships within himself and society. The common goal of each, then, was the achievement of "inner tranquility."

To this their later followers simply grafted on the beliefs and practices of already existing religions, together with the deification of the great teachers themselves. Thus, in its principal form, Buddhism really represents an amalgamation of Buddha's teachings about proper ways of conducting oneself to achieve complete "enlightenment," with the worship of Buddha himself and devotion to the beliefs and rituals of Hinduism and various primitive religions. In a similar way, Confucianism is also an amalgam of different beliefs and practices.

An understanding of these distinctions and some awareness of the backgrounds out of which the Oriental faiths developed make them less bewildering and mysterious to the Western mind. They also serve to explain why they are so different from Judaism. For the dissimilarities between the teachings of Judaism and Hinduism that we have already observed apply in the main to Buddhism as well. Many Buddhists, too, subscribe to practices that to us appear largely polytheistic and idolatrous, and the life Buddhism recommends, though in many respects based upon worthwhile teachings, is designed chiefly to attain Nirvana and a higher form of reincarnation after death.

Hinduism in the Time of Buddha   Just about the time the Jews were settling down to life in the Babylonian exile, and the Hindus were beginning to develop their beliefs about Brahman, reincarnation, and the way of supreme bliss, a child named Siddhartha Gautama was born in Nepal, in northeast India. He was later to become known as Buddha, "the Enlightened One," and his teachings, originally a protest against certain aspects of Hinduism, were destined to sweep across Asia.

Today, Buddhism in its many varieties and sects is the religion of some 152 million people in Burma, Thailand, Tibet, China, Ceylon, Korea, Japan, Mongolia, portions of Manchuria,

and elsewhere. Interestingly, however, although Buddhism started in India, it has comparatively few followers in that country. In large measure this is due to the coming of the Moslems who, with fanatic insistence upon the worship only of Allah, uprooted Buddhism wherever they found it. Whatever survived of it in India was then most likely absorbed by Hinduism with its great hospitality to other interpretations of religion.

The rise of Buddhism may be traced to two main factors. The first has to do with certain developments that had taken place within Hinduism by the middle of the sixth century, the time Buddha appeared on the scene.

By then the caste system had firmly established the privileged position of the Brahmins, the upper caste among the Hindus. Only they possessed authoritative knowledge of the faith, since the important sacred writings and other key sources of religious information were maintained in Sanskrit, a language which was no longer known to the masses. Hence, they were dependent upon the Brahmins for an understanding of their faith and its effective rites.

Furthermore, through the process of interpretation, Hinduism had come to represent a fatalism in which the individual was helpless to achieve his own salvation. The rounds of endless rebirths made it appear that the human being could do nothing to end the cycle, and had to submit passively to enduring the many thousands of lifetimes that lay before him. Nor could the untouchables or lower castes hope to rise to the position of the Brahmins within a predictable number of lifetimes. Hence, the caste system became frozen, and there appeared to be no remedy for all of the disabilities of those outside the upper caste.

The consequences were that the Hindu religion was being sapped of its religious vigor. To the intellectual, on the one hand, Hinduism had become an endless debate over the meaning of its teachings. What, for instance, was the nature of the various worlds that made up the Hindu cosmos, or what part of the individual underwent rebirth after death? For the masses, on the other hand, Hinduism represented an

प॰ ४ । सू॰ ५६—५८] ऋग्वेदप्रातिशाख्यम् १४७

पादादिरन्तश्च दिवस्परीति च ॥ ५६ ॥

दिवस्परि इत्येतद् द्वैपदं निपात्यते पादादौ पादान्ते च वर्तमानम् । दिवस्परि सुमखिं तदाद् (ऋ॰ १ । १२१ । १०) । अयं ख यो दिवस्परि (ऋ॰ ८ । ३८ । ४) । पादादिरन्तश्चेति किम् । वृष्टि दिव: परि स्रव (ऋ॰ ८ । ८ । ८) । नन्वकारपूर्वविसर्जनीयानुवृत्तौ सत्याम्—पादान्तगते परि (४ । ४४) इत्यनेनैव सिद्धत्वाद्दिहान्तश्च दिवस्परीत्युच्यते तदतिरिक्तमिति । नातिरिक्तम् । तस्यावकाश:—दिवे अन्तेभ्यस्परि (ऋ॰ १ । १४८ । ३) इत्यादिष्वेव । इहान्तग्रहणे क्रियमाणे पादादिग्रहणेनैवैतद् द्वैपदं निपातितं स्यात्पादादावेव । न त्वन्ते । तस्मान्नातिरिक्तम् ॥

दिवस्पृथिव्या अधमस्पदीष्ट पूर्वं पादादौ यदि ॥ ५७ ॥

दिवस्पृथिव्या: । अधमस्पदीष्ट । एतद् द्वैपदद्वयं निपात्यते । अत्र पूर्वं द्वैपदं पादादौ यदि स्यात् । दिवस्पृथिव्या: पर्योज उद्भृतम् (ऋ॰ ६ । ४७ । २७) । विश्वस्य जन्तोरधमस्पदीष्ट (ऋ॰ ७ । १०४ । १६) । पूर्वं पादादाविति किम् । प्र ये दिव: पृथिव्या न बर्हणा (ऋ॰ १० । ७७ । ३) ॥

सस्पदीष्ट ॥ ५८ ॥

एतद् द्वैपदं निपात्यते । यो नो द्वेष्ट्वधर: सस्पदीष्ट (ऋ॰ ३ । ५३ । २१) ॥

अवसा मह: सहस इळाया:
पात्विद्येकं पुच्छग्रब्दे पराणि ॥ ५९ ॥

(१) B², -दिव्वेवासति इहांतग्रहणे क्रियमाणे B³, -दिव्वेव । सति इहांतग्रहणे क्रियमाणे I², -दिव्वेव इहांतग्रहणेनैव Bⁿ. (२) B³I², एतद्द्वैपदं Bⁿ, इति एतद्द्वैपदं B². (३) अत्र B²Bⁿ, अस्य द्वैपदद्वयस्य B³I². (४) द्वैपदं omitted in B².

SANSKRIT. The sacred writings of the Hindus, such as the **Vedas**, were written in this ancient Aryan language. Buddha, however, preferred to speak and write in the vernacular understood by the masses. (The notes at the bottom are commentary.)

overemphasis upon rituals, most of them plainly magical in nature, by which the gods could be influenced in their behalf. And for all of this, the priests, of course, expected handsome payment.

It was to bring about necessary reforms that Buddha originally directed his efforts. But his life, personality, and teachings achieved far more. And it was the man himself who became the second and undoubtedly more important factor in the birth of the new religion.

The Life of Buddha   What of this man, Siddhartha Gautama, who became the Buddha?

Most of what we know about his life comes from legends and traditions that arose centuries after his death. These appear in a number of sacred books written in Pali, the language he spoke, as well as in Sanskrit and Persian. Those in Pali are believed to be the oldest, and three collections of them have been adopted by one of the largest Buddhist sects as its official Scriptures. This is called the *Pali Canon* or, among the Buddhists, *Ti-Pitaka*, "Three Baskets," each a collection of many writings.

The *Ti-Pitaka* comprises (1) the "Basket of Discipline," describing the duties of Buddhist monks and nuns, (2) the "Basket of Doctrine," teachings concerning Buddha's beliefs, and (3) the "Basket of Higher Learning," presenting deeper thoughts about the beliefs of Buddhism. But, since most of the information that they and other traditional materials tell us about the life of Buddha is clearly legendary, scholars have had to sift through them for the facts. The following, we believe, represents a reasonably accurate account.

Born about 563 B.C.E. into an aristocratic Hindu family of the warrior caste, Siddhartha Gautama was reared in luxury. According to legend, his father hoped that some day his son would become the emperor of all India, and unite the country. But even at his birth, the prediction was made that the child would reject the ambitions of his father. So we are told in this account found in *The Jataka Tales*, or "Birth Stories" that are part of the *Pali Canon*:

On this same day [of Buddha's birth] the happy and delighted hosts of heaven held a celebration . . . because there had been born a son who should sit at the foot of the Bo ["enlightenment"]-tree and become a Buddha.

Now it came to pass at that time that after his daily meal an ascetic named Kaladevla, a friend of the boy's father, went to the heaven of the thirty-three [deities] to take a noonday rest. And as he was sitting there resting, he noticed these gods, and said, "Why do you frolic so joyously? Let me know the reason."

"Sir," replied the gods, "it is because a son has been born . . . who shall sit at the foot of the Bo-tree, and become a Buddha, and cause the wheel of [true] doctrine to roll. . . ."

On hearing this, the ascetic descended from the world of the gods in haste and entered the dwelling of his friend, the King [father of Buddha]. "Great King, I hear that a son has been born to you. I would like to see him."

Then the King had the Prince [Buddha] magnificently dressed and brought in and carried up to do reverence to the ascetic. [But instead, the baby had the ascetic do reverence to him.]

Then said the King, "What shall my son see to make him retire from the world?"

"The four signs: a decrepit old man, a diseased man, a dead man, and a monk."

"From this time forth," said the King, "let no such persons be allowed to come near my son. It will never do for my son to become a Buddha. What I wish to see is my son exercising sovereign rule and authority [over all India]...." And when he had spoken he placed guards . . . in all four directions in order that none of these four kinds of men might come within sight of his son.

But the father was unsuccessful in spite of all of his efforts. For years he kept his son in a life of sheltered luxury. He even arranged for him in early manhood a marriage with a beautiful young woman who bore him a fine son.

By all standards Siddhartha Gautama should have been happy, but he was not. For despite all his father's precautions, he had come across the four individuals as predicted. Now he was aware of the suffering of the aged, the ill, and the dying, and he was deeply troubled. It moved him to wonder about the purpose of life and how man could find release from suffering. The example of the monk and his retirement from the world began to appeal to him.

So, determined to solve the riddle of life, Gautama bade farewell to his wife and child as they slept and took up the life of a wandering beggar, with shaved head and the yellow robes of a monk. First, he tried the way of meditation, immersing himself in the sacred writings of Hinduism and pondering their teachings, but their answers did not satisfy him. Then he turned to the disciplines of Yoga and intense asceticism, denying himself food

LEGENDARY BUDDHA. Numerous legends about Buddha promptly sprang up after his death. Here is one showing him flying across the Ganges River on a winged steed.

CENTERS OF BUDDHISM

TOTAL BUDDHISTS
152 MILLION

ASIA

U.S.S.R.

MONGOLIA

MANCHURIA

JAPAN

Korea

CHINA

Tibet

Kashmir

Afghanistan

Pakistan

Pak.

Burma

INDIA

Thailand

Malaya

INDONESIA

AUSTRALIA

Ceylon

Indian Ocean

IRAN

IRAQ

TURKEY

SAUDI
ARABIA

EGYPT

EUROPE

AFRICA

until he almost died of starvation. Even this brought him no closer to his goal. Finally, after six years of fruitless effort, Buddha sat himself down in despair beneath an Indian fig tree and resolved not to move until he had found the answer.

For forty-nine days he sat there. According to Buddhist tradition he was repeatedly attacked by the "evil tempter," who offered him every kind of reward if he would abandon his quest. But Gautama persisted and finally arrived at the "enlightenment" he sought. Hence his name, *Buddha*, "the Enlightened One."

Now that he had the truth about life and its suffering, he immediately went to the holy city of Benares, where he preached his first sermon to the men who had instructed him in Yoga. Then for 45 years he traveled throughout northern India, attracting numerous disciples, especially among the monks.

From all we know of him, evidently his warmth and compassion toward others, as well as the quality of his character and mind deeply impressed everyone who came into contact with him. His teachings spread, and more and more Hindus were converted.

Then, around the year 483 B.C.E., at the age of eighty, Buddha died. Tradition declares that his final words to his disciples were, "Work out your salvation with diligence."

Buddha's Teachings   What was it Buddha discovered?

To begin with, he seems to have been aware that changes were necessary in the ways Hinduism was then being carried on. Therefore, by asserting that the individual need not build his faith upon the traditional Hindu writings, he put an end to the strangle-hold that the Brahmins held on the sources of religious knowledge. Similarly, he also refrained from teaching in Sanskrit, but spoke in Pali, the language that the masses understood.

But Buddha went much further. He scoffed at the various Hindu rituals and viewed the involved arguments over the meaning of its doctrines as profitless. He even spoke of the futility of any appeal to the gods. He also re-

jected the fatalism that bound the individual to his caste for an unending series of lifetimes. Since all men, he held, were capable of following his doctrine, they were able to work out their own salvation and thereby escape the consequences of previous reincarnations. And, in place of the Hindu caste system, all his followers, laymen as well as monks, formed a common community of their own.

Indeed, as Buddha saw it, the answer lay in the willingness of each person to work away at his own salvation with determination. He even assured his followers that this was possible within a single lifetime. Said he, "Let a man of intelligence come to me, honest, candid, straightforward; I will instruct him . . . and if he practice according as he is taught, then he will come to know for himself and realize that supreme religion and goal."

With Hinduism, Buddha was in full agreement that everything in the universe underwent birth and rebirth. Also, one's previous existence, he maintained, did largely determine—especially in the formation of his character—the form of reincarnation one would enjoy after death. And with the Hindus, Buddha felt that to find release from the burdens of the world, the individual must learn to curb his desires.

But neither the Hindu Way of Knowledge, with its study of the *Vedas*, speculation, and asceticism, nor the Way of Devotion, with the worship of the various gods, satisfied Buddha. Rather, he proposed the practice of the "Middle Way," which means following a course of moderation and avoiding extremes which inevitably produce frustration. To him the excessive concern of Hinduism with curbing one's desires was simply another form of unrealizable desire, bound to be frustrating and, therefore, to be avoided. In the matter of appetite, for example, one was neither to crave for food nor yearn to hunger. Both represented forms of insatiable desire. Rather, it was to seek to make eating of no real consequence and to take the matter of food as it came.

As tradition has handed it down, this is the way Buddha himself is said to have expressed this doctrine in his first sermon:

And the Blessed One [Buddha] thus addressed the five monks: "There are two extremes, monks, which he who has given up the world ought to avoid.

"What are these two extremes? A life given to pleasures . . . this is degrading, sensual, vulgar, ignoble, and profitless.

"And a life given to mortification, this is painful, ignoble, and profitless.

"By avoiding these two extremes, monks, Buddha has gained the knowledge of the middle path which leads to insight, which leads to wisdom, which is conducive to calm, to knowledge, to supreme enlightenment, to Nirvana."

Some scholars claim that Buddha did not frown upon those desires that could be satisfied, but only upon those that were unrealizable, and hence frustrating. At any event, as his teachings came to be understood by his followers, he appeared to be opposed to *every* form of desire. It was this interpretation that they placed upon his "Four Noble Truths," the answers he was said to have found to the meaning of life. In effect these declared:

1. All of life, from birth through death, soon becomes dislocated and produces much anguish for the individual. From the very moment we

SACRED WHEEL. In the Buddhist faith the wheel has come to represent a sacred symbol. With 8 spokes, it stands for Buddha's Eightfold Path. Here it symbolizes the series of lives and reincarnations of man.

are born, with our very first cries, we encounter suffering. Sickness, fear of death, old age, separation from those we love, and the like, add to our pain. As a result, life soon gets out of focus, and we never succeed in achieving true happiness.

2. However, the real cause of our misery is self-centered desires. To satisfy them we shut ourselves off from the real essence of life. We become so concerned with ourselves, for instance, that we fail to see our fellow man as of equal importance in the universe. Interest in our own welfare prompts us to think of life chiefly in terms of our desires, which grow until we are hopelessly enmeshed in them. But, since they cannot be satisfied, our lives become a continuous round of frustration, suffering, and pain.

3. The answer, of course, is to eliminate all self-centered desires. Overcoming selfish concerns inevitably puts an end to our craving, and to the pain that must accompany it.

4. However, this can only be achieved by practicing the Middle Way, the way of selflessness and no-desire. To this end Buddha offered man his "Noble Eightfold Path," the doctrine represented in Buddhist symbolism by the wheel with its eight spokes converging at the axle, the central essence of life.

The Noble Eightfold Path has remained the basic way of life for the Buddhist, the way that leads to no-desire. Certain important assumptions underly it. One is that it can only be implemented by the will of the individual. Another is that it requires arduous training and rigorous practice. And a third maintains that we can be helped by association with others whose counsel and example we can follow.

The Eightfold Path calls, first, for "Right Belief," that is, an understanding of the Four Noble Truths, their view of life, and the manner in which we can come to live it in genuine happiness.

The second is "Right Intention," the wish to put an end to all suffering-producing desire and the willingness to concentrate our energies upon this goal.

The third is "Right Speech," to listen intently

to what we say and become aware of our real motives as they are revealed through our statements. Understanding them will compel us to speak the real truth and avoid saying whatever is harmful to others.

The fourth is "Right Conduct." Here we strive to gain insights into our behavior so that we may avoid hurting any creature, acting impurely or falsely, taking that which is not ours, indulging in intoxicants, and the like.

The fifth essential the Eightfold Path requires calls for the "Right Means of Earning a Livelihood." Buddha recognized that the sort of occupation a person pursues has great influence upon his life. For example, one who works at gambling for a living will inevitably become contaminated by it. Consequently, one should follow a vocation that promotes life's spiritual objectives.

The sixth is "Right Effort," the exercise of the will so that one comes to distinguish between what is wise and unwise. Yet we must not expect to achieve this quickly or without great patience.

The seventh is "Right Mindfulness," overcoming ignorance of what is the real truth and attaining complete knowledge of oneself. This is to be accomplished by rigorously disciplined thought.

The eighth and final point is "Right Concentration," which at last produces the sought-for "Enlightenment." Here, through deepest meditation, the individual arrives at a trance-like state where all illusion and self-centered craving vanish. Now one is on the path to "sainthood" and man's final objective, Nirvana, that spiritual condition which releases him from the process of endless rebirths.

The Development of a Buddhist Faith   As we have already noted, the worship of deities as such played no part in Buddha's teachings. At best, as some claim, Nirvana to him meant the merging of the individual with Brahman, the Supreme Reality. Consequently, among his immediate followers no reverence to the various Hindu deities was practiced. Nor was Buddha himself ever regarded by his followers during his lifetime as more than a great teacher. In fact, he discouraged anything else.

But after his death the masses eventually turned him into a deity, and his doctrines into a religion. Doubtlessly they were affected by Hinduism with its numerous gods and rites. At any event, shortly after Buddha's death, traditions arose in which he came to represent the living embodiment of his teachings. It was now said that he had never really died, but was immortal, and actually the Supreme Being "who turns the wheel of the True Doctrine."

In the years that followed, the religion grew only slowly. However, in the third and second centuries B.C.E. it began to spread rapidly throughout Asia, thanks to the vigorous missionary activities of two powerful rulers of northern India. An expanded message of ethics and good works helped give Buddhism universal appeal so that it found a warm welcome beyond the borders of India.

During this period, too, different interpretations of Buddha's teachings led to the creation of a number of sects. Very early, we are told, there were already eighteen such sects. The two most important sects had already come into being by the time Buddhism reached its peak.

The first of these two was South Asian Buddhism, found today chiefly in Ceylon, Burma, Thailand, Cambodia, and Laos. It was nicknamed by its adversaries "Hinayana" Buddhism, "the *Little* Vehicle." The use of the term "vehicle" suggests a religion that can successfully transport the individual through the whole of life and on to salvation. Its followers today object to this name, and prefer to be called "Theravadists," that is, those who are loyal to the Theravada, "the Way of the Elders," or the original teachings of Buddha.

By the third or second century B.C.E., "Mahayana" Buddhism, "the *Great* Vehicle," was already challenging the Theravadists. Its followers, living mainly in northern and eastern Asia, disagreed with Theravadist teachings as being too difficult to practice and lacking in emotional appeal. Consequently, the Mahayanists adopted other interpretations that won for them the great majority of Buddhists today.

Mahayana Buddhism The Theravadists were essentially orthodox in that they held fast to the teachings of Buddha as contained in the oldest traditions, the "Three Baskets." Hence, they interpreted the doctrines virtually as Buddha had pronounced them and regarded him as the Supreme Sage. For them, the monk and nun, organized in monastic orders, represented the ideal person, the one who renounced life in the quest for complete detachment from desire.

This had only limited appeal to the masses, who sought greater comfort from their religion and a program of living more in touch with worldly realities. This was offered by Mahayana Buddhism with its more liberal interpretation of tradition that incorporated materials produced much later than Buddha.

While Nirvana, the state of complete Enlightenment, remained the goal of both sects, in Mahayana Buddhism the ideal was not the saint who simply attained his own salvation and the end of his reincarnations. Rather, it was the person who had the capacity of achieving Nirvana but preferred to renounce it in order to remain in the world and make his "knowledge" available to others.

The saint, then, is a would-be Buddha. Not only does he possess knowledge of the Way of Enlightenment, but also deep concern for the spiritual welfare of all others. Gautama, they said, was the divine embodiment of this ideal. He possessed both the wisdom to attain complete Enlightenment, and the overwhelming compassion that moved him to appear among men and share his knowledge so that others, too, might gain Nirvana and Buddhahood for themselves.

Indeed, according to the Mahayanists, everyone—priest and layman alike—may aspire to Buddhahood. In fact, a great many Buddhas and would-be Buddhas are needed to reveal the Way of Enlightenment and relieve the suffering of mankind. And it is to those who have already appeared that one should turn with his whole self.

Today, the Mahayanists revere three types of Buddhas. The first, naturally, is Gautama himself and others like him who assumed Buddhahood in different ages. They are principally divine teachers, who as Compassionate Beings, inspire mankind toward Nirvana. Most of the Buddha figures one sees are generally of this variety, and their different poses indicate meditation, teaching, comforting, protecting, and the like.

The second type of Buddhas consists of certain superhuman beings, identified with sun-gods and other deities who have postponed entry into Nirvana in order to help the individual in the higher regions. They have become the lords of the various heavens and hells through which the souls of people must pass before being reborn.

The third type is the most important for the purposes of worship: Bodhisattvas, "Buddhas-in-the-making," heroes who could have attained Buddhahood but, out of compassion for mankind, postponed their enjoyment of Nirvana to help others. Since they accumulated so much merit during their lives, they are believed to share it with those seeking to obtain a higher form of reincarnation, and their images are worshipped much as the gods of the ancient religions. In some instances, there are female Bodhisattvas, and in Tibet, the Grand Lamas are regarded as living reincarnations of the Bodhisattvas.

The existence of Bodhisattvas stimulated the development of an important Mahayana teaching that has had great influence upon modern Buddhism. In essence, it is the belief that just as the Bodhisattvas postponed entrance into Nirvana for the sake of humanity and made their merit available to others, so each individual is capable of imitating them. By vowing to become a Bodhisattva—though it may take an eternity to come to pass—the person is inspired to postpone Nirvana for himself and embark upon the path of benevolence for the good of others.

The adherents of Mahayana Buddhism, living principally in Tibet, China, Manchuria, Mongolia, Formosa, and Japan, greatly outnumber those of the South Asian branch. However, in each country different varieties have developed.

In recent times some efforts have been made

by the main branches of Buddhism to find a common basis of unity. As a result of a series of world-wide conferences, Mahayana and Theravadist groups are currently engaged in a number of joint projects, including the preparation of an encyclopedia of Buddhism.

The Practices of Buddhists In the course of time, certain features of Mahayana Buddhism ultimately found their way into the Theravadist form of the religion. Thus it too has come to regard Buddha as divine, though not a Savior, and it also stresses compassion as a major virtue.

In both branches Buddha himself, in the form of images, is worshipped in connection with his relics. Informed Buddhists, however, do not look upon this as idolatry but merely as an expression of reverence for him. From him they seek guidance on the Way of Enlightenment so that the effects of the Law of Karma may be meritorious for them.

The custom of preserving the relics of Buddha is an ancient one that led to the creation of numerous temples built in the form of pagodas. Originally, whenever some relic was discovered, it was placed under a parasol, a symbol of royalty. However, to show it even greater respect, people placed parasols on top of parasols, creating a tapering tower-like effect. This in turn led to the erection of actual pagodas to house the sacred relics. Even today, Buddhists consider the building of a pagoda or the care of one a very virtuous deed.

Buddhism centers about the lives of the great Brotherhood of Monks who are easily recognized by their yellow robes, clean-shaven heads, and alms-bowls. Practicing poverty, chastity, and "inoffensiveness," the monks conduct the funerals, carry on various ceremonies in their monastery temples, and educate the young. In certain countries, many Buddhists spend several months of their lives as monks.

Normally, the Buddhist has no regularly scheduled services. Rather, the important feature of his worship is the meditation designed to prepare him to pursue the path of Enlightenment. However, there are certain set periods

PRAYERS FOR THE LAMA. The religion of Tibet is part of Mahayana Buddhism. The Dalai Lama, for whom these Tibetans are praying, was both their spiritual and political ruler until he was forced to flee from the Chinese Communists in 1959.

of worship, especially the celebration of significant events in Buddha's life, as, for example, the Flower Festival, held in honor of his birth.

Acts of worship are performed at shrines in one's home, both morning and evening. These are decorated with images and offerings of flowers, water, incense, and sometimes food. In Japan, tablets with the religious names of ancestors are also placed beside the image of Buddha.

Certain folk-versions of Buddhism call for the worship of various local deities. Among the masses, too, all sorts of good and evil spirits often play an active part in daily religion. To cope with demons and win the aid of the good spirits, they resort to the use of charms, magic, dances, and many kinds of rituals.

There is no system of life-cycle ceremonies comparable to that found in other faiths. The principal rites are reserved for death and the funeral. It is generally not even customary for Buddhist priests to officiate at marriages.

Yet, within Buddhism, practices differ widely. In various places certain ceremonies are held marking particular stages in the life of the individual. Such a case is the feast held among certain Buddhists when boys are about the age of four and are initiated by living for a day as a monk. The child is first adorned with rich clothes at a lavish banquet. Then the garments are removed, the child's head is shaved, and he is clothed in a yellow robe. Finally, he is taken off to spend the night in a nearby monastery. Thus he is initiated into the ways of Buddha.

Shin Buddhism   Two forms of Buddhism are of special interest to us because they are currently found in the United States. The first is Shin Buddhism, the faith practiced by most of America's 20,000 Buddhists.

Originating in Japan and probably influenced by certain forms of Christianity, Shin Buddhism centers about the worship of Amitabha, better known as Amida, one of the five great Buddhas of the Mahayana faith. According to tradition, Amida was originally a monk who made forty-eight vows of compassion to be fulfilled when he became a Buddha. One, the eighteenth, promised that those who trusted in him would enjoy rebirth in the Pure Realm of the West over which he has charge. There the individual would achieve his Enlightenment and gain Buddhahood.

Appeal to Amida is central in the Shin faith. Prayers to other gods or spirits, it maintains, are futile. Nor can the individual achieve Enlightenment by himself since he cannot rise above the sin, selfishness, and error that dominate his life. Salvation, therefore, can come only through the power bestowed upon him by Amida, and particularly effective in winning his grace is the recitation of Buddha's name.

Here, contained within the funeral service for a Shin Buddhist, is a characteristic expression of the reverence in which Amida is held:

> You, perfect Master,
> Who shine upon all things and all men
> As gleaming moonlight plays
> Upon a thousand waters at the same time!

> Your great compassion does not pass by a single creature.
> Steadily and quietly sails
> The great ship of compassion across the sea of sorrow.
> You are the Great Physician for a sick and impure world,
> In pity giving the invitation to the Paradise of the West.

Featured in Shin worship, which in this country very much resembles a church service, are lectures and sermons that seek to stimulate belief in salvation through Amida. The service is conducted by persons considered to be neither monks nor laymen, and centers about the recitation of the name of Buddha. It also provides for the use of rosaries.

In the temple one usually finds an image of Amida or a scroll bearing his name, together with a picture of Shinran, the thirteenth century monk who founded the sect and after whom it is named. Art, music (especially gospel-like singing), and drama—well-known in the form of Japanese Noh-plays—are important in Shin religious activity.

Some of the more important ceremonies in Shin temples are weddings and funerals, and the ritual in which the child is brought there soon after birth to hear the reading of the creed and the scriptures. The death of Shinran is also commemorated annually with special rites.

Zen Buddhism   In recent years a second form of Buddhism coming out of Japan has had special appeal to some Westerners. This is Zen Buddhism.

Though it first appeared around the sixth century C.E., its followers trace the origins back to a legend in the life of Buddha himself. A disciple is said to have brought him a gift of a golden flower and asked him to explain the secret of his teaching. Buddha took the flower, held it up and looked at it in complete silence. Thereby, he was said to have indicated that his doctrine could not be explained in words, but only through one's own personal experience.

This is the heart of Zen teaching. Words, its followers insist, can never convey true understanding. Rather, it must come about through direct experience. A Zen Buddhist would say that one may tell a person all he knows about fire, but to comprehend what fire really is the person must see it for himself, feel it, smell it burning, and the like.

Consequently, if one is to achieve Enlightenment, it can only be by experiencing the mind of Buddha. Each person, says Zen, originally possessed Buddhahood, and it can be restored to him only as he succeeds in regaining that former state of mind. To this he can be guided by one who has already learned the process, the Zen master.

What is involved is undergoing certain kinds of experiences, described by three terms. The first is *zazen*, "seated meditation," usually remaining seated for hours in the "lotus" position (with crossed legs) and meditating with eyes open, designed to encourage sudden flashes of intuition.

The second is *koan*, "a problem" that one concentrates on as part of his instruction or meditation. To the uninitiated these seem quite strange, because the pupil may be given some such *koan* as:

> What is the sound of one hand that is clapping?
>
> Where there is nothing, what do we find?
>
> What was the appearance of your face before you were born?

To deal with such problems, something other than normal logic is required. One must "experience" the matter and arrive at sudden flashes of insight, say Zen Buddhists.

The third is *sanzen*, "consultation" about one's meditation with his master. Periodically, the pupil meets with him briefly to give him the answers that he has found to his *koan*. The master informs him whether or not he has been successful. On other occasions the master may test him by asking him the meaning of some paradox like "To die the great death is to gain the great life." When a pupil shows that he does not comprehend, the master may turn away,

roar at him, or even slap at him, indicating his failure to understand Zen.

The goal of this process is to enable the individual to achieve continuing flashes of inner insight, known as *satori*. This is described as a sense of being at one with everything in the universe in which all awareness of oneself has disappeared. As a result, say the followers of Zen, one comes to look upon all of life in a new way so that everything seems good. At that point the person has succeeded in bringing out the Buddha in himself.

Out of the practice of Zen in the United States has arisen a type of literature known as "beat," a term describing its general indifference to things, an attitude incomprehensible to the average person. Yet, in so far as it flows out of the experience of Zen, it typifies the "beat" writer's view of life in terms of the inner intuitions he has gained.

Still Farther Eastward How Buddhism came to China is the subject of many interesting legends.

According to one, a Chinese emperor who lived shortly after the beginning of the Common Era became interested in Buddhism through a dream. In his sleep he is supposed to have seen Buddha's image, glowing like the sun, fly into his room. When he awoke, he dispatched messengers to India and they brought back a number of Buddhist books, some statues of Buddha, and two monks. The emperor is then said to have become a fervent Buddhist and helped spread the faith.

Though it is possible that Buddhism may have come into China as early as the beginning of the Common Era, most scholars doubt that it had much influence or gained many followers until four or five centuries later. In the fourth and fifth century C.E., many tribes from Central Asia broke through the Great Wall of China, and among them were some who brought Mahayana Buddhism with them. Only then did the existing beliefs and practices of the Chinese people come into full contact with Buddhism.

The eventual outcome of this encounter was the religion known today as Confucianism. . . .

TOPICS TO DISCUSS

1. What does Buddhism establish as the main goal of life? Why?

2. In what ways is Buddhism different from Hinduism? What do they share in common?

3. How do the central teachings of Judaism differ from those of Buddhism in general? How do you explain this?

4. How do you account for the fact that some people of the Western world have been attracted to Zen Buddhism?

THINGS TO DO

1. Prepare a picture-chart showing the development of Buddhism.

2. Produce a playlet designed to bring out some of the main differences between the beliefs and practices of Jews and Buddhists.

3. Prepare a dictionary of key Buddhist ideas and terms.

OTHER THINGS TO READ

BALLOU, ROBERT O., *The Portable World Bible*, Viking, "The Buddhist," pp. 95-159.

FITCH, FLORENCE MARY, *Their Search for God*, Lothrop, Lee, and Shepard, "The Way of the Buddha," pp. 110-155.

GAER, JOSEPH, *How the Great Religions Began*, Signet Key, Book 1, Part 1, "Buddhism," pp. 18-41.

————, *The Wisdom of the Living Religions*, Dodd, Mead, Part 1, "The Sayings of Buddhism," pp. 3-41.

KITAGAWA, JOSEPH M., *Religions of the East*, Westminster, Chapter 4, "Buddhism and the Samgha," pp. 155-221.

MORGAN, KENNETH W., *The Path of the Buddha*, Ronald Press.

NOSS, JOHN B., *Man's Religions*, Macmillan, Chapter 5, "Buddhism in Its First Phase," pp. 155-179; Chapter 6, "The Religious Development of Buddhism," pp. 181-222.

SMITH, HUSTON, *The Religions of Man*, Mentor, Chapter 3, "Buddhism," pp. 90-149.

The World's Great Religions, Time, "The Path of Buddhism," pp. 39-70.

19

GREAT RELIGIONS OF THE EAST:

3. Confucianism

The Religion of Confucius   Chinese tradition claims that when Confucius, its great sage, was thirty-four years old, he already had more than three thousand pupils.

Over the centuries, however, that following was destined to grow so enormously that today there are some 301 million Confucianists who live principally in China, Korea, Manchuria, Japan, and parts of Mongolia. Though at the present time Confucianism is under serious attack by the Communist rulers of most of these lands, the influence of this great teacher and the doctrines he taught remain an important factor in the people's way of life.

Confucianism arose in China during the sixth century B.C.E. Actually, this was a time of great religious awakening in many other parts of the world. Among the Jews, it was the period of Jeremiah, Second Isaiah, and Ezekiel. In India, it marked the age of Buddha, and in Persia, of Zoroaster, the founder of an important religion known as Zoroastrianism. Similarly, among the Chinese, it was the time of two of their greatest teachers, Lao Tzu and Confucius. The blending of their teachings, though very different, with Buddhism and various ancient religious beliefs and practices has given the Chinese people the religion commonly known as "Confucianism."

To understand the Chinese religion, therefore, we must know each of the four elements that have gone into its making: the ancient Chinese faiths, the teachings of Lao Tzu, the teachings of Confucius, and the ideas of Buddhism, which was imported later on.

The Ancient Religions of China   Long before Confucius appeared, the people of China had already developed many of their religious beliefs and practices. Some were based upon their regard for nature; others, respect for society.

As an agricultural people, the early Chinese centered much of their worship around local gods who were felt to be responsible for crops. In addition, people believed there were various spirits in trees, fields, mountains, rocks, and the like. Eventually, a great Earth-goddess, the Mother of all life, became one of the more powerful deities, and her chief function was to insure the fertility of the soil. Many of her duties in turn were assigned to lesser spirits, some good, some bad. To the Chinese, it was essential to win the favor of the good spirits and drive away the evil ones.

Many Chinese ceremonies today still concern themselves with these spirits. To ward off the evil of demons, the people provide special rice offerings at weddings and shoot off firecrackers, especially on the New Year. Also, as protection against them, magic sayings are inscribed on red paper—an imitation of the peach-blossom which is a symbol of the fertility of the soil—and hung in various places. Likewise, articles made of peach-wood itself are believed to free the individual from the evil of demon spirits.

At a very early time, too, another powerful deity had come into existence. This was Heaven. To the ancient Chinese, the heavens, with their sun, moon, stars, winds, rain, clouds, and lightning, seemed especially awesome. They came to believe in a "ruler of the heavens," or Heaven, the great spirit who could be influenced by proper forms of worship. Gradually a number of lesser deities under his control appeared— deities representing, for example, the sun, the moon, and other aspects of nature. Over the centuries, the worship of Heaven began to assume even more importance than that of Earth, and the Chinese emperors introduced a number of public ceremonies in honor of the "Spirit of Heaven."

In addition to these beliefs, the early Chinese found another chief concern, reverence for one's ancestors, whose spirits also were said to bring good or evil. Regard for ancestors has remained a very important feature of China's religion. In fact, among the Chinese today the individual thinks of his family as including not only living relatives, but also long generations of his deceased ancestors.

This respect for the dead eventually led to many rites and ceremonies. The deceased must be properly sent off into the land of the dead with appropriate sacrifices, funeral rites, and mourning. In place of the actual articles of food and clothing they are believed to need, paper objects have come to be substituted, and these are usually burned so that they can ascend to heaven in the smoke. The grave-site of one's ancestors is considered very sacred; and in one's home a room is generally set aside as a shrine in memory of at least five generations of the dead. Special home rituals are performed, including "three kneelings" and "nine knockings" of the forehead against the ground, called *kow-tow*.

In the main, these features of Chinese religion were well-established prior to the sixth century B.C.E. When Lao Tzu and Confucius made their appearance, the Chinese people merely incorporated their teachings into their existing faith. Later they added the worship of both sages.

The Life of Confucius Though Lao Tzu preceded Confucius by more than a half-century, we know a great deal more about the latter. Hence, we shall begin with him.

What we know of Confucius comes to us from two main sources. One is the collection of many sayings ascribed to him. These were gathered together over a period of years by disciples and appear in a volume known as the *Analects*, "Sayings," one of the "Four Books of the Philosophers" that deal with Confucianism. The second source is various late traditions about Confucius' life. Though the information about his teachings is generally reliable, many of the details of his life are clearly legendary. However, the following seems to us to be an accurate account.

Confucius, whose name has been Latinized from K'ung Fu-Tse, "the Great Master K'ung," was born around the year 551 B.C.E. into the poor but noble K'ung family, who lived in the Shantung province of coastal China. His father died when he was young, and, with great personal sacrifice, his mother undertook to have him educated for a career in the government.

At about the age of nineteen, he entered the employ of the Duke of the region as a minor collector of taxes. At the same time, he devoted a great deal of his energy to training boys for what he considered to be the proper kind of government service. For, all during these years, Confucius had become more and more disturbed by what he felt was the people's indifference to desirable conduct in social and political affairs.

Unquestionably, the times during which Confucius lived influenced his feelings, for the ancient Chinese feudal system was gradually decaying. Powerful lords with armies of their own were practically independent of the emperor, and civil war was frequent. Many of the old noble families, as in the case of Confucius' own family, had been reduced to poverty, and their place was being taken by a rising merchant class and a group of former serfs, who had now accumulated land of their own. Many of these people were opportunists who often took the law in their own hands to the detriment of the ordinary man.

CONFUCIUS. This great Chinese sage of the sixth century B.C.E. sought to establish ways of conduct that would bring harmony to both the individual and society.

Confucius looked upon all of this as improper and wished to restore the social order as it had formerly been, though in a purer, nobler form. He was convinced that if the ruling classes set the right example in their own conduct, the old and correct ways could be reestablished with the wholehearted approval of the people. Therefore, while continuing to serve the Duke, he engaged in preparing the children of many of the best families for future service in the government.

Gradually, tradition tells us, Confucius rose to a position of some importance in the Duke's cabinet. But in his fifties he became the victim of a plot and was forced to resign. Then for many years he wandered from state to state seeking a position. Though the rulers received him courteously, they did not engage him. Evi-dently they were afraid of his candor as well as his idealistic plans.

Finally, at about the age of 67, he returned home to retire. However, he continued to attract disciples, and before his death in 479 B.C.E he enjoyed a considerable following. He may also have produced several books which, together with some of the older Chinese works, are known as the *Five Classics*. These and the writings of later Confucianists served for centuries as the basis of all Chinese education.

What Confucius Taught   What did Confucius teach?

He was concerned, not with beliefs about the deities or their worship, but with the development of rules of proper conduct to achieve a desirable social order. "People must understand how to conduct themselves," he taught. "Otherwise there is bound to be disharmony and confusion which produce human suffering." For just as Chinese thought regarded the well-being of the world as dependent upon harmony between Earth and Heaven, so Confucius taught that society also demanded harmonious relationships between the government and its subjects, among the people themselves, and within each family.

The mark of the "Ideal Man," Confucius taught, is revealed by his devotion to four main principles of conduct. The first, *Jen*, may be translated as "Mutual Regard," or "Reciprocity," expressed by Confucius' own Golden Rule, "What you do not want done to yourself, do not do to others." Hence, in each situation, a person must first judge the feelings of others by how he himself would feel, and then act accordingly.

The second is *Yi*, the right way of doing things, or "Duty." Each person, observed Confucius, is automatically obliged by his situation in life—be it as a member of his family, a citizen of the community, an official in the government, and the like—to perform certain duties for others. In each situation, a person must consider not what is best for himself, but what is right according to the principle of *Jen*, "Mutual Regard."

DEVELOPMENT OF HINDUISM, BUDDHISM, AND CONFUCIANISM

DEVELOPMENT OF HINDUISM

Before 1200 B.C.E. Invasion of India by Arians. Beginning of important gods, priesthood, caste system.

About 700 B.C.E. Beginnings of *Veda* literature.

About 600 B.C.E. Start of belief in Brahman as the indefinable source of all in universe. Belief in reincarnation.

About 200 B.C.E. Duties of castes prescribed. Way of return to Brahman without reincarnation created. Beginning of literature about Rama, Krishna, and other gods.

DEVELOPMENT OF BUDDHISM

Before 1000 B.C.E. Development of primitive religions of India and other Asian countries.

About 563 B.C.E. Birth of Siddhartha Gautama (Buddha) who introduced reforms in Hinduism.

About 483 B.C.E. Death of Buddha. Development of *Pali Canon*. Gradual deification of Buddha.

About 250 B.C.E. Spread of Buddhism from India to other lands. Development of Mahayana Buddhism.

About 6th century C.E. Appearance of Zen Buddhism.

DEVELOPMENT OF CONFUCIANISM

Before 1000 B.C.E. Development of original Chinese religious beliefs and practices involving Heaven and Earth and spirits under their control.

About 604 B.C.E. Birth of Lao Tzu.

About 551 B.C.E. Birth of Confucius.

About 479 B.C.E. Death of Confucius.

About 350 B.C.E. Connection of eternal life with Tao through mysticism.

About 195 B.C.E. Beginning of the deification of Confucius.

About 100 C.E. Taoism becomes magical cult.

During 4th and 5th centuries C.E. Introduction of Buddhism; deification of Lao Tzu.

KEY DEVELOPMENTS IN JUDAISM

About 1000 B.C.E. Hebrew Kingdom.

926 B.C.E. Division of the Kingdom.

About 750 B.C.E. Amos, Hosea, Isaiah, and Micah.

586 B.C.E. Babylonian exile, Jeremiah and Ezekiel.

550 B.C.E. Second Isaiah.

331 B.C.E. Greeks conquer Palestine.

165 B.C.E. Maccabean victory.

70 C.E. Romans destroy Jerusalem. School at Yabneh. Oral Law develops.

Li, perhaps best expressed by the word "Propriety," is the third principle to be followed by the "Ideal Man." This involves a sensitivity to the kind of conduct called for by the particular relationship between people in each different situation. For, though one's actions should be governed by his sense of Mutual Regard and Duty, these take different forms, depending upon his relationship to the other person. For instance, one is expected to behave differently toward his father than toward a brother or a friend.

In this connection, Confucius maintained, conduct among human beings should be regulated according to what he called "The Five Relationships." These cover the basic social relations that should exist between parents and children, brothers and sisters, husbands and wives, older and younger people, rulers and their subjects. All should be governed by Mutual Regard, but in terms of the respect due the parties involved.

He later expanded these "Five Relationships" to the following ten rules that established responsibility for each person's behavior in accordance with his relationship to others: (1) love on the part of the father, and (2) filial piety on the part of the son; (3) gentility in the oldest brother, and (4) humility and respect on the part of the younger brother; (5) righteous behavior in the husband, and (6) obedience in the wife; (7) humane consideration on the part of elders, and (8) deference in younger people; (9) benevolence on the part of rulers, and (10) loyalty in their subjects.

The last essential principle is *Chih*. This is the "Wisdom" at which one finally arrives when, spontaneously, he can act according to the principles of Mutual Regard, Duty, and Propriety. It is then that a person has gained confidence in himself, the complete good will of others, and the inner satisfaction which comes of leading the good life. At last he enjoys that contentment which is the true goal of every person.

This, undoubtedly, was what Confucius had sought for himself. For in the *Analects* he tells his pupils:

At fifteen I had my mind bent on learning. At thirty I stood firm. At fifty I knew the decrees of heaven. At sixty my ear was an obedient organ for the reception of truth. At seventy I could follow what my heart desired without transgressing what was right.

Confucius and Religion   The essence of Confucius' teachings, then, was the establishment of a harmonious society, based upon a fixed idea of what each person's position and conduct demanded. His main concern was that everyone do the "right thing," especially in his relations with others.

Convinced that each individual was fully capable of training himself to carry on the right relationships according to the principles of Mutual Regard, Duty, Propriety, and true Wisdom, Confucius found it unnecessary to build an ethical system upon faith in a deity. Hence, any concept of righteousness based upon the will of God, as in Judaism, is missing. Nor did Confucius engage in any real discussion of the nature of the deity and his worship. Consequently, from the point of view of Western man, the teachings of Confucius do not constitute a "religion" in the usual sense, with God the focus of man's aspirations and his conduct ordained by Him.

This is not to say that Confucius was an atheist. He seems to have believed in the power of Heaven. Thus, when he was urged by his disciples to flee from a certain army officer who was pursuing him, he replied, "Heaven produced the power that is within me. What have I to fear from such a person?" And he often spoke of the will of Heaven as sustaining him in his mission.

Moreover, he advised the individual in the performance of his duties to pay proper attention to his religious obligations. Traditional rites and ceremonies were to be carried on. Concerning the spirits themselves, Confucius is reported to have said:

How wonderfully great they are! Looking, we cannot see them; listening, we cannot hear them. Embodying them—

CHINESE STUDENTS. For many centuries, the classic texts of Confucianism were the universal subject of study. This old tradition of learning still motivates Chinese secular education.

TAOIST PRIESTS. There are two principal kinds: those who lead celibate lives in monasteries, and those, pictured here, who live in the villages. They normally work at regular occupations, and they may marry if they wish.

CHINESE RELIGION

GOLDEN BUDDHA. Since Chinese religion has incorporated much of Buddhism—especially its temple rites and ceremonials, and its concern with the after-life—many varieties of Buddha images are found in Chinese homes.

CONFUCIANIST TEMPLE. At one time, temples to Confucius existed in every district of China, but now only a few remain. These contain no statues of Confucius, but only tablets inscribed with his name.

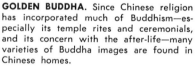

selves in all things, they are not to be neglected; they make all men breathe. Fast, put on sacrificial clothing and worship them. Vague and yet all-pervading, they seem to be above and all around us.

But, at the same time, the answers to man's needs here on earth were not to be found through religious speculation. "Absorption in the study of the supernatural," said Confucius, "is most harmful." And when one of his disciples asked him what was involved in doing one's duty to the spirits of the dead, he replied, "Before we are able to do our duty to the living, how can we do it for the spirits of the dead?"

Consequently, for Confucius, man's salvation upon earth lay in the manner in which he carried out his responsibilities to others within the context of the proper social system. While meriting respect as part of man's duty, Heaven and the spirits did not provide people with answers to the challenges of living effectively within society.

Yet, ironically, history succeeded in converting this man and his teachings into the religion known today as Confucianism. At first, after his death, Confucius was widely revered as a sage. Then, after many centuries, he came to be looked upon as a deity. In 1906, the emperor of China officially declared him to be a god, equal to Heaven and Earth. And today, wherever the religion is practiced, Confucius is worshipped by the masses, though in his case without any images.

Lao Tzu and Taoism   Taoism is said to have begun with the man named Lao Tzu, sometimes written "Lao-Tse." Little is actually known about him, and some scholars consider his existence purely legendary. However, old Chinese traditions provide us with this picture of his life.

Lao Tzu, literally "Old Boy," but best translated as "Revered Sir," is said to have been born with a white beard, thus indicating his great wisdom. The date of his birth is commonly believed to have been around 604 B.C.E., some fifty years before Confucius.

For a while he served as a royal librarian. Then he began to look upon all government as unnecessary and complicating the natural life of man. He resigned from his position and determined to lead a life of meditation among the hills. At the final stage of his journey, a gatekeeper recognized him and persuaded him to write down his teachings, which he did in the *Tao Te Ching*, "The Book of the Tao and Its Activity." He then disappeared forever.

The teachings of the *Tao Te Ching* reflect the ancient Chinese idea of a universal, indefinable power called Tao, "the Way." It is this principle which has brought into harmony the operation of two great opposite forces that make up all things. So living and dying, good and evil, love and hate, etc.—expressions of the opposing forces *yang* and *yin*—are balanced against each other and yet found within one another, all within the unity of Tao.

Traditionally, this has been pictured in this Chinese symbol:

Note that though *yang* and *yin* oppose each other, a part of each lies within the very heart of the other. Moreover, as they revolve within the circle that represents the unity of Tao, they are constantly changing places.

Life, then, consists of the continuous movement of these opposites back and forth, and frequently they are intermingled. Therefore, no one can really say that something is totally good or bad. If, for example, we fall down and hurt ourselves, that is bad; but it may also be good, if it has prevented us from driving our car and being involved in a much more serious accident.

Containing the movement of both opposing forces within itself, Tao is the ideal, natural "Way" that everything goes. Its rhythmic movement flows throughout the world and must be maintained if true order is to be preserved. As Tao brought Heaven and Earth into harmony, so man and society can achieve well-being only if they remain in tune with Tao. Says the *Tao Te Ching:*

> Before heaven and earth existed, there was something,
> Which, unmoved and unseen, neither begins nor ends.
> Present everywhere and inexhaustible, it is the perpetual source of everything else.
> For want of a better name, I call it "Tao."
> If I am forced to describe it, I speak of it as "Supreme" . . .
> Tao is supreme, heaven is supreme, earth is supreme,
> And the wise person is also supreme.
> Man follows earthly laws;
> Earth follows the laws of heaven;
> Heaven follows the laws of Tao;
> And Tao follows the laws of its own nature.

The root of man's difficulties lies in his failure to be in harmony with Tao. In seeking to exert his own will, he disrupts the natural order Tao has established. Instead, man must not interfere with the course of things; the individual must let things follow their natural bent. For practical living, then, here is the formula that the *Tao Te Ching* would have man follow:

> Banish wisdom, discard knowledge,
> And the people shall profit a hundred-fold;
> Banish love, discard justice,
> And the people shall recover love of their kin;
> Banish cunning, discard utility,
> And thieves and bandits shall disappear.
> As these three touch the externals they are inadequate.
> The people have need of what they can depend upon:

> Reveal your simple self,
> Embrace your original nature,
> Check your selfishness,
> Curtail your desires.

These teachings of Lao Tzu may be summarized as a program of "being oneself," that is, allowing one's own nature to come through. For working within man is Tao, which, in this instance, means the power of his natural self to exert itself if it is not thwarted. Hence, he must not act differently because someone else wishes him to; nor should he impose his will on others so that he restricts Tao from operating in them. Rather, he should allow their own inner nature to prevail, recognizing that each person's way is best for him. One might, in fact, call this the very opposite of Judaism's position, with its emphasis upon obeying commandments that say "Thou shalt . . ." and "Thou shalt not. . . ."

Yet, as Lao Tzu contends, this is the course that will be followed by the wise person. As one permits Tao to flow unhindered in his life, he maintains, it will not only produce its own pattern of desirable human relationships but also enable the individual to attain gentleness, frugality, and humility, the "Three Jewels" of Taoism.

The Blending of the Chinese Way   With the teachings of its two great sages, China now possessed two opposing Ways by which life could be lived. The one of Confucius prescribed precise forms of proper conduct, while that of Lao Tzu disapproved of all imposed rules of behavior because they interfered with the natural operation of Tao. Yet, ultimately, the paths of both came to be blended within the daily life of the Chinese, with the kind of conduct called for by Confucius now regarded as the natural course of Tao. To this were added also the ways of both the ancient Chinese religions and Buddhism to form that faith we now call Confucianism.

How did this come about?

We recall that Confucianism underwent many changes over the centuries until it became a religion which worshipped Confucius

A DIGEST OF BUDDHISM AND CONFUCIANISM

MEMBERSHIP

152 million — chiefly in Ceylon, Tibet, Burma, Thailand, Mongolia, Manchuria, Korea, Indochina, Japan.

301 million — chiefly in China, Mongolia, Manchuria, Korea and Japan.

ORGANIZATION

Many sects: 2 main forms of Buddhism— East Asian (Mahayana Buddhism) which is the larger, and South Asian (Theravada Buddhism).

Clergy: Brotherhood of monks, priests.

Many interpretations stemming from the ancient Chinese religions, the teachings of Confucius and Lao Tzu, and Buddhism.

No clergy as such.

PRACTICES

Sacred writings: The Pali Canon, others in Sanskrit, Chinese, and other languages.

Holidays primarily connected with life of Buddha.

Some life-cycle ceremonies, especially in connection with death.

Reverence of relics and Buddhas in pagoda shrines.

Sacred writings: *The Five Classics, The Four Books of the Philosophers*, and others.

Holidays connected with coming of the seasons, New Year, Dragon Boat Festival and Festival of Eighth Moon. Holidays honoring Confucius and Lao Tzu.

Life-cycle ceremonies of birth, marriage, death, with special emphasis upon the honoring of ancestors.

DISTINCTIVE BELIEFS

Since man's cravings disrupt the order of the universe, he should rid himself of desires through following the Middle Way and attaining Enlightenment.

The Eightfold Path calls for Right-Belief, -Intention, -Speech, -Conduct, -Means of Livelihood, -Effort, -Mindfulness, -Concentration.

Worship of different kinds of Buddhas and Bodhisattvas, with acceptance of belief in reincarnation after death.

(Confucius) Disharmony is the result of improper conduct. This can be overcome by a life devoted to Mutual Regard, Duty, Propriety (as explained in the Five Relationships), and true Wisdom.

(Lao Tzu) Tao is the indefinable power that maintains harmony between the 2 conflicting forces in the universe. Man should not disrupt this harmony but simply attune himself to it by "being himself." Attempt through later Taoism to gain eternal life with Tao.

as a deity. In a similar way, Taoism also developed into a religion of its own.

The generations that followed Lao Tzu soon found his teachings difficult to understand and much too hard to put into practice. Gradually, Lao Tzu's doctrines underwent certain radical changes. Tao came to be looked upon as giving great powers to those who possessed it, particularly the gift of eternal life. Thus, it was taught that everlasting life could be attained through aloofness to material things so that one's spirit would be open to receive the "truth of Tao." Once this was experienced, the individual would find that ecstasy which insured his immortality.

The notion of everlasting life through Tao captured the imagination of the masses, and gradually practical measures were devised by which it was believed this could be achieved. By the end of the first century C.E., priests of Tao were offering magic potions that were said to insure immortality, and these were usually conceived of as some form of edible gold. In addition, all sorts of charms against dangers or for other purposes were offered. Among them were pills said to enable the individual to walk on water, and seals to protect him from demons.

With the coming of Mahayana Buddhism into China during the fourth and fifth centuries C.E., the followers of Taoism proceeded to imitate it by deifying Lao Tzu as the "Emperor of Mysterious Origin." Gradually, he was joined by other gods and spirits, chiefly those that had long been part of ancient Chinese religion. Now, too, all of the sacred writings were collected, and worship in temples, conducted by orders of priests, was begun. The final stage was the introduction into Taoism of a Heavenly paradise for the dead, as well as a fearsome Hell.

At about the same time, probably as a consequence of challenges posed by both Buddhism and Taoism, Confucianism itself began to take on more of the characteristics of a popular religion. New rituals were introduced into the worship, and miracle stories began to be told about the life of Confucius. All this was stimulated, too, by the fact that, over the years, Confucianism had been made into the official religion of China. In 630 C.E., every district was ordered to erect a temple to him in which regular sacrifices were to be performed. Gradually, images of Confucius and pictures of his chief disciples were placed in them so that more and more they came to resemble those of the Buddhists. Only in much later times did reformers succeed in removing the images of Confucius.

Today, Confucianism as a state religion has ceased to be. With the Chinese Revolution in 1911 and the establishment of the Republic, the state discontinued its support of the religion. Nearly all the Confucianist temples were closed.

Taoism, too, has languished. Its devotion to magic brought it into disrepute, and its opposition to the power of centralized government has caused its followers to be severely persecuted by the Communist regime in China.

Only Buddhism manages to maintain itself as a formal faith in China. Despite the opposition of the Communists who seized power in 1949, it has evidently retained the loyalty of many of its followers. At least the Communists appear to be cautious about arousing the anger of the Chinese Buddhists by open attacks on their shrines and temples.

Nevertheless, Confucianism lives on within the daily lives of the Chinese people. Over the centuries, the essentials of all three of their faiths—Taoism, Confucianism, and Buddhism—together with elements of the ancient religions of the land, have been blended into a particular type of family and community life. Basically, as some have pointed out, the Chinese wants to live according to the noble rules of conduct developed by Confucius, but he also wants to enjoy his religion according to the colorful observances of China's ancient faiths. However, when he is in difficulty or ill, he consults Taoist priests for a cure, and near the time of death he calls in a Buddhist priest to insure a happy after-life.

And it is this whole way of life that really makes up Confucianism.

Some Practices of Confucianism   In what sense can we consider Confucianism a "religion" in today's world?

There are some who would deny that it is a

COMPARISON OF KEY
BELIEFS OF JUDAISM, ISLAM, AND THE

	DEITY	MAN	SIN
JUDAISM	One universal God with whom man stands in direct relationship.	Man has the capacity to be righteous or sinful; hence he has freedom of will.	Disobedience of God's Law.
ISLAM	Allah is the one universal God. However, there are angels and evil spirits.	Man must submit to the predetermined will of God (most).	Unfaithfulness to Moslem belief and practice which represents the will of Allah.
HINDUISM	Many deities, such as Krishna, Vishnu, as well as goddesses. Brahman is underlying essence of everything.	Through the operation of the Law of Karma, man's actions determine the state of his succeeding reincarnations.	Evil is to regard the world which is illusory as real. Also unfaithfulness to one's caste responsibilities and the Way one has chosen.
BUDDHISM	Essentially Buddhas and Bodhisattvas, some of whom are female.	Through the operation of the Law of Karma, man's actions determine the state of his succeeding reincarnations, particularly in the area of character-formation.	Evil is equivalent to desire. Failure to follow the Middle Path and practice the requirements of the Eight-fold Path represents wrong-doing.
CONFUCIANISM	Many deities including Heaven, Earth, Confucius, Lao Tzu, and others. Also many spirits.	Man is originally designed to be in harmony with the universe (Tao).	Evil is the failure to follow the conduct demanded by the Five Relationships, ignoring ancestors, failure to worship the deities properly. Self-assertiveness disrupts the order established by Tao.

EASTERN FAITHS

(Note: Such terms as "sin," "salvation," "authority," etc., appearing in the first column arise out of Judeo-Christian tradition. The Eastern faiths do not think in these terms. Hence, as we might otherwise assume from this chart, their use here is only for the purposes of broad comparison.)

	SALVATION	HEREAFTER	AUTHORITY
JUDAISM	To bring about the Kingdom of God on earth through a life lived according to His righteous Law and dedication to the Mission of Israel.	Perfected society of mankind on earth. Reform Jews believe in immortality of the soul which returns to God.	The Written and Oral Law.
ISLAM	To gain eternal life in heaven through faithfulness to Moslem belief and practice, representing the will of Allah.	Resurrection and Final Judgment with reward in heaven and punishment in hell.	Primarily the *Koran*. Also acceptance of the Traditions, 5 Books of Moses and Christian Gospel.
HINDUISM	Ideally, to merge self with Brahman and end process of rebirth by attaining Nirvana. Practically, to achieve a higher form of reincarnation through 4 Ways: Works, Knowledge, Devotion, and Concentration.	Nirvana. Heaven and hell are merely waiting places until rebirth takes place.	Many sacred works, including the *Vedas*, *Upanishads*, *Ordinances of Manu*, *Ramayana*, *Bhagavad-Gita*, etc.
BUDDHISM	Ideally, to attain the state of Buddhahood and Nirvana which end the process of rebirth. Practically, to achieve a higher form of reincarnation through following the Middle Path which involves renunciation of desire, understanding of the Four Noble Truths, and practice of the Noble Eightfold Path.	Nirvana. Heaven and hell are merely waiting places until rebirth takes place. (Shin) Paradise.	Many works in Pali, Sanskrit, Chinese and other languages. The Buddhist Scriptures for many are those works found in the *Pali Canon*.
CONFUCIANISM	To gain eternal life in heaven(?) with one's ancestors through (Confucius) a life lived according to Mutuality, Duty, Propriety and Wisdom; and (Taoism) to seek to be in tune with Tao. Also through worship of deities and regard for spirits, especially of the dead.	Eternal life in heaven(?) with one's ancestors.	*The Five Classics, The Four Books of the Philosophers,* and others.

religion. Certainly, from the Western point of view, Confucianism as originally expounded was essentially a philosophy and a code of ethics. Even as it is carried on today, Confucianism is by no means an organized religious system, such as we find in Judaism or Christianity.

Yet, as it has come to be practiced by its followers—especially in the reverence they show various deities and spirits, and their observance of rituals and ceremonies—there is little doubt that Confucianism falls within the broad definition of a religion.

Among the different Confucianists, a wide variety of beliefs and practices exists. Yet, virtually all traditional Chinese homes have a family shrine located in the main hall. In the center are the tablets of the family's ancestors, going back five generations, and on both sides of the

NEW YEAR'S A LA CHINESE. Oriental garb, massive green dragons, pounding drums, and much more, add to the festivities of the Chinese New Year's Day Parade.

shrine are other tablets bearing the names of various Confucianist, Taoist, and Buddhist deities. Elsewhere in the house are still other tablets with the names of the deities and spirits that arose out of ancient Chinese religion. During different phases of the moon and on particular festivals, offerings of incense, wine, and food are set before them.

Practically all Confucianists observe appropriate ceremonies connected with the life-cycle of the individual. Before the birth of a child, there are certain rites to insure that the baby will enjoy a life of good fortune. Announcements of his birth are sent on red paper—the color symbolizes good luck—and gifts are acknowledged with eggs dyed red. Thanksgiving offerings are made on each birthday of the child.

The wedding ceremony involves drinking from cups tied with a red cord and bowing before the household shrines. Death, of course, is accompanied by elaborate provisions for the safe departure of one's ancestor into the land of the dead.

In addition to particular observances honoring Confucius and Lao Tzu, traditional Chinese celebrate many holidays connected with the seasons. The coming of spring, winter, summer, and harvest time are all festivals. Interestingly, an exchange of gifts takes place during the winter festival that begins around December 21.

The Chinese New Year, occurring between January 10 and February 19, is also a period of great celebration. It commences on New Year's Eve with ceremonies at the family shrine remembering one's ancestors with messages, gifts, and feasting. New Year's Day centers around the burning of an image of Chang, the fat, jolly household god, so that he may bring a good report of the family as he goes up in smoke to heaven. (Four days later the family provides a new image of Chang for the household.) Public parades with firecrackers, drums, and dragons—which, according to Chinese legend, help bring rain and a good harvest—are supposed to rid the new year of evil spirits.

The people also observe the Festival of the Eighth Moon, as well as the colorful Dragon

252

Boat Festival, a thanksgiving observance held once every three years. At this holiday the gods are believed to come to earth, only to return to heaven when the beautifully decorated boat containing their images is burned.

Yet how much longer such practices will continue or whether Confucianism itself will survive is a matter of uncertainty because of the spread of Communism to China and most other areas inhabited by its followers. However, the religion is still practiced wherever the people are free to do so.

Let's Compare Religions   With this brief account of Confucianism, we complete our study of the great religions of the modern world.

The study has covered many thousands of years and has probed into the very origins of religion. We have circled the globe, from East to West and back again. We have observed the origins and development of the major faiths of today, and have examined their distinctive beliefs, practices, and forms of organizations.

We have also noted in what principal ways Judaism differs from them.

Now we are ready to take a final look at the major religions, this time to compare them. . . .

TOPICS TO DISCUSS

1. In what ways does modern Confucianism reveal the fact that it represents the blending of various religions?
2. In what sense can Confucianism and Taoism be said not to be religions? In what respect is modern Confucianism a religion? Yet in what ways is it different from Judaism?
3. What insights into the way religions develop do we gain from the history of Confucianism?
4. From your knowledge of Communism in China, what are some of the main reasons

for its incompatibility with religion in general and Confucianism in particular?

THINGS TO DO

1. Create a dictionary of key terms and concepts as found in Confucianism and Taoism.
2. Prepare a picture-chart portraying the way in which modern Confucianism developed.
3. Using Confucianism and Judaism as illustrations, write an essay on the subject: "How religions influence the life-goals, society, and character of its people."

OTHER THINGS TO READ

ARCHER, JOHN CLARK and CARL E. PURINTON, *Faiths Men Live By*, Ronald Press, Chapter 3, "An Introduction to Religions in China," pp. 53-68; Chapter 4, "Confucianism," pp. 70-118; Chapter 5, "Taoism," pp. 120-137.

BALLOU, ROBERT O., *The Portable World Bible*, Viking, "The Confucianist," pp. 483-529; "The Taoist," pp. 533-574.

FITCH, FLORENCE MARY, *Their Search for God*, Lothrop, Lee, and Shepard, "The Way of Confucius," pp. 52-66; "The Way of Lao-Tzu," pp. 66-83.

GAER, JOSEPH, *How the Great Religions Began*, Signet Key, Book Two, Part 1, "Confucianism," pp. 71-88; Part 2, "Taoism," pp. 90-104.

———, *The Wisdom of the Living Religions*, Dodd, Mead, Part 3, "The Sayings of Confucianism," pp. 93-112; Part 9, "The Sayings of Taoism," pp. 259-271.

KITAGAWA, JOSEPH M., *Religions of the East*, Westminster, Chapter 2, "Chinese Religions and the Family System," pp. 40-98.

NOSS, JOHN B., *Man's Religions*, Macmillan, Chapter 9, "Chinese Religion and the Taoists," pp. 294-336; Chapter 10, "Confucius and Confucianism," pp. 338-397.

SMITH, HUSTON, *The Religions of Man*, Mentor, Chapter 4, "Confucianism," pp. 151-182; Chapter 5, "Taoism," pp. 183-199.

The World's Great Religions, Time, "The Philosophy of China," pp. 71-98.

20

A COMPARISON OF RELIGIONS

How Man Found Religion   The earth was already formed. So were the sun, moon, and stars, the trees and grasses, even the birds, fish, and beasts. Then God declared it was time to create man.

A stir went through the ranks of the angels. One finally spoke up. "O Lord, Your angels wonder about the wisdom of creating man. . . ."

Another broke in, "We foresee that man will suffer much pain. . . ."

". . . And he will not take proper care of the world You have created," added a third. "The beautiful earth will be burned by his carelessness, and the lovely gardens will be trampled."

"He will mistreat the animals . . . and even destroy his fellow humans," said another.

God was saddened by the objections of the angels, for according to His plan man was to be the climax of creation. Yet He knew that the angels were not wrong.

"Well, then," God told them, "not only shall I create man with the five senses I had planned for him, but I shall give him another. . . ."

"An extra sense, Lord?" they asked.

"Yes, one that will remind him of Me. Whatever he sees—the trees, the hills, the plants, the seasons, the sun, moon, and stars, the harvest, even his fellow man—everything in the universe will remind him of Me if he uses this sense. And, eventually, he will yearn to be like Me in all his ways."

The angels broke into songs of rejoicing, and God proceeded to breathe His spirit into the dust of the earth to form Adam.

Why Religion Is Universal   Though this is only a legend, it does contain a kernel of real truth. The experts declare that religion is found everywhere in our world, among primitive peoples who outwardly seem to have no formal faith, and even in Communist lands where the official position scoffs at religious belief. Man does seem to have what we may call an extra sense for religion, which everything about him, and especially nature, tends to sharpen. Remember the words of the Psalmist?

> I lift up my eyes to the mountains;
> From whence shall my help come?
> My help comes from the Lord
> Who made heaven and earth.
> —Psalm 121:1-2

Scientists offer us several explanations for the world-wide existence of religion. One maintains that it was transmitted directly from one people to another, probably springing up first in the region of Mesopotamia or in the Nile Valley. As these peoples migrated, they carried their beliefs and practices to different lands, until gradually a sense of religion became universal.

Another theory holds that, as the result of circumstances common to the whole human

A COMPARISON OF RELIGIONS

race, religion came into being in a number of different places at about the same time. All peoples shared certain experiences with nature and life. The sun, moon, stars, and earth were there for all to observe; so were the seasons, the winds, rains, and clouds. Everyone witnessed birth and death; all human beings knew inner feelings of joy, doubt, fear, despair. And all yearned for a way of life that would bring inner contentment and hope for the future.

Once religious feelings arose in man, he connected them with nature and his life, depending on the needs he felt and the circumstances of the locality in which he happened to live. Those who dwelt in cooler climates found the sun a friendly force; in hot areas, the sun could be a great source of evil. In areas of few trees, the spirits that dwelt in them came to be regarded with special awe, and where there were mighty rivers that flooded in the spring, their spirits were viewed as extremely powerful.

Unquestionably, there is some truth in both explanations. In the past, just as today, religious ideas have been transmitted from place to place and from people to people. Surroundings, too, were bound to influence the nature of a people's beliefs and practices. But neither theory entirely explains certain facts. For students of primitive peoples have long observed that

religions of neighboring tribes, subject to essentially the same needs and natural surroundings, often differ widely.

Evidently other factors—the special experiences of the group, the appearance of certain more sensitive religious personalities, or feelings of direct communication with the Supernatural—have also played an important part in shaping religion. Certainly, as we have observed with all the major faiths and particularly with Judaism, there is ample evidence to confirm this.

Consequently, in their origin and growth, the different religions appear to be no less the product of mankind's sense of the Supernatural. As a result, many—and especially those in the Western world—look upon the universality of religion as evidence of God's revealing Himself to man whom He created in His own image. Judaism, we must remember, gave this idea to the Western world when it taught in Genesis that God made a covenant, not simply with the Jews through Abraham, but *with all men*, through His covenant with Noah at the time of the Flood.

And because of religion's universality, we are not surprised to find that, on the surface at least, Judaism, Christianity, Islam, and the Eastern faiths have certain things in common.

POTLATCH. A particular type of religious festival celebrated by Eskimos and others with gift-giving. Gifts are exchanged with the expectation that they will bring double their value in return.

Difficult as it has been to speak of so many great religions as briefly as we have thus far, we now face the even more difficult task of quickly comparing them. Naturally, this means that we shall have to summarize in a sentence or two the essentials of complex faiths that have inspired vast numbers of people over many centuries. Exceptions must also be skipped over, and only the most general characteristics of the great religions as they are currently practiced by most of their followers can be dealt with. Recognizing, therefore, that such summaries can only hold true in general, we nevertheless believe the following observations may prove valuable.

Bearing these limitations in mind, suppose we now note what it is that the great religions seem to have in common.

What the Religions Share in Common

First, of course, all of the faiths—even Bud-

SUKOS. With their rabbi, Reform Jewish children participate in the Harvest Festival by holding the lulov and esrog as they stand within the decorated booth.

dhism and Confucianism, not in their original form but as they have come to be—share a belief in the existence of the Supernatural to whom man can appeal for aid. Faith in some Power (or powers), who created the universe and who controls and sustains it, is common to every one of the great religions, though, as we have seen, this is expressed in widely different ways.

Secondly, they all regard individual and group prayer or meditation as an important element in establishing a relationship and communicating with the Supernatural. In some instances, as in Judaism, man appeals directly to God; in others, he may pray for the intercession of certain divine beings, saints, heroes, or sages. But prayer in some form is common to all.

Thirdly, worship of God (or deities) through the observance of particular ceremonies and holidays is universal. Though the rites differ greatly, all religions have some observances in connection with the life-cycle of the individual, from birth through death, and the changing of the seasons, especially those originally having to do with the agricultural cycle of planting and harvesting.

Fourthly, all religions possess some approved pattern of behavior or code of ethics and morality. Those of Christianity, and to a large extent of Islam, are based upon Jewish ethics; the Eastern faiths have developed their own standards along considerably different lines. But, as we have seen in the case of the so-called "Golden Rule," there are certain types of human conduct demanded by all faiths.

Fifthly, all religions deal with many questions that are basic to life. Practically every one offers explanations about the nature of man and the universe, what constitutes evil or sin, the purpose of life, why humans suffer, what happens after death, the role of the deity in the world, and many other important matters.

Sixthly, certain religious institutions are shared by almost all. Nearly every faith has a priesthood of some sort and particular places of worship. (Confucianism is the exception, but

BELIEFS ABOUT ITSELF AND OTHER FAITHS

ABOUT ITSELF	ABOUT OTHER FAITHS

JUDAISM

It is the highest form of religion and the true religion for Jews.

All religions contain some truth if they demand righteousness from their followers and thereby contribute to the establishment of God's Kingdom. All righteous people share in salvation.

ROMAN CATHOLICISM

It is the true religion and represents the one true Church

All other religions are in error. Salvation is denied those willfully refusing to join its Church.

PROTESTANTISM

Christianity is the true religion.

In most Protestant groups, only Christians can achieve salvation. All others are in error.

EASTERN ORTHODOXY

It is the true religion and represents the one true Church.

All other religions are in error. Salvation can come only through its Church.

ISLAM

Only it is the true religion.

Other monotheistic faiths have some truth but are inferior to Islam. Salvation can only come to its followers.

HINDUISM

It is the true religion but accepts a wide variety of beliefs.

Other religions contain some truth.

BUDDHISM

It is the true religion but accepts a wide variety of beliefs.

Other religions contain some truth.

CONFUCIANISM

It is the true religion but accepts a wide variety of beliefs.

Other religions contain some truth.

its followers do turn to the Buddhist or Taoist priest when necessary, and they have shrines in their own homes.) All of them have a sacred literature, teachers who instruct the young, and great sages, prophets, or leaders who have appeared in the course of their history.

Finally, we note that all religions believe in an existence after death. Though there are important differences in what each teaches, they nevertheless insist that man, or some portion of him, continues to live on in some form.

Thus we find that the religions of the world do share certain things in common.

Important Differences between Religions

Yet these similarities appear mainly on the surface, for on closer examination the various religions disclose much deeper differences.

The most obvious, of course, lies in the area of observances. Judaism has its own distinctive cycle of annual holidays. Christianity, Islam, and all the other faiths have their own holidays. Similarly, with life-cycle practices. Judaism and Islam insist upon the circumcision of all males; Christianity and the religions of the Far East do not. Roman Catholicism and Eastern Orthodoxy have certain sacraments without which people cannot gain salvation. Judaism has none. Each religion also has its own approved mode of worship, with different prayers frequently recited in a language other than one's native tongue. Thus, in addition to basic differences in the liturgy, the Jewish service uses Hebrew; the Roman Catholic, Latin; the Eastern Orthodox, Greek; and so forth.

On the simplest level, then, it is *institutions* and *practices* which make religions different.

But even within the broader areas of *belief* which the various faiths seem to share, there are deep-seated differences. Some, like Roman Catholicism, Eastern Orthodoxy, and various Protestant denominations, require belief in a specific creed. Judaism and the Far Eastern religions do not. Though most followers of all the major religions today believe in some form of deity, Judaism insists upon the worship of only one God, while those of the East permit many deities. There are important distinctions,

too, between the view of God held by Judaism and that of practically all of Christianity, with its insistence upon belief in the Trinity.

Actually, we find that in terms of beliefs the great religions of the world differ in five important areas. These are: (1) each religion's belief about itself and other faiths, (2) beliefs concerning the deity and prayer, (3) beliefs about the nature of life, (4) beliefs about man and his salvation, and, finally (5) its views of the hereafter. And, as we shall see, this is not just a matter of theory, but something that profoundly affects man's actions as well.

Let us look more closely at each of these areas of difference. . . .

1. Each Religion's Belief about Itself and Other Faiths

In their beliefs about themselves and other faiths, the great religions differ in certain respects. Some, such as Judaism, Christianity, and Islam, demand that their followers accept only the teachings and practices of their own faith. Since they believe in only one God, they feel that there is a best way of serving Him. Hence, they do not believe one can add the worship of other gods, or pick and choose among the practices of other religions and still serve Him. However, the Oriental faiths, in which polytheism is widely practiced, do permit the beliefs and rituals of other religions to be carried on alongside their own without any difficulty. Hinduism, with its adoption of the practices of so many other faiths, is a good example.

Naturally, all religions maintain that they possess the truth, but they differ on the question of whether they represent the *only* true faith. If they do, then all others are held to be in error. If not, then other religions are considered to contain some truth. Thus, while Judaism regards itself as the true faith for Jews, it finds some truth in other religions as they demand righteous conduct from their followers and thereby contribute to the eventual establishment of God's Kingdom on earth. On the other hand, Roman Catholicism, with its exclusive scheme of salvation for man, views all other faiths—including other forms of Chris-

258

BELIEFS CONCERNING THE DEITY AND PRAYER

	THE DEITY	THE DEITY'S NATURE	PRAYER
JUDAISM	One God.	Completely pure, holy, righteous.	Man prays directly to God.
ROMAN CATHOLICISM	Trinity (Father, Son, Holy Spirit).	Completely pure, holy, righteous.	Man prays to God through Christ. Intercession of saints and the Virgin Mary.
PROTESTANTISM	Trinity (Father, Son, Holy Spirit) in most Protestant groups.	Completely pure, holy, righteous.	Man prays to God through Christ.
EASTERN ORTHODOXY	Trinity (Father, Son, Holy Spirit).	Completely pure, holy, righteous.	Man prays to God through Christ. Intercession of saints and the Virgin Mary.
ISLAM	One God (Allah) whose will determines man's fate. Also various spirits who stem from Allah.	Completely pure, holy, righteous. However, certain spirits are evil.	Man prays directly to God.
HINDUISM	Belief in Brahman (unknowable basis of all), and spirits. Also a variety of gods, chiefly Vishnu (Creator-god) and Siva (Destroyer-god), and associates.	Gods share many human characteristics.	Man prays directly to the deities and spirits.
BUDDHISM	A variety of Buddhas, Bodhisattvas (divine heroes), and spirits.	Gods share many human characteristics.	Man prays directly to the deities and spirits.
CONFUCIANISM	Heaven, Earth, a variety of deities including Tao (the force that maintains harmony in the universe), Confucius, Lao Tzu, and spirits.	Gods share many human characteristics.	Man prays directly to the deities and spirits.

tianity—as being in error, and denies that salvation is possible to anyone who consciously refuses to join the Church.

From the chart appearing on page 257 we observe the teachings of all the great religions in this area.

2. Beliefs Concerning the Deity and Prayer

Though all religions now believe in some form of deity who is worshipped through prayer and other rites, we discover three principal differences in the nature of their God-concepts. The first has to do with whether there is only one God, as in Judaism, or more than one, as among the Eastern religions. The second concerns the nature of the deity; that is, whether He is completely pure, holy, and righteous, as in Judaism, or whether the deity shares certain human characteristics, as in most of Hinduism and Buddhism. The third concerns man's relationship to his deity—whether he prays directly to God, as in Judaism, or whether there are other beings who can intercede with the deity in his behalf, as, for example, in Roman Catholicism and Buddhism.

The chart that was presented on the previous page offers us a comparison of the great religions in this area.

3. Beliefs about the Nature of Life

In its system of beliefs, each religion makes certain judgments about the basic nature of life, as well as the kind of life it considers ideal. Here again, we discover significant differences.

With regard to the nature of life, the religions differ all the way from Judaism's belief that, though life does contain evil, man is able to overcome it with the aid of God and His Law, to Christianity's essential view that, without the direct intervention of God through Christ, man is unable to save himself from the evil that dominates both himself and the whole of life.

These views, in turn, determine the nature of the ideal life for man. In Judaism, for instance, it is one lived righteously and fully in this world, in which man engages in a suitable occupation, marries, has a family, and enjoys every worthwhile aspect of human existence. According to its view, righteous living to the full is indispensable to the creation of God's Kingdom upon earth. In Roman Catholicism, on the other hand, the ideal life remains one of dedication to Christ, which, in its purest form, demands renunciation of certain aspects of normal living, such as in the case of the priest, monk, or nun, who live out their years unmarried, in poverty, and in complete obedience to the Church.

We note the difference between the various religions from the chart that appears on the next page.

4. Beliefs about Man and His Salvation

Just as their views of life do not agree, so the great religions differ about the nature of man, sin, and the way he achieves his salvation. Concepts of man's nature range from those religions, chiefly Christianity, which regard him as contaminated by original sin, to Judaism which views him as sinless at birth and capable of either sinning or leading a righteous life.

Religions differ, too, as to what constitutes sin or evil-doing. In Judaism and Islam, it is disobedience to the will of God. In Christianity, it is this, as well as the fact that man has inherited original sin by simply being a descendant of Adam. Considerably different, however, is the view of the Eastern religions which, in general, see evil in man's human strivings.

Achieving salvation, therefore, is basically a matter of overcoming sin, or that which is considered the wrong way to live, according to the particular conception of the religion. Similarly, the whole goal of salvation is bound to differ. In Judaism, salvation is primarily conceived of in terms of the establishment of God's Kingdom upon earth through the faithfulness of the Jewish people to their covenant with God and obedience to His Law. In Christianity and the Eastern religions, it centers about rewards to be gained after death. Hence, the means to salvation also differ. In Christianity, the prime emphasis is upon faith in Christ, while Judaism, in turn, stresses the righteousness of each person's deeds in accordance with God's Law.

The chart on pages 262 and 263 summarizes the teachings of the great religions in this area.

NATURE
OF LIFE

	NATURE OF LIFE	IDEAL LIFE
JUDAISM	Capable of being good or evil.	The person who lives life fully in this world, in accordance with the laws of God.
ROMAN CATHOLICISM	Capable of becoming good through the Church and God's grace.	The person who abandons wealth, marriage, worldly desires, and dedicates self to Christ through the Church and its teachings.
PROTESTANTISM	Essentially corrupting (most sects), though capable of redemption.	The person who develops inner faith in Christ which leads to righteous deeds and the overcoming of evil in the world.
EASTERN ORTHODOXY	Capable of becoming good through the Church and God's grace.	The person who abandons wealth and worldly desires, and dedicates self to Christ through the Church and its teachings.
ISLAM	Of little consequence. Man's fate is determined by Allah (most).	That of the holy man or mystic who surrenders himself to Allah.
HINDUISM	Basically unreal. Man determines his future life according to the operation of the Law of Karma.	The individual who successfully merges self with Brahman through meditation, devotion and disciplines (Yoga).
BUDDHISM	Life is in a constantly-changing state which makes it unreal. Man determines his future life according to the operation of the Law of Karma.	The saint who rids self of desires, avoids extremes and seeks absolute bliss (Nirvana), and then foregoes Buddhahood to bring true knowledge to mankind.
CONFUCIANISM	Life is good, particularly when it follows according to the harmony of the universe established by Tao.	The person who conducts himself according to the rules of Confucius and seeks a life in harmony with the order established by Tao.

MAN
AND HIS SALVATION

JUDAISM	ROMAN CATHOLICISM	PROTESTANTISM	EASTERN ORTHODOXY
NATURE OF MAN			
Born sinless, but has capacity either to sin or live righteously.	Born evil because of original sin. Has tendency to sin.	Born evil because of original sin (most sects). Has tendency to sin.	Born evil because of original sin. Has tendency to sin.
SIN OR WRONG-DOING			
Man's disobedience of God's will.	Original sin at birth, and man's disobedience of God's will.	Original sin at birth (most), and man's disobedience of God's will.	Original sin at birth, and man's disobedience of God's will.
GOAL OF SALVATION			
To establish God's Kingdom on earth through the faithfulness of the Jewish people to their covenant with God.	To gain eternal life in heaven and eventual resurrection.	To gain eternal life in heaven; resurrection (many sects).	To gain eternal life in heaven and eventual resurrection.
MEANS OF SALVATION			
Through righteous living in accordance with the will of God, and participation in the Mission of Israel.	Through belief in Jesus Christ as taught and practiced by the Church.	Through faith in Jesus Christ as interpreted from Scripture.	Through belief in Jesus Christ as taught and practiced by the Church.

ISLAM	HINDUISM	BUDDHISM	CONFUCIANISM
NATURE OF MAN			
Has capacity for good and evil, though his actions are determined by Allah (most).	Determined by previous rebirths.	Determined to large extent by previous rebirths, especially in terms of character-formation.	Has capacity for good and evil.
SIN OR WRONG-DOING			
Man's disobedience of Allah's will.	Regarding life as real. Faithlessness to the pursuit of one's chosen Way.	Being moved by one's desires and failing to follow the Middle Path.	Failing to maintain harmony of Tao and to live according to the principles of mutual regard, duty, propriety and wisdom.
GOAL OF SALVATION			
To achieve eternal life in paradise.	To achieve a higher form of reincarnation after death, or ideally to end the process of rebirth.	To gain Nirvana and a higher form of reincarnation after death, or ideally to end the process of rebirth.	To maintain harmony with the universe and gain eternal life in heaven(s) with one's ancestors.
MEANS OF SALVATION			
Through belief in Allah and acceptance of His will according to the teachings of Mohammed, His Messenger.	Merging with Brahman through Ways of Works, Knowledge, Devotion to the various gods who intercede for one, and Concentration.	Through renunciation of desire, and following the Middle Path through understanding the Four Noble Truths and practice of the Eightfold Path.	Through seeking to live in harmony with Tao; living according to the principles of Mutual Regard, Duty, Propriety and Wisdom. Worship of various deities and spirits.

5. Views of the Hereafter As we have seen, all religions believe in some form of existence after death. However, in the Western faiths its nature varies from the belief of the Reform Jew in immortality of the soul, to that of the Moslem and many Christians in an actual heaven and hell. The Hindus and Buddhists, of course, believe in reincarnation after death as well as the possible attainment of Nirvana.

In addition, certain religions hold to a belief in an "end of days." These range from a time of Great Judgment with the resurrection of the dead, as in Islam and many forms of Christianity, to that of a Messianic Age of universal peace, justice, and righteousness, as found in Reform Judaism. The whole concept of an "end of days" is lacking, however, in Buddhism and Confucianism, and is quite different in Hinduism, which conceives of history in terms of a series of destructions and rebirths of the entire world.

The differences here between the teachings of the various religions may be noted from the chart presented on the next page.

Do the Differences Matter? Are these differences really important? Judaism says "Yes," and for good reason. True, as we have seen, Judaism shares certain features with other religions. Thus, for example, because Christianity adopted most of Jewish ethics, we find great similarity here. But there is a vast difference between the role that righteous living plays in Judaism and Christianity. In Judaism, righteousness is the principal means by which mankind achieves salvation; in Christianity, salvation comes through faith in Jesus Christ. Judaism tends to emphasize salvation through man's efforts to improve his society (salvation through deeds); while most Christian groups stress belief in Jesus as the main goal of life (salvation through faith).

But every religion is more than a series of individual beliefs, practices, and institutions that can be compared. Religions must also be considered as a whole, because when seen this way everything in them adds up to a particular point of view that is central in their peoples'

way of thinking and living. In other words, every great religion expresses a distinctive philosophy of life, and we need only examine Judaism's to see how important this is.

Rooted in a belief in the One God who is completely spirit and thoroughly holy and righteous, Judaism calls upon its followers to sanctify their lives by the practice of holiness and righteousness. Hence, at the very heart of the Jewish faith stand the principles of ethical, righteous conduct.

The fact that God created the world and all that is in it, and that He continues to sustain it, makes life capable of being good. Similarly, man, created by God in His image, is endowed with the capacity for righteousness. Thus man becomes a partner with God in their joint effort to produce a thoroughly righteous world. In short, Judaism views life, man, and the universe optimistically and hopefully.

To aid man, God has revealed to Israel those principles of the moral law by which the salvation of the whole human race can be achieved. With God's help and through his own efforts, each person can overcome evil and help bring about His Kingdom of universal and everlasting righteousness, justice, brotherhood, and peace here upon earth. Because all men are the children of God and capable of living righteously, Judaism denies salvation to no one.

Having entered into its eternal covenant with God, the people of Israel have been especially taught His demands, and these are embodied in the Torah. Worship, ceremonies, and study have been designed to aid them to carry out their obligations to live according to them. More than this, the Jews are charged with being His "servant" in sharing His truths with all mankind, chiefly by practicing them. This, in turn, has committed them all the more to righteous living as an "example" to the world, and obligated them with a deep sense of personal responsibility for the well-being of their fellow men.

Thus we note how the distinctive elements that comprise Judaism combine to form a unified, consistent pattern of belief. And more than any other religion, its teachings appear to be

VIEWS OF THE HEREAFTER

WESTERN

END OF DAYS	LIFE AFTER DEATH

JUDAISM

Reform: Messianic Kingdom of God on earth; Orthodox: Coming of Messiah, with resurrection, final judgment, and return of Jews to Palestine.

Orthodox: Life in Paradise; Reform: Immortality of the soul which returns to God.

ROMAN CATHOLICISM

Return of Christ, Last Judgment, resurrection.

Life in heaven, hell, purgatory.

PROTESTANTISM

Wide differences, but many denominations accept belief in return of Christ, Last Judgment, resurrection.

Wide differences but many accept belief of life in heaven and hell.

EASTERN ORTHODOXY

Return of Christ, Last Judgment, resurrection.

Life in heaven, hell, and intermediate states.

EASTERN

END OF DAYS	LIFE AFTER DEATH

ISLAM

Last Judgment with rewards for those saved and punishment for the damned.

Life in Paradise and the various hells.

HINDUISM

There is none. History is a cycle of the eventual destruction of the world and then its rebirth.

Return to heaven and hell where the soul awaits rebirth. Release from the cycle only when the soul reaches Nirvana and merges with Brahman.

BUDDHISM

None. History is unreal.

Return to heaven and hell where the soul awaits rebirth. Release from the cycle only when the soul reaches Nirvana which is pure bliss. (Shin) Return to the Pure Realm of the West.

CONFUCIANISM

None.

(Possibly life in heaven where one's ancestors dwell.)

in closest agreement with the realities of human experience.

For, reviewing the history of mankind, the Jew finds constant confirmation of the truth of his faith. He observes how, over the long centuries, man has sought to advance morally, so that some of the very teachings of Judaism—such as the Ten Commandments—have become basic to the law of most lands. With the development of democracy, he has noted how society has become more and more concerned with the welfare of all its people; and in the establishment of the United Nations, he witnesses the attempt of mankind to realize the Jewish quest for universal peace. He sees, too, how various religions—some of the forms of Protestantism, for instance, with their emphasis upon the social message of Jesus—have turned to basically Jewish teachings for the improvement of society. Moreover, he finds that those nations that have defied the moral law of God, as, for example, Nazi Germany in our own time, have eventually been destroyed.

The beliefs of the Jew also seem to be borne out by the experiences of his own people. Though the mighty empires of the past, such as Assyria, Babylonia, Greece, and Rome, are no more, the Jews are still very much in existence. Furthermore, they have survived despite repeated persecution and, for long centuries, lack of even a land of their own. Truly, this is one of the great miracles of history, and, to the Jew, it testifies to his divine Mission, a role ordained by God Himself as part of His ancient covenant with Israel.

To the Jew, this also serves to explain the remarkable religious creativity of his people.

DEVASTATION OF GERMANY. The war that the Nazis unleashed upon the world in 1939 eventually led the Allies, in turn, to bomb and destroy virtually every important German city.

The Jew has not just survived. Every century of his history has had its scholars, saintly men, and leaders, not to mention its countless ordinary men and women, whose lives Judaism filled with holiness.

The Religious Contribution of the Jew   All faiths, of course, have made contributions to the development of religion. Christianity produced the New Testament, the doctrine of the Trinity, the practice of the sacraments. Roman Catholicism introduced a new concept of church organization, as well as great religious art and pageantry. Protestantism developed the doctrine of "justification by faith," and stimulated advances in religious music and in upholding the liberty of individual conscience. Hinduism produced a belief in reincarnation; Buddhism and Confucianism contributed distinctive rules of conduct with their "Eightfold Path" and "Five Relationships."

But none has been more creative than Judaism. In the realm of beliefs, it introduced the concepts of a universal God of spirit, ethical monotheism, and repentance of sin. It developed the idea of a Messianic Age with the establishment of the Kingdom of God on earth. In the area of practice, Judaism substituted prayer for sacrifice, instituted a system of regular worship according to an established liturgy, introduced the concept of study as a religious obligation, and developed the idea of the Sabbath as a day of rest. And, in terms of institutions, Judaism contributed the synagogue as a unique house of worship, the Bible and Oral Law as a great body of sacred literature, and the rabbinate as a distinctive ministry of learning.

The importance of these contributions may be measured by the fact that both Christianity and Islam have drawn so heavily upon them. The church and mosque are both patterned after the synagogue. The creation of the New Testament and *Koran* were inspired by the Hebrew Scriptures. Much of the worship of the Christian is based upon the Jewish prayer book, and all of the religions of the West have adopted the more important Jewish beliefs, including those having to do with a universal God, ethical mono-

266

theism, and the concept of a Messianic Age.

Moreover, all through the centuries, as the Jews have carried on the search for further religious truth, Judaism has continued to be creative. The interpretations of the rabbis produced many new religious insights, and the thinking of philosophers like Maimonides provided a systematic, logical basis for religious belief and practice. Similarly, from time to time, various movements have arisen to keep the message of Judaism vital and fresh in line with the developments of the age. In our own day alone, we have witnessed the growth of Reform, Conservative, and Orthodox Judaism, Reconstructionism, Zionism, and other movements. And, as in the past, other religions continue to be influenced by Jewish thought. Thus, today, many Protestant thinkers have been strongly attracted to the writings of Martin Buber, the modern disciple of Chasidism.

The fact that the Jewish people has enjoyed this remarkable record of religious creativity once more points to the truth of its teachings, especially its conception of itself as the "Servant" of the living God, with a Mission to all mankind.

Religion in the Future   Thus far we have viewed religion only as it has developed up to the present. What about its future?

Certain things seem clear. For one, we can be sure that the great religions of the world will continue to exist as such. Most people can be counted upon to remain loyal to the faiths in which they have been reared, and finding satisfaction and value in them, they will continue to claim that theirs is the true faith. As a matter of fact, as far back as the fifth century B.C.E., the famous Greek historian Herodotus observed that "If one were to offer men to choose out of all the customs in the world that which seemed to them the best, they would examine the whole number, and end by preferring their own, so convinced are they that their own practices far surpass those of all the others." Hence, it is safe to predict that the great religions of the world will carry on into the future.

PHILOSOPHER MARTIN BUBER. Greatly influenced by Chasidism, Dr. Buber interprets religious faith as a dialogue between man and God. Here the scholar is surrounded by students of the Hebrew University in Jerusalem, where, prior to his retirement, he was professor of the sociology of religion.

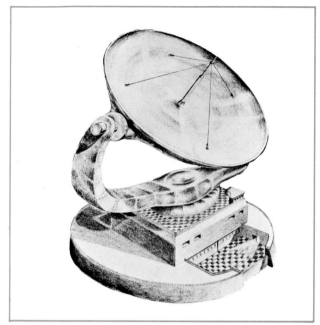

RADIO-TELESCOPE. By picking up radio signals from remote stars and galaxies, astronomers are extending their knowledge of our universe.

And, despite the destructive efforts of Communism, religion will most likely grow even stronger in the years that lie ahead. For, with the increasing uncertainties of life as a result of the great scientific revolution of our times and the growing threat to the survival of the world, more and more people are turning to religion for understanding, hope, and courage in meeting the many new challenges they face. This is borne out by reports of the very large increases in church and synagogue membership today, and there is every reason to believe that the trend will continue.

Moreover, as science progresses, people are finding stronger motivation for a belief in a Power higher than man. The more powerful the telescope scientists invent and the more new worlds man discovers in outer space, the greater his reverence for the Architect of the universe. The deeper he probes into the secrets of the atom, the more wonderful life appears and the greater its mystery. The more knowledge he accumulates about himself, his physical structure, his emotions, his intellect, the more he stands in awe of his Creator.

Yet, it also seems evident that these very scientific discoveries will produce certain changes in all religions. For, just as we have seen them respond to the discoveries of other ages, so we can expect new religious developments as man's knowledge about himself and his universe expands. To some extent we have already seen evidence of this in modern religion's growing interest in the discoveries of archeology, psychiatry, and sociology, and we can expect other important advances as new truths in these and many other fields appear.

Finally, religion is bound to be affected by the even smaller world of tomorrow. As contact between the followers of the different faiths grows, the process of religious borrowing that has gone on ever since the beginning of history is certain to increase. Undoubtedly, too, all religious peoples will develop greater understanding of one another's faiths, and out of this should come new ways in which the various faiths can cooperate effectively.

In all of this Judaism has nothing to fear and much to gain. Its search for truth these past 4000 years serves only to make it eager to learn more. Its continual creativity in the past gives it every confidence that this new knowledge will bring new ideas, new practices, and an even stronger sense of holiness in its dedication to God's purposes.

Judaism and Our Neighbor's Religion From our study of Comparative Religion, we have good reason to be proud of our Judaism and to regard it as man's highest form of religion. If this is so, what attitude can we take toward the religion of our neighbors?

Out of Jewish tradition comes a tale that has direct bearing on this question. Two rabbis long ago were discussing the creation of man. "What is so miraculous about the creation of man?" one asked the other. "After all, God certainly has the power to create anything He wishes."

"You are right," agreed his colleague. "However, the miracle is not that God was able to create man. Rather it is that, though all men are created in God's image, each one is different!"

Unfortunately, all too often people look upon

A COMPARISON OF RELIGIONS

differences of color, race, and creed as though they are something evil. They fail to realize that this is the wonderful part of God's creation. For how drab, colorless, and monotonous life would be if all peoples were exactly the same! It would be like an orchestra composed of only one kind of instrument.

Judaism teaches us that at the very birth of the universe God planned that difference should be part of life. The world is richer because of it, and mankind is more blessed because of the struggle of each of the many religions to catch a reflection of the Creator.

As Jews we remain faithful, of course, to Judaism. For it offers us that view of God, life, man and the universe which appears closest to the truth and a way of living that seems most realistically to promise salvation for all mankind. But this should not bind us to a wider view of religion that gives our neighbors the right to their own way of faith and keeps us ever mindful of the opportunities we have to work together in the historic Jewish task of creating God's Kingdom on earth.

So we pray each day:

> O may all, created in Thine image, recognize that they are brethren, so that, one in spirit and one in fellowship, they may be forever united before Thee. Then shall Thy kingdom be established on earth. . . . —*Union Prayerbook*

TOPICS TO DISCUSS

1. In what basic ways do you and your non-Jewish neighbor agree in matters of religion? Where do you differ?
2. What are some of the factors in your community that make for religious intolerance? In what ways do people of the various religions cooperate? How does their religious faith contribute to this?
3. In what respect does Judaism offer you important incentives for living your life effectively? How do these compare with those offered by the other great religions? In what ways is Judaism superior here? In what other ways does it appear superior?

4. In what particular ways do you find religion undergoing changes as a result of the modern world? How are these affecting the various religions in your own community? How, in particular, is it affecting Judaism?

THINGS TO DO

1. Prepare a chart showing the various elements that each of the world's great religions shares in common with the others.
2. Plan a "Congress of the World's Great Religions" with different individuals representing the various faiths. Then have each representative discuss the merits of the particular religion he represents.
3. Prepare a large map of the world and show by means of different colors the centers of the major religions today. Then beneath the map, list the principal beliefs of each and the number of its followers as currently given by the *World Almanac*.

OTHER THINGS TO READ

ARCHER, JOHN CLARK, and CARL E. PURINTON, *Faiths Men Live By*, Ronald Press, Chapter 1, "An Introduction to the Study of the Living Faiths," pp. 3-20.

HUME, ROBERT E., *The World's Living Religions*, Scribners, Chapter 13, "A Summary Comparison of the Living Religions," pp. 270-288.

KITAGAWA, JOSEPH M., *Religions of the East*, Westminster, Chapter 1, "Introduction: 'One World' and Religions," pp. 17-39.

ROSTEN, LEO, *A Guide to the Religions of America*, Simon and Schuster, "Can a Scientist Believe in God?" by Warren Weaver, pp. 158-165; "What Catholics, Jews, and Protestants Believe: A Comparison Chart," by Stanley I. Stuber, pp. 175-178; "Comparison of Religious Beliefs: 15 American Denominations," by Robinette Nixon and Barbara J. Kaplan, pp. 178-194.

SILVER, ABBA HILLEL, *Where Judaism Differed*, Macmillan.

SMITH, HUSTON, *The Religions of Man*, Mentor, Chapter 9, "A Final Examination," pp. 317-322.

The World's Great Religions, Time, "Introduction," by Paul Hutchinson, pp. 1-8.

SELECTED
TEACHER'S
REFERENCES

The following works are recommended for the teacher, though most students can also profit from many of them. Each has been selected for its non-technical style, readability, and usefulness in providing background and illustrative material for the teacher's use.

Archer, John Clark, and Carl E. Purinton, *Faiths Men Live By*, Ronald Press, New York.

Ballou, Robert O., *The Bible of the World*, Viking Press, New York.

Bamberger, Bernard J., *The Story of Judaism*, Union of American Hebrew Congregations, New York.

Browne, Lewis, *This Believing World*, Macmillan, New York.

Fitch, Florence M., *One God*, Lothrop, Lee, and Shepard, New York.

——, *Their Search for God—Ways of Worship in the Orient*, Lothrop, Lee, and Shepard, New York.

Gaer, Joseph, *How the Great Religions Began*, Signet Key Books, New York.

——, *The Wisdom of the Living Religions*, Dodd, Mead, New York.

Hume, Robert E., *The World's Living Religions*, Scribners, New York.

Manwell, Reginald D., and Sophia Lyon Fahs, *The Church Across the Street*, Beacon Press, Boston.

Noss, John B., *Man's Religions*, Macmillan, New York.

Pike, E. Royston, *Encyclopaedia of Religion and Religions*, World Publishing Company, Cleveland.

Potter, Charles F., *The Faiths Men Live By*, Prentice Hall, New York.

Rosten, Leo (ed.), *A Guide to the Religions of America*, Simon and Schuster, New York.

Smith, Huston, *The Religions of Man*, New American Library, New York.

Spence, Hartzell, *The Story of America's Religions*, Holt, Rinehart, Winston, New York.

Steinberg, Milton, *Basic Judaism*, Harcourt, Brace, New York.

The World's Great Religions, Time Incorporated, New York.

(The Mentor pocketbooks, published by New American Library, offer inexpensive and good translations of many religious classics such as the *Koran, Bhagavad-Gita,* Lao Tzu's *Tao Te Ching,* etc. These can be extremely useful aids.)

GLOSSARY

ABSOLUTION. Forgiveness of one's sins. In Roman Catholicism, granted by the priest after hearing confession.

ADVENT. The period beginning on the fourth Sunday before Christmas and ending with the coming of Christmas. Also, the second coming of Christ.

ALLAH. The Moslem name for God.

ANGLICAN COMMUNION. Those churches associated with the Anglican Church or Church of England. In the United States, the Episcopal Church.

ANIMISM. The belief that regards all objects and beings as possessed by "spirits."

ANTICHRIST. A powerfully evil being whose coming and reign will precede the second coming of Christ.

APOCALYPSE. A revelation of the events believed to lead to the "end of days" or Messianic Age.

APOCRYPHA. A collection of ancient Jewish writings not considered sufficiently holy to be included in the Hebrew Bible.

APOSTLE. Originally, one of the twelve disciples of Jesus sent forth to spread the message of Christianity. Used also to include Paul and others who served as missionaries in early Christianity.

APOSTLES' CREED, THE. The first official statement of Christian belief, appearing during the middle of the second century C.E. Incorporated into the belief and worship of various churches, including the Roman Catholic Church and Anglican Communion.

APOSTOLIC. Claiming the succession of its bishop or bishops from Peter or the Apostles as a whole.

ASCETICISM. The practice, for religious purposes, of severe self-denial and turning one's back upon normal ways of living.

BAAL. The name of the chief Canaanite deity and used in connection with various other Canaanite deities.

BAHA'I. A Universalist faith that grew out of the teachings of a Moslem sect and became a separate movement under the leadership of Baha'ullah (1817-1892) after whom the faith was named. Drawing upon some of the teachings of the major religions, it affirms a belief in the unity of God and seeks to unite the whole human race into one common, universal brotherhood.

BAPTISM. Sprinkling or immersion in water. The rite or sacrament by which the individual identifies himself with Christ and the Church.

BODHISATTVAS. "Buddhas-in-the-making," semi-divine heroes who could have attained Nirvana but who out of compassion postponed its enjoyment to help others.

BRAHMAN. In Hinduism, the indefinable, unknowable source and essence of everything in the universe.

BRAHMIN. A member of the Hindu priestly caste.

BUDDHA. Literally, "the Enlightened One." The name given to Siddhartha Gautama and others in Buddhism.

CADI. The Moslem judge who decides cases on the basis of Islamic religious law.

CALIPH. Literally, the "successor" (to Mohammed). The title of political and religious rulers of Moslem countries.

CANON. Referring to the approved contents of the Scriptures.

273

CANONIZATION. The process employed by certain forms of Christianity of officially declaring an individual a saint and worthy of veneration.

CASTE SYSTEM. Within certain Eastern religions, the division of followers into permanent classifications with varying duties and privileges. In Hinduism, the four major hereditary castes, subdivided into numerous sub-castes.

CATHOLIC. Originally, "universal, world-wide." Hence, a world-wide body of believers. Also, a particular world-wide religious organization, as the Roman Catholic Church.

CHALICE. The special silver and gold cup used for the wine of the Eucharist.

CHASIDISM. A Jewish religious movement in Eastern Europe beginning in the eighteenth century with the Baal Shem Tov and stressing the intimate love of God and man, and the joy of Jewish living.

CHRIST. Originally, the Greek word for "messiah." Applied to Jesus who was regarded by his early followers as the promised Messiah. Later, the divine son of God.

CHRISTMAS. The Christian holiday occurring at the time of the winter solstice (the period of the shortest day of the year), and commemorating the birth of Christ, with the promise of his return.

CODE. A work embodying the collection and organization of Jewish teachings, particularly laws, in a systematic, orderly fashion.

COMMUNION. The ceremony or sacrament of the Last Supper of Jesus, employing the bread and wine, and symbolic of his death and resurrection. Also called the Lord's Supper, the Eucharist, and Mass.

CONFESSION. The admission of one's sins in the presence of a priest. Also called "Penance."

CONFIRMATION. A ceremony or sacrament for children or young people when they are able to understand and affirm the teachings of their faith.

CONVERSION. The spiritual change associated with the discovery or adoption of a new religion. An emotional state of religious exaltation. Also, the ceremony of adopting another religion.

COUNTER-REFORMATION. In connection with Roman Catholicism, the movement in the sixteenth century (following the Protestant Reformation) designed to overcome the Church's ills and oppose the spread of non-Catholic Christian teachings and practices.

COVENANT. The ancient agreement entered into by the Hebrew people with God.

CREED. A brief formulation of religious beliefs required of all followers of a particular faith.

CRUCIFIX. A representation of Jesus on the cross, as distinguished from the plain "cross" which is always empty.

CRUCIFIXION. A Roman form of execution of criminals by binding or nailing to a cross; referring to the death of Jesus.

CRUSADES. A series of seven attempts by military force, organized by the Church from the end of the eleventh through the thirteenth centuries, to wrest the Holy Land from the Moslems. So named because of the emblem of the "cross" worn by the soldiers.

DERVISH. A member of a Moslem ascetic sect.

DIASPORA. All Jewish settlements outside of Palestine.

DIOCESE. A large administrative church district, composed of many parishes.

DISCIPLE. A follower of Jesus during his lifetime. Also, a leader in an early church, the follower of any religious leader; a member of the Disciples of Christ.

DISSENTER. One who objects to the beliefs or practices of the Church of England or who disputes its authority. Also called a "non-conformist."

EASTER. The spring holiday commemorating the resurrection of Christ.

ECUMENICAL. Literally, "world-wide in extent." Referring to a movement of cooperation between denominations or churches within Christianity or any religion.

EIGHTFOLD PATH, THE NOBLE. The basic way of life prescribed by Buddha by which the individual can overcome desire. It calls for Right Belief, Right Intention, Right Speech, Right Conduct, Right Means of Earning a Livelihood, Right Effort, Right Mindfulness, and Right Concentration.

EMANCIPATION. Literally, "freeing." Specifically, the granting of political equality to the Jews of modern times, beginning in the late eighteenth century.

END OF DAYS. Messianic times, or the period of the Kingdom of God.

EPISCOPAL. Referring to church organization governed by bishops. From the Greek word for "bishop."

EPISTLE. "A letter." Hence a communication by Paul and other early Christians appearing in the New Testament.

ETHICAL CULTURE. A movement founded in New York in 1876 by Felix Adler and asserting the supreme importance of ethics in all relations of life, but the irrelevance of theological beliefs. It conducts its own "services" and engages in numerous educational activities.

ETHICAL MONOTHEISM. The belief in one righteous God of the universe who demands righteous conduct as an essential of His worship.

EUCHARIST. The ceremony or sacrament of the Last Supper of Jesus, symbolic of his death and resurrection. Also called the Lord's Supper, Mass, and Communion.

EVANGELICAL. From "evangel," "the message of man's redemption through Christ as contained in the Gospels." Hence, referring to any Protestant denomination stressing the Gospel teachings of man's need for redemption from sin by faith in God's grace through Christ.

EVANGELIST. A preacher of the Gospel, especially for the purpose of revivals and conversions to Christianity.

EXCOMMUNICATION. To cut off from association with a religious body, and particularly, from the "saving" sacraments of the Church.

EXTREME UNCTION. The sacrament administered to Roman Catholics at death.

FETISH. An object, such as an amulet, believed to possess supernatural powers.

FIVE DAILY OBLIGATIONS, THE. The five daily practices of the orthodox Hindu, involving the offering of food and a water-libation to the deity, reading from the *Vedas*, a food-offering to animals, and care of guests or giving alms.

FIVE RELATIONSHIPS, THE. In Confucianism, the principles governing the relations between parents and children, brothers and sisters, husbands and wives, older and younger people, and rulers and their subjects.

FOUR NOBLE TRUTHS, THE. The statement containing the answer Buddha found for the meaning of life; essentially, that desire is the cause of suffering and to achieve Nirvana, one must eliminate desire.

FUNDAMENTALIST. One who accepts the literal word of the Bible as true.

G'MORO. One of the two major sections of the Talmud. Basically, the discussions by various rabbis of the reasoning behind the decisions of the Mishnah.

GENTILE. A term used by Jews and Christians to refer to a non-Jew, generally a Christian. (Originally Christians applied it to heathens.) In Mormonism it means all non-Mormons.

GOLDEN AGE, THE. The period from approximately 1000 to 1400 C.E. marking great religious and cultural creativity in post-biblical Judaism.

GOLDEN RULE, THE. The statement, "Whatever you wish that men would do to you, do so to them," ascribed to Jesus in Matthew 7:12 and Luke 6:31, as well as to other religious leaders, such as Hillel, in slightly different form.

GOOD FRIDAY. The holiday occurring on the Friday before Easter commemorating the crucifixion of Jesus.

GOSPEL. Any one of the first four books of the New Testament offering an account of the life of Jesus.

GRACE. The mercy or forgiveness of God which enables man to attain forgiveness of sin or salvation.

GURU. A personal teacher of the *Vedas* to Hindus.

HASKALA. A cultural movement, principally through the medium of Hebrew, beginning in the nineteenth century in Eastern Europe to bring "enlightenment" or acquaintance with modern thought to the Jews. Later converted to the support of Zionism.

HEGIRA. The flight of Mohammed in 622 C.E. from Mecca to Medina.

HELLENISM. The culture and civilization of the classical period of the Greeks, ending roughly with the death of Alexander the Great (323 B.C.E.).

HERESY. An opinion held in opposition to the accepted doctrine of a religious body.

HIERARCHY. The organization of the clergy by rank or orders, especially referring to the Roman Catholic clergy.

HIGH CHURCH. In the Anglican Communion, those churches whose services more closely resemble Roman Catholic worship, in contrast to "low church."

HINAYANA BUDDHISM. The Buddhism of South Asia, more closely related to the original teachings of Buddha. More properly called Theravada Buddhism.

HOLY GHOST or HOLY SPIRIT. The Spirit of God through which He appears to man. One of the three aspects of the Trinity.

HOLY ORDERS. The sacrament required of all who wish to be clergy in the Roman Catholic Church.

HOLY ROMAN EMPIRE. The medieval and modern empire of the German-speaking peoples of central Europe, extending from 800 to 1806.

HOST. The rounded bread wafer used in the sacrament of the Eucharist.

"IDEAL MAN," THE. The superior individual, according to Confucius, whose life embodies the principles of Mutual Regard, Duty, Propriety, and Wisdom, the attainment of which is an essential goal of Confucianism.

IMAM. In Islam, the person who stands at the head of the congregation and recites the prayers.

IMMACULATE CONCEPTION. The doctrine that Mary, the mother of Jesus, did not receive the guilt of original sin (as all people do) when she was conceived by her mother.

INCARNATION. The miraculous process by which Christ was transformed from pure spirit into the bodily form of Jesus, retaining the nature of both true God and true man.

INDULGENCE. Technically, the forgiveness of sins by the Church. Likewise, at one time, a certificate bearing the seal of the Roman Catholic Church and assuring the individual of forgiveness for his sins.

INQUISITION. An organization established by the Roman Catholic Church to discover heresy and punish heretics, especially in Spain during the fifteenth through seventeenth centuries.

INVINCIBLE IGNORANCE. The Roman Catholic doctrine which permits salvation to those outside the Church who in any age live in lands where Catholic teachings are so badly distorted that people find them impossible to accept.

JAINISM. A religion of India, with about a million and a half followers, that arose in the sixth century B.C.E. as a form of protest against Hinduism. Its essential doctrines, calling for no belief whatever in a deity, are that the individual's spirit retains consciousness of its identity through successive reincarnations and that after nine incarnations its followers attain Nirvana. However, even after achieving this, the soul may undergo further births in order to help weaker spirits attain salvation. Asceticism is stressed, and the taking of life in any form whatever is strictly forbidden.

JEHOVAH. The early Christian mispronunciation of the original Hebrew name for God. In Judaism God's name is never pronounced but instead is read "Adonoi," "My Lord."

JEHOVAH'S WITNESSES. A Christian sect originating in the United States with Charles Taze Russell in 1872. Its doctrine centers around the second coming of Christ, which is believed to be already under way. His final coming will be preceded by a great battle between the forces of good and evil, called "Armageddon" (probably from "Megiddo," the great biblical battlefield in Palestine). Then sinners will be given another chance for salvation. Its followers believe that they must preach this urgent message to all men.

JINN. In Islam, male and female supernatural beings, often demons.

JOHN THE BAPTIST. A Jew who lived during the early part of the first century C.E., dwelling in the desert-like regions of Palestine and practicing baptism to wash away sins. His baptism of Jesus is said to have had a profound affect upon him.

JUSTIFICATION THROUGH FAITH. The Protestant doctrine that the Christian attains salvation, not through the Church, rites, deeds, etc., but solely through his own faith in Christ, which reconciles him to God and cleanses him of sin.

KA'ABA. The black stone preserved in the cube-like shrine in Mecca and held sacred by the Moslems.

KABALA. A form of Jewish mysticism that was widely practiced in the Middle Ages. (Also spelled Cabala.)

KARAISM. The movement in Judaism, beginning about the middle of the eighth century C.E., calling for the elimination of the Oral Law and a return to just the teachings of the Bible.

KARMA, LAW OF. In various Eastern religions, the principle that the effects of one's acts determine his present and future forms of reincarnation.

KINGDOM OF GOD. The establishment of God's reign over all mankind, a period characterized by complete righteousness, peace, justice, brotherhood. Often also referred to as the Messianic Age and the "end of days."

KORAN. The Moslem Scriptures, containing the revelations received by Mohammed.

KOW-TOW. The special ritual of kneelings and knockings of the forehead against the ground that is part of Chinese reverence for one's ancestors.

LAST JUDGMENT. A final judgment of the dead by God at the "end of days." Usually accompanied by the resurrection of the dead.

LAST SUPPER. The last meal (Passover or Sabbath) shared by Jesus and his disciples on the eve of his crucifixion.

LENT. The period of forty days before Easter commemorating Jesus' fast in the wilderness. Often marked by restrictions upon the diet of Christians.

LOST TEN TRIBES, THE. The Hebrews of the Northern Kingdom of Israel who disappeared after being taken off as captives by the Assyrians in 721 B.C.E.

LOW CHURCH. In the Anglican Communion, those churches whose services are simpler and with less emphasis upon Catholic-like ritual, in contrast to "high church."

MAHAYANA BUDDHISM. The Buddhism of Northern and Eastern Asia, marked by the worship of many gods and divine beings.

MANA. An impersonal spiritual force that attaches itself to an object or individual.

MARRANO. A Jew of Spain who, under compulsion, publicly adopted Christianity but secretly continued to practice Judaism.

MARY. The mother of Jesus. Also called the Virgin Mary and the Holy Virgin.

MARY MAGDALENE. A woman healed by Jesus who accompanied him to Jerusalem where she witnessed his crucifixion and resurrection.

MASS. The ceremony or sacrament of the Eucharist, symbolic of Jesus' death and resurrection, as well as the service embodying the sacrament of the Eucharist. Also called the Lord's Supper, Communion, the Eucharist.

MENNONITES. A Protestant sect deriving its name from Menno Simons (d. 1561), leader of the Anabaptists in Holland. The faith originated in Switzerland about 1525 and from there spread to other European countries and America. Each congregation decides its own form of worship, but all agree upon baptism only of those old enough to accept Christ, the necessity for man's regeneration, refusal to bear arms or take oaths, and rejection of worldly concerns. The group is marked by simplicity of dress and habits. One of the most conservative branches is the Amish.

MESSIAH. Literally, "the anointed one" (of God); a deliverer sent by God to usher in His Kingdom.

MESSIANIC AGE. The Kingdom of God upon earth, the "end of days."

MIDDLE WAY, THE. In Buddhism, following a course of moderation and avoiding extremes so that one's desires become of no consequence to the individual.

MIDRASH. Literally, "interpretation." Generally, a collection of rabbinical interpretations of the Bible, especially for sermonic purposes.

MISHNAH. A collection of rabbinical interpretations of biblical law completed about 200 C.E. and later incorporated within the Talmud. Also, each individual rabbinical interpretation.

MISSAL. The book containing all of the directions and texts necessary for the conducting of the Catholic Mass.

MITZVAH. The Commandment of God as revealed through His Written and Oral Law.

MONASTICISM. Organized asceticism, generally in monasteries and convents.

MONOTHEISM. Belief in one God of the universe.

MONK. One who has retired from worldly life to devote himself to asceticism. Found today within Roman Catholicism, Buddhism, and other faiths, living in a cloister as a member of some religious order.

MORTIFICATION OF THE FLESH. An intense form of asceticism designed to destroy the vigor of the body.

MOSLEM. A follower of Islam.

MUTUAL REGARD. The principle of Confucius that one's actions should be governed by feelings of respect, sympathy, and compassion for his fellow man.

MYSTERY RELIGION. Any one of a number of faiths in the Greco-Roman world connected with a great Mother-goddess and the "death" and "rebirth" of her divine son, and involving special rites of participation in this myth. So called because the beliefs and rites were revealed only to those initiated into the religion.

MYSTICISM. A direct and immediate sense of God's presence, attained through inner faith or spiritual insight rather than through reason or observation. Hence, a religious movement characterized by the intense inward religious feelings of its followers.

NATIONAL RELIGION. That form of religion in which the power of the deity (or deities) is limited to the nation, its people, and land.

NAZARENES. The early Jewish followers of Jesus of Nazareth, led by Peter and James; Jewish Christians.

NEW TESTAMENT. The collection of twenty-seven writings originally in Greek, comprising the literature produced by the early Christian movement. The central element of the Christian Scriptures which include the Jewish Bible as well.

NIRVANA. The extinction of one's self; the achievement of a state of complete bliss or "enlightenment."

NOBLE EIGHTFOLD PATH, THE. In Buddhism, the eight essential principles of the way of life that leads to the attainment of the Middle Way and ultimately to Nirvana.

NON-CONFORMIST. One who does not conform to the beliefs or practices of the established Church of England. A dissenter.

OLD TESTAMENT. The Christian name for the Hebrew Scriptures which are also part of the Christian Bible. Literally, the "Old Covenant," since according to Christian belief, the coming of Christ marked the end of the ancient covenant of God with the Jews.

ORAL LAW. The reinterpretations of biblical teachings produced by the rabbis and found in such works as the Mishnah, Talmud, Codes, etc.

ORIGINAL SIN. In Christianity, the result of Adam's disobedience of God which at birth inclines man to sin and corrupts him.

ORTHODOX. Literally, "right doctrine." Hence, those who adhere to the "true" doctrines, beliefs, and practices.

PALI CANON. The official Scriptures of many Buddhists, written in the Pali language, a dialect of Sanskrit.

PALM SUNDAY. The Sunday occurring a week before Easter and commemorating the entry of Jesus into Jerusalem.

PAPAL INFALLIBILITY. The Roman Catholic doctrine that when the pope speaks officially on the subject of Catholic belief, he voices the absolute truth. To disagree with such statements is therefore heresy.

PARADISE. The Garden of Eden, or heaven.

PARISH. The smallest administrative unit of the Church.

PATRIARCH. One of the early forefathers of the Hebrew people: Abraham, Isaac, or Jacob. Also, the head of a branch of the Eastern Orthodox Church.

PENANCE. A sacrament of the Roman Catholic Church calling for the confession of sins and the granting of absolution by the priest. Also, certain religious acts prescribed by the priest as a sign of the Catholic's repentance.

PENTECOST. In Christianity, a holiday coming 50 days after Easter, which commemorates the descent of the Holy Spirit upon the apostles and marks the traditional start of the Catholic Church. Sometimes, also, the name given to the Jewish holiday of Shovuos, which occurs 50 days (7 weeks) after the beginning of Passover.

PENTECOSTAL. Referring to any Protestant sect which stresses the inspiration of the Holy Spirit, especially as revealed through the strong emotional response of the worshipper.

PHARISEE. A member of the Jewish religious party in Palestine headed by the scribes and rabbis, which came into existence during the first century B.C.E., and supported the reinterpretation of biblical teachings.

PHILOSOPHY. The study of the principles of life, human nature, and conduct, generally systematically and on the basis of human reason.

POLYTHEISM. Belief in many gods.

POPE. The Bishop of Rome and supreme head of the Roman Catholic Church. Also called the "Pontiff," from the Latin for "one who makes a bridge," or a "pathfinder."

PREDESTINATION. God's choice beforehand of a particular individual for salvation.

PRESBYTERIAN. Designating a church or churches governed by "presbyters," or elders.

PROPHET. In Judaism, one of a number of inspired individuals who spoke God's word, insisting particularly upon righteousness from the Jewish people as part of the fulfillment of their covenant with God. Also, the term used by Moslems for Mohammed as the chief spokesman of Allah.

PROTESTANTISM. The general Christian religious movement arising out of the Reformation beginning in the sixteenth century. Its common characteristic is its refusal to recognize the authority or absolute power of salvation of the Roman Catholic Church, but places its emphasis instead in personal faith in the Christ.

PURGATORY. In Catholicism, the place designed to "purge" the soul after death of its remaining sins.

RECONSTRUCTIONISM. A modern movement arising out of Conservative Judaism and designed to "reconstruct" Judaism for the circumstances of modern life. It views Judaism as a "civilization" in which religion plays an important part.

REFORMATION. The religious movement in Western Christianity, beginning in the sixteenth century, which resulted in the appearance of various Protestant denominations.

REINCARNATION. Rebirth after death.

RENAISSANCE. Literally, "rebirth." The intellectual and cultural movement occurring in fourteenth to sixteenth century Europe and arising out of the revival of the study of the classics. It marks the transition from the medieval to the modern period of history.

REPENTANCE. Confessing one's shortcomings, often accompanied by prayer, and amending one's deeds to overcome one's sinful acts.

RESURRECTION. The rising again of the dead in bodily form. Also, in Christianity, the rising of the crucified Jesus on the third day after his death.

REVELATION. That which is disclosed by God to man. Also, the process by which such disclosures occur.

REVIVAL. An evangelistic meeting or series of meetings designed to awaken or renew religious faith.

ROSARY. Beads used in worship by various faiths. Chiefly a set of small and large beads attached to a cross and generally used for private meditations and prayers by the Roman Catholic. Also, the devotion carried on with these beads.

SACRAMENT. A rite of the Roman Catholic Church which is believed to confer God's grace upon the individual so that he is redeemed from sin.

SADDUCEE. The member of a Jewish religious party in Palestine headed by priests, wealthy land-owners, and the ruling classes, which came into existence during the first century B.C.E., and opposed reinterpretation of the Bible as advanced by the Pharisees.

SALVATION. In Christianity, the saving of the individual from the spiritual consequences of sin, which in a number of faiths leads to eternal damnation. In Judaism, the redemption of the Jewish people for its Mission as the servants of God, ultimately bringing about the redemption of all mankind with the establishment of God's Kingdom upon earth.

SALVATION ARMY. A separate Christian denomination, with centers in 85 countries, founded in England in 1878 by William Booth, a Methodist minister. It is organized along military lines and emphasizes the salvation of God and the need for deliverance from sin. As part of its purpose of bringing the "saving" message of Christianity to the masses, it engages in many varieties of social service work. Since it has no formal creed, there is great freedom of worship. Its officers perform all the functions of clergy.

SAMARITAN. A descendant of the foreign peoples who were settled in northern Palestine by the Assyrians after 721 B.C.E. Today, a small sect in Jordan and the State of Israel which carries on certain ancient Jewish practices.

SANSKRIT. The ancient Aryan language of the Hindus in India in which the *Vedas* and other sacred writings appear.

SEPARATION OF CHURCH AND STATE. The principle prohibiting the establishment of a state church or the intervention of the government in religious matters as well as the interference of religion in the affairs of government.

SHI'ITES. An important Moslem sect which traces the descent of its caliphs from Ali, the cousin and son-in-law of Mohammed.

SHIN BUDDHISM. A form of Mahayana Buddhism, originating in Japan and found in the United States. It features the worship of Amida, the Buddha whose grace can accomplish the salvation of the individual by securing forgiveness of his sins.

SHINTOISM. The ancient religion of Japan, but modified by the influence of Buddhism and Confucianism. The name Shinto means "the way of those above" and refers to many supernatural beings or deities, generally beneficent personifications of various forces of nature. The faith is built around love of country, reverence for ancestors, ceremonial and bodily purity, and loyalty to ancient customs. One of its more important features has been a code of military conduct, akin to rules of chivalry, for service to Japan. Until 1946 the Emperor of Japan was believed to be descended from the gods and served as the chief priest of the faith.

SIKHISM. A religion of India which was founded by Nanak (b. 1469) in opposition to Hinduism's priesthood and caste system. However, in the seventeenth century, the last of its great teachers (called "Gurus") raised all members of the sect to the warrior caste and introduced the practice of wearing the turban, carrying a dagger, and never cutting the beard. Thereafter, the Sikhs were welded into a military community and today carry on caste practices and various beliefs typical of Hinduism.

SIN. A violation of the will of God as expressed, frequently, in divine law.

SINS, VENIAL AND MORTAL. In Roman Catholicism, sins are of two kinds, "venial," or less serious offenses against God's will, and "mortal," those mighty transgressions against the moral law which can condemn the soul to eternal punishment in hell.

SOCIAL JUSTICE. Having to do with measures for the promotion of just and fair treatment of all segments of society. Also called "Social Action."

STOICISM. A school of Greek philosophy arising about the beginning of the third century B.C.E., which believed in the existence of one great universal Force, akin to nature, worthy of respect and aspiration. It stressed living a virtuous life, in accordance with the natural principles, through self-control and self-discipline.

SUFIS. Monastic orders of Moslem ascetics.

SUNNIS. The largest sect in Islam. It traces the descent of its caliphs from among the members of Mohammed's own tribe.

SUPERNATURAL. A Power (or powers) in, above, and beyond nature which exerts control over human and natural happenings.

SWAMI. A member of a Hindu religious order.

SYNOD. A church council composed of clergy and laymen.

SYNOPTIC GOSPELS, THE. The first three gospels of the New Testament, Matthew, Mark, and Luke, so named because they contain a great deal of information in common, in contrast to John, the fourth gospel.

TABOO. An object or person believed so charged with supernatural power that all contact with it should be avoided.

TALISMAN. An amulet or charm believed to possess special supernatural powers.

TALMUD. One of two rabbinical works bearing the same name which served to reinterpret the teachings of the Bible for the period following its completion and thereafter. The best-known and most influential is the Babylonian Talmud which appeared in final form about 500 C.E. The other and smaller work is the Palestinian Talmud, completed about 425 C.E.

TAO. Literally, "the Way." The universal, indefinable power, combining the opposing forces of *yang* and *yin*, that brings harmony and order into everything.

THEOLOGY. Literally, "the study of God." The study of religious knowledge, chiefly in terms of religious history, ideas, and experiences, generally in systematic form.

THERAVADA. Literally, "the Way of the Elders." South Asian (Hinayana) Buddhism, which traditionally follows more closely the original teachings of Buddha.

"THREE BASKETS," THE. A collection of writings in Pali (the popular language of India) held sacred by many Buddhists. Called *Ti-Pitaka*, it contains early information about the duties of Buddhist monks, descriptions of Buddha's teachings, and discussion of the deeper thoughts involving Buddhist doctrine.

"THREE JEWELS," THE. The attributes of gentleness, frugality, and humility which, according to Taoism, the individual gains by following the Way of Tao.

TITHING. The practice of giving a "tithe," or tenth, of one's earnings to one's religion.

TOTEM. A particular object or creature regarded as mystically bound up with the life of a clan, tribe, or family.

TRANSUBSTANTIATION. The miraculous transformation of the wine and bread of the Eucharist into the blood and body of Christ, though they remain unchanged in outward appearance.

TRINITY. In Christianity, God the Father, the Son (Jesus), and the Holy Ghost or Spirit, in which all are one, the same, and equal.

TZADIK. A righteous man. The term is also used to designate some of the outstanding leaders of Chasidic groups.

UNTOUCHABLE. A member of the lowest caste in Hinduism, with whom contact is believed to be defiling.

VATICAN ECUMENICAL COUNCIL. An official convocation of Roman Catholic bishops called by the pope to discuss and recommend church doctrines and practices. The first, held in 1869-1870, declared the infallibility of the pope. The second began in 1962 and made significant changes in worship procedures, church organization and doctrines.

VEDAS. The sacred Hindu books of religious "knowledge," comprising four major works.

VIRGIN BIRTH. The doctrine that Jesus was conceived by his mother, Mary, who miraculously remained a virgin.

VIRGIN MARY. The mother of Jesus.

VOLUNTEERS OF AMERICA. A Christian organization founded along military lines in 1896 in the United States by General and Mrs. Ballington Booth after their withdrawal from the Salvation Army. It operates many missions to reach the unchurched, and in connection with its evangelism carries on an active social work program for transients, orphans, the aged, prisoners, etc. It conducts its own worship with the rituals of the Lord's Supper, baptism, and marriage, but also encourages converts to join denominations of their own preference.

WAY OF CONCENTRATION, THE. In Hinduism, one of the means of attaining Nirvana through a series of difficult, arduous, mental and physical disciplines that are designed to gain for the individual single-minded concentration upon the "Ultimate Truth," Brahman.

WAY OF DEVOTION, THE. In Hinduism, one of the means of attaining a higher form of reincarnation, chiefly through self-dedication to particular gods and goddesses.

WAY OF KNOWLEDGE, THE. In Hinduism, one of the means of attaining a higher form of reincarnation, chiefly through the study of the sacred writings, Yoga disciplines, and intense concentration upon Brahman.

WAY OF WORKS, THE. In Hinduism, one of the means of attaining a higher form of reincarnation through properly carrying out religious obligations according to the demands of one's caste.

WRITTEN LAW. The Bible, and particularly the Torah.

YAHVEH. Believed to be the name of God among the Hebrews starting with the time of Moses.

YOGA. A program of intense mental and physical discipline, often involving severe asceticism, designed to help the individual attain Nirvana.

YOGIN. In Hinduism, one who has renounced worldly life to practice his particular discipline, a "saint" or "holy man."

ZEMZEM. The holy well in Mecca.

ZEN BUDDHISM. A form of Mahayana Buddhism, originating in Japan and found in the United States, which stresses disciplined meditation in order to gain knowledge of the "real truth" or "enlightenment."

ZOROASTRIANISM. A religion originally of Persia and founded by Zoroaster (possibly seventh century B.C.E.), but with many later additions. Today it is mainly the religion of the Parsis of India, with about a million followers. Its basic teachings divide numerous deities into good spirits, headed by Ahura Mazdah, the supreme god and represented in many forms but especially by fire, and the evil ones, headed by Ahriman. There is constant warfare between them, especially within man's soul, and man's conduct may aid either side. If wicked, the individual goes to hell after death; otherwise, he goes to the "realm of light." The ultimate triumph of Ahura Mazdah with the general resurrection of the dead is predicted. Today many more gods are worshipped, including Mithra and Zoroaster himself, and the worship is connected with the use of the sacred fire.

INDEX

INDEX

INDEX

INDEX

INDEX

PHOTO CREDITS

PAGE		CREDIT
133		Unitarian Association
136		Theodore Hetzel, Haverford, Penn.
139		United Lutheran Church in America
141		New York Public Library
143	Left	Church of Jesus Christ of Latter Day Saints, Utah
143	Top	Church of Jesus Christ of Latter Day Saints
143	Bottom	Church of Jesus Christ of Latter Day Saints
145	Inset	Seventh Day Adventist
145		Seventh Day Adventist
147		Christian Science Publication Society
147		Christian Science Publication Society
150		Art Shay
160		New York Public Library
162		UAHC—Department of Experimental Education and Audio-Visual Aids
165		Jewish Museum, Frank J. Darmstaedter, Photographer
166		Jewish Museum, Frank J. Darmstaedter, Photographer
172		New York Public Library
173	Left	New York Public Library
173		New York Public Library
176		Joint Distribution Committee, N. Y.
179		Religious News Service
181	Right	Israel Office of Information
181	Center	Israel Office of Information
181	Left	Israel Office of Information
182		Hebrew Union College—Jewish Institute of Religion
185		UAHC—Department of Experimental Education and Audio-Visual Aids
186		Hebrew Union College—Jewish Institute of Religion
187		Union of American Hebrew Congregations
188	Top Left	Culver Pictures, N. Y.
188	Bottom Left	Wide World
188	Bottom Center	Wide World
188	Bottom Right	Wide World
189	Top	Union of American Hebrew Congregations
189	Center	Hebrew Union College—Jewish Institute of Religion
189	Bottom Left	Hebrew Union College—Jewish Institute of Religion
189	Bottom Right	Hebrew Union College—Jewish Institute of Religion
190		Jewish Museum, Frank J. Darmstaedter, Photographer
192	Top Left	Reconstructionist
192	Top Right	United Synagogue of America
194		Shearith Israel, New York
196	Top Left	Justin Kerr
196	Top Right	United Synagogue of America
198	Top Left	Jewish National Fund
198	Center	Israel Office of Information
202		Religious News Service
204		Ewing Galloway, Inc., N. Y.
207		Ewing Galloway, Inc., N. Y.
209	Top	Ewing Galloway, Inc., N. Y.
209	Bottom	Bettmann Archive, Inc., N. Y.
210		State of Israel
216		India Information Service
217		Metropolitan Museum of Art
221	Left	Ewing Galloway, Inc., N. Y.
221	Right	Bettmann Archive, Inc., N. Y.
222	Top	India Information Service
222	Bottom	India Information Service
223		Ewing Galloway, Inc., N. Y.
228		New York Public Library
229		Bettmann Archive, Inc., N. Y.
232		New York Public Library
235		Religious News Service
242		Bettmann Archive, Inc., N. Y.
245	Top Left	Chinese News Service, N. Y.
245	Top Right	Chinese News Service, N. Y.
245	Center	Hamilton Wright
245	Bottom	Chinese News Service, N. Y.
252		Wide World
255		American Museum of Natural History
256		Union of American Hebrew Congregations
266		Wide World
267		American Friends of the Hebrew University
268		American Museum of Natural History

COMMISSION

ON

JEWISH

EDUCATION

OF THE UNION OF AMERICAN HEBREW CONGREGATIONS
AND CENTRAL CONFERENCE OF AMERICAN RABBIS
AS OF 1963

Union Graded Series

Union of American Hebrew Congregations

297